WOMEN, THE NEW YO
AND OTHER TRUE ABSTRACTIONS

WOMEN, THE NEW YORK SCHOOL, AND OTHER TRUE ABSTRACTIONS

BY MAGGIE NELSON

University of Iowa Press, Iowa City

University of Iowa Press, Iowa City 52242
Copyright © 2007 by Maggie Nelson
www.uiowapress.org
All rights reserved
Printed in the United States of America

Design by Teresa W. Wingfield

The University of Iowa Press is a member of Green Press Initiative and is
committed to preserving natural resources.

Printed on acid-free paper

ISBN-13: 978-1-58729-615-4, ISBN-10: 1-58729-615-2 (cloth)
ISBN-13: 978-1-60938-109-7, ISBN-10: 1-60938-109-2 (pbk)

LCCN: 2007924052

CONTENTS

ACKNOWLEDGMENTS

First thanks go to Wayne Koestenbaum, whose impassioned and omnivorous writing, reading, teaching, scholarship, and friendship—not to mention his own example of when to "care" and when not to—have greatly expanded my sense of liberty, possibility, and pleasure, both in regard to this project and otherwise. I have no doubt that I will be eternally grateful.

Thanks also to Mary Ann Caws, for opening my eyes wider to beauty, chance, and art; Joan Richardson, for being a spiritual and intellectual anchor from our first meeting onward; Eve Kosofsky Sedgwick, for her astonishing pedagogy and permission; Nancy K. Miller, for her keen advice and *affidamento*; and to all the other scholars and friends who offered invaluable insights and support along the way, especially Brian Blanchfield, Libbie Rifkin, Susan Rosenbaum, Daniel Kane, Louis Menand, Joshua Wilner, Melissa Dunn, Deborah Lutz, Rebecca Reilly, Charlotte Deaver, Andy Fitch, Christina Crosby, Janet Jakobsen, Mark Bibbins, Rodney Phillips, and Mark Hitzges. Thanks also to David Lehman, for introducing me to the pleasures of this topic so long ago, and to the Graduate Center of the City University of New York, for all the support that helped make this book possible. Invaluable assistance was also provided by the Creative Capital/Andy Warhol Foundation Arts Writers Grant Program. I also thank my new community at CalArts—especially Nancy Wood, dean of the School of Critical Studies, and the wise and visionary Janet Sarbanes, for further expanding my notion of what a school can or might be.

For help with obtaining images, I thank Carolyn Somers and Allison Hawkins at the Joan Mitchell Foundation, Hadley Haden-Guest, Jason Murison at P.P.O.W. Gallery, Jessica Marx at Art + Commerce, Brooke Davis Anderson and Nicole Whelan at the American Folk Art Museum, Anselm Berrigan, and Nathan Kernan. I also heartily thank Joseph Parsons, Holly Carver, Charlotte Wright, Allison Thomas, Karen Copp, and Gail Zlatnik at the University of Iowa

Press for all their hard work in bringing this book into being. Thanks too, and as always, to PJ Mark of McCormick & Williams, for his ongoing guidance.

This book would have no meaning or context without all of the friends, writers, artists, performers, activists, and publishers who have constituted my own personal "New York School" over the years—a list way too long to print here, but which would include everyone I've learned from and worked with at the Poetry Project at St. Mark's Church (Anselm Berrigan, Ed Friedman, and, in the basement long ago, Elaina Ganim); all the devoted provocateurs in and around the first and second incarnations of Soft Skull Press; Robert Hershon, Donna Brook, and all the good people of Hanging Loose Press and magazine; New York dancers from a previous life, especially KJ Holmes, for teaching me to think on my feet, and Adrienne Truscott (of the Wau Wau Sisters and so much more) for all the bad education; the indefatigable ladies of *Fort Necessity* magazine, along with all the other pioneering spirits from Eileen's NYC workshops; Robert Polito and my students and colleagues at the New School; Thad Ziolowski and my students and colleagues at Pratt Institute of Art; Suzanne Snider, who braved the Storrs archives with me long ago and who has forged the path of so much more since; and the late, great Robert Creeley, the best kind of poetry father one could have hoped for.

Last but not least, I dedicate this book to my excitement sister/not-sister Cynthia Nelson, for unwittingly drawing me east, and for all subsequent speech.

"G-9" from *Powerless: Selected Poems 1973–1990* by Tim Dlugos. Copyright © 1996 by Tim Dlugos. Reprinted by permission of the Estate of Tim Dlugos.

Excerpts from "On the Way to Dumbarton Oaks," "Parachutes, My Love, Could Carry Us Higher," "Green Awnings," "A Reason," "The Poetess," "Santa Fe Trail," "An Emphasis Falls on Reality," and "Roses" by Barbara Guest, originally published by Sun & Moon in *Selected Poems*, copyright © 1995 by Barbara Guest. Excerpts from "The Screen of Distance," "Sunday Evening," "The Location of Things," "Sadness," and "The Open Skies" by Barbara Guest, originally published by Random House in *Poems: The Location of Things, Archaics, The Open Skies*, copyright © 1962 by Barbara Guest. All forthcoming in *Collected Poems*, to be published by Wesleyan University Press and reprinted here by permission of Wesleyan University Press.

Excerpts from *Rocks on a Platter* by Barbara Guest, copyright © 1999 by Barbara Guest. Reprinted by permission of Wesleyan University Press.

Excerpt from *Selected Poems* by Robert Lowell. Copyright © 1976 by Robert Lowell. Reprinted by permission of Farrar, Straus and Giroux, LLC.

Excerpt from "Failures in Infinitives" by Bernadette Mayer, from *A Bernadette Mayer Reader*, copyright © 1992 by Bernadette Mayer. Reprinted by permission of New Directions Publishing Corp.

Excerpts from *Midwinter Day* by Bernadette Mayer, copyright © 1982 by Bernadette Mayer. Reprinted by permission of New Directions Publishing Corp.

"To a Politician" and excerpts from "Sonnet Welcome" by Bernadette Mayer, from *Scarlet Tanager*, copyright © 2005, 2004, 2003, 2002, 2001, 2000, 1999, 1997, 1996, 1995 by Bernadette Mayer. Reprinted by permission of New Directions Publishing Corp.

Excerpts from *Another Smashed Pinecone* by Bernadette Mayer, copyright © 1998 by Bernadette Mayer, reprinted by permission of the author.

Excerpts from *The Desires of Mothers to Please Others in Letters* by Bernadette Mayer, copyright © 1994 by Bernadette Mayer, reprinted by permission of the author and Hard Press Editions, Inc.

Excerpts from "An Urban Convalescence" by James Merrill, copyright © 2001 by the Literary Estate of James Merrill at Wash-

"Poem," "Homosexuality," "Song," "Spleen," "F. (Missive & Walk #53)," "To My Mother," "Biotherm (for Bill Berkson)," "Today," "Getting Up Ahead of Someone (Sun)," from *The Collected Poems of Frank O'Hara* by Frank O'Hara, edited by Donald Allen, copyright © 1971 by Maureen Granville-Smith, Administratrix of the Estate of Frank O'Hara. Used by permission of Alfred A. Knopf, a division of Random House, Inc.

Excerpts from "Three Women: A Poem for Three Voices," from *Winter Trees* by Sylvia Plath. Copyright © 1968 Ted Hughes. Reprinted by permission of HarperCollins Publishers.

Excerpts from "Elm," "Fever 103°," "Ariel," "A Birthday Present," "Lady Lazarus," and "Getting There" from *Ariel: Poems* by Sylvia Plath. Copyright © 1961, 1982, 1963, 1964, 1965, 1966 by Ted Hughes. Foreword by Robert Lowell. Reprinted by permission of HarperCollins Publishers.

"Magi" from *Crossing the Water* by Sylvia Plath. Copyright © 1971 by Ted Hughes. Reprinted by permission of HarperCollins Publishers.

Excerpts from *Collected Poems* by James Schuyler. Copyright © 1993 by the Estate of James Schuyler. Reprinted by permission of Farrar, Straus and Giroux, LLC.

A revised version of this book's introduction first appeared in a *Mississippi Review* issue devoted to the New York School, vol. 31, no. 3, 2003. Thanks to Angela Ball.

A revised portion of chapter 5 first appeared in an issue of *Interim* magazine devoted to Alice Notley, vol. 23, nos. 1 and 2, 2005. Thanks to Claudia Keelan.

TALES IN AND OUT OF SCHOOL

AN INTRODUCTION

American Abstract Artists, the Irascibles. *Photograph by Nina Leen/Getty Images*, Life, *15 January 1951: 34. Top row, lr: Willem de Kooning, Adolph Gottlieb, Ad Reinhardt, Hedda Sterne; middle, lr: Richard Pousette-Dart, William Baziotes, Jackson Pollock, Clyfford Still, Robert Motherwell, Bradley Walker Tomlin; bottom, lr: Theodoros Stamos, Jimmy Ernst, James C. Brooks, Mark Rothko. Copyright © Getty Images, used by permission.*

THIS INITIAL IMPULSE behind this project was to document and explore the myriad roles women have played in and around the so-called New York School of poets. In painting, the term "New York School" generally refers to the Abstract Expressionists working in New York City at midcentury; in poetry, it has come to refer to the close-knit, albeit diverse group of poets who were their friends and artistic peers, a group which includes John Ashbery, Kenneth Koch, Frank O'Hara, and James Schuyler (and, perhaps less often, writers such as Kenward Elmslie, Harry Mathews, and Edwin Denby, and their so-called descendants—writers such as Ted Berrigan, Ron Padgett, Joe Brainard, Bill Berkson, David Shapiro, Tony Towle, Michael Brownstein, Paul Violi, Dick Gallup, Peter Schjeldahl, and many others).[1] Given these oft-repeated lists of male "leading figures," the question immediately arises: who were (or are) the women of the New York School?

One tempting response to such a question would be to provide a list of names—a list which would probably include painters such as Helen Frankenthaler, Lee Krasner, Grace Hartigan, Elaine de Kooning, Jane Freilicher, and Joan Mitchell; the poet Barbara Guest; the poet and playwright V. R. (Bunny) Lang (though she lived most of her short life in Boston); and, perhaps most important, so-called second-generation writers associated with the scene such as Bernadette Mayer, Alice Notley, Eileen Myles, Maureen Owen, Anne Waldman, and many others—and then to write a cultural history which systematically charted their work and interactions.[2]

My study has shades of this approach, but for a variety of reasons it takes a different path. Excellent and thorough social histories of the period and its immediate aftermath have already begun to appear—perhaps most notably Daniel Kane's 2003 *All Poets Welcome: The Lower East Side Poetry Scene in the 1960s*, which spends some real time discussing the increased visibility, influence, and even predominance of women poets—along with the difficulties they faced—in the downtown poetry scene loosely centered around the Poetry Project at St. Mark's Church in-the-Bowery, the influential "anti-institution" formed in 1966 (the year of O'Hara's death). Libbie Rifkin has also written well on the subject in essays such as "'My Little World Goes On at St. Mark's Place': Anne Waldman, Bernadette Mayer, and the Gender of an Avant-Garde Institution," and writers such as Rachel Blau DuPlessis, Kathleen Fraser, Lynn Keller, Linda Kinnihan, Chris

Kraus, Sara Lundquist, Susan Rosenbaum, Anne Vickery, and many others (including Mayer, Notley, and Myles themselves) have all usefully touched on the subject to varying extents.[3]

The present study offers more of a textual history than a social one. To this end, it combines close readings of a wide range of poetry with an overarching philosophical and theoretical meditation on the relationship of gender and sexuality to the particular set of aesthetic issues that have accumulated around the idea of the New York School. I choose this approach partly out of temperament; partly because I want to give the poetry itself the attention it deserves; and partly because I very much want certain questions—questions about the critical urge to consolidate a "school" (even, or especially, an "avant-garde," as the New York School is often deemed), questions about whether and how work by women can be effortlessly slotted into such structures, and so forth—to remain unsettled, and unsettling. For this reason, while I aim to call attention to the prominent—indeed foundational—roles that women have played over the years (Waldman, Mayer, and Myles each directed the Poetry Project for a period of time; Daisy Aldan, Barbara Barg, Myles, Mayer, Notley, Owen, and others ran important workshops, literary magazines, small presses, and so on), I do not suggest here that these roles can or should be facilely folded into normative narratives of literary history.

"The writing of literary history inevitably takes mythic forms," Michael Davidson cogently observes at the start of his study of the San Francisco Renaissance (1), and indeed, most retrospective narratives do. But given that these "mythic forms" have historically tended to exclude women, and given that the critical mythology around the New York School of poets has just begun to accrue in earnest (the mythology surrounding the painters has been in full swing for some time[4]), it seems to me a critical moment to consider in depth the various contributions and critiques women have made in and around this particular milieu. None of the full-length considerations of the school to appear thus far—David Lehman's *The Last Avant-Garde: The Making of the New York School of Poets*, William Watkin's *In the Process of Poetry: The New York School and the Avant-Garde*, and Geoff Ward's *Statutes of Liberty: The New York School of Poets*—offers a feminist perspective, and none includes Barbara Guest (the only first-generation female poet) as a principal subject of interest. Thus, in addition to calling attention to work by women associated with the New York School and the complexities of its various contexts, my study also hopes to offer an alternative to the logic of exclusion which can still underlie and perpetuate so much literary mythmaking.[5]

In an interview with Judith Goldman, Notley offers her take on this logic as follows: "Men lead movements and argue with each other over the present and future of poetry, insuring that they get more space in the so-called discourse. It's like they're still doing all the real thinking. We're geniuses, they say, and then go back to arguing with each other. . . . It's also a fact that the ways in which poetry gets published . . . not to mention the whole idea of a literary movement, the academy, the avant-garde, are all male forms" (8). There's much to debate here, and the debate is an important one. It raged, for example, at a 1999 conference at Barnard College titled "Where Lyric Tradition Meets Language Poetry: Innovation in Contemporary American Poetry by Women," organized by Claudia Rankine and Allison Cummings. In a statement published after the conference, Rankine and Cummings reiterate Notley's sentiments, and push at them further:

> Most discourse on late twentieth-century poetics has been written by men, and has aimed to delimit various aesthetic positions or movements. Given that the (slight) majority of poets writing today are women, the dearth of aesthetic spokeswomen for various aesthetic positions is striking. . . . Why is it that so many women poets—or is it simply most poets?—do not want to describe—or is it reify?—their poetics? Perhaps they are not in the habit of theorizing poetry, leaving that to critics or other poets so inclined. Perhaps the wish not to anatomize one's aesthetic position stems from a core belief in slippery subjectivity and a fear of reductively fixing one's position, limiting one's vision of what is possible. Could this belief, this fear, have particular urgency for women writers? . . . Many poets are feeling their ways through an era of turgid, competing aesthetics; are women more likely to respond with reticence, as opposed to braggadocio? Whose nature abhors a vacuum?[6]

These are good questions, and ones this study aims to address throughout. In an effort to counter this "reticence," I have also tried to provide ample space for Guest, Mitchell, Mayer, Notley, and Myles to describe their work and methods in their own words, as I have personally learned so much from listening to them speak for themselves in interviews, lectures, conversation, essays, performance, on the canvas, and/or on the page.

My approach here also differs from surveys such as Lehman's or Ward's in that I do not attempt to seal off the New York School from other concurrent literary or artistic movements in order to valorize or canonize it. While I consistently point out important distinctions between various trends of the postwar period, from the Confessionals to Warhol to Black Arts to L=A=N=G=U=A=G=E writing to so-called identity-based spoken-word performance poetry, generally speaking I treat them here as "one flow," as Myles has put it.[7] I don't see this as fence-sitting as much as the natural result of a certain kind of feminist perspective. For example, while there exist real differences between New York School writing and, say, the less romantic or less expressivist art of Language writing, critical attempts to police their borders become complicated when one considers them through the lens of gender. Language writing is remarkable for being one of the first avant-garde movements with many—perhaps a majority—of female innovators, including luminaries such as Lyn Hejinian, Rae Armantrout, Harryette Mullen, and Leslie Scalapino, and there has been a great deal of fluidity and affinity—personally, textually, and critically—between women writing in the New York School vein and women associated with Language writing.[8] The reasons for such an affinity are complex, but some certainly stem from the fact that many of the women who came to writing in the seventies shared a developing feminist consciousness—a consciousness which challenged and expanded both the New York School's famed antipathy to politics and the male Language writers' occasionally monomaniacal focus on warring economic systems. As Notley recently put it, "If I were to say what I feel most a part of, it's not the New York School, but it is the generation of women poets who are my age, who cut across all of the ways that American poetry is written."[9] In keeping with this cutting across, I hope here to celebrate the specifics of New York School aesthetics as I understand them without holding them up as examples of, or prescriptions for, what poetry "should" do. In a 1995 lecture, Notley's second husband, the late British poet Douglas Oliver, offered up the following aphorism: *"Each narrowing of what contemporary poetry is supposed to do bears with it an equivalent narrowing in the definition of a human being."*[10] The expansive, humane sentiment which urges against such a narrowing has served as a guide and inspiration for me throughout this undertaking.

When I first started writing this book I imagined a simpler title, such as "Women of the New York School." As it soon became apparent that although women have been there all along, they have never been simply *of* or *in*, I shifted to "Women *and* the New York School." Then, after suffering fits of irritation with the (marketing? literary-historical? Platonic? Aristotelian? misogynist? feminist?) demand that all experience or experiment be tamed, or at least made palatable, by categories or captions, I felt increasingly tempted to abandon both "women" and "the New York School" altogether.

But the sly phrase "true abstraction," lifted from O'Hara's 1959 mock manifesto "Personism," helped me to stick with them both. "Personism," O'Hara explains, "a movement which I recently founded and which nobody knows about, interests me a great deal, being so totally opposed to this kind of abstract removal that it is verging on a true abstraction for the first time, really, in the history of poetry" (*Collected Poems*, 498). On the one hand, this "true abstraction" could designate something deeply and truly abstract, with no concrete referent; on the other, it could designate something seemingly abstract that turns out to be "true," that is, real, literal, or materialized.[11] Though I doubt O'Hara had feminism on his mind (indeed, the term had yet to be invented), the tension in his phrase can be productively linked to the longstanding feminist debate over the viability of the categories of "woman" or "women" themselves. In fact many of the arguments against the unexamined use of literary or art-historical groupings or labels have much in common with certain radical feminist arguments against the category of "women."[12] Treating both "women" and "the New York School" as "true abstractions" thus seemed to me one way to keep the terms expansive and alive, and to understand that while their definitions may necessarily remain in flux, they are not without real referents or pragmatic power.

For while O'Hara's "Personism" mocks the seriousness of other twentieth-century isms, as many have noted, it isn't entirely a spoof. His quip about reaching "true abstraction" via a flood of personal details breezily dismantles the age-old opposition of the concrete and the abstract—another prototypical (if, again, unintentional) feminist gesture, and one which lies at the heart of the two thematically linked chapters which constitute part 1 of this study. Chapter 1 considers the problem of women and abstraction via a discussion of Joan Mitchell's abstract painting and the increasingly abstract poetry of

Barbara Guest, while chapter 2 takes up the reverse, as it were, and considers the distinct ways in which the work of three gay New York School men—O'Hara, Schuyler, and Ashbery—contends with the quotidian, the domestic, and the particular. Taken together, these two chapters call attention to an intriguing inversion that developed in this particular art scene at midcentury—an inversion which upends the misogynistic equation that figures women as matter and men as form ("matter" derives from the Latin *mater,* for mother); women as detail and men as generality; women as aberration and men as essence; women as incapable of abstract thought or art and men as their natural practitioners.

Though my study is primarily concerned with literature, when considering the "feminine abstract" and its relation to the New York School, it would be a tremendous oversight not to explore, however briefly, the accomplishments of female Abstract Expressionist painters of the period. Despite earnest and accurate assessments of Abstract Expressionism as inhospitable (to put it mildly) to female artists, I worry that the observation (here made by Michael Leja in *Reframing Abstract Expressionism: Subjectivity and Painting in the 1940s*) that "Elaine [de Kooning] and other female Abstract Expressionists were structurally excluded from the construction of subjectivity embedded in the full experience and production of Abstract Expressionist art" (266) may unintentionally lead to overlooking what the female painters *did* do, whether "structurally excluded" from the terms of the movement or no. Leja is right to note that "[a] dame with an Abstract Expressionist brush is no less a misfit than a *noir* heroine with a rod" (262), but it's crucial to note that for the female painters, such a predicament marked the beginning of a journey, not the end of one. There are many female painters whose work merits discussion here, and I regret that my literary focus momentarily displaces the possibility of a more comprehensive consideration of their work. For my purposes here I have chosen to focus on Mitchell, because she worked solidly in an abstract idiom for forty years, because of the importance of poetry in her life and work, because she was closely tied to O'Hara, Ashbery, and Schuyler as collaborator, muse, fan, and friend, and because I find her painting astonishingly beautiful.

Chapter 2 begins with the supposition that the idea of the New York School as the "last avant-garde" is not nearly as interesting as the ramifications of its being one of the first gay avant-gardes. Here

I aim to show how the continual, often vague alignment of the New York School of poets with Abstract Expressionism (as famously enacted by Donald Allen in his introduction to the influential 1960 anthology *The New American Poetry*) has at times deflected attention from a very potent distinction between the two—namely, the apparent gulf between the stereotype of the serious, macho New York School painter interested in "transcendence," on the one hand, and that of the campy, frivolous, queer poet interested in the quotidian and "deep gossip," on the other. The critical commonplace that poets such as O'Hara and Ashbery were trying to "do" with words what the Abstract Expressionists were "doing" with surface (i.e., flatness, "all-overness," "push-pull," speed, performativity, improvisation, gesture, etc.) is by no means meaningless. But its rush to sublimate the poetry into a formalist paradigm can elide some very interesting questions about sexuality and aesthetics. For while many of the Abstract Expressionists are infamous for casting their art in deeply macho terms (most famously epitomized by the ongoing myth of Jackson Pollock as the artist-hero on a quest into the feminized deep of the unconscious), the first generation of poets have a very different reputation: that of faggy aesthetes, with more controversial sorts of feminine identifications.

I pause over this difference in chapter 2 in order to highlight the fact that the New York School of poets was unique in midcentury America for having a core of openly gay men as its primary practitioners (not to mention a gay man, John Bernard Myers, as their original publisher and the source of their moniker). Indeed, as the gay giants of the New York School era pass on (and here I'm thinking not only of O'Hara and Schuyler, but also of Warhol, Cage, Ginsberg, and others), I think it quite important not to erase their queerness under the guise of not wanting to "reduce" their work to its sexuality. Such a concern—with its assumption that there still exists a need to protect these figures from a homophobia presumed to come from without—strikes me as outdated, confining, and unnecessary.[13] As the feminist critic Shoshana Felman has smartly pointed out, sexuality takes on the status of an answer to a text only in the relation of interpretation; in the relation of transference, it takes on the status of a question (171).

Chapter 2 explores some of these questions, primarily through a roving examination of the poets' various feminine identifications. That said, nowhere do I mean to suggest that male homosexuality and effeminacy are inevitably or intrinsically linked, nor am I particularly interested in delimiting any monolithic "gay sensibility."[14] Rather, I consider the subject here in the context of a larger conversation about the various roles played by the feminine in the history of male lyric poetry and its critical reception—a complex issue which has been lucidly explored by Barbara Johnson (especially in *The Feminist Difference*) among others. In light of this conversation, I have become increasingly wary of any critical attempts to exalt O'Hara's localized "I do this, I do that" poems, or Schuyler's "things to do" laundry-list poems, which blithely skip over gender issues. In her book *Reading in Detail: Aesthetics and the Feminine*, Naomi Schor considers the recent theoretical privileging of "the detail" by Jacques Derrida (not to mention Freud, Barthes, Foucault, Lacan, de Man, Habermas, and so on), and poses the following important questions: "Does the triumph of the detail signify a triumph of the feminine with which it has long been linked? Or has the detail achieved new prestige by being taken over by the masculine, triumphing at the very moment when it ceases to be associated with the feminine?" (6). When considering the related "triumph" of "contingency over universality"—or of "self-resistance and uncertainty" over the model of an autonomous, stable self—which characterizes so much twentieth-century philosophy and theory (as well as many critical conversations about New York School aesthetics), one may indeed find oneself wondering whether such ideas maintain their power and panache only when partitioned off from feminist inquiry.[15] One point of my study is to abolish such partitions, and to avert yet another scenario in which, as Jane Gallop has put it, "being antiphallic becomes the new phallus, which women come up lacking once again."[16]

To do so, one needs to find a way to talk about the role of the detail, the contingent, and the quotidian in New York School writing which does not repress the fact that "the detail does not occupy a conceptual space beyond the laws of sexual difference: the detail is gendered and doubly gendered as feminine" (Schor, *Detail*, 4). To celebrate, for example, the "abundance of localized detail" in O'Hara's poem "The Day Lady Died" (the poem begins: "It is 12:20 in New York a Friday / three days after Bastille day, yes / it is 1959 and I go get a shoeshine / because I will get off the 4:19 in Easthampton / at 7:15 and then go straight to dinner"), and then to argue that the poem is great because "historians a century hence" could use such detail to "piece together the New York of that moment in the same way that archaeologists can reconstruct a whole extinct species of dinosaur from a single fossil bone" (Lehman, 202), is to construct a peculiar double bind: O'Hara's "abundance of localized detail" represents a departure from—indeed a threat to—the traditional gender equation that figures women as "attentive to their immediate surroundings, the finished product, the decorative, the concrete, the individual," while "men prefer what is most distant, the constructive, the general and abstract,"[17] but by degendering such a reversal—and by insisting that O'Hara's details will somehow *matter* to future historians the same way a precious fossil will—the critic notes O'Hara's difference only to sublimate it into a traditional conception of literary value.

For it isn't just a matter of celebrating the details qua details, or of returning them to their more traditional role as thruways to the "archeological" or the "universal" (that age-old ticket to literary seriousness and durability). As Schor eloquently explains: "By reversing the terms of the oppositions and the values of hierarchies, we remain, of course, only just barely able to dream a universe where the categories of *general* and *particular*, *mass* and *detail*, and *masculine* and *feminine* would no longer order our thinking and our seeing" (*Detail*, 4–5). The poetry associated with the New York School—like any art grouped under a label—is incredibly diverse. But if I had to make one tactical generalization about the writing I will be discussing here, it might be this: when considered together, its paradoxical commitment to "true abstraction" offers a rich field from which to rethink, or re-experience, these presumably opposing categories (to which I would also add *personal* and *public*, *world* and *word*, *daily* and *epic*). It is my contention—indeed, it has been my experience—that the different ways in which New York School–related poetry has gone about this task can have a truly liberating effect on those writing and reading in its wake. For whatever the New York School may be, one of its effects has been to allow male writers to explore a different relationship to materiality and immanence, and, conversely, female writers a claim on abstraction and idealism. The poetry itself rarely gets bogged down in lofty, humorless claims about such matters, but the stakes of this exchange could not really be higher, as they concern nothing less than the question of how "being-man" and "being-woman" can both be thought as "primary, originary forms."[18]

THE STAKES OF A DISCUSSION about the New York School, its particular nexus of gender and sexuality, and its status as an avant-garde are also both higher and broader than they may initially appear. For if, as Lehman has argued, the New York School was indeed "the last authentic avant-garde" in the United States, and if that last avantgarde coincided with everything from the "the death of the public intellectual" to "the expansion of the purview of academe" to "the triumph of a slick, mass-produced globalization" to the rise of "irony" at the expense of "sincerity," to a kind of doomed infatuation with poststructuralist theory and its unpopular (if not a bit outmoded) association with moral relativism (whatever that might mean), one might fairly ask why such a bell tolls for the American avant-garde precisely at the cultural moment of the triple "liberations" of the civil rights movement, the women's movement, and the gay/lesbian rights movement, and the consequent rise to prominence of art from these corners. To declare the death of an art form—or of the civic value of the academy, for that matter—just as its demographics and fields of interest undergo a profound and hard-won diversification—strikes me as deeply troubling. Lehman and others are right to diagnose the disturbing and daunting impediments facing the avant-garde impulse today—the ever-increasing commodification of literary production; the absorption of so many writers and intellectuals into the academy, coupled with the increasing corporatization of the academy itself; a widespread loss of faith in personal and/or collective potency in the face of a homogenizing, globalizing capitalism; and so on. But I would also ask hard questions of any nostalgia for a time—or the fantasy of a time, as the case may be—when the so-called avant-garde was safely dominated by white men (many of whom, in the case of the New York School of poets, came to New York straight out of Harvard).

For nostalgia notoriously works to create a mythic past, which it then mourns. This cycle, while arguably quite human, can engender a blindness to new impulses and movements that do not fit into previous models.[19] Part 2 of my study, which consists of career studies of Mayer, Notley, and Myles, counters this cycle by examining how the work of these three women has enlarged the scope of possibilities for poetic project, feminist imagination, and even political action (especially in the case of Myles, who conducted an "openly female" write-in campaign for president in 1992). These three chapters pay special attention to the ways in which certain New York School tropes necessarily morph when their practitioners are women, whose historical relationship to detail, the personal, the local, and the quotidian is somewhat overdetermined. At times, as we shall see, this morphing has entailed a wholesale rejection of some of these tropes: Mayer has testified to having an "incredible resistance to New York School writing"; Myles has called "third- or fourth-generation New York School poetry . . . too decadent to be believed"; and Notley recently told me, "I don't like the quotidian much any more either as new writing or as living."[20]

In addition to examining this vexed stance toward the fetishized daily (or more than vexed—"The everyday makes me barf," Myles recently wrote [*Sorry Tree*, 73]), part 2 also considers a number of other mutations. For example, while chapter 2 discusses the campy domesticity at play in Ashbery, it is quite a leap to the domesticity in Mayer's *Midwinter Day* (written as a piece on December 22, 1978), and *The Desires of Mothers to Please Others in Letters* (written during the period of a pregnancy in 1979–80), both of which perform the difficulties of the domestic quotidian for a woman who feels herself ensconced in a certain form of "female anonymity," as Myles has put it.[21] This difficulty deepens when that woman is a mother (as discussed in the chapters on Mayer and Notley), and/or a lesbian (as discussed in the chapter on Myles). Likewise, as dirty-minded as the men in chapter 2 get, we shall also see how the celebrated "trash aesthetic" of male artists from Duchamp to Schwitters to Rauschenberg to Ashbery inevitably reads differently when its practitioners are women, as women have a historically distinct—again, overdetermined—relation to pollution.[22] And as my consideration of Myles makes clear, the literary tradition of the writer as *flâneur*—a tradition of great importance to O'Hara, for example—simply cannot remain intact when the *flâneur* becomes a *flâneuse*.

But perhaps the most persistent, most compelling mutation running through part 2 has to do with these three writers' take on the vacillation between "caring" and "not caring" that characterizes so much New York School writing and attitude. In the conclusion of her book on O'Hara, Marjorie Perloff cuts to the heart of the problem: "All his life, O'Hara refused to *care* in the conventional sense; he would not fight for publication or scramble for prizes. But perhaps he adopted this stance because he knew, all along, that we would indeed be looking" (197). In his study, Lehman extends this idea to argue that this "not-caring" stance was primarily a put-on—that underneath it all, the New York School poets cared deeply about poetry, about fame, and about creating lasting and complex works of art that would rise to the top of the heap in posterity. "They were dedicated to the new, and implacably opposed to the poetry of the academy," he writes. "But they did not confuse the new with the ephemeral. They never forgot that the aim of a poem was to live forever" (290). There may be some truth in this statement, but its sudden downgrade of the ephemeral, along with its dismissal of the poets' aversion to mainstream, reverential notions of artistic success or merit, is jarring. *Celebrating the ephemeral or marginal is all fine for fun and games*, it seems to say. *But in the end, this is no sand painting. It's Poetry, and with a capital P.*

No one can pretend to know the extent of the inner fantasies of fame, recognition, and adulation that the male New York School poets harbored (or still harbor)—and surely they harbored some, as most human beings, and certainly most artists, do. But I think we lose something pivotal when an intense drive toward canonization leads us to discount O'Hara's statement—"I don't think of fame or posterity (as Keats so grandly and genuinely did), nor do I care about clarifying experiences for anyone or bettering (other than accidentally) anyone's state or social relation, nor am I for any particular technical development in the American language simply because I find it necessary" (*CP*, 500)—as a simple fronting, evasion, or deception. Here I am more interested in the wavering between "caring" and "not-caring"—about literary stature, about politics, about "good writing," about posterity, about the role of the poet in the world, about P/poetry itself, about publication, about "bettering anyone's social relation," about the fate of the avant-garde, and so on—than on making an eventual decision between which stance is "code" and which "real." In fact I would argue that it is precisely this wavering—with all its attendant skepticism, indecision, insubordination, and insouciance—which has helped make the New York School so attractive and useful to women poets writing in its wake, who found (and to some extent continue to find) themselves charged with navigating their way through a male-dominated literary scene and history which has never "cared" about their voices in the same way that it has about those of men.

Despite this attractiveness, however, it is also the case that the stakes of this caring/not caring inevitably differ for women as compared to both gay and straight men. In the online journal *Narrativity* Myles lays it out as follows:

> Let's face it, [the male New York School poets] were just as New Critical as everyone else in the fifties. They would all assert that the poetry was not about them. It's about skimming the surface of the self. Using that facility to shape the poem. My dirty secret has always been that it's of course all about me. But I have been educated to believe I'm no one so there's a different self operating and I'm desperate to unburden my self of my self so I'm coming from nowhere and returning. That's sort of classic. You just cannot underestimate the massive difference in writing out of female anonymity. It blows all styles out of the water. (n.p.)

Part 2 zeros in on this "massive difference," and argues that the various ways in which Mayer, Notley, and Myles have combined this irreverent, nonchalant "skimming the surface of self" with feminist urgency, political conviction, and literary bravado have produced some of the most alive and necessary poetry to date.

Further, while all three women at issue in part 2 "care" about the art of poetry, the role of the poet in the world, and what it means to commit one's life utterly to practicing and inhabiting both, as much as or more than any other contemporary American poets I can think of, it's worth noting that this caring never leads them into the morose, nostalgic conversations about the fate of the art that have recently preoccupied so many poets and critics, epitomized by book titles such as Dana Gioia's *Can Poetry Matter?*, Vernon Shetley's *After the Death of Poetry*, or even Lehman's *The Last Avant-Garde*.[23] It's notable—though not surprising—that not one book-length epitaph for "popular" poetry or the avant-garde has been penned by a woman (or, I might add, by a person of color). There's simply too much other work to do. Recent years have in fact seen an explosion of critical work on the avant-garde and its relation to women and feminism, in the form of critical studies such as Elizabeth Frost's *The Feminist Avant-Garde in American Poetry* and Juliana Spahr's *Everybody's Autonomy*, anthologies such as *American Women Poets in the Twenty-first Century: Where Lyric Meets Language* (edited by Rankine and Spahr) and *The New Fuck You: Adventures in Lesbian Reading* (edited by Myles and Liz Kotz), not to mention a flood of adventuresome writing by women from all quarters. The purview of the present study is more local, but I remain grateful for and indebted to the energy, experiment, and nerve of all of this work.

Over the past few decades it has become something of a feminist maxim that the "anxiety-of-influence" model that still implicitly and explicitly shapes so much thinking about literary history cannot be easily mapped onto women writers, who are so often engaged in the opposite activity: actively searching out predecessors and models instead of feeling oppressed by them. In her essay "The Lesbian Poet" (in *School of Fish*) Myles reiterates this gesture, asking "Where's the mothers," before answering herself: "Gertrude. Gertrude Stein, of course. And all the living women I know" (127). The present study—which pays a significant amount of attention to Stein, and also to several living women, many of whom I know—also follows along this path. Later in her talk Myles says: "Women I know are turning around to see if that woman is here. The woman turning, that's the revolution. The room is gigantic, the woman is here" (130). If it isn't obvious by now, I'd like to add that this project is clearly a result of my own "turning"—my own (gratified) desire, as poet, fan, and feminist, to recognize some of the others I've found in the room.

PART ONE

1

ABSTRACT PRACTICES

THE ART OF JOAN MITCHELL,

BARBARA GUEST, AND THEIR OTHERS

TOP: *Joan Mitchell in her studio in Vétheuil with her dog, Bertie, 1972.*
Copyright © 1972 Nancy Crampton. Used by permission of Nancy Crampton and
courtesy of the Joan Mitchell Foundation. BOTTOM: *Barbara Guest in Sermoneta, Italy,*
1965. Photograph by Gloria Finn. Reprinted courtesy of Hadley Haden-Guest.

As THE DUST of the twentieth century settles, it's quite possible that many artists, writers, and critics would identify the move away from "the impediment of 'representation,' all that easy mimicry, etc." (as Robert Creeley has put it) and toward differing forms of "abstraction" as one of—if not the—defining impulse in both verbal and visual art. In the seventies Creeley went so far as to assert that this move "gave us, in short, what art we have had in the last 50 years. At least that" (Yau, 52), and many would probably (if grudgingly) agree.

But throughout the modernist period, for every Wallace Stevens who stayed busy elaborating the idea of a Supreme Fiction that "must be abstract," there was also a William Carlos Williams proclaiming "No ideas but in things!" As Wendy Steiner has observed about the many literary modernists who came out "on the side of things" (whatever that might mean), "writer after writer—no matter how hermetically his work was cut off from the 'average reader'—vowed his hatred of abstraction" (183). And while Creeley himself celebrates abstraction as *the* major event of twentieth-century art, he also adds this caveat: "Danger is very much present in the too simple concept: 'abstraction.' The idea of it, rather than the practice" (Yau, 52). Similarly, Gertrude Stein—who perhaps worked harder than any other writer in the twentieth century to disrupt the tradition of mimesis as metaphor for or goal of artistic practice—was also quite wary of abstraction, which she famously deemed "pornographic."[1]

Given these recurrent tensions, it may make more sense to highlight not abstraction per se as the twentieth-century's overriding obsession, but rather the negotiation a work of art makes between its dual status as a sign of the thing-world and a part of the thing-world. This negotiation certainly has its roots in modernism (in Duchamp's readymades, in the cubist collages of Picasso and Braque, in Stein's nonrepresentational still lifes and portraiture, and so on), but in retrospect also appears the animating force of much else: Pollock's drip paintings, Rauschenberg's combines, Warhol's soup cans, Robert Smithson's earthworks, Carolee Schneeman's body art, and so on. It also continues to shape much contemporary debate about American poetry—a debate which still worries over whether poetry should privilege "the word over the world." In the past few decades, the varying debates about Language writing and its challenges have presented the most salient example: in his 1993 book *After the Death of Poetry*, for instance, Shetley compares the chilly poles of New Formalism and Language writing to conclude that poetry's cultural reputation has been lost, and can only be restored if it manages to strike some kind of balance between the two extremes—that is, if the poetry of the future can "bring together the authority of skeptical reflection with that of experience. Neither is adequate by itself" (191).

Some feminists might scoff at this fuzzy, seemingly outdated dichotomy of "reflection" vs. "experience," but a similar split continues to run through feminist conversations about women's writing. The 1999 Barnard conference, for example, hopefully titled "Where Lyric Tradition Meets Language Poetry: Innovation in Contemporary American Poetry by Women," ended up mostly underscoring the divide; as Frances Richard later observed about the event in the spring–summer 2000 issue of *Fence* magazine, it was as if "the poetic spectrum had collapsed to navel-gazing lyric or egg-headed language and the twain could never meet" (87). In another statement published in *Fence* after the conference, the organizers (Rankine and Cummings) asked almost plaintively, "Might the opposition between object and representation be addressed in other, less combative terms?" (126)

This chapter addresses this question through a consideration of the "abstract practices" of the painter Joan Mitchell and the poet Barbara Guest. Creeley's phrase is important here not only because it emphasizes the decades-long commitment to her artistic practice that both Mitchell and Guest made, but also because it serves as a helpful reminder of the fact that "abstract is not a style," as Mitchell was fond of saying. Indeed, regardless of its hold on the twentieth-century imagination, abstraction is not any one thing (as a cursory walk through a gallery containing works by artists such as Kandinsky, Miró, Rothko, Agnes Martin, Robert Ryman, Bridget Riley, and Amy Sillman, for example, would quickly make clear). Similarly, the various kinds of abstraction explored by writers of the past century or so are nothing if not diverse: no one would say that Mallarmé, Stein, Creeley, Celan, and Ashbery, for example, contend with abstraction in the same, or even similar, ways. What's more, as Wendy Steiner reminds us, when it comes to abstraction, the painting-literature analogy is by no means a simple one, complicated as it is by "the ability of painting to be utterly abstract and the corresponding inability of literature to be so, since it is composed of words that have preexisting meanings" (*Colors*, 65–66). The complexity of this analogy only deepens when one contends with the broad, slippery, and often vague employment of the word "abstract" by critics, artists, and writers alike, and the confusions that can arise when the word gets dragged across multiple disciplines.[2]

The work of both Mitchell and Guest speaks generously and provocatively to Rankine and Cummings's question—"Might the opposition between object and representation be addressed in other, less combative terms?"—but I want to make clear at the outset that I'm not holding them up as examples of artists who've somehow bridged the gap, so to speak. Such a goal doesn't strike me as possible or even desirable. As O'Hara demonstrated in his statement for Allen's *New American Poetry*, it's the mysterious movement between the concrete and the abstract that can be so much fun: "It may be that poetry makes life's nebulous events tangible to me and restores their detail; or conversely, that poetry brings forth the intangible quality of incidents which are all too concrete and circumstantial. Or each on specific occasions, or both all the time" (420). In keeping with this vacillating spirit, I hope here to underscore how Guest and Mitchell are each central to their fields and periods, and at the same time to chart the ways in which their specific "abstract practices" represent an important mark of difference within them: Joan Mitchell's slowed-down, landscape-oriented practice of abstraction differs tremendously from the better-known and mythologized accounts of New York School action painting; likewise, while Barbara Guest is endlessly referred to as the only woman poet in the first generation of the New York School, her work is often strikingly different from that of Ashbery, Koch, O'Hara, and Schuyler, and for a variety of reasons has not found an easy home in their "school."[3] As far as I see it, one could easily consider each woman's work as either emblematic or disruptive of the terms of the movements with which it is associated—the first move aims to shifts them to the center, the second, to preserve the power of the margin. Both gestures have their temptations, but I suspect the tension between them is more engaging if left unresolved.

At first this approach may appear to resemble the one taken by Ward in his review of Guest's *If So, Tell Me* (in *Jacket* 10), in which he writes:

It is possible to reconfigure the New York School showing Barbara Guest to be of marginal, or equally, of major importance. There are obvious links. She connected with the world of visual arts, and indeed her work may be more genuinely influenced by abstract painting than is the male poets'. . . . However it is in part the quality of the *parallel* that finally sets her apart from the male poets with whom she conversed, and for much of the time her work does not resemble theirs at all. . . . The two wider traditions in which it might be even more useful to situate her work would be those of modernist women's poetry (particularly given her biography of H.D.), and ultimately, aestheticism. (n.p.)

I agree with Ward's tacit point, that there's no "correct" way of constructing a movement—that the very construction of one endlessly invites being "reformulated, expanded, or exploded by reading different texts," as he says elsewhere. Surely that's all part of the critical dance, and without it, many would be out of a job. But despite Guest's real affinity with H.D. and other modernists, the idea of situating her work with other "women's poetry" gives me pause, as it cleaves Guest from her milieu—a redundant gesture, at this point—not to mention modernist women from modernist men.

For while there's intrigue and excitement in the idea of a parallel tradition, there's real conflict, too. There also exist profound aesthetic differences between the male members of the New York School of poets and painters that should not be overlooked (a Schuyler poem rarely "resembles" an Ashbery poem; a painting by Kline rarely "resembles" one by Pollock), but the problem remains that profound differences between male artists do not always preclude their membership in a group or club. In fact, critics often treat such differences as necessary to the formation of a sort of gang of superheros, in which each wields his own special power (i.e., "If each of the four [poets] had a role to play, Ashbery's was that of the Poet . . . O'Hara was the hero . . . Koch was the madcap," and so on [Lehman, 72]), or as paradigmatic of important shifts in purpose or sensibility (i.e., the alleged split between the camps of Pollock and Willem de Kooning, or the alleged "defacement" of Abstract Expressionist gesture by artists such as Rauschenberg and Cy Twombly, etc.). In the case of the male Abstract Expressionist painters, the more vociferous the differences among them, the more these differences were heralded as proof of their "irascible" individuality—a club-by-divergences which famously took a literal form for some time as "The Club."[4]

On a more basic level, the construction of a parallel tradition also airlifts women out of the scene in which they lived and worked. In his memoir *Tracking the Marvelous: A Life in the New York Art World*, John Bernard Myers describes the New York School milieu as follows: "Grace Hartigan and Jane Freilicher divided O'Hara and Ashbery between them. Nellie Blaine latched onto Koch. Helen Frankenthaler and Mary Abbot took up with Barbara Guest, as did Robert Goodnough" (147). Later, in discussing the Artists Theatre formed in 1953, Myers writes:

> Our program that first year consisted of four one-act plays written for us: Tennessee Williams' *Auto-Da-Fé*, with décor by Robert Soule; *Try! Try!* by Frank O'Hara, décor by Larry Rivers; *Presenting Jane* by James Schuyler, film sequence by John Latouche, décor by Elaine de Kooning; and *Red Riding Hood* by Kenneth Koch, set by Grace Hartigan. . . . We moved to the Comedy Club for our next presentation. . . . We used for this program a play by John Ashbery, *The Heros*, décor by Nellie Blaine, *The Lady's Choice* by Barbara Guest, décor by Jane Freilicher, and *The Bait* by James Merrill, décor by Albert Kresch. (166)

I reprint this brief snapshot not only to suggest the flavor of the artistic production of the place and time, but also to call attention to the novelty of men (primarily gay men) and women working side by side in that production, taking each other's writing and art seriously—a trend that didn't necessarily extend to other midcentury avant-garde scenes, such as the more homosocial environments of the San Francisco Renaissance or Black Mountain College (a point chapter 2 explores in more detail). In tribute to this fact, this chapter pays a significant amount of attention to the work of Mitchell and Guest on its own, and also in relation to, and sometimes collaboration with, the work of other male figures of the period, including Schuyler, Ashbery, O'Hara, and Joe Brainard, while it also sets forth larger questions about women, abstraction, and the processes of literary and art history.[5]

IT'S A DAUNTING TASK to bring a feminist perspective to bear on artists famous for bristling at the very presence of the words "women" and "artist" in the same sentence. When asked to write a response to Linda Nochlin's famous 1971 article "Why Have There Been No Great Women Artists?" Elaine de Kooning sent the following:

> I was talking to Joan Mitchell once at a party ten years ago when a man came up to us and said, "What do you women artists think . . ." Joan grabbed my arm and said, "Elaine, let's get the hell out of here." That was my first response to Linda Nochlin's essay. I was curious about how a man would react. Alex Katz thought it would be a cop-out to answer the piece. Sherman (Drexler) thought it would be a cop-out not to answer it. John Cage thought the question "divisive and an over-simplification." I agree with all of them. (Hesse, 56)

"Let's get the hell out of here" seems to me an understandable response. But the progress of de Kooning's comment is telling, insofar as her next response is to canvass the important men in her life, as if a chorus of male opinion were a prerequisite to knowing what she wanted to say. She then takes an undeniable pleasure in agreeing with the men, and aligning against the feminist scholar. It's not an unusual stance, especially at that particular cultural moment: before the feminist movement (and, I'm sure some would argue, long after) such an attitude was something of a prerequisite for women to get in and stay in the conversation—the way to get ahead, get seen, get heard. Looking back on this period in a 1986 conversation with Nochlin, Mitchell elaborates on this aspect of the painting scene:

JOAN MITCHELL: . . . I think the women were, some of them, more down on women than the men.

LINDA NOCHLIN: Yeah, that's perfectly possible.

JOAN MITCHELL: [A lot, Like], you know.

LINDA NOCHLIN: But I just wondered whether the generally nonsupportive atmosphere for women artists, whether it's by fellow women, or by men, or by a general atmosphere, or what?

JOAN MITCHELL: Oh, I don't know. I adulated the men so much they sort of liked me. I mean, I thought Bill [de Kooning] was a great painter. They liked me.

LINDA NOCHLIN: Yeah, but I mean, they would have liked you if you weren't a painter, too. I mean, was there any feeling that . . .

JOAN MITCHELL: I don't think. . . . No, no, [Conrad] Marca-Relli [shows at McGee now] and Nic Carone [teaches at Studio School] in the

Stable Gallery, they . . . Hans Hofmann was very supportive—of me. I used to run into him in the park. I'd be dog-walking at nine in the morning, he'd say, "Mitchell, you should be painting." Very nice. (both chuckle) I don't think women in any way were a threat to these men, so they could encourage the "lady painter."

LINDA NOCHLIN: Umm. But what if you . . .

JOAN MITCHELL: Oh, no, I was very seriously involved in painting, they knew that.

LINDA NOCHLIN: Yeah.

JOAN MITCHELL: Philip Guston was very nice to me.

LINDA NOCHLIN: Yes. So you didn't feel any difference?

JOAN MITCHELL: Well, about what?

LINDA NOCHLIN: I mean, if you'd been a man painter?

JOAN MITCHELL: I would have had a lot easier time.

LINDA NOCHLIN: Yeah, okay. (n.p.)

At a different point in the conversation, still undaunted by the task of trying to needle some feminism or protofeminism out of Mitchell, Nochlin pushes at her to say more about how it felt to be a woman painter amidst so many men. Mitchell responds: "How did I feel, like how? I felt, you know, when I was discouraged I wondered if really women couldn't paint, the way all the men said they [the women] couldn't paint. But then at other times I said, 'Fuck them,' you know."

As the above conversation may indicate, Mitchell was not big on feminism per se. But her "fuck them" sentiment is certainly of a piece with the immense effort made by feminists over the past thirty years or so to lay bare the misogyny which for centuries has posited women as the antithesis to abstraction or transcendence. Paul Valéry summed up this attitude cogently in his remark: "*The more abstract an art, the fewer women there are who have made a name for themselves in that art*" (see Schor, *Detail*, 17). Annoying as it is, I'd like this comment to haunt this chapter, as it may serve as a constant reminder of what was at stake for the women at the heart of the Abstract Expressionist enterprise.

A slightly more complicated but equally necessary feminist approach to keep in mind is the one staged by the French feminist Luce Irigaray. In a paraphrase of Irigaray, Butler articulates the shift in the terms of the debate that Irigaray's work makes as follows: "The problem is not that the feminine is made to stand for matter or for universality; rather, the feminine is cast out outside the form/matter and universal/particular binarisms. . . . Irigaray insists that this exclusion that mobilizes the form/matter binary is the differentiating relation between masculine and feminine, where the masculine occupies both terms of binary opposition, and the feminine cannot be said to be an intelligible term at all" (*Bodies*, 38–39). Irigaray's subsequent wager, of course, is that the repressed feminine—which is precisely that which cannot be named, being neither a particular nor a universal (these are Plato's terms)— "emerges within the system as incoherence, a threat to its own systematicity" (*Bodies*, 39). It's important to remember that Irigaray is talking about the feminine, not about women; as she says tartly elsewhere, "for the elaboration of a theory of woman, men, I think, suffice" (*This Sex*, 123). The distinction matters, for without it, one might slip into the expectation that women artists and writers should or could somehow exemplify in some direct way a *peinture* or *écriture féminine*—which is precisely what the female Abstract Expressionists feared most. As Mitchell once complained, "A man can put on pink [paint] and it's 'sensitive.' A woman puts it on and it's 'feminine,' which is a dirty word" (Benstock, 163).

This study makes no claims on discovering the "repressed feminine," but it does take Irigaray's desire to disrupt the form/matter binary seriously. And in the twentieth century, no writer concentrated harder on this problem than Gertrude Stein. As Wendy Steiner concludes *Exact Resemblance to Exact Resemblance*, her study of Stein's tenacious experiments in nonrepresentational portraiture: "A literalist interpretation of the direction set for western art by the mimetic program could only lead to defeat, and if for no other reason, we must credit Stein with forcing herself to full consciousness of this fact. The demands of artistry and reference make possible only an uneasy mutual compromise, a compromise in which Stein refused to take comfort" (204–205). In *The Autobiography of Alice B. Toklas*, Stein describes (in third person, of course) her discomfort with this compromise as follows: "She was, and is, tormented by the problem of the external and the internal" (119). Precisely because of her dogged confrontation of this torment—and her generosity in sharing it with others—Stein stands as the towering figure over any discussion of the problem of referentiality and abstraction in twentieth-century writing.

While Stein is generally assumed to be a patron saint of Language writing, her relationship to the New York School has gone fairly unexamined. Ward's study mentions Stein in passing three times, each time only to tell us that she was "a favourite" of O'Hara's, and that O'Hara's work "may owe something" to her work. But what, exactly, O'Hara might have loved about Stein never becomes clear. (She does, however, get more airtime in Lehman's study.) Stein in fact thought and wrote obsessively about many issues intimate to any conversation about New York School writing: the relationship between poetry and painting; the particular relationship Americans have to abstraction ("like Spaniards, [Americans] are abstract and cruel," she says in *The Autobiography* [91]); the problem of "flat depth" (or, as T. J. Clark puts it in reference to Picasso's *Ma Jolie*, a "relentless shallowness" in which "farce and metaphysic" coexist simultaneously [178]); the ontology of the avant-garde; the relations (or lack thereof) between aestheticism and politics; the problems of artistic coterie and general audience; a commitment to charting the "continuous present" and the habits of attention that form consciousness; the related fascinations of identity, money, sexuality, and temporality, and their roles in the creative process; and so on.

Stein's enormous body of work in fact reminds us over and over again how misleading the opposition of the abstract and the concrete can be. For the more abstract her writing gets, the more concrete it feels; as Ashbery once said about *Tender Buttons*, the writing ends up imparting "an unfathomable solidity" (*Reported Sightings*, 108).[6] Of course this phenomenon is quickly recognizable as one of the primary lessons of modernist experimentation: when referentiality drops out, the materiality of the form (in this case, of the words) tends to become more acute, as Stein's mantra "A rose is a rose is a rose is a rose" famously exemplifies. But although Stein was converted by Cézanne's turn to "the reality of the composition," she remained equally enraptured by the endless task of "expressing the rhythm of the visible world" (*ABT*, 119). Mary Jo Haronian and others have usefully connected this dual commitment to Stein's medical training—specifically, to her study of the brain at Harvard, where she researched how thought patterns function as actual neuronal modes (Haronian, 193).

The connection is an important one—as is Stein's kinship with the philosophy of William James and Alfred North Whitehead—for it reminds us that the abstract/concrete dyad only makes sense within a certain mind/body split that Stein spent her early career troubling as a medical researcher, and her later career troubling as a writer. And while she may have been tormented by the split, her elaborations of this torment have carried for many readers the charge of liberation. The experience of reading a work like *Tender Buttons*—which was, as Stein puts it, "the beginning of mixing the outside with the inside" (*ABT*, 156)—not only makes palpable the notion that "we awake in the same moment to ourselves and to things," as philosopher Jacques Maritain once put it, but also suggests that one simply cannot choose between them. As Stein might say, you're better off liking what you have—and in a real and mysterious sense, we seem to have both.

In a recent essay titled "Voice," Notley writes, "There is nothing in Stein but—I'm tempted to say—voice; hardly ever anything but . . . a voice so whole that it is an abstraction" (*Interim*, 152). If New York School poetry is indeed "chatty abstraction," as Myles has said, Stein's paradoxical method of troubling referentiality by "flooding the world with her details" is a crucial forerunner of such (see Myles, *Mississippi*, 228; *Fish*, 131). O'Hara's wager about "Personism"—that it is "so totally opposed to this kind of abstract removal that it is verging on a true abstraction for the first time, really, in the history of poetry"—can be read as yet another testimony to this Steinian revelation. O'Hara, Koch, Schuyler, and Ashbery all understood the potentiality in this flood of details, with its love for proper nouns, intemperate speech, and the redundancy of objects. Of course the fact that Stein was a woman, and a butch lesbian at that, complicates any patrilineal "anxiety of influence" model—a problem Lehman solves (in his reading of the O'Hara poem "Memorial Day 1950") by including Stein on a list of O'Hara's "freely elected father-substitutes" (181). For my purposes here, I'd prefer to let Stein stand as yet another marker of difference in the field—as the apparitional lesbian, to use Terry Castle's phrase—whose life and work haunts, and perhaps mocks, the supposition that "the more abstract an art, the fewer women there are who have made a name for themselves in that art."

Joan Mitchell, with her forty-year career of vigorous abstract painting, is another figure who defies such a dictum. Mitchell is constantly referred to as one of the strongest painters of the so-called second generation of the New York School (a label that the so-called second-generation painters always chafed against, as one might expect). In the summer of 2002, the Whitney Museum housed a

Mitchell retrospective at the same time that four New York galleries showed her work,[7] hopefully further evidence that she is continuing to gather attention in the United States since her death in France in 1992. Mitchell had a lifelong investment in literature and in poetry in particular—her mother, Marion Strobel, was a poet and a coeditor of the influential magazine *Poetry*; Mitchell was married for a time to Barney Rosset, the founder of Grove Press; O'Hara, Schuyler, and Ashbery were all important friends to her; she and Samuel Beckett were intimate confidantes in Paris; and she was a devoted fan of many other poets, including Rilke, Wordsworth, and Eliot. Mitchell often titled her paintings after poems by O'Hara (such as *To the Harbormaster* [1957] and *Ode to Joy* [1970–71]); in his Mitchell monograph, Klaus Kertess usefully relates the "extreme one-to-oneness between viewer and painting" in Mitchell's work to the kind of intimacy proposed in O'Hara's manifesto "Personism" (25). Mitchell also titled paintings after Schuyler poems (such as *A Few Days After II [After James Schuyler]* [1985]), and in the mid-seventies she did a series of "color abstracts" to accompany the Schuyler poems "Sunset," "Daylight," and "Sunday." She also collaborated with John Ashbery: in 1960, Tiber Press published 225 copies of a book of Ashbery poems accompanied by prints of Mitchell silkscreens, called *The Poems*. In addition to reviewing her work regularly, Ashbery also wrote the foreword to a 1992 Mitchell monograph.[8]

For all of these reasons, nearly every monograph on Mitchell begins by citing the importance of poetry to her painting. (Judith Benstock's, for example, begins: "Several themes predominate in Mitchell's painting. Poetry, generally, lyrical and rooted in nature, is foremost among these" [11].) In contrast, very few literary critics have paid much attention to the relationship between Mitchell's particular abstract idiom and New York School poetry, though Mitchell unavoidably pops up in historical accounts as a close friend of O'Hara's and one of the few female regulars at the Cedar Tavern (and one of the most ornery). In O'Hara's case, for many years the focus has remained on the parallel between his famed writing style of "playing the typewriter" and the spontaneity of Action Painting (as epitomized, for example, by the lively poem-paintings he made with Norman Bluhm in 1960), or, more recently, on O'Hara's kinship with the camp and collage of Rauschenberg and Johns.[9] In Schuyler's case, the attention has usually fallen on Fairfield Porter, whom Schuyler freely admitted was his favorite painter, and whose soft-focus realism—a realism which presents "an aspect of everyday life, seen neither as a snapshot nor as an exaltation" (Schuyler, *Selected Art Writings*, 16)—makes for a quick corollary to Schuyler's own role as a scribe of days. These parallels are useful and necessary, and I see no need to displace them; my goal here is to add Mitchell's presence to the conversation.

IN A SENSE, Mitchell's career stands apart from the oft-repeated art history narrative that charts the move from the high "metaphysical heat" of the first generation of Abstract Expressionists to the "blague" of Johns and Rauschenberg to the cool vacancy of Pop, minimalism, and conceptualism(s). Her rage and vigor also set her apart from the quiet realists associated with the New York School, such as Porter, Freilicher, John Button, and so on. Kertess succinctly describes Mitchell's alienation from the critical terms set forth by Clement Greenberg and Harold Rosenberg, the two theorists famous for championing (and perhaps delimiting) New York School aesthetics as follows: "Mitchell made no effort to secure a place in either one of these camps. . . . Greenberg's [formalist] theories seemed to foreclose the possibility of a congruence of painting, nature, and consciousness that she was seeking. Nor could her paint, step back, paint, step back, deliberations qualify her for the ranks of Rosenberg's macho warriors armed with gesture" (20). (Kertess explains elsewhere that Mitchell's "step back, paint, step back, paint" method was "in part necessitated by Mitchell's farsightedness, present since childhood" [18].) Like Stein, Mitchell was known for an unremitting dedication to her art—once Mitchell discovered abstract painting in the late forties, she never went back, not even to flirt with figuration. As Rosset once said, "There was no stopping it. . . . In a society that didn't allow abstract painting she would have gone to jail" (Benstock, 19). What's more, Mitchell's characterization of her painting method—"Call it . . . whatever you want. I paint with oil on canvas—without an easel. I do not condense things. I try to eliminate clichés, extraneous material. I try to make it exact"—would remain accurate throughout her long career (*Theories*, 33).

There are, in fact, several intriguing parallels between Mitchell and Stein. Both pursued their work with an unrelenting largesse and little to no concern for artistic trends, and both were deeply interested in the overlaps between visual and verbal arts. And while both were known as quintessentially "American" artists, each relocated to

France in early adulthood and essentially never came home. Both worked big: Stein on interminable projects such as writing "everybody's autobiography," Mitchell on huge canvases hung vertically—two examples of what Sedgwick might call "fat art," and which stand as challenges to the assumption that a voracious desire to cover space—to "think big"—is an inherently virile impulse. There are also more subtle connections between them, one of which gets triggered by Mitchell's above insistence, "I try to be exact." "Exact" was one of Stein's favorite words, as dramatized at length in her "Completed Portrait of Picasso": "exact resemblance to exact resemblance, the exact resemblance as exact as a resemblance," etc. In *The Autobiography*, Stein boils down her own artistic temperament as follows: "Gertrude Stein, in her work, has always been possessed by the intellectual passion for exactitude in the description of inner and outer reality. . . . She has produced a simplification by this concentration, and as a result the destruction of associational emotion in poetry and prose. . . . [Poetry or prose] should consist of an exact reproduction of either an outer or an inner reality" (211). Stein's distaste for emotion as a source of art-making certainly separates her from Mitchell, who repeatedly described her paintings as "remembered landscapes which involve my feelings" (Benstock, 31)—a phrase which recalls O'Hara's "In Memory of My Feelings" (a poem O'Hara dedicated to painter Grace Hartigan, with whom O'Hara also collaborated). Upon scrutiny, however, Mitchell's approach to the relationship between "inner" and "outer" reality (or "feelings" and "landscape") is quite subtle, methodical, and even scientific. As Ashbery once quoted her as saying: "I'm trying for something more specific than movies of my everyday life: to define a feeling" (*Reported Sightings*, 101). Stein and Mitchell both remained deeply committed to nonrepresentational investigation, but unlike so many of their comrades, they did not conduct their investigations in service of the mythic, the transcendent, the sublime, or even the unconscious. Rather, both were interested in charting the fact of feeling, and its relation to "outer reality," exactly.

Another provocative parallel between the two has to do with the question of audience. It would be an erasure of both artists' ambition to imply that neither cared about finding an audience or achieving worldly success—each worked hard to get her work into the world, and each had, I think, a truly audacious conviction of her own genius. But this phenomenon doesn't interest me quite as much as the question of what kind of audience each had in mind while composing. And both women often conceptualized—or actualized, as the case may be—this audience as a dog. Stein famously said that she wrote for herself and strangers, but she also consistently connected her identity—specifically her creative identity—to that of her dog (presumably her beloved poodle, Basket). In *Everybody's Autobiography*, which documents the identity crisis and writing block that followed the publication of *The Autobiography*, Stein's primary conflict vacillates between "I am I because my little dog knows me" and "perhaps I am not I because my little dog knows me." As Koestenbaum has observed in contemplating Stein's impossible career, "she wrote without an audience, and she wrote against the idea of an audience. . . . Stein's ideal audience is a dog, mute and loyal" (*Cleavage*, 327). In Mitchell's case, when asked in a 1986 interview, "Whom do you paint for?" Mitchell responded, "I suppose I must paint for me and my dogs. We are in the studio and they watch" (*Theories*, 33). Some of Mitchell's best and best-known paintings—*George Went Swimming at Barnes Holes, but It Got Too Cold* (1956), *Skyes* (1960–61), and *Iva* (1973)—refer to her dogs (George was a poodle; Skyes a terrier; Iva a German shepherd). Mitchell had thirteen dogs throughout her life—many were gifts, and her sister was a breeder. In one interview, she unhesitatingly names "music, poems, landscape, and dogs" as the things in life that make her want to paint. She is frequently quoted as saying she prefers the company of dogs to people (Benstock, 43).

So, what's with the dogs? Part of the reason why I'm drawing attention to the dog-as-audience or dog-as-muse concept—beyond the fact that it demonstrates, in Mitchell's case, the pleasure to be found in her deadpan deflation of Abstract Expressionist rhetoric—is that it stands in such sharp contrast to the notion of inspiration, artistic identity, and creative performance as necessarily tethered to the human audience of literary or art history, as in Bloom's every-poem-is-really-about-another-poem schema. And while many might agree with Patricia Yaeger's statement that "the claim of the sublime is that we can—in words or feelings—transcend the normative, the human" (192), I imagine that only a few would immediately link this sublimity to a canine audience. It also throws a wrench—a third term, if you like—into the customary binaries of "artist" and "Nature," or "artist-as-subject" and "world-as-object," and instead suggests a different question: What happens when the human is not the only measure or witness?[10]

Like Schuyler, who is also known for his urban pastoral, Mitchell regularly blurred the division between city and country, perhaps reminding us that in the New York School, getting *out* of the city is often as important as being *in* the city. In 1958, Mitchell told an interviewer, "I am very much influenced by nature as you define it. However, I do not necessarily distinguish it from 'man-made' nature—a city is as strange as a tree" (*Theories*, 31). (The structural similarities between the early paintings *Evenings on 73rd Street* and *Hemlock*, for example—both from 1956—seem to bear this out.) At times Mitchell goes a bit further: in a 1986 interview, she tells the following story of her paintings leaving her studio for a show in New York: "I was in the garden and the trees and the garden were beautiful and there was a beautiful light and I saw the paintings moving. A big strong man lifted moved them with great ease and I saw all their colors between the trees moving and it was like a parade and I was happy" (*Theories*, 34). The anecdote indicates something of the deep pleasure to be found in the blurring of boundaries between art and nature, pigment and color, human and nonhuman, aesthete and naturalist, and so on—not to mention the profound gratification of evacuation, of getting rid of one's art, and of watching it join the procession of objects in the world (as Warhol celebrated with his floating silver pillows).

Unlike Stein, however, who explicitly envisioned modernist experiment (hers and Picasso's, primarily) as necessarily destructive of that which had come before (i.e., the entire nineteenth century, the mimetic direction of Western art since the Renaissance, etc.), and unlike many of her fellow New York School painters, Mitchell did not invest much in the avant-garde fetishes of innovation or knocking down one's predecessors. "Lots of painters are obsessed with inventing something," Mitchell explained. "When I was young, it never occurred to me to invent. All I wanted to do was paint" (*Theories*, 34). Consequently, Mitchell was not enthralled by the work of Picasso or the Surrealists. Her list of favorite painters included Matisse, Van Gogh, and Monet—hardly the usual roster of influences for an Abstract Expressionist associated with "the greatest painting adventure of our time," as Motherwell famously termed it. In fact, Mitchell's move to France in 1959 (a move which parallels that of Ashbery, who lived in Paris from 1958 to 1965, as well as, much later, Notley's) removed Mitchell from the heyday of New York School painting at a critical juncture, and served instead to align her with the very "School of Paris" that others slightly before her had worked to "overthrow." I don't want to make too much of these moves—people relocate, after all, for all kinds of reasons—but Mitchell's move gains in significance when linked to broader cultural currents, some of which have to do with gender and sexuality. As Leja argues in a chapter entitled "Narcissus in Chaos," during the postwar period, Abstract Expressionism's "aura of masculinity" and obsession with originality together served as "a crucial component of cold war U.S. national identity, differentiating the nation politically and culturally from a Europe portrayed as weakened and effeminate" (256). Seen in this light, a withdrawal from the New York scene at this time and a relocation to Europe (Mitchell in fact ended up living on the same property as Monet had in Vétheuil) cannot help but appear as an abstention from, if not an aversion to, this differentiation.

While many of Mitchell's paintings bespeak a tremendous urgency —indeed a violence—they don't necessarily feel reactionary or iconoclastic. As Ashbery wrote in a 1965 review of her work, "There are new forms, new images in this work, but no more than were needed at a given moment. . . . These unelaborated planes happened to suit Joan Mitchell only once or twice, after which she discarded them, for the time being at least" (*Reported Sightings*, 99–100). While it may be justly impossible to hammer out the specifics of a relationship between Mitchell's gender and her skepticism about innovation, I still think it possible that one exists. A commitment to innovation qua innovation presupposes an investment in lineage—a feeling, perhaps teleological at its core, that one's work will somehow *matter* in the scheme of things, that it will have a significant part to play in the course of art or literary history. Though there are certainly women who have had this feeling (Stein, for one)—and certainly many men who have not—it isn't one that can be divorced from the historical fact of women's presumed irrelevance to these histories.[11]

This fact becomes particularly acute within Abstract Expressionist rhetoric, which, as Leja has pointed out, worked together with "a broad range of cultural productions from this time . . . popular psychology, *film noir*, cultural criticism, and popular philosophy" to construct a discourse he calls "Modern Man discourse," from which women were structurally excluded (258). Mitchell's negotiation of subjectivity and landscape did not necessarily form in reaction to this discourse, but it nonetheless stands apart from the dominant Abstract Expressionist trend of replacing the tradition of female-as-subject-matter (specifically, the female nude) with a journey toward a feminized "other within," which could then stand for "primarily the unconscious, primitive instincts and residues, vague irresistible forces, or all of these" (Leja, 258)—a good example of which might be Pollock's 1953 painting in Duco allegorically titled *The Deep*, which hovers between the abstract and the vaginal.

In contrast, Mitchell describes her work as follows: "My painting is not an allegory or a story. It is more like a poem" (*Theories*, 33). Though Mitchell uses a simile here, when considering her "field composition" paintings from the seventies, one might be inclined to take her comment more literally. As a critic once remarked about her haunting triptych *Clearing* (1973), the panels seem to communicate three "self-contained episodes—or, better, interrelated stanzas" (Livingston, 35). *Stanza* is an Italian word meaning "an apartment, chamber, or room," which traces back to the Latin verb *stáre*, "to stand." As its etymology indicates, *stanza* signifies a stopping place, a place to stand, a space for a "stance," that is, for an idea or conviction. Many of Mitchell's paintings from this period are polyptychs—such as the overwhelming *Wet Orange* (1972), or the exquisitely muted *Field for Skyes* (1973)—each of whose panels represents a stanza, a "room for an idea." ("I want to paint the feeling of a space," Mitchell said [*Theories*, 34]). Further, *within* each of these panels, Mitchell often paints a variety of rectangular blocks clearly reminiscent of stanzas on a page of poetry. Her polyptychs are thus doubly stanzaic, in that they echo the part of poetry that has to do with holding or vacating space—of intimating the places in a form where words might appear (as in the generalized outline of a sonnet or sestina), but, in this case, have not.

In paintings such as the gigantic *Wet Orange*, there are dozens of such placeholders—skinny and fat rectangles in a spellbinding array of colors (orange, most notably, but also brick red, lavender, a thin red, veridian, a watery lime, ochres and browns, and so on). The orange brushstrokes in the foreground of *Wet Orange* dance over the entire structure, unifying the panels even as they smutch them up. In contrast, works such as the triptych *Field for Skyes* present fat, squarish blocks that dominate the foreground in primarily one color—here, a deep viridian verging on teal—and block out whatever might have lain behind them. (Mitchell repeats this effect at the top of the central panel, where lavender blocks obscure an anemic red.) The overpainting has a violent beauty to it, reminiscent of official documents in which enormous sections of controversial text have been blacked out. On the one hand, the move here is towards silence, as the ever-encroaching white impasto on the edges suggests; on the other, the painting also hoists images of text—or, rather skeletons of text—before us, and lets their green say what it has to say.

Paintings such as *Field for Skyes* may bring to mind what Charles Olson termed "composition by field" in his influential "Projective Verse" manifesto of 1950. But Mitchell's practice diverges from the scenario envisioned by Olson's manifesto—which remains fixated on the white page and the performance of the authorial body composing upon it ("Action Painting" by typewriter)—in several interesting ways. For her interest in "fields" never elides those of nature—that is, the actual green fields that a dog might play in, as her title suggests. Thus the fascination of *Field for Skyes* lies in its ability to invoke green fields of nature *and* fields of textual or stanzaic composition, while also calling attention to its status as a material art object via its immense size and the autonomous wonder of its pigments. Mitchell always insisted she was "a visual painter"—hostile to linguistic explication, and averse to issuing "pithy statements about her work," as Bill Berkson put it in a short essay on the gallery card for Mitchell's 2002 *Working with Poets* show at the Tibor de Nagy Gallery. It is more customary to talk of, say, Twombly as a "literary" painter, because of his many poetic allusions and his scribbling on the canvas—scribbling which borders on, develops into, or wipes out actual script. But Mitchell's painting incorporates her interest in writing just as fiercely as Twombly's, albeit in a different way—one which has less to do with *language* and the authorial hand, and more to do with *poetry*, or poetry as form.

Indeed, her polyptychs address two fundamental compositional questions in poetry: "How does this look next to this?" and "Should this stay or should this go?" Side-by-side comparisons were key to Mitchell's process, especially as she did not compose the panels of her polyptychs together, but rather worked on them separately, then decided on their sequence after the fact. (Her studio at this time could apparently fit only two panels next to each other at one time, so she had to move them around quite a bit—see Livingston, 64.) Mitchell does not unite her polyptychs, as do many other painters, with brushstrokes that bleed from one panel onto the next;

consequently, her panels retain a sense of isolation within their unity. And although I once overheard a docent at the Whitney Museum instructing her group to consider the endpieces of Mitchell's quadriptych *La Vie en rose* as prologue and coda to the central action, personally I have found that Mitchell's large works repel a narrative tack—or in this case, as the central panels of *La Vie en rose* chronicle a heart-wrenching degeneration into embers, a kind of extinguishing, or vanquishing, of the choppy black strokes— it must be said that if Mitchell is telling a story, she means to emphasize the hollowness at its center. Mitchell often arranged her work in sequence, but she did so with the goal of creating an overall effect, ideally taken in all at once from a distance, not read left to right. (Mitchell hung long-distance mirrors in her studio for this reason.) Given the New York School obsession with spontaneity (an obsession shared by the Beats, the Black Mountain writers, and many others at midcentury) it makes sense that poets such as O'Hara would deeply envy this "all-at-onceness," that is, painting's failure to unfold sequentially. And it was precisely this element of painting that enraptured Mitchell, who loved the idea that "painting never ends, it is the only thing in the world which is both continuous and still" (*Theories*, 32). In this sense, Mitchell's endless, stanzaic paintings may best represent the dream of a poetry in which form is truly content.

In addition to negotiating these "stanzas," many of Mitchell's paintings also negotiate a dialectic between white space (or white paint, as is often the case) and intense clots of color (as in *Girolata Triptych* [1964]). As with all of Mitchell's colors, however, "white" is never a stagnant entity, but rather always on the cusp of shifting into the palest of yellows, grays, blues, etc. The phenomenon of color—the materiality of pigment, and its transcendent emanations— presents us with yet another sort of true abstraction, in that color somehow brokers out—indeed, is somehow paradigmatic of—the mysterious relationship between subjective and objective reality. As Wittgenstein summarizes the paradox: "An object must occur, if it occurs at all, in a certain colored state of affairs, though in itself it is, so to speak, colorless." And Mitchell's paintings are justly famous for being "colored states of affairs." To stand in front of paintings from the seventies such as *Blue Territory*, *Salut Sally*, or *Mooring* is almost to hear Mitchell say: *Here are the most beautiful colors in the world, no holds barred. Enjoy.* The paintings are not exactly spontaneous outpourings—Mitchell was known for planning each brush stroke—but in her chromophilia, she holds nothing back. Her use of color is shockingly generous, to the point of extravagance. By all accounts, Mitchell was enthralled by the rush of glorious pigment, and while she had the money to buy high-quality paint, she tended to privilege instant color gratification over longevity. As a friend once explained, "She was focused on *color*, not the durability. . . . She used a lot of turpentine, repeatedly thinning and rethinning her paints, which would sometimes sit in her studio (usually in large dog-food cans), often unlidded, for months, and even years, waiting to be reconstituted when the need arose" (Livingston, 26).

Mitchell's unrestrained chromophilia plays an undeniably large part in the visual pleasure of her work. This pleasure, however, has also engendered a certain amount of critical wavering. Near the beginning of his *New York Times* review of Mitchell's 2002 Whitney retrospective, Michael Kimmelman writes: "The impact of her works, especially the later ones (she died of lung cancer 10 years ago, at 66), is so immediately intoxicating that a natural reaction is to distrust the art. Paintings this suave and sure-footed must be glib and manipulative, you may be excused for telling yourself" (31). Though the next paragraph advises the reader to "distrust your distrust," the suspicion with which he opens his review interests me, especially as it recurs in many reviews of Mitchell's work. On the one hand, a patent distrust of beauty can be read as a modernist tic, and the urge to judge it as "glib and manipulative" perhaps a postmodernist extension of the same. (Not to be myopic, I should note that a distrust of beauty—especially when aligned with the feminine—goes back a long way. At least to Eve in Eden, probably earlier.) On the other hand, in Mitchell's case, I wonder if it also has something to do with the tacit relationship between chromophobia and gender. As Mitchell (and Frankenthaler) well knew, being labeled "a colorist" is about as feminized a designation as art history has to offer. While the robustness and size of Mitchell's paintings disallows a dismissal of them as decorative, her paintings remain peculiar in the Abstract Expressionist pantheon for their furious insistence on over-the-top visual pleasure. This insistence may partially explain why Mitchell never found a Greenberg or a Rosenberg to champion her work in writing: its commitment to pleasure, and specifically to the pleasure of color, has produced a sort of forcefield around it, and a certain imperviousness to words.

In his slim and lovely book *Chromophobia*, David Batchelor meditates on precisely this problem. First he charts how Western art has an "intimidating and ancient tradition of *disegno versus col-ore*"—line versus color—in which line is figured as masculine and color as feminine (53). (The nineteenth-century French color theo-rist Charles Blanc articulated the hierarchy in this idea with the utmost of clarity: "The union of design and colour is necessary to beget painting just as is the union of man and woman to beget mankind, but design must maintain its preponderance over colour. Otherwise painting speeds to its ruin: it will fall through colour just as mankind fell through Eve" [Batchelor, 23].) Batchelor then explores how for centuries various Western artists and art theorists have linked color—specifically color-as-corruption—with the femi-nine, the "Orient," the infantile, and the homosexual. In a chapter on color and language, Batchelor argues: "To attend to colour, then, is in part to attend to the limits of language. It is to try to imagine, often through the medium of language, what a world without lan-guage might be like" (79). If you put together these two lines of inquiry—the characterization of color as "feminine, oriental, cos-metic, infantile, vulgar, narcotic, and so on," and the observation that the visceral experience of color somehow repels verbal expres-sion—you get an enriched sense of the problem Mitchell's work presents. It's too butch to write off or exalt as an instance of femi-nine chromophilia, just as it's too involved with poetics to write off or celebrate as simply "beyond words."

In his book *On Being Blue*, William Gass considers the question of how written texts become visual, and argues, seemingly against conventional wisdom, that "fiction becomes visual by becoming verbal." Mitchell in fact discovered something of the same when she attempted to collaborate with Beckett on his 1959 radio play *Embers*. The collaboration was to focus on the role of color in Beck-ett's play, with Mitchell painting watercolors to accompany the text. But she eventually abandoned the project, deciding that the play was already visual enough "without a single visual description in it." Speaking about Beckett's work elsewhere, Mitchell praised a related phenomenon: "If something is green you know it's green but he doesn't say it's green" (Benstock, 108). The exact opposite might be said about Schuyler's writing, which labors endlessly at visual description and, in particular, at the task of describing colors. (Green is in fact one of Schuyler's obsessions, as evidenced by the

"November 7" part of "A Vermont Diary," in which he aims to distinguish three particular kinds: "In the sky a gray thought / ponders on three kinds of greens: / Brassy tarnished leaves of lilacs / holding on half-heartedly"; "behind the lilac / on a trunk, pale Paris green / as moonlight," and "another green, a dark thick green / to face the winter, laid in layers on / the spruce and balsam" [*CP*, 109]). It would not be a stretch to read Schuyler's entire *Collected Poems* (and, perhaps, his diaries as well) as a testament to Wittgenstein's remark: "Colors present us with a riddle, a riddle that stimulates us—not one that disturbs us"(*Culture and Value*, 67e).

The notion of the riddle is crucial here, for although many laud Schuyler's humble desire "merely to say, to see and say, things as they are" ("Dec. 28, 1974"), Schuyler is no spokesman for certainty. He constantly questions his powers of perception, and constantly gauges his desire or responsibility for exactitude: "I have always been / more interested in truth than in imagination. I / wonder if that's / true?" ("A Few Days," 362). In an essay on Schuyler's poetics, Koestenbaum repeatedly calls attention to this aspect of Schuyler's writing—Schuyler's "this is this, this is not this" manner of identifying and misidentifying, his habit of asserting then self-correcting; Koestenbaum keenly locates this stutter at the center of one of the repeated lines of Schuyler's villanelle "Poem": "What is, is by its nature, on display" (45). What is, is, indeed; but the comma necessary for clarification also renders the proclamation awkward, revealing that even for the nominalist, the act of perceiving what's "on display" and then translating it into language inevitably courts a certain self-consciousness and cleavage. But—and this is the crucial point—it is a cleavage that Schuyler experiences more as a koan than as postlapsarian trauma.

Consider, for example, the following riddle of color Schuyler relates in "The Cenotaph": "I have a red toenail. / It is red dye from orange socks bought in Vermont. / If sweat causes the sock to dye the nail red why won't the dye wash off of the nail? / It is incomprehensible. / I cannot understand it" (95). Such mysteries occasionally make Schuyler a bit cranky, but never despondent. More often than not they provoke a bemused sense of wonder, often of the synesthetic variety: "'What is that gold-green tetrahedron down the river?' / 'You are experiencing a new sensation,'" he writes in "Freely Espousing" (3). As much as Schuyler aspires to the simple task of "seeing and saying," he is equally aware of the fact that the action goes both ways: by perceiving, and by extension, by writing, he also colors the world: "September day, how shall I color you?" he asks in "A Few Days" ("In blue / and white and airy tones," he then answers [374]). At times he takes great pleasure in such activity; at other times he grows agitated, as in the middle of "Hymn to Life": "I hate fussing with nature and would like the world to be / All weeds. I see it from the train, citybound, how the yuccas and chicory / Thrive. So much messing about, why not leave the world alone?" (218). As with Mitchell's *Field for Skyes*, one of the great tricks of Schuyler's work is that it seems to accept Emerson's dictum that "the universe wears our color," while also giving off the impression of—or making space for—the feeling of a world left "as is." In this sense, a ray of relation passes between Schuyler, Emerson, and Mitchell, insofar as all seem to offer a conception of the world as "at once a succession of moods (inner matters) and a succession of objects (outer matters)," which are not at odds, but rather enjoined in a state of romance.[12]

Part of this trick has to do with privileging juxtaposition over metaphor—a typical New York School move. A miniature example is "Daylight," one of the Schuyler poems from *Hymn to Life* that Mitchell chose to accompany with a color abstract. In entirety, the poem reads:

And when I thought,
"Our love might end"
the sun
went right on shining (183)

Benstock interprets this poem as being about "the indifference of nature to man's personal sorrows," and I suppose in a sense, it is. But "indifference" may put too fine a point on it. There are other dances going on here—most notably, the dance between one's emotion and one's thought-in-language—an interaction Schuyler calls attention to with quotation marks. And more than indifference, the poem postulates relation via the dialectic of a haiku: the two thoughts—each taking up equal halves of the poem—somehow need each other.

Mitchell's "color abstract" painted on, or with, the poem suggests as much: a stout, Rothko-esque block of yellow dominates the page, and gives way at the bottom to the typed poem; the words are then set off by a diminutive smear of violet-blue pastel, a few marks of which stray off into the yellow above. Of course the small typed words cannot bear up under the intensity and weight of the yellow, and the scribbling, delinquent blue suggests that they don't even try. Nonetheless, together they create a ratio, a ratio in which mass and detail presuppose each other (recalling, perhaps, the fact that our experience of color itself is essentially the apprehension of a ratio of frequencies). As Schuyler's poetry suggests elsewhere, the presumed oppositionality of the abstract and the concrete is often a misunderstanding produced by the problem of scale. Look closely enough at anything, he shows us, and it becomes abstract, as in the opening lines of "Running Footsteps"—"A thin brown stain / down the white brick wall" (114). But pull back a bit further, and it becomes concrete, "I guess yes / the new roof leaks." Then pull back further still, and it becomes abstract again: "sleet down the chimney: / a rustle broken / into dots and dashes," and so on.

In reviewing a 1965 Mitchell show, Ashbery was perplexed by a related phenomenon. Noting that the forms in her *Girolata Triptych* "look very much like a fairly literal impression of the face of a cliff pocked with crevices," Ashbery then asks, "Ought abstract painting to stay abstract? Things are not clarified by artists' statements that their work depicts a 'feeling' about a landscape, because in most cases such feelings closely resemble the sight which gave rise to them. What is the difference, then, between Joan Mitchell's kind of painting and a very loose kind of landscape painting?" (*Reported Sightings*, 100). Later in the review, he comes up with this answer: "There will be elements of things seen even in the most abstracted impression; otherwise the feeling is likely to disappear and leave an object in its place. At other times feelings remain close to the subject, which is nothing against them; in fact, feelings that leave the subject intact may be freer to develop, in and around the theme and independent from it as well" (100). This comment may represent Ashbery at his most elliptical, but one way of interpreting his remark is to say that Mitchell's work creates a space similar to that of Schuyler's poetry: one in which self-expression and leaving the world "as is" need not contradict or compete with each other, in which "feelings" and "objects" move in and around each other in an intimate dance. Both Mitchell and Schuyler are enthralled by the riddle of subject-object relations, but neither has a compulsion to settle the matter. Each seems instinctively to appreciate the fact that despite centuries of philosophical speculation, "no one has ever come close to explaining the objective appearance of perception," as Gass has bluntly put it (65).

Taken as a whole, Schuyler's *Collected Poems* speaks eloquently to the befuddlement and relaxation produced by this admission. In *Principles of Psychology*, William James describes consciousness as "that which we habitually choose to pay attention to," and as "a theater of simultaneous possibilities," and bit by bit, Schuyler builds a poetics out of this vacillation between observation and omission. His daily poems thus seem to say, *Here is today's poem, but it could have been otherwise. There could have been a different one; there could have been more; there could have been no poem at all.*

Schuyler's poem "February" revels in this wavering. Ostensibly a list of what he can see from where he's sitting, it begins: "A chimney, breathing a little smoke. / The sun, I can't see / making a bit of pink / I can't quite see in the blue" (4). He sees and says, but often reports only failure: he squints at the world as much as, or more than, he stares it down. The poem goes on to extend the trope: "The green of the tulip stems and leaves / like something I can't remember, / finding a jack-in-the-pulpit / a long time ago and far away." The desire for exactitude is real, but not rigorous; there's pleasure in remembering, but also in forgetting. As far as colors go, again, there's another riddle: "a woman who just came to her window / and stands there filling it / jogging her baby in her arms. / She's so far off. Is it the light / that makes the baby pink?" Who knows? The unanswered question accepts color as the most relative of phenomena, one whose appearance depends entirely on its context. As Josef Albers, famed painter and teacher of color theory, puts it in his classic *Interaction of Color*, "We are able to hear a single tone. / But we almost never (that is, without special devices) see a single color / unconnected and unrelated to other colors" (5). "February," like so many other Schuyler poems, ends up as a hymn to such interrelatedness. "I can't get over / how it all works together," he writes, echoing Mitchell's late-in-life comment about painting: "The way to do it is relationship, relationship. That is what you learn as you grow up" (Benstock, 35).

In an essay entitled "Sight into Insight," Annie Dillard tells how the blind, upon having their sight restored, often initially see the world "as a dazzle of 'color-patches.'" Dillard mourns the fact that, for a normally seeing person, the color-patches of one's infancy get lost as soon as meaning fills them: "I live now in a world of shadows that shape and distance color, a world which makes a terrible kind of sense." She can momentarily force herself to see an orchard of peach trees, for example, as a color-patch, but she can't sustain it: "Form is condemned to an eternal danse macabre with meaning: I couldn't unpeach the peaches" (1190). Schuyler and Mitchell meditate together on this "eternal dance," as is illustrated by their joint interest in bluets. In 1973, Mitchell painted a large triptych called *Les Bluets*; in 1981, she returned to the subject, albeit in a very different style, with a series of smaller canvases all entitled *Bluet*. Each panel of the 1973 painting contains color-patches—a variety of blues, some violet and white—against a cream background. The painting feels quite textual, as the patches are arranged on the white surface roughly in quadrants, each patch suggesting a different mood or possibility (a dark cobalt square stays intact; a bright solid disintegrates into drips; others implode; others bespeak a hollowness; one is translucent). Schuyler knew the painting, and celebrates it in a prose nugget entitled "Footnote":

> The bluet is a small flower, creamy-throated, that grows in patches in New England lawns. The bluet (French pronunciation) is the shaggy cornflower, growing wild in France. "The Bluet" is a poem I wrote. *The Bluet* is a painting of Joan Mitchell's. The thick, hard blue runs and holds. All of them, broken-up pieces of sky, hard sky, soft sky. Today I'll take Joan's giant vision, running and holding, staring you down with beauty. Though I need reject none. Bluet. "Bloo-ay." (*CP*, 238)

The address of the piece is funny, in that its earnest desire to clarify and inform contrasts with its floating status: it bobs up in the middle of the *Collected*, seemingly untethered to any root text, simply to tell us that there are many bluets—some verbal, some visual; some art, some life; some American, some French—and Schuyler's self-appointed job is to clue us into the list. Wittgenstein (predictably) always treated color as a problem of language ("How do I know this is the colour red?—It would be an answer to say: "I have learnt English" [*PI*, no. 381]). Schuyler veers this way, too, by calling attention to the word "bluet" via repetition, and by finishing his footnote with an emphasis on its sound. In the end, however, he doesn't choose—or, rather, choosing Joan's vision today doesn't preclude a different choice tomorrow, or in five minutes. "Though I need reject none" is the key line here—it's as if he's suddenly talking to an invisible interlocuter, one who threatens to make him choose between the many pleasures he has laid out before him. Then, as if to reassure himself that he doesn't have to reject any of them, he repeats the word he loves, which now, perversely, stands for all—then pushes it further still, into the realm of the queer: "Bloo-ay." Though Schuyler was often known as a miniaturist, by proclaiming his solidarity with Mitchell's "giant vision" in "Footnote," he asserts his own fat art. Likewise, Mitchell's love of Schuyler draws attention to the detail at play within her work, which is otherwise known for its more grandiose drama.[13]

Beyond the affinities between Schuyler and Mitchell, there also exist many intriguing parallels between Mitchell and her other New York School peers. The ebb and flow of an Ashbery poem like *Flow Chart*, for example, which was written in part while he traveled up and down the Hudson River by train, bears a compelling relation to the chaotic yet curiously serene motion of a Mitchell painting such as *Hudson River Day Line* (1955). In "The New Spirit" Ashbery writes, "I thought if I could put it all down, that would be one way. And next the thought came to me that to leave it all out would be another, truer way"; famously, he never really decides. Mitchell's career evidences a similar rage to include that vies with her rigorous commitment to "eliminating all extraneous material," and her body of work runs the gamut from deeply melancholy, frozen paintings such as *Mooring* (1971) to the hyperactive chaos of paintings like *Two Sunflowers* (1980). (Remember, too, that Ashbery's first five books of poetry have been collected under the title *The Mooring of Starting Out*.) Further, Ashbery's description of Mitchell's work as driven by "an energy that seemed to have other things in mind than the desire to please," as well as "a fierce will to communicate and an equally frantic refusal to make this task any easier for the sender and the receiver," could easily serve as an apt description of his own process and temperament (*Joan Mitchell*, 1992).

There also exist rich links between Mitchell and O'Hara. Beyond the obvious (though not exhausted) relationship between his poem "To the Harbormaster" and Mitchell's painting of the same title—an overlap which draws attention to the less insouciant side of O'Hara, the side that maintains a consistent dialogue with collapse, violence, and mortality—there are other connections: their dual interest in charting "the memory of a feeling"; their compulsion to capture the texture of events, especially as that texture swerves from commotion to order and back again; the kinship between the blazing particularity of Mitchell's colors—her "theater of color," as Ashbery once termed it—and O'Hara's euphoric celebration of the specific; and so on. But I leave these discussions to another time and place, and turn now to the poetry of Barbara Guest—the entire body of which could also be called a "theater of color."

GUEST'S ONGOING COMMITMENT to potential fluidity of poetic form and the mysteries of color-in-language constitutes perhaps the strongest testament of all the New York School poets to Schuyler's oft-quoted statement (from Allen's *The New American Poetry*) that "New York poets, except I suppose the color blind, are affected most by the floods of paint in whose crashing surf we all scramble" (418). Guest's poems explore color as relentlessly as do Schuyler's, but in a different way: she doesn't fumble to describe the colors of the world accurately as much as she creates a synesthetic universe in which it makes sense to say "Sometimes this mustard feeling / clutches me also" ("A Reason") or "he felt a little blue tinge in his arm" ("Green Awnings").[14] In her poem "The Screen of Distance," Guest writes: "I / created a planned randomness in which color / behaved like a star" (*Poems*, 132); such a line could easily serve as a sort of artist's statement for Guest's work at large. A stanza from an early Guest poem, "On the Way to Dumbarton Oaks," provides a good example of the kind of movement between concrete and abstract color that Guest's poetry often charts:

> Chinese tree
> your black branches and your three yellow leaves
> with you I traffick. My three
> yellow notes, my three yellow stanzas,
> my three precisenesses
> of head and body and tail joined
> carrying my scroll, my tree drawing (*Selected*, 15)

The lines begin with attention to landscape, then quickly move into the realm of "yellow stanzas"—a near-exact rendition of Mitchell's process. In both cases, the goal isn't to represent the tree's yellow leaves, but rather to "traffick" with them. The effect of this trafficking is odd, for Guest's continual naming of colors eventually creates a universe that often feels colorless, or at least one in which color hovers between sensation and idea, never quite landing in either place. Like Mitchell and Schuyler, Guest couldn't really care less about being saddled with the feminized or queer designation of colorist. As her poem "The Poetess" makes clear, Guest embraces the roles of both "poetess" and "colorist" alike (though not without some irony): "coriander darks thimble blues / red okays adorn her / buzz green circles in flight / or submergence?" (78). In a critical piece titled "The Color Green in the Art Work of Richard Tuttle," Guest observes that "color initiates form" (*Dürer*, 16); something of the same could certainly be said of Guest's work, whose increasingly atmospheric, "spaced-out" quality has much in common with the bled-out, meditative color-stains of the painting of Helen Frankenthaler, who was renowned for her "abstract practice" of drawing with color.

The four poems of Guest's that appeared in Allen's 1960 *The New American Poetry* anthology may have borne many similarities to those of her New York School comrades also appearing there (Schuyler, Edward Field, Koch, O'Hara, and Ashbery), but her repeated mantra "I go separately" from one of her included poems ("Santa Fe Trail") announced—perhaps inadvertently—her difference, or her difference to come. Though Guest and O'Hara were good friends, and though their work most certainly overlaps—specifically in their adaptation of a Surrealist sensibility to an American idiom—in a sense Guest's unironic investment in aesthetic theory and philosophy couldn't stand further apart from O'Hara's "there's nothing metaphysical about it" attitude as performed in "Personism." And while Ashbery certainly gets metaphysical, none of the New York School men really holds a candle to the degree of abstraction of Guest's writing, which approaches (and even occasionally surpasses) Mallarmé in its commitment to lyrical opacity. As Guest said in a 1986 talk appropriately titled "Mysteriously Defining the Mysterious": "In whatever guise reality becomes visible, the poet withdraws from it into invisibility" (Gevirtz).

Even Ashbery's famed evasiveness (i.e., his writing "as though to protect / What it advertises," as he wrote of Parmigianino's hand in "Self-Portrait in a Convex Mirror") doesn't court the same withdrawal Guest is talking about here, a withdrawal which is more mystical, more Platonic, and, perhaps, more hopeful about lyric poetry's capacity to contain, veil, and act as guardian to wonder. Read a Guest poem once, quickly, and you might feel as though nothing happened; in fact, you may feel as though you missed it altogether. (Here is a whole page, for example, from *Rocks on a Platter*, with the white space condensed: "Wet earth disinters itself. / With aplomb / bestows / 'The Kiss Behind the Counter'" [9]). Ashbery also plays with this sense of fleetingness, as he explains on the opening page of *Flow Chart*: "*It seems I was reading something*; / I have forgotten the sense of it or what the small / role of the central poem made me want to feel. No matter." But where Ashbery's "not caring" allows—indeed encourages—a kind of amnesia ("No matter"), the carefully scored quality of Guest's work suggests something quite different: that to hear it we must listen very closely, as if listening to something that isn't entirely sure it wants to be heard, more like a Morton Feldman composition. And whereas Ashbery and Guest have each had blessedly long and productive careers, Ashbery's voluminous poetic output has often plastered the radar screen, visually as well as critically, while Guest's poetry, especially her later work, gives off the feeling of quiet but steady beeps flickering across the screen, then returning to the void whence they came. This feeling has increased over the past forty-odd years, up until Guest's death in 2006 (she died just as this book was going to print). Guest published voluminously—twenty-one volumes of poetry since 1960—but with an ever-increasing commitment to a firm and mystical minimalism. (Her 2002 book, aptly titled *Miniatures*, uses the following epigram from Chekhov: "I, too, am an ardent defender of Miniature Pieces.") If there is a "fatness" in Guest's art, it has less to do with rage or voraciousness and more to do with this strange and steady output, and with her use of the page as an open compositional field, a practice which increased markedly over her career.

Robert Kaufman has suggested that Guest's work evokes the problem of "hearing lyric at all in our culture; and of hearing a specifically difficult lyric whose seeming abstractness or hyperdistillation may appear willfully recondite" (12). (It's tempting, and perhaps somewhat accurate, to charge the hyperstimulation of contemporary culture with creating and abetting this difficulty, but it may help to remember that back in the 1890s, Mallarmé was addressing himself to the same issue, and offered the following reminder: "I become obscure, of course! if one makes a mistake and thinks one is opening a newspaper."[15]) Kaufman's above use of the word "distillation" offers a good inroad into Guest's particular kind of "abstract practice." The common slippage in Abstract Expressionist rhetoric from "abstract" to "nonobjective," "nonfigurative," or "nonrepresentational" doesn't really make sense in relation to Guest, whose poetry is quite concerned with objects. (The title of her first book is, in fact, *The Location of Things* [1960].) Guest's abstract practice leads us back to the root of the word "abstract" itself, which derives from the Latin *abs* (off, away) + *tractus* (past participle of "to draw")—thus, "to abstract" means "to draw away." It is this etymology that lends the word its scientific usage—in chemistry, "abstraction" is used synonymously with "distillation." While my discussion of Mitchell focused on how her painting complicates the definition of "abstract" as meaning "to consider apart from material embodiment, or from particular instances," here I want to consider how Guest's poetic practice locates itself at the literal heart of the verb "to abstract," which has withdrawal, removal, and distillation as its core gestures. "In whatever guise reality becomes visible, the poet withdraws from it into invisibility."

In *Other Traditions*, Ashbery poses the question of whether there is "something inherently stimulating in the poetry called 'minor,' something that it can do for us when major poetry can merely wring its hands" (6). It's possible that Guest's work finds its home—indeed, its freedom—in such a place. As Kaufman has observed, "[Guest's] work—judged, for example, in terms of the language poetry or mainstream lyric which it is not—does not behave according to any current canons" (12). Curiously, it is also true that compared to the men of the New York School, Guest's work is by far the most explicitly involved with "canonical" writers and issues. Whereas Schuyler, O'Hara, and Ashbery all cultivate the camp pleasure of eschewing the major and privileging the minor, Guest's work converses throughout with heavy hitters, reaching a sort of peak in 1999's *Rocks on a Platter: Notes on Literature*, each of whose four sections begins with an epigraph from a notable male: 1. Hölderlin ("To live is to defend a form"); 2. Dr. Samuel Johnson ("To invest abstract ideas with form, and animate them with activity has always been the right of poetry"); 3. Hegel ("The empirical inner and outer world is just what is not the world of genuine reality, but is to be entitled a mere appearance more strictly than is true of art, and a crueller deception"); and 4. Adorno ("The Moment a limit is posited it is overstepped, and that against which the limit was established is absorbed.") As is apparent from these epigraphs—particularly from the Adorno—Guest's experimentation is of a far more skeptical sort than the brash, anti-academic battle cry of Koch's "Fresh Air" (1968). As Lynn Keller summarizes, "Guest's poems don't have the same counter-cultural flair, the in-your-face defiance of social convention that catches us up in the fifties and sixties work of Ginsberg, O'Hara, Duncan, Olson, or even Ashbery" (Keller, 215).

Taken together, these epigraphs from *Rocks on a Platter* also testify to Guest's distrust of "the empirical inner and outer world," which, as Hegel has it, "is just what is not the world of genuine reality, but is to be entitled a mere appearance more strictly than is true of art, and a crueller deception." Coming from Hegel, this prescription sounds quite dire. Guest has considerably more fun with it, as in the opening lines of the poem "The Location of Things":

> Why from this window am I watching leaves?
> Why do halls and steps seem narrower?
> Why at this desk am I listening for the sound of the fall
> of color, the pitch of the wooden floor
> and feet going faster? Am I to understand change, whether remarkable
> or hidden, am I to find a lake under the table
> or a mountain beside my chair
> and will I know the minute water produces lilies
> or a family of mountaineers scales the peaks? (*Poems*, 11)

And thus Guest begins her (published) poetic career with questions—big, unanswerable questions, such as *Why am I here, and not somewhere else? Do objects change, or only our perception of them? Does color make sound, i.e., can there be true fluidity between distinct sense-perceptions? Is the marvelous right around the corner, indeed right under the table? How can any of us presume to know what will happen next? Are all material events somehow interrelated? If so, how attuned am I as an instrument to perceive their correspondence; how attuned can (my) poetry be?* These are not necessarily depressing questions, and Guest is not melodramatic about them. Still, Hegel's notion of the perceivable world as a cruel deception lurks not too far off in the distance. Especially in her early poetry, Guest's surrealist buoyancy ("a lake under the table / or a mountain beside my chair") coexists with a real sense of dread—a dread that comes, perhaps, out of her dual urge "to cement connection while insisting at times alarmingly on the separateness of things," as Ward has put it (*Jacket* 10).

Though Guest often delights in specificity, she doesn't echo O'Hara's jubilant celebration of objects, as in his poem "Today": "Oh! kangaroos, sequins, chocolate sodas! / You really are beautiful! Pearls, / harmonicas, jujubes, aspirin! all the stuff they've always talked about // still makes a poem a surprise! / These things are with us every day / even on beachheads and biers. They / do have meaning. They're strong as rocks" (*CP*, 15). Instead, for Guest, "solid objects are merciless" (*Rocks*, 16). The poem "The Location of Things" ends with a related, albeit muted species of this dread:

> through this floodlit window
> or from a pontoon on this theatrical lake,
> you demand your old clown's paint and I hand you
> from my prompter's arms this shako,
> wandering as I am into clouds and air
> rushing into darkness as corridors
> who do not fear the melancholy of the stair. (*Poems*, 12)

The syntax is tricky, but the implication seems to be that the corridors don't fear "the melancholy of the stair," but that the speaker may. (Note the similarity of this phrase to O'Hara's comment in "Personism" that "the choice between 'the nostalgia *for* the infinite' and 'the nostalgia *of* the infinite' defines an attitude towards degree of abstraction. The nostalgia *of* the infinite representing the greater degree of abstraction, removal, and negative capability [as in Keats and Mallarmé]" [*CP*, 498].) Standing at the head of Guest's career, the above stanza functions as an odd self-portrait and invitation: she passes off the comical, phallic shako—a "stiff, cylindrical military dress hat with a metal plate in front, a short visor, and a plume" (*American Heritage Dictionary*, 1125); she won't be needing *that* on her journey—and then wanders off, not as a hero charging off into the great abyss, but as a drifter among the drifting, the "clouds and air."[16] "Air" only gains in meaning throughout Guest's oeuvre—the title of her 1978 novel *Seeking Air* makes use of a phrase from her 1973 poem "Roses" in *Moscow Mansions*: "there are nervous / people who cannot manufacture / enough air and must seek / for it when they don't have plants, / in pictures. There is the mysterious / traveling that one does outside / the cube and this takes place / in air" (*SP*, 71). This last line practices a Hegelian inversion: where one might customarily think life is the vast action that takes place apart from, or alongside, art, here life suddenly shrinks to "the mysterious / traveling that one does outside / the cube," and art remains the less cruel deception.

As the Language poets who celebrate Guest's work know well, her abstract wandering does not imply a withdrawal from the materiality of language, but more often heightens and dramatizes her connection to it. While O'Hara exalts the things that "are with us every day," happily calling them "strong as rocks," the rocks in *Rocks on a Platter* refer more metaphorically to the act of arranging words on a page as one might rocks on a platter (not that one arranges rocks on a platter too often, but no matter). "Dreams set by / typography," Guest calls such a process (*Rocks*, 3). She explicitly sets out to conflate word and object ("Rocks, platter, words, words . . ."). Consequently, she does not spend much time ruing the supposed rift between them, the rift that bothered Jack Spicer so much, for example, in *After Lorca*, when he writes, "Dear Lorca, I would like to make poems out of real objects. The lemon to be a lemon that the reader could cut or squeeze or taste—a real lemon like a newspaper in a collage is a real newspaper" (Spicer, 33).

A wry anecdote from Guest's *Rocks on a Platter* treats this desire with a very different tone:

It had been a vagabond voyage and the entrepreneur was fatigued, yet held up his head inflamed with "LITERATURE, the ABSURD." Ideas dropped out of vines and into his mouth. An idea fell off a SECULAR vine roaming his head: BAKED APPLES!

Among his listeners, a waterer of his vines, was a beautiful girl who hand-typed A BOOK CALLED "BAKED APPLES." THESE ARE STORIES THAT "MELT IN YOUR MOUTH," said the critics.

THE KING READ *BAKED APPLES 100*,
AND GAVE HER AN APPLE TREE GROVE.
THE KITCHEN MAIDS, who had written JONQUIL TALES, asked the king for a jonquil grove. "I prefer BAKED APPLES," said the King.

TEARFUL, THE KITCHEN MAIDS CLOSED THEIR KITCHEN
AND OPENED A JONQUIL STORE IN BUDAPEST, WITH

YELLOW DOORS, and GREEN CEILINGS THAT VERY SOON
APPEARED IN A FILM, "THE BRIGHTENING OF BUDAPEST."

(The King, who liked the film, donated 25 white Palace chairs.) (4)

Characteristically, this short tale offers many enigmatic pleasures, many of which would be squashed by reducing them to paraphrase or allegorical wrangling: the strange freshness of the words "Baked Apples" and "Jonquil Tales"; soft jesting at a Newtonian narrative of inspiration; vague but potentially trenchant innuendo about the alliance of art and business; confusion about authorship and gender—does the beautiful girl act as creator, thief, or scribe?; a loose mockery of literary taste and critical reception (the King's taste is, apparently, all in his mouth); a postmodern doubling in which the King donates chairs only because he is moved by a cinematic representation of gentrification; and so on. Spicer may gape after the taste of real lemons, but here it is the critic, not the poet, who wants "stories that melt in your mouth." One senses the speaker's skepticism about such a leap, particularly as it casts literature as a consumable good.

In the end, however, the tale is too cryptic to proselytize. Guest is more concerned with the construction of an imaginative language game in which "Baked Apples" (like "Bluet") signifies more than one thing. She then plays within the game, finding subtle, multivalent comedy in the King's proclamation, "I prefer BAKED APPLES." The tale reminds you that, as Robert Creeley once put it, "Words are things just as are all things—words, iron, apples—and therefore they have the possibility of their own existence" (*Tales*, 50). But while Creeley's main goal is the deflation of lofty poetic principles such as the "objective correlative," Guest has a more extreme vision in mind. For Guest—as for Mallarmé, and, perhaps, Stevens—poetry is not just a part of reality. It is also a reality unto itself—and a separate, perhaps truer one at that. And here Guest differs in sensibility from some of the Language poets who have learned from her work, for while Guest's writing certainly speaks to Charles Bernstein and Bruce Andrews's wish for a poetry that "does not involve turning language into a commodity for consumption; instead, it involves repossessing the sign through close attention to, and active participation in, its production" (*The Language Book*, x), Guest customarily shuns the communal ramifications of such a project, and insists instead on separateness. As she says in *Fence*, "The poet is always outside society. The moment the poet enters society, strange things happen" (123). And although Guest's work has much in common with that of Hejinian, Hejinian's deep-felt conviction that "a poetics gets formed in and as a relationship to the world" (*Fence*, 114) chafes a bit against Guest's desire to keep poetry as far as possible from "anything that is going to damage it as it moves along the page."

Clearly there's a puritanical streak here: Guest's poems are experimental compositions, but not in the neo-Dadaist sense celebrated by Duchamp, Cage, and Ashbery, who welcome background noise and garbage into the fabric. An early Guest poem, "Sadness," ends with the lines: "A speck of coal dust floated down and settled on my lapel. / Quickly with your free hand you rubbed out the spot. / Yet do you know I shall carry always / that blemish on my breast?" (*Poems*, 33). The sadness of the title seems to be located right there, in that blemish. Guest doesn't try to rub it away, but it's clear that the world's arbitrary markings are not always easy to celebrate. The blemish evokes *The Scarlet Letter*: like Hester's "A," the blemish is actually on the speaker's lapel, not on her body; nonetheless, she will always carry it. But while Hester is tortured, Guest is quietly bemused by the disjunct. In fact this scene in "Sadness" may have more in common with the also bemused opening lines of the George Oppen poem "Myself I Sing," in which Oppen inverts Whitmanic boast to showcase existential uncertainty: "Me! he says, hand on his chest. / Actually, his shirt. / And there, perhaps, / The question" (35). Guest is nowhere averse to accident, but her acceptance of it coexists with a drive toward an ideal of purity more Surrealist than Dada or New York School in spirit. As with Breton, chance for Guest is exalted, but also somehow overdetermined. As Guest explains in her statement in *Fence*, "[The poem] goes from place to place trying to find an identity. It goes anywhere it wants to go. . . . A poem will find its own subject. . . . I think that it is 'the beautiful voyage'" (124).[17]

It seems that for Guest, William James's definition of reality as "that which we habitually choose to pay attention to" does not go quite far enough. She would prefer to propel the problem beyond the bounds of the subject-object dyad, as evidenced by the title of her poem "An Emphasis Falls on Reality," in which the perceiver has apparently vacated the field. No heroic subjectivity dividing the world into the "me" and the "not-me" here—rather, an emphasis simply falls, like light or rain, unprovoked.[18] Myles once remarked that Ashbery could be considered the theorist of the New York School; based on "An Emphasis Falls on Reality," I could imagine a similar case being made for Guest. Here are its final stanzas:

> The necessary idealizing of you reality
> is part of the search, the journey
> where two figures embrace

> This house was drawn for them
> it looks like a real house
> perhaps they will move in today

> in ephemeral dusk and
> move out of that into night
> selective night with trees,

> The darkened copies of all trees. (*Selected*, 124)

In light of this poem, one might ask: In what ways do O'Hara's "I do this, I do that" poems, and Schuyler's "things as they are" poems idealize reality? In what ways does O'Hara's "Personism," which imagines the poem "at last between two persons instead of two pages," also angle toward "the journey / where two figures embrace"? The idea of a poem drawing a house for two people to live in has a potentially queer inflection as well: will the domicile remain, like gender itself, "*a kind of imitation for which there is no original*," to use Butler's famous phrase ("Imitation," 313)? Indeed, the lovely, final phrase "the darkened copies of all trees" leaves little space for an original. Instead, Guest puts a different spin on Platonic form: the trees the poet draws for us are not simply shadows of other, real trees, neither are they simply multiple derivations of one, original "treeness." The phrase "all trees" echoes the title of Ashbery's first book, *Some Trees* (1956), but with a difference: while "some trees" reflects Ashbery's aversion to absolute gestures, Guest's "all trees" reflects her drive toward mystification. The deft doublings in Guest's final lines—"night / selective night," "trees / the darkened copies of all trees"—postulate a universe in which the relation between the particular and the universal is denser, more mysterious, more pro-lific, and more playful than that found in Plato's cave.

Guest's poems repeatedly return to images of "homemaking," often to pose a parallel between the construction of a house and the architecture of a poem-on-the-page (as in the "this house was drawn for them" moment in "Emphasis," the passive voice of which shifts the attention away from the composing poet, and disappears the authorial hand). In doing so, Guest slyly converts stereotypically domestic, feminine images into tropes of heroic—albeit diffuse—artistic adventure. This play with domesticity and heteronormalcy is pleasurably on display in the comic-strip collaborations "Joan and Ken" and "Thinking" that Guest did with Brainard, published in *C Comics* in 1964 (see *Dürer*, 3–4). "Joan and Ken" showcases a noirish couple who converse not in romantic platitudes but in Guest-speak: while in each other's arms, one says, "You were there in the arcade reading winsome"; the other responds, "I broke my arm stroking that cat." Then, in a "reunion with the kids" panel, the family appears with their faces violently scratched out under the caption: "The reunion made them feel better, even if the mystery increased." In the last panel, the woman offers a spaced-out parody of 1950s advertising speech: "The secret is violet soap and living in an old house and never making repairs . . . I mean using consciences that repeat." "Thinking" is even more spaced-out still: the panels blur into each other across their gutters, and eventually give way to a large head of a woman with a flower in her hair who says: "Black Cherry Blossom Miyako Stare A Bed in Air Before I Put Up My Hair." Both comics are too playful, their speech bubbles too opaque, to push at for meaning—their pleasure lies in the dissonance between their Pop idiom and their mysterious, non-sequitur speech, and in their collaborative performance of "chatty abstraction" made visible.

In an essay comparing Guest with Mallarmé, DuPlessis notes that while the subject of *Un Coup de Dés* is "absence, struggle, the void, shipwreck, and the intangible," Guest's work—specifically, her 1996 book *Quill, Solitary, Apparition*—centers on "presence, pleasure, adequacy, buoyancy—and the intangible" (212). Part of what constitutes this difference is Guest's understated feminist consciousness, which generally stands in the shadows but from the start of her career onwards occasionally stepped out to mock—however faintly—the kind of access to the transcendent or intangible traditionally offered to women (i.e., mediated through a male figure). If one takes the "my love" in the early poem "Parachutes, My Love, Could Carry

Us Higher" (1960) as a male addressee—and it seems fairly certain that the poem is toying with conventions of heterosexual romance— the opening lines of the poem take on a particular resonance: "I just said I didn't know / And now you are holding me / In your arms, / How kind. / Parachutes, my love, could carry us higher" (*SP*, 16). For a poet known for her tact and civility, "how kind" pushes as close to sarcasm as Guest gets; it would seem as though this patronizing protector is pushing her quite close to the brink. In fact the speaker is irritated from the get-go—*I just said I didn't know, and now look*. Plus, later on she has to repeat herself: "Now the suspension, you say, / Is exquisite. I do not know." Elsewhere Guest privileges a state of suspension, but here it's clear that this version is not going to do the trick. For the time being, apparently, a man's kind arms will only be an impediment to the kind of transcendence she imagines in a poem such as "The Open Skies": "Noiseless hour / span of float and flight // Sky without lever or stress . . . Tough the cone to shelter / Ecstatic harking to upward dome," and so on (*Poems*, 82).[19]

Though I would hate to tether Guest down from this "ecstatic harking," by means of conclusion I would like to consider this aspect of Guest's work in relation to "a discourse, which is fully and historically specific, in which transcendence is not a way of being that women seize for themselves but something handed to them with all the weight of male sexual fantasy and demand," as Jacqueline Rose has put it (149–150). In her book on Plath, Rose identifies this discourse as one of the principal problems running through Plath's work, and reads Plath's multitude of rising, burning, and otherwise self-immolating female figures as returning us again and again to the problem of "the very form in which (female) transcendence can be thought" (149). While the introduction of Plath may seem incongruous here, her "haunting" may also suggest that her so-called confessional poetry and the more abstract, ekphrastic idiom associated with Guest are not necessarily as far apart as they may initially seem. Though we save a lot of time and trouble by simply admitting that Guest and Plath come from different poetic climates and have divergent poetic projects, I've also found it worthwhile to consider their work together. The opening lines of Guest's novel *Seeking Air*, for example, seem to me quite engaged with what Foucault has called "the imperative to confess," though the speaker defines herself by withdrawing from it: "*Begin with telling her everything, she had said. This provoked me into wanting to say less and less. Yet there was such a marvelous, such an extraordinary circumference around what I might or might not tell."* The speaker then meditates on this circumference "into the reaches of the night" (7).

This opening also bears a relationship to the Ashbery lines from "The New Spirit" cited earlier: "I thought that if I could put it all down, that would be one way. And next the thought came to me that to leave all out would be another, and truer way." At first one might be tempted to cast Plath on the confessional, "put it all in" side, and Guest on the anticonfessional, "leave it all out" side, but Plath's form is incredibly lean and chiseled—certainly as deliberately scored as Guest's, though in a different idiom, and Guest's voluminous production of "willfully recondite" distillations presents a compelling paradox. In her essay "Reading Barbara Guest: The View from the Nineties," Linda Kinnihan usefully unearths a 1962 review in which William Dickey disdains Guest's work as reflecting "a self . . . curiously without coherence," and applauds Plath, on the other hand, for her "consistent, personal tone of voice" (Kinnihan, 233). Clearly Plath's form of address is more "blood-hot and personal," but thematically speaking, the idea of "a self curiously without coherence" obsesses both poets. Everywhere in Plath's work, first-person speakers are dissolving: "I break up in pieces that fly about like clubs," ("Elm"); "all night / I have been flickering, off, on, off, on," ("Fever 103°"); "And now I / Foam to wheat, a glitter of seas," ("Ariel"); "I am your valuable, The pure gold baby // That melts to a shriek. I turn and burn" ("Lady Lazarus"); "I am breaking apart like the world" ("Three Women"); and so on. Far from postulating a coherent identity, Plath's poetry—particularly the later poetry—devotes itself to the endless chronicle of "selves dissolving, old whore petticoats" ("Fever 103°").

For Plath, this dissolution is both desirable and traumatic, and its pain seemingly stems from the fact that it remains tethered to a speaker who can testify to the experience of it. Guest's relationship to such dissolution is less tormented and more elliptical, as in these lines from "Sunday Evening" (1960): "I am talking to you / with what is left of me written off, / On the cuff, ancestral and vague, / As a monkey walks through the many fires / Of the jungle while a village breathes in its sleep" (*Poems*, 26). Somewhat typically for Guest (as for Ashbery), the lines begin with a first-person speaker addressing the reader, but with each line that follows, that speaker leads us further and further away from the self that began, so that by the time the sentence draws to a close, we are out in the jungle with no hand to hold. For Guest this dissolution is desirable, if sometimes melancholic; at times it is the deliverer of ecstasy. As Gevirtz has said of Guest's work, "The body by itself is ecstatic, flying to pieces, marvelous in its occupation of the place no story can fully enter" (*Jacket* 10). Yet as the similarity between Gevirtz's phrase "flying to pieces" and Plath's "I break up in pieces that fly about like clubs" suggests, the interest in transcendence shared by Plath and Guest at midcentury draws them toward uncannily related imagery. (Compare, for example, Plath's famous combustion in "Lady Lazarus"—"Ash, ash— You poke and stir"—to Guest's "Ash and ember / creature and skin // Soft body of unprotected gilt" in "The Open Skies.") Again, Guest's ascents are often rapturous affairs—"Ecstatic harking to upward dome"—while Plath's tend toward the pissed-off and gory (as in "Lady Lazarus," which ends with the revenge of the incinerated spirit: "Out of the ash / I rise with my red hair / And I eat men like air"). Given such divergences, it's easy to see why people have felt the need to take sides—to many Plath fans, Guest's ascent into "float and flight" seems hopelessly "ancestral and vague"; to many Guest fans, Plath can seem mired in loathsome sexual scenarios that some feel we'd be better off without.

Much feminist criticism of Plath throughout the 1970s and 1980s was in fact fierce in this latter sentiment. As Jane Marcus said of Plath in her 1988 book *Art and Anger: Reading Like a Woman,* "May her nets and hooks soon be in a mausoleum of memory of what a dependent woman's pain and anger looked like, and Plath's name on its wall as its best recorder" (65). Though Marcus is herself a feminist, one can hear in her remark an echo of Elaine de Kooning's earlier distaste for Linda Nochlin's feminist inquiry—an impatience with an emphasis on dependence or difference as opposed to an empowered assumption of equality. De Kooning is in fact quite extreme in this view, and extends it beyond the bounds of the "woman question." As she writes in her response to Nochlin, "To be put in any category not defined by one's work is to be falsified. We're artists who happen to be women or men among other things we happen to be—tall, short, blonde, dark, mesomorph, ectomorph, black, Spanish, German, Irish, hot-tempered, easy-going—that are in no way relevant to our being artists. . . . There are no obstacles in the way of a woman becoming a painter or sculptor, other than the usual obstacles that any artist has to face" (57). *Stop complaining and just do it* seems to be the message—or, as Mitchell put it more simply, "Fuck them"—and certainly it has its attractions.

I think, however, that reading Plath and Guest together can keep the need to take sides in abeyance. Guest herself is known for non-polarizing (if somewhat vague) statements such as "I think all poetry is confessional"; at the Barnard Conference in 1999, she stated, "I don't think that there's a poem written that isn't experimental, because the poem presents itself on the page to us and has its own way of being. That's the glorious part of what is known as 'the beautiful voyage' that Ulysses made. We don't always know where we're going" (*Fence*, 122). In her essay about the Plath-Guest divide, Kinnihan explains how this "critical division between the expressive (those advocating the accessible voice of female experience) and the experimental (those concerned with the coded play of language)" has "become standard in literary criticism," then makes the following critical point: "This oppositional division, taken up by and experienced by women poets, seems sustained by an unfortunate resistance to examining its contradictory connections to male-derived discourses already set up, in the late fifties and early sixties" (234, 236). This point is especially important, as it wrenches our attention away from symptom and back to cause, and thus back to the questioning of the gendered underpinnings of the abstract/concrete dyad that began this chapter.[20]

ALMOST THIRTY YEARS after Nochlin published her infamous 1971 article "Why Have There Been No Great Women Artists?" *Art Journal* conducted a forum on feminism entitled "Contemporary Feminism: Art Practice, Theory, and Activism—An Intergenerational Perspective," in which the editors asked several women artists and feminist theorists to answer a series of questions, such as "How would you place your own work within a historical continuum from 1970s feminism to the present? Has the influence of feminist theory affected your practice as an artist, teacher, critic, or historian, and has that changed in the last (five, ten, fifteen, twenty) years?"[21] One of the respondents, Johanna Drucker, explained her personal progression as follows: "[In the early seventies], I was terrified by the idea of becoming a feminist. . . . I longed for transcendence out of gendered identity through my work, not identification with it. It took a decade of professional life and attendant subtle and not-so-subtle abuses for me to understand the need for feminist conscious-ness." She then adds: "But it has always seemed to me that the real triumph of feminism is the moment when women can work without a sense of obligation to overt feminist concerns. . . . I'm not sug-gesting ignoring the lived realities of feminist politics, but I support the possibility of separating them from artistic expression if one so desires" (13). Some might call this separation postfeminist, and perhaps it is. But it is a mistake, I think—especially given the many ongoing and forceful efforts from conservative quarters to stem or repeal the cultural and political effects of feminism—to think of postfeminism as feminism-that-has-done-its-job, or feminism-thankfully-evaporated, or, worse, feminism-after-being-scaled-back-and-redemonized-by-backlash. Instead, I think we might be better off finding ways to live with and in the paradox Drucker articulates above—how to maintain a feminist conscious-ness while also taking, making, or emptying the space to allow for "abstract practices" of all kinds, including the varying explorations into "female transcendence" that Stein, Mitchell, Plath, and Guest all performed in distinct ways throughout the last century.

In 1991 the painter Shirley Kaneda observed that "some femi-nists and postmodernists seemingly cannot get beyond abstract painting's association with modernism and formalism and tend to privilege more conceptual or mimetic forms of representation";[22] thankfully, there are countless young women artists working today who do not labor under such a restrictive burden. Likewise, when considering the question here posed by the painter–feminist critic Mira Schor (sister to Naomi), "Does feminist practice, in art, teach-ing, and critical writing, always have in some sense to be represen-tational?" (*Art Journal*, 23), the answer seems increasingly to be no—or at least not with "representational" considered in any simple sense. Part of the thrill of paying attention to feminist art and liter-ature is watching younger generations of women (and sometimes men) collage, steal from, worship, denigrate, or simply ignore the diversity of practices that have come before them, be they abstract, representational, gestural, conceptual, formalist, prefeminist, post-feminist, antifeminist, all or none of the above. But just as I don't want to seal Plath's name off in a "mausoleum of memory," I'm not quite ready to leave behind the trove of intrigue and difficulty produced by the mere coupling of the words "women and abstraction," and I hope this chapter has at least pointed toward the liveliness of the subject.

After all, as recently as March 10, 2006, Jerry Saltz began a *Village Voice* review of the work of the German abstract painter Charline Von Heyl as follows:

> Given that for every five solo shows of a living artist in a New York gallery only one is by a woman, and that only a small percentage of these are by women painters, and an even smaller proportion of those are by women who paint in what could be called an abstract manner, for a woman to be painting in a nonrepresentational, vaguely gestural mode right now is, consciously or not, a political act. If that woman is over 35 it could be called revolutionary. Some would say it's suicidal.

Suicidal or no, over the past few decades, painters such as Louise Fishman, Mary Heilmann, Suzanne McClelland, Susan Rothenberg, Joan Snyder, and Nancy Spero have worked hard at mocking, reclaiming, transforming, eroticizing, politicizing, deforming, and expanding the tradition of abstract painting, with younger painters such as Ghada Amer, Cecily Brown, Lucia Dole-Recio, Jutta Koether, Ruth Root, Amy Sillman, Sue Williams, and countless others following suit.[23]

Perversely, however, I think I want to give the last word to Plath, as her poem "Magi" remains one of the most memorable and incisive meditations on the so-called "dangers of abstraction" that I know:

> The abstracts hover like dull angels;
> Nothing so vulgar as a nose or an eye
> Bossing the ethereal blanks of their face-ovals.
>
> Their whiteness bears no relation to laundry,
> Snow, chalk or suchlike. They're
> The real thing, all right: the Good, the True—
>
> Salutary and pure as boiled water,
> Loveless as the multiplication table.
> While the child smiles into thin air.

Six months in the world, and she is able
To rock on all fours like a padded hammock.
For her, the heavy notion of Evil

Attending her cot is less than a belly ache,
And love the mother of milk, no theory.
They mistake their star, these papery godfolk.

They want the crib of some lamp-headed Plato.
Let them astound his heart with their merit.
What girl ever flourished in such company? (*CP*, 148)

Plath wrote this poem in 1960—the same year that Tiber Press published Guest's first book of poems, as well as Ashbery and Mitchell's poetry-silkscreen collaboration; the same year which saw Mitchell's first solo exhibition in Europe; and the same year in which Donald Allen published his *New American Poetry* anthology. It would be a good decade before the women's movement got under way, a movement whose very first move was to trouble the public/private divide that Plath here pictures as the Platonic whiteness of "the abstracts" vs. that of laundry and milk. Whether abstraction always need imply the loveless realm of "dull angels" and "papery godfolk," and whether Plath's final question—"What girl ever flourished in such company?"—need remain a rhetorical one, I leave up to the reader.

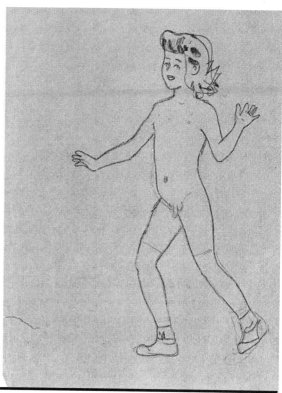

<h1>2</h1>

GETTING PARTICULAR

GENDER AT PLAY IN THE WORK OF JOHN ASHBERY,

FRANK O'HARA, AND JAMES SCHUYLER

LEFT: *Anonymous newspaper fashion illustration of two little girls in bathing costumes,* 9 ½" by 5 ½". *Collection of the American Folk Art Museum, New York, 2003.7.13A copyright © Kiyoko Lerner.* RIGHT: *Henry Darger (1892–1973), Untitled [Little girl with bathing costume removed], carbon tracing of image with pencil on paper,* 11" × 8 ½". *Collection of the American Folk Art Museum, New York, 2003.7.13B copyright © 1998 Kiyoko Lerner. Both used courtesy of the American Folk Art Museum.*

MANY CHAMPIONS of the New York School of poets, from the sixties to the present, have downplayed its gay import, perhaps feeling as though an emphasis on the poets' homosexuality somehow diminishes or misconstrues the work. Likewise, those who have recently focused on the issue on either a textual or biographical level (such as John Shoptaw, in his study of "homotextual cryptograms" in Ashbery, or Brad Gooch, in his much-maligned biography of O'Hara, *City Poet*, which many felt unfairly painted O'Hara as a "gay gigolo") have sometimes found themselves at odds with those who would rather soft-pedal the role of the poets' gayness in their life and work—a group which has included, on occasion, the poets themselves.[1] Certainly there are exceptions to this trend, which has changed with the times—Joe LeSueur's lively 2003 memoir, *Digressions on Some Poems by Frank O'Hara*, for example, is perhaps the queerest portrait of the scene yet. This chapter also calls attention to the queerness of the scene and of the writing, and considers it in relation to the valorization of contingency, detail, dailiness, and "personalism" that has become associated to varying degrees with the writing of O'Hara, Schuyler, and Ashbery.[2] Yet as my larger focus on women artists and the "true abstraction" of the feminine indicate, I am also interested in how questions of gender interweave with those of sexuality, and this chapter thus treats the two categories as "distinct though intimately entangled axes of analysis," rather than as "continuous and collapsible categories," as Sedgwick puts it in *Tendencies* (157).

In contrast to those who would downplay the role of homosexuality in New York School writing, in the introduction to the 1997 reprint of her 1977 book *Frank O'Hara: Poet among Painters*, Marjorie Perloff seems genuinely astonished that she missed the importance of O'Hara's gay sensibility on the first go-round. Perloff reconsiders several early reviews of O'Hara—reviews that remark on his "late Victorian camp," "Paterian pop," and "mental chatter and drift"—and notes that while "twenty years later, we recognize these as code terms for 'queer,'" throughout the sixties and seventies, "no direct reference [was] made to the poet's homosexuality," even (or especially) amongst O'Hara's friends (xii). She continues:

> I remind the reader of these conventions of the seventies so as to
> provide the context for my own historical/critical study on the role

the sexual played in O'Hara's oppositionality. That he was a radical and "different" poet was my premise, but I regarded that oppositionality (to the aesthetic, not only of Robert Lowell, which he criticized openly, but also that of the then counterhero, Charles Olson) as a question of individual ethos rather than as, in any profound way, constructed by the poet's culture or sexual identification. (xiii)

Perloff and others may have missed (or intentionally coded or ignored) the difference of O'Hara's sexuality, but his contemporaries did not. The Beats thought the New York poets "silly and effete" (Lehman, 335), as evident in the infamous 1959 exchange at the Living Theater between Gregory Corso and O'Hara, in which Corso said (onstage) to O'Hara, "You see, you have it so easy because you're a faggot. Why don't you get married, you'd make a much better father than I would." (When Ginsberg then interjected, "Shut up and let him read," Corso shot back, "And you're a fucking faggot too, Allen Ginsberg.") The evening ended with O'Hara walking out on his own reading after being relentlessly heckled by Kerouac, who earlier had told O'Hara backstage, "I'm sick and tired of your 6,000 pricks" (Gooch, 322–323). But lest it seem as though the phrase "gay sensibility" could ever possibly refer to one monolithic voice, style, or program, it's crucial to remember that other gay poets of the period also took pains to differentiate themselves from the New York School. Jack Spicer, for example, found the New York School poets unbearably effeminate, as Michael Davidson relates in an important essay, "Compulsory Homosociality: Charles Olson, Jack Spicer, and the Gender of Poetics": "When asked about Spicer's relation to the New York School, Landis Everson said that 'he didn't like them. He disliked John Ashbery intensely. He called him 'a faggot poet.' John's first book was called *Some Trees* and Jack always made a point of pronouncing it 'Some Twees'" (209).

O'Hara had the aplomb to shrug off such scenes ("It really was quite a witty evening all in all," he wrote of the Living Theater exchange); he also tolerated Pollock's calling him a fag to his face at the Cedar Tavern, forgiving such behavior, as Gooch writes, "in the name of genius and art" (204). As much as one might admire O'Hara's resilience—which was, by all accounts, a key part of his personality and aesthetics—I think it would be a mistake to let it entirely obscure the implications of such ridicule, which extended beyond the jeering in the Cedar and into the literary and art world at large. As the poet-performer John Giorno recently put it in an interview in *Nerve* magazine: "The art world of de Kooning and Pollock hated gay men. I mean, their wives were fag hags, and they knew a lot of gay men, but to them, a gay man could not be an artist of their caliber or on their level. Andy [Warhol] and Bob [Rauschenberg] and Jasper [Johns] were terrified that they weren't going to sell their work. . . . If you ever mentioned anyone was gay [in *Artforum* and other publications], you'd risk being excommunicated."[3] Likewise, though O'Hara was never closeted, and was generally "relieved and content to be queer," as LeSueur describes it (68–69)—in the 1950s and early 1960s there was clearly no place in the mainstream for overtly gay poems. As LeSueur says in reference to O'Hara's poem "At the Old Place," "Frank couldn't have gotten it published even if he had tried, since in those days, in the unenlightened fifties, there was no place to send it. Significantly, it saw the first light of day a few months after Stonewall, in the November 1969 issue of a short-lived magazine called *New York Poetry*" (54).

Yet despite this homophobic atmosphere, and despite the intense machismo of Abstract Expressionism, gay men occupied the very center of the art world in New York. Indeed, from a certain perspective, you could say they ran it: think of prominent gallery owners such as Myers, poet-critics such as O'Hara or Denby, up-and-coming visual artists such as Rauschenberg, Johns, and Warhol, composers such as Cage, choreographers such as Merce Cunningham and Alvin Ailey, celebrity poet-activists such as Ginsberg, and so on. And despite the real and often dangerous problems faced by gay men in the period, and despite (or because of) their air of insouciance, the male New York School poets most definitely found comfortable—and occasionally powerful—positions at the center of the New York art world.[4] By LeSueur's account, many of their friends experienced being queer as having as many or more freedoms and advantages as dangers and estrangements: "'Be glad you're gay'— that was how Jack Larsen put it once, trying to talk some sense into a confused, self-pitying youth who didn't understand that turning queer was his escape hatch from the dreary middle-class existence fate had assigned him. . . . Going to bed with our own sex was just part of it, the great freedom we enjoyed assuming such importance that in [O'Hara's] view it was more than sufficient for being thought of as sexual pariahs and, in some quarters, detested perverts"

(68–69). For these reasons and others, more often than not the poets seemed quite confident that their voices mattered.[5]

As intriguing as this paradox can be, the phenomenon of an artistic gay male brotherhood at the heart of a heterosexist, homophobic culture is not new or unfamiliar. Further, in and of itself, it makes no guarantee against the kind of misogyny that can exist in homosocial circles, be they gay or straight or any variation thereof. As Davidson points out in "Compulsory Homosociality," one should not assume that "because underground literary movements are marginal to the dominant culture, they are therefore more tolerant and progressive. Such assumptions need to be historicized by asking *for whom* progress is being claimed and *by what* aesthetic and social standards" (197–198). For example, though there were many queer Beats—Ginsberg, Burroughs, Spicer, Paul Bowles, and so on—generally speaking, Beat rhetoric treated homosexuality as yet another way in which a heroic male individual could escape the deadening, indeed castrating, influence of familial obligation, that is, of women, children, and the shackles of domesticity.[6] Radical as the Beats may have been, Ginsberg's early rants about men who "lost their love-boys to the three old shrews of fate the one eyed shrew of the heterosexual dollar the one eyed shrew that winks out of the womb" also link up with more mainstream and academic counterparts, from Jung's mythos of the Terrible Mother, to Freud's anxiety about the "universal tendency to debasement in the sphere of love," to Robert Lowell's gothic depiction of heterosexual pathos in suburbia, to Robert Graves's elaboration of the White Goddess, the psychotic flip side of the "one eyed shrew" who imposes domestication on the male.[7] In short, one strain of Beat male bonding, via its championing of the "rough camaraderie of men 'on the road,'" was always at pains to distance itself from the "faggy," and, by extension, the feminine (as the OED reminds us, "faggot" was originally "a term of abuse or contempt applied to a woman" [949]).

Yet on both a social and a textual level, the New York School writers at issue in this chapter actualized a different kind of environment, one in which women were present and pivotal as fellow artists, collaborators, friends, and literary predecessors. Though in some sense predicated on a gay male coterie, the environment nonetheless differed from the homosocial environments of, say, the San Francisco Renaissance or Black Mountain College, in which the absence of women "was a structural necessity for the liberation of a new, male subject," as Davidson has put it ("Compulsory Homosociality," 198).[8] LeSueur makes this point again and again throughout his memoir, in which he characterizes "the way O'Hara lived his life as a homosexual" as follows: "[O'Hara was] adamantly opposed to the gay ghetto principle as exemplified by Cherry Grove on Fire Island, Lenny's Hideaway downtown, the Bird Circuit uptown, any gay gathering where straights were excluded or not wanted—in other words, a way of life that promoted compulsive cruising, misogyny, and homosexual separatism." LeSueur insists, however, that O'Hara also remained deeply committed—"as a point of pride and as a moral obligation"—to "hammer[ing] home to straight people the clear, unmistakable message that he was an uncontrite, arrogant queer who was not about to sing *miserere* or fall on his knees to anyone" (227).

LeSueur elaborates on the subject in a discussion of the marriage of Patsy Southgate and Mike Goldberg, in which he conjectures that

> Patsy wouldn't have fallen in love with Mike, much less married him, if his rough manner and bravado had not been offset by what his two gay friends [i.e., O'Hara and LeSueur] embodied, a homosexuality that was gracefully assimilated into straight society without being closeted, a homosexuality that was carefree without being giddy, a homosexuality that was also gentle, amused, and ironic, and a homosexuality that embraced what so many gay as well as straight men abjure, the inner feminine part of the male personality known as the anima, of which my analyst made me aware. Oh, and one more thing, actually, what's most important, what I suppose is related to the Jungian concept of the anima, a homosexuality whose proscription of misogyny Patsy could only have found novel and reassuring, a comfort and a boon she'd doubtless never known in heterosexual circles dominated by sexist, egocentric males who thought of themselves as, to use Patsy's most damning epithet, "entitled." (178)

LeSueur's assessment may sound utopian—and, I suspect, a hair self-congratulatory—but the difference he is describing matters, in part because it points us toward at least one reason how and why the New York School subsequently found so many female—indeed feminist—admirers.

On a textual level, the writing of Ashbery, Schuyler, and O'Hara has become known for the following decidedly not-macho set of characteristics: a mixture of high/low sensibilities, including the impertinent habit of venerating "minor" artistic figures over "major" ones; the repeated use of localized names, dates, and places, along with a positive focus on the detritus of "everyday life," including (or especially) that produced by consumption and domesticity; a distaste for grandiosity of all kinds, from institutional pretense to linguistic tropes that grope at metaphysical symbolism; a love of chatter, via such ephemeral modes of communication as lunch dates, telephone calls, and postcards; an interest in collaborative practices which complicate or erase the possibility of the individual genius author; an abiding commitment to the occasional and the ephemeral, and a related fascination with nonlinear time—with how phenomena such as lacunae and amnesia structure, or disrupt, a life in writing; an attention to the action at the margins of consciousness, be it background noise, a Proustian web of involuntary memory, or simply the random flow of changes that constitute life on a city street; and so on. All the items on this list have been historically aligned, in some way or another, with the feminine. But unlike other "revolutionary" poetic movements—and I'm thinking here of Wordsworth's Romanticism, Breton's Surrealism, and the Imagism of T. E. Hulme and Pound, to cite just a few examples—the New York School poets did not use these feminized modes as a springboard from which to depart in order to take their place as serious artists—artists who then only gain in seriousness by bemoaning their alienation from these modes as the source of an irreparable sense of rupture and loss.[9]

As Ward and others have pointed out, the particularly macho rhetoric of Pound, Hulme, and other modernist "Men of 1914" can be traced, at least in part, to their fierce desire to contradict the effects of Oscar Wilde's 1895 trial, which Ward aptly terms "the queer birth of the English avant-garde," as it cemented the alliance of "the Artist with the Homosexual." But while Wilde's trial may have crystallized this alliance, Ward also points out that

> the stereotyping of the Lake Poets as Nature-lovers, together with the shrillness of Shelley and the aestheticism of Keats, had already compromised the social normality of the Poet before first Swinburne and then Arthur Symons' 1890's Decadents dished it entirely. T. S. Eliot, of course, never got into fistfights: but then Eliot drew directly on *fin de siècle* Dandyism, and had been corrupted by the exposure to the feminine Frenchness of Baudelaire and Mallarmé. (122)

The issue of corruption via feminine (not to mention French) identification is critical. As feminist scholars such as Barbara Johnson have pointed out, one main tendency in male Western lyric poetry throughout the ages has been its urge to idealize, identify with, or perform the feminine while also taking care to disavow it. In her 1998 essay "Gender and Poetry" (in *The Feminist Difference*) Johnson sets forth the fascinating—if somewhat alarming—argument that femininity is not only "the privileged topic of male lyric poetry," but that the male appropriation of the "right to play femininity" constitutes the condition of possibility for male privilege itself (127–128). "Why is it," Johnson asks, "that Petrarch is not called a masochist, even though Louise Labé, using exactly the same conventions, is? Why are there books published on Baudelaire's sadism but not on his masochism? Why is male masochism the secret that it is lyric poetry's job to keep?" (123).

These are good questions, and Johnson returns to them in a related essay, "Muteness Envy," in which she considers how and why female muteness has served as "a repository of aesthetic value" in lyric poetry. Johnson traces the problem back to one of Western literature's primal scenes—that of "Apollo's pursuit of the nymph Daphne and her transformation into a laurel tree." At the end of this pursuit, Daphne turns into a tree "in a last desperate attempt to avoid rape"; Apollo subsequently plucks the leaves of the tree, and makes a wreath that henceforth serves as a "sign of artistic achievement." Thus, at the very core of one of lyric poetry's most persistent stories and symbols lies the notion that Apollo's failed rape is a "tragic loss," a loss for which his poetic crown stands in as a sort of "consolation prize" (135, 153).[10] This is a deeply vexed scenario for the female subject, not to mention the female poet. When considered against this backdrop, the poetry of O'Hara, Ashbery, and Schuyler seems astonishingly uninterested in this dance of displaying yet disavowing the feminine or the faggy, or in shoring up male privilege by means of standing apart from it in various postures of conquest, admiration, lament, nostalgia, condescension, or disgust.

To insist simultaneously on the importance of the poets' homosexuality and their various feminine identifications is tricky business. It could be seen, for example, as falling directly into the trap of trying to make "male homosexuality *about* women," as Butler has put it in regard to a certain mode of feminist analysis.[11] "At its extreme," Butler explains, "this kind of analysis is in fact a colonization in reverse, a way for feminist women to make themselves the center of male homosexual activity (and thus to reinscribe the heterosexual matrix, paradoxically, at the heart of the radical feminist position)" (*Bodies*, 127). (O'Hara himself notes this problem, albeit more lyrically, in "Meditations on an Emergency": "Heterosexuality! you are inexorably approaching. [How discourage her?]") Such a focus also neglects the rich variety of same-sex imaginings in the poetry, as in O'Hara's phenomenal oral sex poem, "Poem": "Twin spheres full of fur and noise / rolling softly up my belly beddening on my chest / then my mouth is full of suns" (*CP*, 405). Needless to say, I don't agree with Helen Vendler, who once wrote with more than a hint of condescension: "[O'Hara's] sex poems aren't very good, though they try hard and are brave in their homosexual details" (194).

Many people (myself included) find the notion that effeminacy is somehow at the heart of every gay man (and masculinity at the heart of every lesbian) antiquated, totalizing, or just plain ignorant.[12] Perloff grapples with just this problem in her 1997 introduction, via a disagreement with another critic's reading of O'Hara's poem "The Day Lady Died." The critic, Andrew Ross, argues that "the hectic itinerary followed by [O'Hara] could just as well be that of a genteel lady about town. . . . 'The day lady died' is an account of a lady's day, played out by a man through an imagined lunch hour that is the very opposite of the power lunches being eaten in restaurants in the same few blocks by the men who make real history" (xvii). In contrast, Perloff rejects the idea that O'Hara's poem necessarily embodies the "social contours of gay masculinity of 1959," as well as any narrow vision that would see such contours as "allow[ing] the poet no choice but to assume a feminine role." Her trepidation is understandable. But her subsequent argument—"to say that the poet's itinerary is conceived as the daily shopping round of a genteel lady glosses over precisely those images and phrases that make 'The Day Lady Died' the bittersweet, poignant elegy it is" (xix)—seems to sidestep the point, and rehearse yet another instance in which femininity and literary value appear as mutually exclusive. Of course it isn't *exactly* a lady's day—not at all. As Perloff points out, the activities O'Hara talks about—such as a shoeshine—along with the implicit claim he makes on public space as observer and *flâneur*—can certainly be gendered masculine. But O'Hara's self-conscious play with the conflation of "lady" and "day" courts Ross's point, even if it eventually subverts it, and the consequent dissonance is the source of much of the poem's energy, specificity, and originality. Given the stakes of "playing femininity" as laid out by Johnson, and given my interest in women influenced by New York School writing, I am not as eager as Perloff to move off the connection.

The question hovering in the wings here—that of the relationships between effeminate signifiers (feminized tropes, queen taste, drag, camp names—all of which add another dimension to the category of women as a "true abstraction") and actual women (fellow artists and writers, predecessors, collaborators, muses, romantic interests [platonic or otherwise], mothers, protégées, and so on—many of whom may not be the least bit "feminine")—is a thorny and perhaps essentially rhetorical one. Feminists and queer theorists have found much to debate here, but at present I want to remain focused on how the poetry at issue often avoids rather than replicates the misogynistic structures that Johnson and others have shrewdly located at the heart of much lyric poetry. For example, in her essay "Manifests," DuPlessis explains how "the ideology of the muse deflects attention from or disengages from the actual historical presence and activities of women" (37). But in O'Hara's case, for example, the exact opposite is true: his use of female "muses" repeatedly returns us to their historical presence and activities. At the same moment that Robert Graves was busy making Laura Riding into the White Goddess, and Ted Hughes and Sylvia Plath were collaborating on her role as such, O'Hara was pinpointing the activities of women he admired in space and time, like Billie Holiday at the 5-Spot ("she whispered along the keyboard / to Mal Waldron and everyone and I stopped breathing"); thanking friends like Lang ("you enable me, by your least / remark, to unclutter myself"); expressing solidarity with both celebrities such as Lana Turner ("oh Lana Turner we love you get up") and peers such as Guest ("oh Barbara! do you think we'll ever / have anything named after us like / *rue Henri-Barbusse* or *canard à l'Ouragan?*"); and memorializing the image of his painter-friends (like Mitchell) at work in their studios (Ah Joan! there / you are / surrounded by paintings"). The range of these examples indicates how far O'Hara goes beyond the stereotype of invoking women only or primarily as fetishized camp icons. In fact, O'Hara reconfigures the writer/muse dyad so completely that the word "muse" no longer seems right. Given the stakes of the claim DuPlessis makes above, O'Hara's difference is a point of real significance.[13]

While some critics may feel a conflict between championing the greatness of New York School writing and focusing on its various feminine identifications, the poets themselves did not. One primal scene of this identification, so to speak, can be located in Schuyler's magnificent long poem "The Morning of the Poem," in which he tells the following story: "When I first knew John Ashbery he slipped me / One of his trick questions (we were looking at a window / full of knitted ribbon dresses): 'I don't think / James Joyce is any good, do you?' Think, what did I think! I / didn't know you were allowed not to like James / Joyce. The book I suppose is a masterpiece: freedom of choice / is better" (*CP*, 286–287). Far from being an incidental detail, the "window / full of knitted ribbon dresses" appears here as the condition of possibility, as they say, from which the freedom to dismiss a literary "master" such as Joyce arises. Schuyler's sly parenthetical comment weaves this literary "freedom of choice" in with the freedom to stop on the street, with another man, to contemplate some knitted ribbon dresses.

There's no way of knowing, of course, how "true" Schuyler's story is, but it doesn't really matter—a quick survey of Ashbery's career reveals a persistent fascination with girlie things, from his early long poem "Europe" (which is a cut-up of *Beryl and the Bi-Plane*, an Edwardian book for girls) to later poems with titles such as "Thoughts of a Young Girl" to his 1999 book-length poem *Girls on the Run*, which takes as its point of departure the work of outsider artist Henry Darger, whose epic narrative-painting *In the Realms of the Unreal* chronicles the adventures of a group of young vigilantes called the Vivian Girls. As Ashbery explains in an interview about *Girls on the Run*: "I was fascinated by little girls when I was a boy, and their clothes and games and dolls appealed to me much more than what little boys were doing. Therefore, I was sort of ostracized" (D'Agata). (I have no idea what Ashbery makes of the fact that Darger's paintings scandalously portray the Vivian Girls as possessing penises [no one knows what Darger was thinking either, as *In the Realms* was discovered in his Chicago apartment after his death], but the question is certainly intriguing, especially as it dramatizes a certain puzzle about Ashbery's career: how he manages to represent both the faggy, "outsider" poet and the famous, major poet, buoyed by big-time critics such as Bloom and Vendler, who at times seem intent on making sure Ashbery's reputation keeps its phallus securely strapped on.[14])

Another notable inclination that O'Hara, Ashbery, and Schuyler all share is a consistent revalorization of female predecessors (as influences) and female contemporaries (as discussed earlier vis à vis O'Hara). Ashbery spends a considerable amount of time discussing the work of Laura Riding in *Other Traditions*; elsewhere he has spoken quite a bit about Bishop, Moore, and Stein, all of whom he mentions in a list of "major writers" who have influenced him. About Moore, he says, "I am tempted simply to call her our greatest modern poet. This despite the obvious grandeur of her chief competitors, including Wallace Stevens and William Carlos Williams" (Shoptaw, 113). Add to this list Jane Bowles, Djuna Barnes, Virginia Woolf, Ivy Compton-Burnett, and Jean Rhys, and you have the beginnings of a list of the women writers that O'Hara, Ashbery, and Schuyler championed. (Note that most all of the women on this list are queer.) There's something refreshing about the image of the young O'Hara confiding to his journal that his literary models are "*Between the Acts, Nightwood, The Tragic Comedians* (in a special way), *The Waves* (perhaps most of all), *Ulysses*, and *Prothalamium*" (Gooch, 131), or of the young Schuyler in the Buffalo Public Library, sitting in his overcoat, poring over Moore's *Selected Poems* (see Schuyler's *Diary*, 279). Schuyler was also a Woolf fan: her diaries were "favorite books of [his] which he reread often," and Schuyler refers to them throughout his own diary, such as in the entry for 19 January 1985: "Now to get ready for Hy Weitzen—shave, shower, wash my hair. Surprise! I have! So I can spend a couple of hours with the depressing last volume of Virginia's diary. Such a waste! Poor lovely lady." Elsewhere, in a poem called "Virginia Woolf," Schuyler celebrates "Angular Virginia Woolf, for whom / words came streaming / like clouded yellows over the downs" (*CP*, 321).

With the exception of Woolf's famed stream-of-consciousness, however, most of the writers listed above are not known for a flowing, jouissance-laden *écriture féminine*, but rather for their terse, often searing, dialogic wit. The prose of Compton-Burnett and Jane Bowles—like that of the queer aesthete Ronald Firbank—is often indistinguishable from their plays. Such prose most certainly served as a model for the joint novel by Schuyler and Ashbery with the decidedly domestic, faggy title, *A Nest of Ninnies*, which consists primarily of witty remarks devoid of the logic of plot, characterization, or even sequential linkage: "'But wouldn't you like to get out of those wet things?' 'I'm afraid some of the details are not clear to me,' Henry said, 'About the pub and the animal hospital, for instance—I don't quite see the connection.' 'There is none,' Fabia said. Henry, taking this for a witticism, said, 'I see,' and laughed heartily" (161). The influence of Dada is obviously important here, yet *A Nest of Ninnies* is not a hostile spoof of the bourgeois family. In fact the novel does not lampoon the nuclear family as much as it ignores it, or treats it as essentially a non sequitur. Much as in Bowles's novel *Two Serious Ladies* (or her stories "A Quarrelling Pair" or "Camp Cataract"), the principal characters of *A Nest of Ninnies* are sets of siblings (Alice and Marshall, Fabia and Victor, and the Parisians Claire and Nadia Tosti), with parents that quickly blur into a mesh of Mr. Bridgewaters, Mrs. Kelsos, Mr. Turpins, and so on. It's nearly impossible to keep the families straight, and the amnesic flow of the novel suggests there's no reason to try. In such a context, W. H. Auden's blurb on the back cover becomes quite amusing: "My! What a pleasant surprise to read a novel in which there is not a single bedroom scene." Indeed, there are no bedroom scenes, no Oedipal triangles. The novel presents a wash of proper names and couplings, and steadily imparts the refreshing feeling that a traveling companion can be as important as one's parent, a waitress as important as one's fiancé, and so on.

Another dominant characteristic of novelists such as Rhys, Barnes, Bowles, Compton-Burnett, and Woolf is a profound impertinence, often nascently or explicitly feminist in nature, that signifies an audacious willingness to take on (or ignore, as the case may be) one's patrician elders. As Ashbery said about Mitchell's painting, their writing most certainly has "other things in mind than the desire to please." They are, in short, difficult women and difficult writers, whose weapon against hateful situations is often a "thorny wit," as Truman Capote once said about Bowles (Capote, viii). This wit can be as humorous as it is devastating, and often reflects a deep distrust of the values and standards of a literary history characterized by a paucity of female voices. And here camp meets up with feminism: as Ward has put it in his discussion of O'Hara's poem "Biotherm" (specifically, in reference to the lines "better a faggot than a farthead / or as fathers have often said to friends of mine / 'better dead than a dope'"), "to be gay is to spit in the face of the patriarch . . . to enclose the word 'father' in 'farthead'" (52). (Ashbery also shares this scatological insubordination: "Excuse me while I fart," he writes in *Flow Chart*, "There, that's better. I actually feel relieved" [201].)

In her discussion of perversion in the writing of Roland Barthes, Jane Gallop makes a similar link: "Feminism shares with Barthes the goal of an impertinent stance toward the father and a reconciliation and valorization of the mother." Gallop claims, via Barthes, that "the writer is that kind of pervert: 'The writer is someone who plays with the body of his mother'" (115). Obviously O'Hara, Ashbery, and Schuyler revered many male writers; my point here is simply that their work also evidences the presence of this perversion—a perversion I wish there were more of: an abiding interest in playing with the bodies of one's mother. LeSueur's discussion of "matriarchal tyranny" vis à vis gay male writers is also relevant here, as he writes, "At this point some readers—straight readers—might be wondering about Dad's role in all of this. Well, only rarely does he figure in the scheme of things—it's Mom who casts her long, intimidating shadow over our lives" (226).[15] If one extends this comment metaphorically into the realm of literary influence, the classic Oedipal scenario no longer seamlessly applies. Camp wit and feminist resistance are distinct phenomena, and the differences between them matter. But in taking the work of their female predecessors seriously, the poets who are the subject of this chapter call attention to—even if inadvertently—their potential nexus.[16]

ONE SUCH POINT of intersection is the talent for finding pleasure in adversity—for treating deadly serious, indeed life-or-death matters, with a certain irony or lightness of touch. The poet and playwright V. R. (Bunny) Lang, O'Hara's good friend and muse, was another woman with this gift for "perfect light tragedy," in her life as well as her art. Lang died of Hodgkin's disease in 1956 at age thirty-two; it wasn't until 1975 that Random House collected her work in a volume entitled *V. R. Lang: Poems and Plays*. The book jacket assures us that "the fame [of Lang's poems and plays] has spread," but I think it's safe to say that this trend has reversed over the thirty years since their publication. The Random House edition is prefaced by a seventy-page memoir by Alison Lurie, who was a friend of Lang's. In her memoir of Lang, Lurie writes, "If [Lang] had lived, she would certainly have taken her place in the so-called New York School of poets, along with her friends John Ashbery, Kenneth Koch, and Frank O'Hara. (Her poems are occasionally so much like O'Hara's that one which was found among his papers, 'To Frank's Guardian Angel,' was printed as his in the recent collected edition)" (xvi).

Indeed, it's easy to see how Lang's sensibility, which remained buoyant and theatrical throughout her illness, would have attracted O'Hara. For example, here is an excerpt from one of Lang's letters to Lurie, in which Lang describes her illness: "I am diseased again, as of this week. Every six months to the day we go through this farce endlessly the dragon said. Bought a really dramatic jacket at the buckingham clothing sale wait till you see it is a burgeoning white fox collar . . . I have got to get out of my nightgown and go to the Death Ray Parlor now. Love, Bunny" (56). As dramatized by Koch's classic anti-academic roast, "Fresh Air," the New York School poets desperately wanted to escape the midcentury seriousness of poets such as Lowell and his aptly titled "Lord Weary's Castle"; Lang's productions at the Poets' Theatre in Cambridge epitomized such an escape. One good example is Lang's disobedient production of Cid Corman's play *The Circle* in 1952. As Lurie recounts, *The Circle* was a "tragic and symbolic" play populated by allegorical figures such as "A Child," "The Old Man," and "The Philosopher." For costumes, Lang chose union suits dyed salmon pink and straw hats with chiffon streamers; for music, "Elephant Polka." At one point during the play, to simulate a mob scene, she had one-half of the cast chant "rhubarb, rhubarb," and the other "vichysoisse, vichysoisse." By the end of the play, after "The Stranger" had been killed and Lang had him lying on the floor in a pose of rigor mortis, an offended Corman stormed out of the production (21–23).

Like Guest in the Tibor de Nagy circle in New York City, Lang was pretty much the sole prominent woman writer on the Cambridge scene. The other writers at the theater included Richard Wilbur, John Ciardi, Richard Eberhart, Hugh Amory, Ashbery, Edward Gorey, Donald Hall, William Matchett, George Montgomery, O'Hara, and Lyon Phelps (Lurie, 13). Lurie notes that Lang was "a feminist before the movement was reinvented, in the dark ages of the early 1950's when it was much less popular to be a single female of independent mind and professional ambition than it is now" (xvii). Indeed, Lang's best-known play, *Fire Exit*, is a protofeminist rewrite of the myth of Orpheus and Eurydice, set in a burlesque house in New Jersey. At its end, Eurydice chooses to be alone rather than get back together with a bullying, self-pitying Orpheus. "Once, / I almost died for grief, because of you," Orpheus complains. "I ate nothing and drank no water. / I lost thirty pounds." "You look fine," Eurydice replies; "I gained them back," quips Orpheus. In the final scene, after Orpheus badgers her, "Get your coat! I don't care / What you are, or what you've been," Eurydice announces, "I'm not going with him." Eurydice then ends the play with multivalent lines: "Perhaps it was better this way. / I wanted him to look at me" (252).

Lang's poetry is uneven, but never boring. Her voice is snappy, driven, and vaguely formal. Sometimes she goes in for Auden-esque or ornate lyricisms ("When you were in despair / I grew there"; "Spring you came marvelous with possibles"); more often she practices a kind of prosy, unlovely poetry which bears some kinship with Riding, and, occasionally, with Moore ("Old crab bit my finger; / Searching under the rock to touch it / As it should be touched, lingeringly, / It bit me. Wicked secret crab."). Her intentional awkwardness can be disquieting, as in "You Kill Me," which reads (in entirety): "You kill me. Yes, you do. / I know no one else who'd / Buy a sparrow (I / didn't even know they *sold* sparrows) / Just to feed it watermelon / And in public, too. // Every afternoon I think of you / Out there, flushed and fair, / Scraping the exhausted rind with a spoon. / Every day! All winter" (115). It pleases Lang's ear to hang phrases like "Every day! All winter" out to dry at the end of a poem, after, for example, the rhyme of "too" and "spoon" has already stitched it up. She also likes to begin poems with weird questions, such as "Why else do you have an English horn if not / To blow it so I'll know to let you in?" She typically addresses surreal conundrums with urgency, as in the title "How to Tell a Diamond from a Burning Baby," and enjoys inscrutable, banal epigraphs such as "'The tongue is a great magnifier, Mrs. Dubois.'—*My sister's dentist.*" She frequently makes grand, romantic gestures, only to undercut them with qualifications: "When I came back up out of the dark (Tuesday)"; when she gets personal, she often unsettles the reader by recounting moments more odd than confessional: "I stayed at home, / I stayed and I stared at a fingernail. / Now I stare at a bird. . . . He isn't like the birds I've known / And I've been places, and I've seen birds" (131). Throughout her poems, one feels the power of a tremendously agile and ambitious mind moving in and out of imitations and exercises, and at moments, striking out with confidence (and sometimes loneliness) into its own queer idiom: "It was desolate, walking alone, / Talking to no one, / Thinking: seeing me like this / Walking, talking to myself / That couple will have said I'm queer" (142).

In the end, the feeling that Lang's work is uneven probably stems less from any incompetence in her writing and more from the visceral sense that she did not live long enough to come fully into her own as an artist. It was precisely this feeling that bothered O'Hara so much after her death. As Gooch writes, "With Lang's death O'Hara came to grapple with the notion expressed in the title of his grieving poem dedicated to her, 'The Unfinished.' She was obviously someone of enormous talent who had not had time to make a coherent statement out of her many talents." But O'Hara was not one to be frightened off by incoherence. To the contrary, in the making of Lang's *Collected*, O'Hara wanted to see her unfinished poems included. As Gooch puts it, "Revealing something about his opinion of his own irregular poems, O'Hara counseled against tidying up" (286). Indeed, in a late poem, "Poems to Preserve the Years at Home," Lang herself sanctions this approach. Lang begins the long poem with the exasperation of feeling buried in the garbage of the mundane:

> . . . all around me boxes, papers, papers, drawers,
> Files, filing cabinets, especial drawers.
>
> The typewriter which jams. The voice downstairs
> That calls. The telephone which enters.
> The emergency. The caller. The hot water heater that breaks.
> I can't remember I can't remember
> I put something here, I had something to do,
>
> Someone to telephone, some letter to answer. (142)

The poem goes on to record the deep frustration of not being able to navigate through it all: "I don't seem to be able to accomplish / *Anything*. Everything begun. / Nothing ever finished. / Heaps and piles of waste." But as the poem moves along over several pages, it ends up charting a move from exasperation to acceptance: "The morning's mail or the bills— / So what. So they'll get put on bureaus . . . The disorder / Is my own." By the end, she has reversed course entirely, and asserts: "*Not to finish* becomes the challenge."

Of course the blunt interpretation of the poem is that to finish is to die, and the poem closes down with the stark admission: "I never once thought about death / Before I started to die. Time grows thin." But if we put aside Lang's biography for a moment, her eventual embrace of the "heaps and piles of waste" that constitute an "unfinished" career or life—that is, all of our careers or lives, until we die—points us in a different direction. It is the opposite direction to the one Eliot famously took in his prose poem "Hysteria," in which he writes: "I decided that if the shaking of her breasts could be stopped, some of the fragments of the afternoon might be collected, and I concentrated my attention with careful subtlety to this end." (Indeed, Lang's celebration of her brief stint as an exotic dancer, as immortalized in her poem "Anne, A Chorus Girl, Quitting the Line, To Society," which begins, "Don't stop loving me when / I leave the Line Next week's routines / are done with roses and balloons / And one with garlands, all the girls in green," shakes its breasts in the face of such a sentiment [96].)

Eliot may remain most famous for *The Waste Land*, but its title signifies a grim and tortured attitude toward waste, not a celebratory one. In a sense, the fame of the *The Waste Land* lies precisely in this ambivalence: the poem is celebrated for both its inclusion of waste into the poem's fabric—the inclusion of languages other than English, the voices of women and people of lower classes (in a poem haunted by the specters of impotence and infertility, what could be more "wasteful" than the woman at the pub blabbering on about inducing an abortion?)—and, at the same time, for the ostentatious erudition of Eliot's footnotes, which scramble to gain mastery over what precedes them. In short, as a professor in graduate school once sagely put it to me, Eliot's notes pretend to explicate, but their truer function is to piss on the poem. If one reads the poem and the notes together as a sort of an anxious dyad, one can see Eliot grappling with Hegel's infelicitous conviction that "the invasion of everyday life by 'the prose' of the world signifies the death of the Gods" (see Schor, *Detail*, 80).

More often than not, this "prose of the world" signifies the domestic realm of drudgery and materiality occupied by women. By this logic, the particular—the second sex—invariably becomes the vehicle for pollution. Clearly this is an old story, older than Eliot's "Hysteria" or *The Waste Land*; older, in fact, than Genesis; and at least as old as Greek antiquity, as Anne Carson makes clear in an illuminating essay, "Dirt and Desire: Essay on the Phenomenology of Female Pollution in Antiquity." Carson here traces the myriad of ways in which Greek society, philosophy, and poetry consistently regarded women as "pollutable, polluted and polluting" (*Men*, 143). Working on this same theme but in a context closer to the present, Schor has usefully tracked the presumed intimacy between women and refuse through the birth of psychoanalysis at the end of the nineteenth century. Schor explains how hysteria, paranoia, and obsessional neurosis—the provinces of primarily female patients— were treated as "pathologies of the detail, reflecting a society sick with the detail, so to speak" (*Detail*, 70). Schor also explains how the deep hope of Freud's "talking cure" was that it could somehow convert, or inflate, "the refuse of the day's residues" into meaning— that interpretation could somehow "connect the detail with the whole which it represents," and thus lead down "the royal way to the unconscious" (71).

Like Stein, who expressed only disdain for the idea of the uncon- scious, and whose love of the infantile both repels interpretation and welcomes the "pollutable, polluted and polluting," Ashbery, O'Hara, and Schuyler were not particularly smitten by the above narratives. O'Hara's oft-cited denigration of Lowell's poem "Skunk Hour"—yet another twentieth-century poem famous for its discon- solate probe of garbage—points us toward this profound difference in attitude. About Lowell's poem, O'Hara said, "I don't think that anyone has to get themselves to go and watch lovers in a parking lot necking in order to write a poem, and I don't see why it's admirable if they feel guilty about it. They should feel guilty. Why are they snooping? What's so wonderful about a Peeping Tom? And then if you liken them to skunks putting their noses in garbage pails, you've just done something perfectly revolting" (Lehman, 347). Lehman rightly points out that O'Hara's scolding stemmed from the fact that "'Skunk Hour' stood for everything that [O'Hara] detested in American poetry: didacticism, symbolism, and the grandiose ego- ism of a speaker who likens the welfare of the body politic to the state of his psyche and quotes Milton's Satan, 'Myself am Hell,' with- out a saving irony" (348), but I would push the difference further still. After all, what's "perfectly revolting" is not the necking or the garbage, but Lowell's metaphor-making, which sets him apart from both in the role of spectator, and evidences a certain skittishness about getting down and dirty. It isn't just that Lowell's poem is sym- bolic, but that its symbolism casts Lowell as literally looking down on a mother skunk getting creamed in the face by a waste product: "I stand on top / of our back steps and breathe the rich air— / a mother skunk with her column of kittens swills the garbage pail. / She jabs her wedge-head in a cup / of sour cream, drops her ostrich tail, / and will not scare" (90).

67

O'Hara's reaction to "Skunk Hour" also deepens in meaning when placed in the context of the specific discourse on privacy that proliferated in cold war America.[17] As Deborah Nelson explains in her study of confessional poetry and constitutional privacy doctrine, *Pursuing Privacy in Cold War America* (2002), the governing paradox of the cold war was that "in the interests in preserving the space of privacy, privacy would have to be penetrated" (xiii)—a paradox that our own "war on terror" has brought to a renewed and heightened state of crisis. Then as now, these penetrations of privacy were unevenly distributed, and Nelson's study lays bare how in the cold war, "categories of citizens—women or homosexuals—rather than unlucky individuals were banished to the deprivation, rather than the liberation, of privacy" (xiii). Nowhere is this distinction sharper than in the comparison of the Supreme Court decisions *Griswold v. Connecticut* (1965)—which affirmed the right of married couples to use contraception in the privacy of their own bedrooms—and *Bowers v. Hardwick* (1986), which denied gay men a right to privacy in theirs. (*"The issue presented is whether the Federal Constitution confers a fundamental right upon homosexuals to engage in sodomy,"* wrote Justice White in *Hardwick*—an issue which, for him, trumped the question of the constitutionality of a policeman barging into someone's bedroom without a valid search warrant [see Nelson, 147].) I don't really want to keep using Lowell as a patsy, for as Nelson rightly notes, "[Lowell's] innovation was to make himself . . . available, not as the abstract and universal poet, but as a particular person in a particular place and time" (45)—a project related, albeit in a complicated way, to the New York School.[18] But O'Hara's negative reaction to Lowell's voyeurism takes on another dimension when we think about the different positions Lowell and O'Hara occupied in a society obsessed with police surveillance and purges of homosexual men. "Why are they snooping? What's so great about a Peeping Tom?" O'Hara asks—questions that one might well have posed to McCarthy himself.

Read in this light, O'Hara's insouciant, "not caring" attitude can also be read as a defensive stance—a kind of preemptive I-wouldn't-want-to-be-a-part-of-your-club-anyhow line, when you already know you aren't going to get in. For if the New York School of poets did, indeed, constitute an avant-garde, it differed profoundly from prior avant-gardes in its lack of interest in affecting, much less revolutionizing, the culture at large. O'Hara's claim that he couldn't care less about "clarifying experiences for anyone or bettering (other than accidentally) anyone's state or social relation" could not stand further apart from the impulses of Futurism, Dada, Surrealism, the Beats, or Black Arts, to name just a few movements which strove to transform the "state or social relation" of both individual and polis. But instead of venerating this "not caring," apolitical stance as desirable and timeless, we might consider it in the context of being queer in the mid-fifties, where explicitly same-sex poems had to wait until after Stonewall to see the light of day, and where, in certain forums outside one's coterie, "if you ever mentioned anyone was gay, you'd risk being excommunicated," as Giorno put it. In such a context, O'Hara's poetry instead celebrates the merits of a "don't bother me and I won't bother you" mode of living. In "Ave Maria," for example, the poet pleads with mothers everywhere to allow their children to go to the movies, where they might be initiated into the rituals of public sex. As in several other O'Hara poems, the movies here represent a space in which one can maintain a sort of privacy in public—a place where a populace can sit together in darkness, sharing the same space without policing each other's activities.

O'Hara wrote often about public gay sex, an activity presumably not as "all-American" as a straight couple necking in a parked car. But like the wedge-headed skunk, O'Hara's poetry "will not scare" off of such probing. In fact, one of his most euphoric embraces of garbage is found in a poem titled "Homosexuality":

I start like ice, my finger to my ear, my ear
to my heart, that proud cur at the garbage can

in the rain. It's wonderful to admire oneself
with complete candor, tallying up the merits of each

of the latrines. 14th Street is drunken and credulous,
53rd Street tries to tremble but is too at rest. The good

love a park and the inept a railway station,
and there are the divine ones who drag themselves up

and down the lengthening shadow of an Abyssinian head
in the dust, trailing their long elegant heels of hot air

crying to confuse the brave "It's a summer day
and I want to be wanted more than anything else in the world."
   (*CP*, 182)

O'Hara starts with his finger to his ear, probing his own orifices,
then segues to his heart, which he describes as a "proud cur at the
garbage can"—a subtle if inadvertent inversion of Lowell's furtive
skunk, and one that instead imagines a cur—"a dog considered to be
inferior or undesirable; a base or cowardly person" (*AHD*, 349), or, as
my thesaurus puts it more simply, "a bitch"—full of pride. The poem
then takes a jump-cut inventory of various public sites around the city
to get laid (notably, latrines—ground zeros of waste emission), and
touches obliquely on one of O'Hara's ongoing fascinations: oral sex
with black men (here coded as "Abyssinian head").[19] While Lowell
snoops around watching for "love-cars" and concludes afterward, "My
mind's not right," O'Hara instead affirms that "it's wonderful to admire
oneself with complete candor," even, or especially, if that means
admiring one's proficiency in negotiating sex in the public sphere.

Throughout O'Hara's poetry, he sings the praises of the bond
between refuse, sexual attraction, and urban living, as in his lovely
poem "Song":

Is it dirty
does it look dirty
that's what you think of in the city

does it just seem dirty
that's what you think of in the city
you don't refuse to breathe do you

someone comes along with a very bad character
he seems attractive. is he really. yes, very
he's attractive as his character is bad. is it. yes

that's what you think of in the city
run your finger along your no-moss mind
that's not a thought that's soot

and you take a lot of dirt off someone
is the character less bad. no. it improves constantly
you don't refuse to breathe do you (327)

Here O'Hara balances the mania of living in a dirty city like New York, where one is constantly worrying, "it is dirty?" or "does it just seem dirty?" with a memorable mantra of acceptance: "you don't refuse to breathe do you." The point is clear (and wildly pre-AIDS): to refuse the dirt is to refuse to be alive. The poem postulates that you are what you ingest, and that in a city full of attractive strangers with whom one is constantly being thrown into close contact, it's nearly impossible not to have a dirty mind. Certainly there are moments in O'Hara's poetry in which he presents this acceptance in a less exalted manner, such as in the opening lines of "Spleen": "I know so much / about things, I accept / so much, it's like / vomiting" (187), but even here the back-and-forth between reception and emission—between, perhaps, getting fucked and fucking—is fluid and guiltless.

In "The Morning of the Poem," Schuyler pays his own tribute to the scavenger-in-the-garbage motif. Here is his account, set in his mother's home in western New York:

> The other evening my mother and I were watching TV in the living
>   room when something fell, a metal clang on the
> Back stoop. I went and put the outside lights on and looked:
>   the trash-can had been knocked off and
> Perched on the can full of trash was the biggest raccoon I've
>   ever seen: he turned his head and looked me
> In the eye, hopped down and walked sedately off into the shrubs.
>   I put the lid back on and dragged the can into
> The vestibule. "I wish you had seen him," I told my mother, "he
>   was beautiful: he was so big!" "Maybe he
> Was a dog," she said, deep in her program. I don't know why,
>   but that breaks me up, like telling someone
> You've seen a rat, and they say, "Maybe it was a fat mouse."
>   I'd love to have picked him up and held him,
> Only, frankly, I thought he might incline to bite. (*CP*, 298)

Schuyler's rendition is remarkable for its humor and compassion ("I would like / to put food out for him, but how could I know / He was eating it and not the dogs that swarm around this hill?" he continues). There's also something erotic about the exchange—"he / was beautiful: he was so big!" he exclaims, then expresses a desire to pick the animal up and hold him. His desire to share his excitement with his mother—who typically deflates the scenario with inadvertent wit: "Maybe it was a dog"—is equally puerile and per-verse. Like O'Hara, Schuyler eschews the self-loathing that ani-mates "Skunk Hour," and instead celebrates the proud animal in the trash and its various attractions. The moment makes clear both Schuyler's appreciation of the subtle amusements of human inter-action as well as his quiet amazement at the grace of the nonhuman.

Ashbery's poetry is in fact famous for its embrace of waste—of "the dump dumped dumping." As he writes in *The Vermont Notebook*: "I will go to the dump. I am to be in the dump. I was permanently the dump and now the dump is me, but I will be permanently me when I am no longer the dump air" (Shoptaw, 31). As Shoptaw points out, this "waste heap" obviously alludes to other famous heaps—*The Waste Land*, of course, and also Stevens's man "taking a dump on the dump"; it also parallels the trash aesthetic elaborated by Duchamp, Schwitters, Rauschenberg, and others. Given such associations, it's not a stretch to imagine a homoerotic circle anally focused on "the dump, dumped, and dumping." But the similarity between this phrase and Carson's "pollutable, polluted, and polluting" points toward another dimension as well. At a recent talk, I was intrigued to hear Ashbery describe his work as kindred in spirit to a *Symphonia Domestica*—a reference, I assumed, to Richard Strauss's 1902–03 symphony which was notorious for polluting itself with "the blatant realism of the 'domestic' scena," that is, "the inclusion of the scream-ing child Franz, the fights with his wife Pauline, and the sheer real-ism of the 'love scene' between composer and wife, which Romain Rolland decried as one of the most audacious challenges Strauss had 'hurled against at [good] taste and common-sense.'"[20]

Of course neither Ashbery, Schuyler, nor O'Hara had a tradi-tional *scène de famille* complete with man, wife, screaming child, and the heterosexual drama of "differentiated male and female orgasms" to include in their work. (Strauss's symphony even includes a sex scene in which "the woman's motive is very excited figuration, the man's quickly subsiding," as Strauss explained in an unpub-lished note on the short score.) So to be clear: when I talk about these poets as embracing the domestic, I don't necessarily mean the normative conception of such, as elaborated in Strauss's symphony. The embrace I'm talking about has more to do with the "urban gay fetish of 'interiors'" that characterized 1950s gay taste in New York, a phenomenon Koestenbaum has explained as follows: "In the bleak McCarthy era, gay culture paradoxically flourished in the home—safer than police-threatened bars and tearooms. The private apartment—or townhouse—became a Joseph Cornell shadow box, a vitrine, an inside-out Brillo carton; in the domiciles, queers amassed artworks, cleansers, masks, records, and receipts" (*Warhol*, 51). At the panel, Ashbery didn't elaborate on the *Symphonia Domestica*, but he did say that he admired its inclusion of the "left-over pieces" of life—a good description of the kind of queer domi-cile Koestenbaum describes. "I think that any one of my poems might be considered a snapshot of what is going on in my mind at the time—first of all the desire to write a poem, after that wondering if I've left the oven on or thinking where I must be in the next hour," Ashbery has said (*Scene*, 37), once again linking his process to fragments of the domestic scene (in this case, the oven).

At the same panel, Ashbery iterated his admiration for Cage—an admiration which has persisted for fifty years, and which many have treated as a kind of latent threat to Ashbery's work (including his fellow panelist that night, Larry Rivers, who quickly intervened to announce that he would never understand what Ashbery got out of Cage's music). As Ward puts it in his chapter on Ashbery, "The aleatory has been felt by both British and American readers to be [Ashbery's] most dangerous temptation, and one that has been there throughout" (89). Regardless of one's opinion about this "temptation," the link between Strauss's symphony and Cage's most famous experiments, such as *Music of Changes* or *4'33"*, is obvious: the intent is to let in the garbage. In remembering a performance of *Music of Changes* in which Cage played the radio at random, Ash-bery recounted how beautiful and hilarious it was when the radio happened upon a Mozart piece amidst the static, and the audience—being so relieved to hear a lovely, familiar piece of music—burst into applause. Ashbery plays with a similar phenomenon in his long poems, which tend to spin, sputter, and drift, occasionally eddying out into more formal, structured moments (such as the double ses-tina with end-rhymes lifted from Swinburne that bobs up in the middle of *Flow Chart*). This pattern is perhaps a microcosm of his career at large, with the following lines from *Flow Chart* serving as an apt description of this ethos: "How all that fluff got wedged in with the diamonds in the star chamber / makes for compelling reading, as does the heading 'Eyesores,' though what comes under it / e.g. 'Nancy's pendant' is a decidedly mixed bag" (168). The phrases "eyesores" and "a decidedly mixed bag" may echo common charges leveled against Ashbery's work, but he happily deems such things "compelling reading," echoing his contention in *Other Traditions* that "good things sometimes come in mixed bags" (6). And as soon as he lets in the "fluff" along with the "diamonds," the feminine, or faggy, streams in—here in the form of "Nancy's pendant."[21]

Unlike the *Symphonia Domestica*, however, and unlike the poetry of O'Hara or Schuyler, Ashbery's poetry does not focus overtly on his own autobiographical and erotic particulars. But as Shoptaw has pointed out, from a certain perspective, his work can be read as an ongoing speculation about—indeed a theorization of—the metaphysics of particulars. Or, better put, it can be read as a constant challenge to the assumed relationship between the particular and the universal. Shoptaw explains: "Traditionally, poets have been said to represent the universal through the particular. . . . Ashbery's misrepresentative poetics operate differently: the poem represents no experience in particular" (43). At the same time, critics such as David Kalstone have gone so far as to assert that in Ashbery's work, "the enemy, over and over again, is *generality*" (*Scene*, 45). Many Ashbery readers might have trouble buying the latter argument, for, as Thomas Lisk has pointed out, "general nouns unsupported by clear relevant details are exactly what we find over and over again in Ashbery's poetry." Lisk proves his point by describing Ashbery's obsession with "the most general possible word, 'thing,'" as well as Ashbery's habit of "linking abstract subjects with concrete verbs, and vice versa" (*Scene*, 45). Faced with this dilemma, I think we might save some time and trouble by recalling a comment Ashbery makes in *Other Traditions*: he says he stands by Williams's famous slogan, "No ideas but in things," but with the crucial caveat: "For me, ideas are also things" (2)—or, in other words, true abstractions.[22]

But despite the real plurality and multivalence of Ashbery's vision—"What I am trying to get at is a general, all-purpose experience—like those stretch socks that fit all sizes," he explains (Shoptaw, 1)—his work is decidedly *not* a direct sampling of the diverse plethora of voices that constitute the polyglot of contemporary America, a project that held more interest even for Williams, say, in *Paterson*, or, across the pond, Eliot in *The Waste Land*. The idiom that attracts Ashbery most consistently is the fuddy-duddy argot of WASPy, early to midcentury American speech, often with an aw-shucks twist: "As for Jenny Wren, she cares, hopping about on her little twig like she was tryin' to tell us somethin', but that's just it, she couldn't even if she wanted to," he writes in "For John Clare," suddenly possessed by the ghost of inept dialect (*Mooring*, 250). This point is an important one insofar as it underscores Ashbery's attraction to the intensely normative, and, perhaps, his dirty desire to transgress it by removing it from its original context. And here I mean "dirty" in all senses of the word, for, as Anne Carson has explained, "'Dirt' may be defined as 'matter out of place.' The poached egg on your plate at the breakfast table is not dirt; the poached egg on the floor of the Reading Room at the British Museum is. Dirt is matter that has crossed a boundary it ought not to have crossed. Dirt confounds categories and mixes up form" (*Men*, 145).

Carson's definition provides an excellent means of describing the impression left by the exhibition of Henry Darger's *In the Realms of the Unreal*, on permanent display at the American Folk Art Museum in New York. ("Returned again to the exhibition," Ashbery writes in *Girls on the Run*. "How strange it is that when we least imagine we are enjoying themselves, a shaft of reason will bedazzle us" [12].) Darger based his drawings of the Vivian Girls on hundreds of clippings of little girls from coloring books, comic strips, and advertisements for clothing, cookery, or other domestic goods gathered from mainstream magazines; he then copied, traced, or collaged these clippings directly into the watercolor paintings that illustrate his epic saga. A Civil War buff, Darger also collected commemorative issues about the war published by *Life* and other magazines, and pored over their illustrations of battle scenes. But whereas everyone is supposed to appreciate the cuteness of cherubic little girls in pigtails stirring cookie batter or toweling off after a bath, and everyone's supposed to take a patriotic interest in the vicissitudes of American military history, you're not supposed to then place those little girls *into* the scenes of war and horrific violence, much less take their jumpers off, paint them with dancing penises, and copy such scenes obsessively throughout a lifetime. In his collecting, collaging, and cutting, Darger revealed his perversion, joining the ranks of those "pioneers in understanding how perverse sexuality interrupts the distinction between public and private space," as Koestenbaum has put it in a different context (*Warhol*, 51).

Further, if you're going to go ahead and indulge your perversion, you're supposed to make something coherent out of it—a narrative epic, for example—but neither *In the Realms* nor *Girls on the Run* is overly concerned with such a goal.[23] It has not even been possible to publish *In the Realms* in its entirety, as it consists of over thirty thousand pages of manuscript, along with enormous watercolors painted on both sides of the paper; many have claimed it to be the longest piece of imaginative prose ever written. (Luckily the Folk Art exhibit, along with the oversized 720-page study with text by Darger scholar John MacGregor, can give you a pretty good idea of the thing.) While not sprawling in length, Ashbery's *Girls on the Run* inherits the meanderingness and eroticism of Darger's vision ("Like a lilac I am coming on your shoe," Ashbery writes; elsewhere, "Sometimes they were in sordid sexual situations; / at others, a smidgen of fun would intrude on our day / which exists to be intruded upon, anyway" [41, 13]). It also shares in Darger's insistent combination of pubescent innocence and impending violence; the opening lines of the book read, "A great plane flew across the sun, / and the girls ran across the ground. . . . Let's get out of here, Judy said. / They're getting closer, I can't stand it." But for the most part Ashbery sidesteps the more troubling and gruesome aspects of Darger's epic, the violence of which apparently merits a warning sign at the entrance to the exhibit, though the most brutal paintings are not on display.[24]

Yet the nature of Ashbery's identification with Darger remains provocative, as clearly a similar kind of imagination fascinates both: namely, that of childhood ("This, only children can know / and some adults who have turned the steep corner into childhood," Ashbery writes, implying that he is one of those adults who has taken the plunge), but, more specifically, that of girlhood.[25] In talking about the inspiration for *Girls on the Run*, Ashbery has said:

> I'm in correspondence with Mary, a girl I had a crush on all through childhood and adolescence. We had a mythical kingdom in the woods; various of our friends had castles in trees, and I was always just trying to get plays that we could produce spontaneously. Then my younger brother died just around the beginning of World War II. The group dispersed for various reasons, and things were never as happy or romantic as they'd been, and my brother was no longer there. I think I've always been trying to get back to this mystical kingdom that Mary and I inhabited. (D'Agata, n.p.)

Though his fixation on prepubescent fantasy is not as extreme as Darger's, Ashbery's anecdote echoes Darger's version of childhood as a mystical place invariably connected to loss. (In an echo of Ashbery's loss of his younger brother, Darger was obsessed with a sister he never knew, who was given up for adoption at birth, and to whom his mother died giving birth.) And notable among these losses is the freedom to toy with gender. *In the Realms* is in fact loaded with episodes of cross-dressing. "What a pretty girl he sure would make," says Vivian Girl Jennie Turmer of a little boy dressed like a girl; in this same scene, Jennie herself is "adapting to her slender and pretty little form a little boy's attire," and cutting her hair into a boyish bob. As John MacGregor puts it, "It seems to be a matter of great importance to Henry that at least some children have the ability to change gender, or to slip in and out of disguises which fool everyone" (528).[26] Ashbery inherits and enjoys this theme, as the name of his character "Uncle Margaret" suggests. Further, in *Girls*, Ashbery's customary play with indefinite pronouns takes on a more explicitly transgender flavor, as his "we's" and "I's" keep him slipping in and out of the forms of a Vivian Girl, or a Darger-like friend and narrator, or one of the many other little boys or androgynous creatures (such as "Tidbit" or "Shuffle") that populate the long poem.

In addition to (but not unrelated to) this gender trouble lies the problem of parasitical detail, surely another facet of Ashbery's attraction to Darger's work. As MacGregor writes of Darger, "He seemed to have possessed no clear awareness that descriptive detail was expected to serve a precise literary goal. His overly concrete and materialistic mind delighted in an endless build-up of material fact for its own sake" (109). Ashbery's mind is not as literal as Darger's, but Ashbery's use of abundant detail throughout *Girls* and his other poetry also jams any movement toward a "precise literary goal." Instead, the poetry provides an overabundance of verbal pleasure, strung along by a syntax that cannot be tamed, and whose clauses take the reader far afield: "In the lane the parson's / ambulance pestered gold pigtails, who were in for a shock / when the fox returned smiling, fanning his great tail in the comet / of the lighthouses the sausages were so concerned about" (14). Whereas Ashbery is ostensibly concerned with the "realms of the unreal," and Barthes is interested in the opposite—the realist novel—Ashbery clearly contributes to the revalorization of useless detail that Barthes theorizes in his essay "The Reality Effect." Schor describes Barthes's theorization as scandalous insofar as it delegitimatizes "the organic model of literary interpretation, according to which all details—no matter how aberrant their initial appearance—can, indeed must be integrated into the whole, since the work of art is itself organically constituted." Schor argues that "to privilege the insignificant detail is to practice a sort of decadent criticism, to promote a poor management of linguistic capital" (*Detail*, 85). Though I don't imagine the New York School was on her mind, Schor's description of writing as poorly managed linguistic capital could certainly serve as an apt description of much of its literary production.

This tendency toward excess has bothered a lot of people. Speaking of O'Hara, Vendler writes: "The longest poems end up simply messy, endless secretions, with a nugget of poetry here and there" (179–180); here I quote from Ward's introduction to his study:

> With the exception of James Schuyler, the writers with whose work this study deals have tended toward prolificity, in Ashbery's case prodigiously so. . . . The structureless structures of the endless list, the pseudo-narrative, the neo-Surrealist collage, can be read as offering procedural analogues for the faintly nauseating terms in which John Bernard Myers describes the New York art-world of the fifties; "a situation which was open, yeasty, limitlessly permissive." . . . The blame for some of this can be laid at the door of Walt Whitman, rather than the painters. Whitman's severance of American from English poetic tradition inaugurated an aesthetics of monstrous absorbency, total inclusion. Perhaps this has gone even wider than Whitman's bequest, and become a common factor in American aesthetics. . . . The most effective poems of the New York group are those whose capacity for tireless exploration and absorption comes up against, if not Steve McQueen's ice-wagon, then some equally cold shower that has consequences for the formless forms of the poetry. (9)

Perhaps as an American, or as someone not faintly nauseated by the "yeasty" or the "limitlessly permissive," and as someone positively mortified by the idea of killing excitement with a cold shower, I can't quite understand why there need be any blame attached to an aesthetics of "monstrous absorbency" or "endless secretions."[27] Not only do such terms ooze gender—Mary Shelley's famous description of her novel *Frankenstein* as a "monstrous dilation" immediately comes to mind (see chapter 3), as does the female body's somewhat regrettable penchant for yeast—but such an assessment does nothing to illuminate many of the writers' greatest achievements, such as O'Hara's deeply logorrheic "Second Avenue," the largesse of Schuyler's "The Morning of the Poem," or the endless secretion of *Flow Chart*. The drive toward excess in the poetry is real and uncontrollable, as epitomized by Schuyler's memory of pissing all over himself at the end of "The Morning of the Poem": "I / inched down my zipper and put my right hand into / The opening: hideous trauma, there was just no way I could / transfer my swollen tool from hand to hand without a great / Gushing forth (inside my pants), like when Moses hit the rock: so / I did it: there was piss all over Paris, not / To mention my shirt and pants, light sun tans" (302). Schuyler's "piss all over Paris" is, perhaps, the New York School equivalent of Plath's aphorism: "The blood jet is poetry, / There is no stopping it." To worry about whether or not the blood jet always produces "good poems" is to miss the point; as O'Hara once pithily suggested, the bad ones will slip into oblivion by themselves.

In fact a crucial part of the legacy of New York School poetry has been its encouragement to give up the battle to protect the "well-wrought urn" from this "monstrous absorbency." In lamenting the experimental pieces in Ashbery's second book, *The Tennis Court Oath* (1962), Ward writes: "What we actually get in the experimental pieces is . . . a casual Surreal pile-up of deconstructed bits and pieces that is partly responsible for the New York poetry-by-the-yard turned out by magazines like *The World* or *Adventures in Poetry* during the Sixties and early Seventies" (111). Ward's distaste for this poetry-by-the-yard is palpable, and, I think, unfortunate. Not only does it bar the obvious and important connection between Ashbery's poetry-by-the-yard and Warhol's painting-by-the-yard—a connection that many critics have opted to ignore or deny[28]—but it also demotes the New York scene precisely at the moment that a rush of speech by women and people of color began to take center stage via the "mimeograph revolution," and the birth of punk, rap, open mics, and a whole host of other explosive forms of speech. As Patti Smith spews in her 1978 "Babelogue": "I would measure the success of a night by the way by the way by the amount of piss and seed I could exude over the columns that nestled the PA"—another classic rush, or "babble," of female speech in which masculine identification (here in the form of exuding seed and wielding her guitar) is paramount. For his part, Allen Ginsberg described the spirit of the time in his foreword to *Out of This World* as follows:

> Liberation of the word. Liberation of minority groups, questions of race. The famous "sexual revolution." The celebrated women's liberation—women writing and reading brilliantly, led by poets Anne Waldman and Diane diPrima, Alice Notley, Maureen Owen, Denise Levertov, Joanne Kyger, also Diane Wakoski and Rochelle Owens and Carol Bergé, others. At least in my circle these were among the stars who gave expression to new independence. There were angry denunciations, manifestos, gay liberation performance pieces; there was romantic love poetry, there were prose poetry journals like Taylor Mead's excellent *Diary of a New York Youth* (Kerouac liked Mead's free style and frankness). (Waldman, xxvii–xxviii)

And it was precisely this "yeasty and limitlessly permissive" aspect of the New York art world that drew an unprecedented diversity of people to the city in the sixties and seventies to partake in the literary scene, including the three women who are the subject of the second half of this study.[29]

In contending with this "monstrous" aspect of New York School writing, it has proved difficult for many critics to resist the urge to normalize it, in an attempt to meld it into traditional narratives of literary value. For example, when Lehman asserts that the details in O'Hara's "The Day Lady Died" will eventually reveal an entire extinct species of dinosaur, he speaks to a deeply ingrained hope that detail not be superfluous—that works of art, and, perhaps by extension, our lives, will add up to something, preferably something with meaning and value. Ashbery addresses this hope in his poem "The System":

> the few who want order in their lives and a sense of growing and progression toward a fixed end suffer terribly. Sometimes they try to dope their consciousness of the shifting but the ineluctable grid of time that has been arbitrarily imposed on them with alcohol or drugs, but these lead merely to mornings after whose waking is ten times more painful than before, bringing with it a new and more terrible realization of the impossibility of reconciling their own ends with those of the cosmos. (*Mooring*, 349)

Depending on your temperament, this picture may strike you as grim—indeed it might strike me that way, were it not part of a poetry that elaborates a different path, a path that partakes in "the under-currency of American literature that assures us that the moment of being is central and true," as Myles has put it in reference to Stein, Emerson, and Thoreau (*Fish*, 131).

The poetry of O'Hara and Schuyler repeatedly awakens to this "moment of being" via an intense attention to the details of both the physical body and its surroundings. It seems only fitting that the poem that contains the phrase that has come to serve as shorthand for O'Hara's poetics ("I do this, I do that") is the chronicle of an awakening. The poem is called "Getting Up Ahead of Someone (Sun)," and begins: "I cough a lot (sinus?) so I / get up and have some tea with cognac / it is dawn / the light flows evenly along the lawn" (341). From its opening cough onward (through lines such as, "it is cold I shiver a little / in white shorts") the poem charts the transient states and desires of O'Hara's body, and ends with the location of his body within the contingencies of space and time: "I make / myself a bourbon and commence / to write one of my 'I do this I do that' / poems in a sketch pad / it is tomorrow / though only six hours have gone by / each day's light has more significance these days." The exact import of this last line is elusive, but it exemplifies the unique combination of acceptance, subtle wistfulness, and eerie foreboding with which O'Hara often noted the passing of time. Though O'Hara wrote this poem in 1959—seven years before he died—it's admittedly hard, in retrospect, to read it without feeling as though time was already rushing him along toward his untimely death.

Schuyler's "The Morning of the Poem" sustains a related attentiveness to his body alongside a meditation on the passing of time, but he distends the process into a fifty-page poem. Notably, his poem also begins with an awakening: "July 8 or 9, the eighth certainly / 1976 that I know / Awakening in western New York" (259). He then quickly moves from the confusion of sleep to the awareness of inhabiting a particular body: "I being whoever I am get out of bed holding / my cock and go to piss / Then to the kitchen to make coffee and toast / with jam and see out / The window two blue jays ripping something white / while from my mother's / Room the radio purls: it plays all night she leaves it on to hear / The midnight news and then sleeps and dozes / until day which now it is." Throughout "The Morning of the Poem," Schuyler moves in and out of the past and the future, but, like O'Hara, he always punctuates his journey by calling our attention back to his body in the present: "ouch: cologne in a shaving cut." Schuyler's last long poem, "A Few Days," elaborates further on this procedure: its sense of time is even more cyclical—"I / can't nail the days down," he admits—the play with the presence of his writing body even more explicit: "Guess I'm ready for lunch: ready as I'll / ever be, that is. / Lunch was good: now to move my bowels. That was good, too" (359).

As the lacuna in this account of lunch and its expulsion demonstrates, both Schuyler and O'Hara (and Ashbery, as in his "Excuse me while I fart" moment in *Flow Chart*) like to play with the gaps that invariably occur when one attempts to get one's body into the body of one's writing. This combination of details and gaps is partly what makes the writing feel sexy. As Schor puts it in regard to the "aesthetics of Eros" developed by Barthes, "Eros resides in the detail, because the detail is always at least partially sited in a real body" (*Detail*, 96). The poetry teases insofar as it offers up the details of a real body while also acknowledging that this body is inevitably shrouded from the reader via the page, the passage of time, and, eventually, the death of both writer and reader. Likewise, though O'Hara may be famous for writing poems that describe the pleasures of walking down a city street—as in his "cock of the walk" poems, such as "F. (Missive & Walk) I. #53," in which he writes: "I'm getting tired of not wearing underwear / and then again I like it / strolling along / feeling the wind blow softly on my genitals / though I also like them encased in something / firm, almost tight, like a projectile" (420)—the writing still courts an illusion. The poem is, after all, a remembered walk, not a poem written while actually walking. Indeed, later in the same poem, O'Hara acknowledges this rift with a wink, and plays with the reader's expectations: "I'm / not going to the Colisseum I'm going to / the Russian Tea Room fooled you didn't I." Likewise, in "Getting Up Ahead of Someone (Sun)," one doesn't know whether the "I do this, I do that" poem O'Hara mentions writing is the one we're now reading, or some other existent, or virtual, poem.

This play with the body constitutes a great deal of the charm in O'Hara and Schuyler. And whether accidental or not, it also has feminist import. For while O'Hara's poetic insistence that "ideas are inseparable from the people who have them" (Berkson, *Art*) could hold true in many contexts, it also has a plainly feminist ring to it. In a 1978 essay entitled "Taking Women Students Seriously," Adrienne Rich wrote: "To think like a woman in a man's world means thinking critically, refusing to accept the givens, making connections between facts and ideas which men have left unconnected. *It means remembering that every mind resides in a body; remaining accountable to the female bodies in which we live; constantly retesting given hypotheses against lived experience*" (*On Lies, Secrets and Silence*, 245, italics mine). If you remove the gender specifications from the last part of Rich's comment, you have a fairly good description of the strain of New York School poetics I am calling attention to here. Is the logical conclusion of this syllogism that O'Hara, Schuyler, and Ashbery thought like women in a man's world? Not really: such terms don't really make a lot of sense to us today, especially as we've "outgrown" the kind of gender polarity and essentialism that Rich, especially at this phase of her career, is known for. But the connection still intrigues me, as it draws our attention to the spectacle of a group of men who loved men whose poetry also elaborated this cornerstone of feminist thought. I think such a spectacle is worth pausing over, and celebrating—especially as it works against "any insistence that the political dreams of a feminist and of a gay man have nothing in common," as Koestenbaum has put it in a different context (*Double Talk*, 8).

The pleasure the poetry takes in scoring the ephemeral and the bodily also represents a way of coping with what can otherwise seem an inexorably cruel fact of life: as Charles Peirce has put it, "Of nothing but the fleeting instant can [we] have absolutely immediate consciousness, or feeling, whether much or little; and this instant is no sooner present than it is gone. In it we can be conscious of no change; because we do that by making a little rehearsal of the process or imitation of it, and that occupies time." A past moment, Peirce frankly reminds us, "though it be past by but the hundredth of a second," is "totally and absolutely gone" (259). In response to this situation, Schuyler offers the simple ethos: "A few days / are all we have. So count them as they pass." But in calling this ethos a way of coping, I don't mean to suggest that I see it as a deception or a defense. And here I differ from Ward, who suggests that many of O'Hara's poems "operate in basic continuity with the Western lyrical tradition, lamenting the passage of time and erecting metaphysical conceits to clog that passage"—conceits that essentially function as "lies against time," in the Bloomian lingo (64). The poems are by no means simple-minded in their attitude toward temporality and mortality, as the haunting of O'Hara's line, "each day's light has more significance these days," or the mournfulness of Schuyler's inventory, "A few days / are all we have," suggests. But Ward's notion of "clogged passages" cannot account for the play of acceptance and evacuation in the poetry—a phenomenon that Myles has described (in relation to O'Hara) as follows: "O'Hara's voice just shifts and shifts and shifts and keeps taking in everything and letting it out" (Richard, 25). This quality of the writing—evident in Schuyler's short, enjambed lines that run with a strong current down the page, the unpunctuated rush of O'Hara's language ("you never come when you say you'll come but on the other hand you do come"), and Ashbery's commitment to an ethos of readerly and writerly amnesia, in which "your only business . . . is the sentence before your eye. Not the sentence you've just finished, or the sentence you're about to begin. Just the sentence unfolding right now," as Koestenbaum has put it in relation to Stein (*Cleavage*, 214–215)—presents an alternative to the unhappy dyad of choices—lament or fight—that Ward lays out.[30] Instead, the poetry can awaken both reader and writer to the sense that "to allow the world to change, and to learn change from it, to permit it strangers, accepting its own strangeness, are conditions of knowing it now," as Stanley Cavell has put it (119).

Cavell is here talking about Thoreau's *Walden*, but his words also provide an excellent description of the kind of openness to change and strangers that city life—particularly New York life—demands of its inhabitants. In his poem "An Urban Convalescence," James Merrill laments that "in New York, everything is torn down / Before you have had time to care for it"; later in the poem Merrill attributes such a process to "the sickness of our time." O'Hara and Schuyler also chart the shifting landscape and juxtapositions of the city, but they don't moralize about it. O'Hara usually takes geographical confusion and transformation in stride, as in "A Step Away from Them": "And one has eaten and one walks, past the magazines with nudes / and the posters for BULLFIGHT and / which they'll soon tear down. I / used to think they had the Armory / Show there" (*CP*, 257). As these lines suggest, O'Hara's New York is made up of a conglomeration of shifting conditions: the needs and activities of one's own body (i.e., eating and walking); ongoing or serial simulacra (as in the nudie magazines); the appearance and disappearance of events and their signs (the posters for BULLFIGHT and their impending disappearance); and a network of personal misunderstandings and fantasies about the essentially unknowable dimensions of urban space ("I / used to think they had the Armory / Show there").

In his great poem "Dining Out with Doug and Frank," Schuyler also muses on the juxtaposition of the old and the new that characterizes the New York City landscape:

> When they tore down
> the Singer building,
> and when I saw the Bogardus building
> rusty and coming unstitched in
> a battlefield of rubble I deliberately
> withdrew my emotional investments
> in loving old New York. Except you
> can't. I really like
> dining out and last night was
> especially fine. (*CP*, 250)

Schuyler here performs the inevitable emotional vacillations that accompany living in a city with both more architectural history and, perhaps, more commitment to rapid change than many other cities in the United States. Yet he doesn't dwell on the issue too long—instead he moves quickly into the affirmation: "I really like / dining out and last night was / especially fine." ("Like" was also an important word for Stein, as in the concluding lines of *Everybody's Autobiography*: "And I like being in London and I like having a ballet in London and I like everything they did to the ballet in London and I like the way they liked the ballet in London . . . anyway I like what I have and now it is today.") The next few lines of Schuyler's poem return to the poignant problem of withdrawing or continuing one's emotional investments, but this time in people: "A full moon / when we parted hung over / Frank and me. Why is this poem / so long? And full of death? / Frank and Doug are young and / beautiful and have nothing / to do with that." But Frank and Doug are mortal, and as the poem ages, they too will have something to do with that.

Taken together, Schuyler's appreciation of beauty that is "just able still to swiftly flow / it goes, it goes," Ashbery's commitment to "charting the flow," and O'Hara's sentiment, "I am foolish enough always to find [joy] in wind," all speak to Emerson's observations: "Our love of the real draws us to permanence, but health of the body consists in circulation, and sanity of mind in variety or facility of association. We need change of objects. Dedication to one thought is quickly odious" (272). Some might think this commitment to rapid juxtaposition gets tiresome in New York School poetry; others may see such restlessness as the sine qua non of modernity or late capitalism. But it is also the case that in a city like New York, this openness to movement, accident, strangers, and heterogeneity is something of a prerequisite to the dance of daily life. Looking back on New York from Paris, Notley remembers the character of her life there as follows:

> The fact is that to live in New York is to be involved with the outer or communal life of the city in all its detail, to be in the face of everyone else looking at you (but giving you license to be eccentric), particular people doing particular things, amid detail of objects, architecture, weather. Everyone is interested in everything; stoop society (in which we participated wholeheartedly at 101 St. Mark's) is a structure of observation, criticism, and solidarity. The ephemeral, the insouciant, the occasional, the contingent—all of that is outside in New York as well as inside. When I first went to New York to go to Barnard College, I was entranced by this aspect of the city and felt instantly at home. I know no other city like it—it is such a force as itself. It is always bigger than one, which is why one has to say I there. And it is a city of humor, sympathy, and very personalized encounters including aggressive ones. This all seems to me to be part of the School. (Email interview, 4 February 2002)

I know of no better way to describe O'Hara's poetry than as "a structure of observation, criticism, and solidarity," as is evident in the muted curiosity (and not-so-muted desire) in "A Step Away from Them": "First, down the sidewalk / where laborers feed their dirty / glistening torsos sandwiches / and Coca-Cola, with yellow helmets / on. They protect them from falling / bricks, I guess" (257). And Schuyler's poetry certainly speaks to Notley's observation that "the ephemeral, the insouciant, the occasional, the contingent—all of that is outside in New York as well as inside." As Schuyler was sometimes not physically or psychologically able to wander the streets, often he wrote from his room at the Chelsea Hotel, and married the interior with the exterior from there, as in his poem "Moon": "Still, I'm sorry / now I didn't go out / to see it (the lunar / eclipse) last night, / when I lay abed instead / and watched *The Jeffersons*, a very / funny show, I think. / And now the sun shines / down in silent brightness, / on me and my possessions, / which I have named, / New York" (321).

Schuyler here names his possessions "New York," but a broader read-ing would include the "me" in there too. It's an intriguing move, as it figures Schuyler's body (which we've just had the pleasure of pictur-ing lying in bed, watching *The Jeffersons*) at one with the city itself, not as metaphor for it.

It's also worth noting that at the same time that the first-generation New York School poets were hanging out in Greenwich Village, an enormous drama was playing out between highway-obsessed urban planners—Robert Moses, mainly—and Village resi-dents, who were engaged in a bitter struggle to protect their streets from "the attrition of automobiles," as Jane Jacobs, their principal advocate, termed it. (Indeed, if Jacobs and her fellow activists had not prevailed, an enormous freeway would run through the heart of the West Village today.) In her landmark 1961 book on urban plan-ning, *The Death and Life of Great American Cities*, Jacobs describes the workings of the city in a way that could almost serve as an aes-thetic manifesto for much New York School poetry:[31]

[The city] is a complex order. Its essence is intricacy of sidewalk use, bringing a constant succession of eyes. This order is all composed of movements and change, and although it is life, not art, we may fanci-fully call it the art form of the city and liken it to dance—not to a simple-minded precision dance with everyone kicking up at the same time, twirling in unison and bowing off en masse, but to an intricate ballet in which the individual dancers and ensembles all have dis-tinctive parts which miraculously reinforce each other and compose an orderly whole. The ballet of the good city sidewalk never repeats itself from place to place, and in any one place is always replete with new improvisations. (50)

Jacobs admired and fought for precisely the same attributes of New York City life that Notley names above as "part of the School": the importance of the human encounter, of the casual surveillance and solidarity of "stoop culture," and of the tangled, improvisatory mesh of "particular people doing particular things." Though Jacobs's main focus lies in the workings of public space and social interactions, she also theorizes on the nature of privacy in city life. She articulates the peculiar way in which most city-dwellers main-tain a certain privacy in public, thus forming a kind of "web of pub-lic respect and trust" that notably *"implies no private commitments"*

(56). "Nobody can keep open house in a great city," she writes. "Nobody wants to. . . . Cities are full of people with whom, from your viewpoint, or mine, or any other individual's, a certain degree of contact is useful or enjoyable; but you do not want them in your hair. And they do not want you in theirs, either" (56). This dynamic may also aid in understanding the differences between "Personism" and a more confessional idiom: as Vendler once observed about O'Hara's poetry, it presents "a version of public poetry which does not abolish the private" (191).[32] We might also hear in Jacobs's notion of an urban trust that "implies no private commitments" another rendition of the New York School vacillation between "caring" and "not caring." At a 1988 panel on the New York School at the Poetry Project, John Yau made precisely this point: the chaos of the city itself, he said, makes it impossible to "care" about what's going on everywhere at all times, and New York School poetry necessarily reflects the competing demands on one's attention (and perhaps, on one's conscience).

This play with the writing body, the body of the city, and the complications of personal address is partly what has held the interest of Language writers such as Charles Bernstein in New York aesthetics. In his essay "Stray Straws and Straw Men," Bernstein considers the terms of O'Hara's essay "Personism" and writes: "Note that O'Hara's word 'personism' is not 'personalism': it acknowledges the work to be a *fronting* of another person—another mind, if you will. O'Hara's work proposes a domain of the personal, & not simply assuming it, fully works it out" (42). I agree that O'Hara's first-person voice (or Schuyler's) is not "natural and direct" in a simplistic way, and I don't wish to undo the important work on O'Hara that Perloff and others have done—work that has struggled for the past thirty years or so to get us to understand that "those 'streamers of crepe paper fluttering before an electric fan,' as [Marius] Bewley called [O'Hara's poems], are actually the most intricate of language games" (Perloff, *FOH*, xxviii). But as I don't share Bernstein's anxiety about what he calls "personalism"—presumably, the deeply personal lyric voice that makes an urgent and intimate demand on the reader's attention—and as I see no conflict between an intensely personal poetry and intricate language games, I admit I'm tempted to push in the opposite direction.[33]

Many advocates of New York School writing champion the fact that it tends to be autobiographical while avoiding the confessional, as if the latter should be avoided like the plague, or as if the borders between the two were ever clear-cut. There are potentially interesting distinctions to be made here, but I think it a mistake to police their borders too vigorously. I have sympathy for the Marxist critique of bourgeois individualism associated with the confessional scenario, and I understand Bernstein's distaste for "the cant of 'make it personal' poetry" that has at least one root in New York School writing. But insofar as these tenets evidence the same allergy to the personal that has plagued literary criticism from (at least) Eliot's famed doctrine of impersonality to the intense, sexualized backlash against Plath and Sexton, for example, I find that I must regard them, too, with a certain degree of skepticism. For in art as in life, the concept of the personal has been simultaneously gendered as female and used as a pejorative. It takes a certain amount of guts to reclaim this scenario, as Myles does when she says in *Narrativity*: "Let's face it, [the first-generation New York School writers] were just as New Critical as everyone else in the fifties. They would all assert that the poetry was not about them. . . . My dirty secret has always been that it's of course all about me."

Perhaps the point is that there are an infinite number of moods and uses of the personal in poetry, just as there exist a multitude of kinds of "privacy," as Jacobs's theorization about city life and Nelson's study on privacy, for example, are at pains to illustrate. Further, while psychologists have traditionally treated "male identity as forged in relation to the world and female identity as awakened in a relationship of intimacy with another person," as Carol Gilligan has summarized it (*In a Different Voice*, 13), O'Hara's "Personism" charts a different course—one in which intimacy precedes identity. In "Personism," an intimate relation with another person becomes the condition of possibility for a statement of relationship between poet and culture. Consequently, this statement of relationship is not the same thing as a "fronting," especially as the latter implies "meeting in opposition," or "serving as a front [i.e., a facade] for" (*AHD*, 536)—terms which resurrect a spirit of confrontation, the ghost of a New Critical interest in masks, not to mention the epistemology of the closet.

For the statement of relationship between poet and culture that O'Hara's poetry proposes is, I think, as personal as it gets. Of course it all depends on what one means by "personal"—and here I'm using it to signify exactly the opposite of what Lyn Hejinian means when she says, "Poetics is not personal. A poetics gets formed in and as a relationship to the world." In an essay that discusses Plath, Creeley, and O'Hara, Charles Altieri has argued that what conjoins the poetics of these three distinct writers is the fact that "their poems are not the development of symbols interpreting life, but the actual enactment of imaginative energies devoted to fleshing out particular life situations" (*Scene*, 362). I see this dedication to "particular life situations" as quite personal, and part and parcel of the sort of radical contingency that leads O'Hara to worry in "A Letter to Bunny": "When anyone reads this but you it begins / to be lost." It is also central to the role that "coterie" has played in New York School writing, with its habit of naming particular people, places, and occasions. Such a habit can be understood in many ways—as constitutive of a queer family; as a reaction to poetry that prefers the royal "we" to the more local "I" or "you"; as a full-fledged crush on contingency; as campy self-absorption; and on. It can also be understood as a performance of "anxious care" about the present moment—a staging of caring for "life" over "art."

In a statement for the Paterson Society, O'Hara once wrote, "It's a pretty depressing day, you must admit, when you feel you relate more to poetry than to life" (*CP*, 511); a line from a Schuyler villanelle—"Art is brief; life and friendship, long"—speaks to a related sentiment. In considering this statement by O'Hara, Vendler writes: "O'Hara refused to take his poems, I would guess, as seriously as he took life. . . . The greatest poets would have found that antithesis unthinkable, and it works to the harm of O'Hara's poetry that he thinks poetry is *not* life" (184). Not only do I disagree, but I also think it possible that Vendler is taking O'Hara way too literally. Personally I take O'Hara's stance as an example of how one might remain utterly devoted to poetry without fetishizing linguistic expression at the expense of other ways of knowing—an occupational hazard for poets and literary theorists alike, so it would seem. This stance is another crucial legacy of the New York School. For example, while Notley takes the "spiritual task" of poetry extremely seriously (as we shall see), she also retains the influence of O'Hara's affable nonchalance, audible in her comment: "Writing poems gets done in a strangely isolated nontemporal space as all poets know, but I'm not really trying to claim anything 'special' for the poet. I think anything we do could be like this; but poetry is especially meditative" (Foster, 87).

Further, if we return O'Hara's statement about art and life to its original context, its complexity becomes clearer. Here is his complete thought: "(it's a pretty depressing day, you must admit, when you feel you relate more to poetry than to life), and as such may perhaps have more general application to my poetry since I have been more often depressed than happy, as far as I can tally it up" (511). This tally not only might come as a surprise to those who think of O'Hara as the bard of happiness; it may also suggest that he spent more days relating to "poetry" than to "life"—testimony that complicates Vendler's criticism. "Life" has become a politicized and confused term as of late, as epitomized, perhaps, by the neologism "pro-life" (you know something very strange is afoot when a politician's statement that he [and sometimes she] stands for "life" is immediately understood as a right-wing position on the fate of stem cells, fetuses, and women's reproductive rights). Then there are the age-old oppositions of "real life" vs. "art," "imagination," or "academia"—that is, the "life of the mind" vs. the "real-er," prole life of the body (yet another gendered dyad). The New York School poets certainly contributed to this fetishization of "real life," with their famed anti-academic stance (hence the joke of the "School" in their moniker), and with poem titles such as Schuyler's "Hymn to Life."[34] It's worth remembering, however, that "life" and "art" are just words, and that one's sense of their independence or interdependence is essentially mutable, both over a lifetime and from moment to moment. This mutability is in fact the main point of O'Hara's statement for the Paterson Society, in which he posits that an artist's statement or manifesto is nothing but "a diary of a particular day" (511). O'Hara's tone is casual, but his insistence that mood trumps dogma is profound, and perhaps a distant cousin of Nietzsche's famous quip that every great philosophy might also be considered as a kind of confession or memoir.

The pose of caring more for life than art might also be seen as a means of replacing a Kantian aesthetic of disinterestedness with an ethos of strong libidinal investment. In reference to the painter Larry Rivers, O'Hara once wrote: "What his work has always had to say to me, I guess, is to be more keenly interested while I'm still alive. And perhaps this is the most important thing that art can say" (*CP*, 515). For O'Hara, this "keen interest" carries a strong erotic charge. We might then wonder, along with O'Hara, what the relationship is between this "keen interest" and happiness. At what point does a jubilant or defiant "not caring" slip into indifference or depression? "It used to be that I could only write when I was miserable; now I can only write when I'm happy. Where will it end?" O'Hara asks in his Paterson statement. O'Hara returns to the question in a letter to Mike Goldberg, in which he reports that he isn't happy, but then adds: "That is not a complaint, since I have long given up the idea of being happy for the idea of being active, or engagé, or whatever it is the French tell us we ought to be and Walt Whitman seems to back up" (LeSueur, 291). Here "keen interest" trumps disinterest and happiness alike. Indeed, the poems of O'Hara, Schuyler, and Ashbery consistently enact this commitment to being "engagé" while not ignoring its many shadows—the shadows of indolence, indifference, depression, impossibility, futility, impotence, and in Schuyler's case, convalescence. O'Hara often dramatizes this struggle ("In placing this particular thought / I am taking up the cudgel against indifference," he writes [384]) while Schuyler and Ashbery customarily let their poems slip into "not caring" with less of a fight—Schuyler often with a languid sigh ("Give my love to, oh, anybody" [256]), Ashbery with mischievous flourish ("I have forgotten the sense of it or what the small / role of the central poem made me want to feel. No matter [FC, 3]). But whether engagé or exhausted, the poetry consistently replaces the drama of "caring" about Poetry and/or literary accomplishment with the drama of "caring" or "not caring" for the moment at hand—a shift that grants the poetry much of its remarkable euphoria, melancholy, and freedom.

In my introduction I noted the allure that this vacillation has had for women writing in its wake, while also pointing out how its stakes differ for women as compared to gay and straight men alike. Here I would remind us that the word "care" is itself rich with feminized associations: caring for others, especially as a mother or nurse; investing too much in what other people think; fretting over one's career instead of resting confidently in one's genius; attending obsessively to details; exercising caution; suffering from anxiety, depression, or excessive worrying; having ensnaring desires or attachments; and so on (see *AHD*, 240).[35] Women traditionally struggle with a much greater psychological (and sometimes physical) burden to care for others—be they infants or otherwise—often at the expense of their own pursuits. Their struggle to place "art" before "life" can be intense and even bitter—as Andrea Dworkin recently described her struggle: "In learning to write, I had to develop a sense that writing was more important than anything else—no person or conflict or tragedy except dying and death could get in the way. I had to break in myself all the habits associated with taking care of or feeling responsible for others" (35). (Compare this conviction, for example, to the exchange between Elizabeth Bishop and Robert Lowell that transpired over the publication of Lowell's collection *The Dolphin*, which included anguished letters written by Elizabeth Hardwick at the time of her and Lowell's divorce. "*Art isn't worth that much*," Bishop famously wrote to Lowell, in a stinging condemnation of his decision to care more for the art than the person.) Generally speaking, women are not culturally encouraged to exhibit the kind of confidence—much less arrogance—that brazenly assumes that their work can or will transform or even factor into the master narratives of art or literary history, or that the pursuit of such influence should trump everything else in their lives. When women exhibit this confidence or arrogance (as Stein did, in spades), the spectacle often courts a certain perversity. It is, as Myles will later say, a sort of fool's journey.

Elsewhere Myles explains that she never had "the same desire to gain approval from men," because as a working-class lesbian, she "knew [she] wasn't going to get in anyhow." "I could only be a tourist," she tells Foster (59). Myles has been called "the last of the New York School of poets," and there's a certain irony in the fact that this last of the School grew up as a "townie" in Cambridge just a few years after O'Hara, Ashbery, Koch, Creeley, and others graduated from Harvard. (Earlier in the interview, in discussing the influence of the men of the New York School, Myles makes a telling comparison: "New York School mimed is worse than academic, it's like my dad being a mailman coming home with the Ivy League clothes from the Harvard dorms where he had his route.") Though neither Ashbery, Schuyler, nor O'Hara came from a particularly illustrious or wealthy background, an undeniably large part of their particular camp aesthetic has to do with a certain kind of class fluency—with wielding high culture well enough to be able to combine it with concerns of the more ordinary consumer. (The humor of *A Nest of Ninnies*, for example, is predicated on the above mixture: "'Work doesn't get done,' a new voice said, 'one abandons it.' This version of Valéry's dictum was spoken by Fabia, who had just entered the office arm in arm with Alice. 'Why, we were just talking about you,' Betty gasped. 'Yes,' Marshall said, closing the catalogue after a lingering look at a suit of thermal underwear" [134].)[36] The poet Paul Blackburn called the first generation of the New York School poets the "MOMA/Edge of Big Money school"; Ted Berrigan once described them (without rancor) as "sophisticated sons-of-bitches, all these Harvard-educated poets who knew very well very talented painters" (Kane, 41, 159). Seen in the light of these apparent contradictions—Harvard grads railing against the academy; bohemian poets with a taste for bourgeois pleasures; art-world insiders who represent an avant-garde; outsider poets who eventually win Pulitzer Prizes; a group of openly gay men in the middle of a straight man's world, not to mention an incredibly macho painting movement; and so on—the tension between caring and not caring in their work seems but a natural, inextricable, and irresolvable part of the "School."

Recently I asked Notley what it was like to live in New York as a young poet in the shadow of the men discussed in this chapter—not to mention as the wife of their chief acolyte, Ted Berrigan—at the same time that anthologies such as *An Anthology of New York Poets* (1970) had begun to establish a patrilineal image of the New York School (only one woman—Mayer—appears in the anthology). She replied: "I was just coming of age when the Padgett-Shapiro anthology came out: I had barely written anything at that moment (I had to develop quickly). What I thought was something like: there's all this space to be filled. Then a little bit later, when I was suddenly a mother writing, I thought: why isn't there anything there to help me? And further: there's all this space to be filled" (email interview, 4 February 2002). One can almost hear in the rhythm of her comment (there's all this space—why isn't there anything here to help me?—there's all this space) an echo of Beckett's "I can't go on I will go on" mantra, but with a feminist twist. Her image of "space to be filled" also evokes Mitchell and her enormous canvases, Guest's love of white space, and Stein's drive toward impossibly epic literary ventures: all torsions of the image of the page or canvas as a white, virgin space to be marked or penetrated by the phallic pen or brush. Unlike Olson's "field composition"—with "field" connoting a finite domain or battlefield—"space" sounds, well, *spacier*—more capacious, more disorienting, more blatantly alien or "other." Indeed, empty space can grant both tremendous permission and tremendous alienation.[37]

In *The Desires of Mothers to Please Others in Letters,* Mayer addresses this space with the following wager: "Women can still wind up writing some unheard of things don't you think, I mean things that have never been written yet" (19). The thought is bold, but characteristically qualified by the relational, slightly insecure tag "don't you think" sandwiched in between her propositions. How does one proceed without the subterranean, cocky assurance that Perloff locates in O'Hara, that perhaps "he knew, all along, that we would indeed be looking"? The remainder of this study keeps this question in mind as it considers the distinct, ambitious, and provocative poetic experiments undertaken by Mayer, Notley, and Myles over the past three decades.

PART TWO

2

3

WHAT LIFE ISN'T DAILY?

THE GRATUITOUS ART

OF BERNADETTE MAYER

Front cover of Memory *by Bernadette Mayer (Plainfield, VT: North Atlantic, 1975), author pictured at bottom. Reprinted by permission of Bernadette Mayer.*

PERHAPS MORE THAN THAT of any of her "second-generation" peers, the work of Bernadette Mayer embodies the legacy of the "open, yeasty, limitlessly permissive" atmosphere of the New York art world at midcentury, along with the Whitmanesque "aesthetics of monstrous absorbency, total inclusion" that Ward worries over in *Statutes of Liberty*. In 1964, Ted Berrigan put forth *The Sonnets*, a lengthy sonnet cycle propelled (as the story goes) by speed, and woven together via collage and repetition; in 1970, Joe Brainard's *I Remember* appeared—a litany of memories each beginning with the line "I remember," which was soon followed in 1972 by *More I Remember*, and then *More I Remember More* in 1973, bringing the total number of entries over the one-thousand mark. But Mayer's self-conscious cultivation of what the *Dictionary of Literary Biography* has called "a startling inclusivity"—an inclusivity that attempts, in a number of different works, "to re-create the innumerable objects, events, memories, and dreams that range into the field of an alert consciousness" (Baker)—may represent the most unapologetic, and, perhaps, the most unmanageable example of "poetry-by-the-yard" from the period. As Mayer's friend and fellow poet Clark Coolidge once noted about the work that he and Mayer produced in the seventies, "We wanted endless works, that would zoom on & on and include everything ultimately, we'd talk about the 'Everything work' which would use every possible bit flashing through our minds" (Baker).

This chapter explores Mayer's desire for and elaboration of the "Everything work"—most definitely another instance of Sedgwick's "fat art," to be placed alongside that of Stein and Mitchell—by focusing on two of Mayer's time-structured projects: *Midwinter Day* (written as a piece on December 22, 1978) and *The Desires of Mothers to Please Others in Letters* (written in 1979–80, over the course of a nine-month term—the time-span of her pregnancy with her third child, Max).[1] Here I consider both works as extensions of the New York School interest in contingency and dailiness, as well as part and parcel of other broader, interrelated contexts, including performance art, conceptual art, and Warhol's pioneering experiments with recording verbal and visual excess; the tradition of the American long poem, especially the kind that collapses the boundary between poetry and prose; and other feminist works from the period (such as Mary Kelly's *Post-Partum Document* (1973–79), an exhaustive, psychoanalytically oriented visual and textual record of Kelly's postpartum experience), many of which act out the productive pleasure to be found in the blurring of public and private spheres.

Ward's word "monstrous" is important here, as it (unintentionally, I imagine) evokes Mary Shelley's *Frankenstein*, a crucial antecedent to the concerns of this chapter. In her 1831 introduction to the book, Shelley addresses the question "so frequently asked of [her]": "How I, then a young girl, came to think of, and to dilate upon, so very hideous an idea?" (1) The question itself, along with Shelley's use of the word "dilate" to describe the genesis of both the "abhorred monster" within her story and the book *Frankenstein* itself, famously link female authorship and childbirth (as does Shelley's sendoff of her book: "I bid my hideous progeny go forth and prosper. I have an affection for it, for it was the offspring of happier days" [5]). *Midwinter Day* and *Desires* explore the many complications of that link, and extend the New York School "aesthetics of monstrous absorbency" to include the many anxieties, frustrations, pleasures, and desires which attend being or becoming a mother, mothering daughters, being a female writer, and having a female body. And like Shelley before her, Mayer embraces both the excitements and the "hideousness" of the undertaking.

Before moving into this discussion, I should note that Mayer's passion for charting consciousness's excesses has not faltered or become dated over the years. In a 1997 interview with Lisa Jarnot, for example, Mayer reiterated this interest (adding a technological twist): "I'd like computers to be able to record everything you think and see. To be like the brain, and to write that out. . . . And somebody said to me, 'who would read it?' But I'm thinking that I would love to read it. Like if you had all these documents of everybody's experience. It would be amazing" (Jarnot, 9). A recent piece entitled "Dream Tape Transcribed—Hypnagogic Images" (published in the Poetry Project's magazine, *The World*, in 2000) testifies to Mayer's ongoing commitment to transcribing the minutiae of liminal consciousness. In this case, Mayer attempts to detail the many shifting colors in her field of vision—one of the effects of a brain hemorrhage Mayer survived in 1994: "i'll watch these some more, i'm waiting for the really thrilling spots of red & blue that sometimes come, i'll just observe the colors for a while and ript [sic] out the commenting on them & then see what happens" (9).

Despite the debilitating effects of Mayer's hemorrhage—including an extended period of time in which she could neither read nor write—she has continued to treat what many would consider an unthinkable scare or tragedy as yet another opportunity to investigate the workings of the mind. As she told Jarnot:

> I've always been interested in the brain and consciousness. I mean it's amazing that I had a cerebral hemorrhage and now I see all these neurologists and am concerned with all these things in a different way. I think it's great actually. I shouldn't say that. I learned in the hospital that you're not supposed to think a cerebral hemorrhage is interesting in any way. Otherwise you get accused of having a sense of unreality. One nurse actually said to me, "You don't realize what happened to you." (8)

Indeed, an abiding feature of Mayer's work is its relentless ability to remain interested where others' attention drops off, and a refusal to be sated by the demarcations of "reality" as defined by others. Though Mayer's sensibility is not really Pop—her penchant for scientized scrutiny of feeling differs from a Warholian focus on emotional vacancy, and one of her primary topics is love—one of the many aesthetic inclinations she shares with Warhol is an aversion to any humanist pabulum that mandates that one "feel the way others feel," as opposed to exploring less culturally endorsed realms of perception and sensation. Furthermore, though in general I would caution against proposing any unproblematic relationship between a writer's work and bodily health, here it seems almost unavoidable, and potentially appropriate, to follow Mayer's lead in finding her cerebral hemorrhage quite interesting—especially as *hemorrhage* means a "copious discharge of blood from the blood vessels," that is, the actualization of Plath's mantra of disruptive (female) excess: "The blood jet is poetry, / There is no stopping it." (Think, too, of Rosset's line on Mitchell: "There was no stopping it. . . . In a society that didn't allow abstract painting she would have gone to jail.")

Plath's mantra takes on a whole different meaning when placed in the context of the so-called mimeograph revolution of the sixties and seventies—a revolution spurred along by the developing technology of photomechanical reproduction, which suddenly allowed for the cheap dissemination of poetry publications of all kinds, including magazines such as *Floating Bear, Kulchur, C, Yugen, Fuck You: A Magazine of the Arts, Angel Hair, Adventures in Poetry, Telephone,* and many others.[2] As Brad Gooch notes in his O'Hara biography, "No phenomenon separated the sixties more distinctly from the fifties among poets than the appearance seemingly overnight of this paper river of magazines, broadsides, mimeos, and poetry chapbooks" (138). In his study, Kane points out that this "paper river"—which coincided with other new technologies, such as the tape recorder— had much to do with the idealization of speed, immediacy, and improvisation that one finds in so much alternative poetry of the period (Kane, 168–172). In the downtown scene swirling around the Poetry Project, Mayer's work as a poet, editor, performer, and teacher was pivotal to the development of this aesthetic. Kane also notes that the reading lists for Mayer's classes—which often included Wittgenstein, Whitehead, and Barthes alongside the *Curious George* books and prepubescent classics such as Paula Danzinger's *The Cat Ate My Gymsuit*—introduced a more theoretical, more ambitious element into a scene known for its distaste for anything too serious or academic, while also continuing the New York School tradition of fusing high and low culture (188). Further, Mayer's experiments with collaborative, performative writing—often enacted in her workshops, and then recorded in the anonymously authored magazine *Unnatural Acts*—explicitly set out to disregard the sanctity of the monolithic author or text. Mayer also became known for her "Experiments" list—an evolving, Oulipo-esque catalogue of potential writing adventures, including directives such as "experiment with theft and plagiarism," "write a soothing novel in twelve short paragraphs," "write the longest most beautiful sentence you can imagine," and "attempt as a writer to win the Nobel Peace Prize in Science by finding out how thought becomes language, or does not."[3]

As one might gather from the above tactics, critics have often aligned Mayer's work with Language writing rather than with the New York School per se. (Vickery's inclusion of Mayer in her "feminist genealogy" of Language writing, along with the title of Kane's chapter, "Bernadette Mayer and 'Language' at the Poetry Project," suggest something of the same.) But as both Kane and Vickery have noted, Mayer's career agitates against delimitations. Not only has she experimented in a wide array of genres, including sonnet sequences, translations of Catullus, epigrams, collaborations, experimental narratives, blueprints for a utopia, and guides to science writing, but throughout all these projects she maintains "a rather tough balancing act" that Kane describes as follows: "Fascinated by the possibilities for linguistic innovation, [Mayer] nevertheless maintained a connection to writing as expressivist, microsocial, and personal" (193).[4] This particular balancing act is precisely what interests me most about her work: not only does it link Mayer's experiments to the "abstract practices" of Mitchell, Guest, and Stein as discussed in chapter 1, all of which search out "the fact of feeling," but it also allows us to consider the real relationship of her writing to the more romantic strain of the New York School.[5]

Mayer began her career not as a fledgling wordsmith, but rather as a performance artist dedicated from the get-go to the art of interminable catalogue. When she was twenty-seven, she exhibited her first major work, *Memory* (1972), at the 98 Greene Street Gallery in SoHo. She describes this work as follows: "1200 color snapshots . . . processed by Kodak plus 7 hours of taped narration. I had shot one roll of 35-mm color film every day for the month of July, 1971. The pictures were mounted side-by-side in row after row along a long wall, each line to be read from left to right, 36 feet by 4 feet. All the images made each day were included, in sequence, along with a 31-part tape, which took the pictures as points of focus, one by one & as taking up points for digression, filling in the spaces between" (Baker). As Mayer explained in a 1989 lecture given at the Naropa Institute, "It was an eight hour show. If you wanted to hear the whole show, you could follow the whole month by walking along with the pictures and spend eight hours in the gallery" (*Disembodied Poetics*, 98). Such a project has obvious roots in Warhol's multi-hour cinematic extravaganzas such as *Sleep* (1963) which starred John Giorno—a friend of Mayer's—as its sleeping star, and which catapulted boredom and endurance into new aesthetic territory. ("I've been quoted a lot as saying, 'I like boring things.' Well, I said it and I meant it. But that doesn't mean I'm not bored by them," Warhol explains in *POPism* [50].)

Memory also belongs to the history of conceptual art, a movement which Lucy Lippard helpfully defines in her book *Six Years: The Dematerialization of the Art Object from 1966 to 1972* as "work in which the idea is paramount and the material form is secondary, lightweight, ephemeral, cheap, unpretentious, and/or dematerialized" (vii). Despite its close ties to Pop, much conceptual art of the sixties and seventies aimed to batter precisely the kind of marriage of art and commerce that Warhol had come to represent. Many thought that by "dematerializing" the aesthetic art object, and promoting art-as-idea, art-as-action, or even art-as-language in its place, one might profoundly disrupt the circulation of art-as-commodity. Lippard explains how in the late sixties, with the utopian spirit running high, the battle plan assumed that "no one, not even a public greedy for novelty, would actually pay money, or much of it, for a xerox sheet referring to an event past or never directly perceived, a group of photographs documenting an ephemeral situation or condition, a project for work never to be completed, words spoken but not recorded; it seemed that these artists would therefore be forcibly freed from the tyranny of a commodity status and market orientation" (263). *Memory* was in fact quite cheap for Mayer to produce: in her 1989 Naropa talk, she explains: "I had a patron at the time, Holly Solomon. She paid for the film and the developing. I shot slides and she made them into prints" (98).

Of course, as Lippard readily admits, she and her comrades underestimated the canniness of the market; Lippard's postscript to *Six Years* laments the fact that "the major conceptualists are [now] selling work for substantial sums here and in Europe; they are represented by (and still more unexpected—showing in) the world's most prestigious galleries" (263). Mayer's *Memory*, however, did not share this fate—neither the photographs nor the text has ever been published in its entirety, despite some talk of it. (In 1975, North Atlantic published a partial collection of the photographs and text, together with an introduction by Mayer's Freudian analyst, Dr. David Rubinfine, who confirmed its status as "an emotional science project.") Mayer's next big project, *Studying Hunger*, was even more unmanageable. It too attempts to track states of consciousness over the time span of a month ("A month gives you enough time to feel free to skip a day, but not so much time that you wind up fucking off completely," she explains [Baker]), and clocks in at about five hundred pages of single-spaced text—text which also includes "a lot of pictures . . . a lot of colored pens" (*Disembodied Poetics*, 99). Only one-fifth of *Studying Hunger* has been published (in 1975); Mayer later admitted, "I knew this was not a publishable work. It's almost masochistic in and of itself to do something like that" (*DP*, 99).

Lippard, herself a feminist critic, notes that "the inexpensive, ephemeral, unintimidating character of the Conceptual mediums" held a special interest for women. She argues that mediums such as "video, performance, photography, narrative, text, and actions . . . encouraged women to participate, to move through this crack in the art world's walls" (xi). Mayer's work from this period is not as explicitly feminist as some of the better-known pieces of the time, but Mayer's work was contemporaneous with them, and rife with shared impulses.[6] In 1973, Mayer's work traveled with an international women's Conceptual show called "c. 7,500," which started at CalArts in Valencia, California, and ended in London, and included the work of Laurie Anderson, Eleanor Antin, Alice Aycock, Jennifer Bartlett, N. E. Thing Co., and Adrian Piper, among others. In the seventies Mayer also coedited the magazine *o to 9* with the performance artist/video artist/sculptor/architect/poet Vito Acconci. (In addition to being Mayer's brother-in-law at the time, Acconci is known for pieces such as 1969's *Following Piece*, which involved twenty-three days of following strangers; 1971's *Zone*, in which he attempted to keep a cat from leaving a ten-foot-square area, marked off with masking tape, for thirty minutes; and, perhaps most notoriously, 1972's *Seedbed*, in which he lay under the ramp of a gallery jerking off and voicing sexual fantasies while gallery-goers walked above.) *o to 9* published many important pieces of the period, including the journals of Jasper Johns and writings by Robert Smithson, Hannah Weiner, Sol LeWitt, and Dan Graham, as well as books by Adrian Piper and the painter Rosemary Mayer, Bernadette's sister.

In her interview with Jarnot, Mayer addresses this time:

LJ: What was the idea behind *o to 9*?

MAYER : It was pretty much the same idea that there is behind any magazine—to create an environment for our own work and to publish all the things we both loved to see published. So we started publishing the works of Robert Smithson, and the journals of Jasper Johns. You know, these really interesting things, but I don't think too many people were publishing them at the moment, or at least we never read them.

LJ: How much were you influenced by New York School writing?

MAYER: Well, you know, I had this incredible resistance to New York writing. I really didn't want to be influenced by it. So I wasn't. We had such a strong resistance that I was going out with Ted Berrigan for awhile and Ted and Ron would do these collaborations and send them to *o to 9* and we would never publish them. We published one called "Furtive Days." But we would never publish them and I guess it was because of their style or something. I really couldn't figure out why it was. I used to go to a lot of those avant-garde concert performance events with John Cage and Yoko Ono. They were pretty amazing. I always liked them, I think they influenced me much more than any of the writing. (6)

Although we're free to disavow Mayer's own disavowal of the influence of the New York School poets that I've discussed thus far, her remarks here underscore the importance of placing her work in a conceptual and performative context as well as a literary one. In this light, the kinship that pieces such as *Midwinter Day* or *Desires* share with Cage pieces becomes quite clear. (Think, for example, of Cage's *4'33"* in which one simply waits to hear what sound occurs within the fixed period of time, or of Cage's essays such as "Where are we eating? And what are we eating?" in which he jauntily describes what he and the Merce Cunningham dancers ate on tour for pages upon pages.)

The general aversion to literary preciousness in Mayer's long works reflects an affinity for writing by figures like Cage, or, to take a fresh example, the designer, inventor, and mathematician R. Buckminster Fuller (whose great aunt was Margaret Fuller)—inventors who were not primarily poets, but who sometimes chose poetry as a medium, often with the goal of conveying information rather than inducing lyric epiphany. R. B. Fuller—who is perhaps best known for designing the geodesic dome—wrote many books of "poetry" (the quotation marks remain for the more skeptical reader) that attempt to communicate mathematical issues, chronologies of American history, design explications, etc., on the principle that readers might be able to remain more attentive to such discussions if he employed line-breaks. In one sense, this interest in information can be traced to the "Objectivist" strain of twentieth-century poetry, that is, the inclusion of historical record and geological fact in William Carlos Williams's *Paterson*, rants about usury and antiquity in Ezra Pound's *Cantos*, the documentary-poetic projects of Charles Reznikoff or Muriel Rukeyser, and so on.[7] The difference in the seventies was that figures from *outside* the realm of "literary poetry"—Cage, Ono, Fuller, Piper, etc.—began producing poetic texts that contended with similar issues.

Further, within downtown poetic circles, the "not caring" attitude I've been discussing throughout was reaching critical mass. As Lewis Warsh, Mayer's husband at the time, testifies: "A lot of my own poems were pretty dumb, but I published them anyway. Type the stencil, run it off, staple it together, and then it's out there. A lot of the anti-intellectual epithets aimed at the Poetry Project had to do with the surface mindlessness of these collaborations. The idea of writing poems that didn't have to be good was one thing—but actually publishing them in a magazine where a lot of other poets wanted to publish—was really nervy, and pissed people off. Who cared?" (Kane, 163). Meanwhile, groups such as Art and Language began calling their writing about art "art," and so on. Such experiments provoked a whole slew of questions, some of which Lippard has articulated as follows: "If written (visual) art is a viable (visual) Art Form, how do you distinguish it from literature? Is the only difference that one is made by an Artist and one by an Author? If an Artist makes up a story and tells it in book form is it Art? If an Author paints a pretty picture is it Literature?" (188). I probably would not be writing about Mayer's work if I didn't consider it "literature," but I want to point out that the literary achievements of *Midwinter Day* and *Desires* deepen when considered in light of such questions.

Indeed, *Midwinter Day* and *Desires* hold the most interest for me because they self-consciously position themselves right on the cusp of literature-as-product and literature-as-process. *Midwinter Day* is more of a performance than *Desires*—as we shall see, Mayer even "rehearsed" for its writing—but as *Midwinter* is shorter and more formally constrained, it also has the aura of a more "teachable" experimental text (like Hejinian's *My Life*, for example, in which the opaqueness of Hejinian's language is counterbalanced by the autobiographical, numerical structure). But unlike the work of Cage, Fuller, and many other artists and/or conceptualists who experimented with art-as-language or language-as-art—many of whom aimed to strip poetry of its traditional foundation in emotional impulse ("My feelings belong, as it were, to me, and I should not impose them on others," Cage explains [*Conversing with Cage*, 213])—both *Midwinter Day* and *Desires* are rich with rage, melancholy, longing, likes and dislikes, sorrow, aggravation, fear, and love. Further, *Midwinter Day*, which vacillates between poetry and prose (and invents some new forms in between) has many traditional lyric moments, and often makes heavy use of rhyme and other standard poetic structures. (The book ends, for example, with the decidedly antiquated *abba* lines: "Welcome sun, at last with thy softer light / That takes the bite from winter weather / And weaves the random cloth of life together / And drives away the long black night!" [119].) And despite her affinity with conceptual art, at times Mayer's *Desires* echoes the vehemence of the artist Carl Andre, who once said in a radio forum: "I have a great anger against so-called conceptual art. . . . I don't really know what conceptions are. I don't have any ideas about art and poetry. I have *desires*" (Lippard, 156–157).

Though some might write off Mayer's stream-of-consciousness "poetry-by-the-yard" as being too easy, Mayer, like Andre, consistently reminds us that its production is hard work. As she says in *Desires*, "Someone once said to me I wanted to write without writing anything so it was just an idea, it was someone who can't stand to sit still for it, as if it were all some medical operation, the violence of an abortion" (32). Given the "plot" of *Desires*, which chronicles the strenuous work of being pregnant, Mayer's irritation with her imaginary interlocutor, who "can't stand to sit still" for the act of writing, as if it were an abortion, seems especially intense. At this point in the text, she isn't entirely sure she is pregnant, but her early comparison of writing that is "just an idea"—not "sat still" for, and not materialized on the page—to the violence of an abortion indicates her clear displeasure at the thought of jettisoning the intense physical labor of writing.

As Mayer is well aware, the word "labor" itself links the work of writing to the work of bearing children, and *Midwinter Day* and *Desires* occupy a privileged place in the history of American feminist poetics in that they represent one of the first sustained attempts to fold the "women's work" of bearing children into the fabric of an experimental lyricism stretched to book-length proportions.[8] At a tribute to Plath at the New York Public Library in 1997, Jorie Graham told of the crisis she experienced upon first becoming pregnant—the crisis of not knowing whether becoming a mother could be compatible with being a poet. When Graham thought about the female poets she admired most (Dickinson, Bishop, and Plath), she was distressed to realize that they were (respectively) a lifelong recluse, a lesbian without children, and a mother who committed suicide while her two small children slept nearby. The prognosis, Graham joked, did not look good. Graham resolved her crisis with a pilgrimage to Dickinson's home in Massachusetts, where, as luck would have it, Dickinson's writing desk was on loan to an exhibit, and had been replaced with a cradle to fill the space.

Other writers might avert such a crisis by turning to Mayer's *Midwinter Day* and *Desires*. Throughout both, Mayer agonizes over the burden of her dual occupation, but in the end, the burden isn't the point. "Could it be this whole thing is about children?" she wonders in the middle of *Midwinter Day*, calling attention to a crucial revelation of her experiment: how much there is to be gained from meditating on children—on their language, their logic, their demands, their desires, and their pleasures—and from refusing to police the border between this meditation and "real" (i.e., "adult") life and/or writing. For those who perpetuate the false choice between poetry and motherhood that undergirded Graham's crisis, Mayer expresses only impatience and annoyance: "Remember that woman I told you about who came to take a picture of Lewis and me and he said I was a poet too, and she looked at me and Sophia and Marie carefully crawling on me and she said, oh really and when do you get to write? There's no use ever saying you're a poet, it's a disservice to yourself except for the wonder you can sustain among the moths, but you'd better say it anyway" (*Desires*, 59).

The idea behind *Midwinter Day*—to write a book-length chronicle of one day's thoughts and events *as they happened,* not in retrospect—lays waste to the photographer's question, "and when do you get to write?" by offering the unexpected answer: *All day long.* As Fanny Howe once observed about the book, "[Mayer] does, in fact, seem to be writing at the same time as she is living." Of course, the distinction between "writing" and "living" is semantic, or nonsensical, in that writing always gets written by living people. "Living" here functions as a euphemism for "not in a room of one's own," not isolated in the ivory tower of "the life of the mind," but rather enmeshed in relations, busy with and/or distracted by tasks other than writing, engaged with matter over (or at least in addition to) mind. When gendered as male, "living" often takes on an exciting, macho flavor—that of the hard-living Papa Hemingway type, photographed more often with large game and a rack of guns than with a slim pencil in hand. But even the more fey images of an exhausted yet dapper O'Hara becoming consumed by his job as an influential curator at the Museum of Modern Art, or of Duchamp famously (if somewhat spuriously) abdicating art-making and dedicating his genius to chess, are capable of sustaining a certain heroic aura. (In Thoreau's *Walden*, to take an earlier example, the very impact of the writing depends upon the artifice of a male speaker who seems to be "living" more than "writing." As Cavell once noted about *Walden*'s narrator, "We seem to be shown this hero doing everything under the sun but, except very infrequently, writing" [5]). When feminized, however, the triumph of living over writing has traditionally suggested a different stereotype: the victory of mind-numbing domestic duty over the possibility of artistic inspiration or production. Children often play into this picture, but not always: imagine the faint, cramped handwriting of Emily Brontë, writing furtively in a corner of a room full of people; it's not a far stretch to imagine Emily giving up, and roaming listlessly over the moors.

The form and content of *Midwinter Day* directly challenge these stereotypes, as Mayer's description of the book in her Naropa lecture suggests:

> Nobody ever believes me when I tell them it was written in one day, but it almost was. I did rehearsals for the first section, which is dreams. I practiced for about 2 weeks before the December 22 date and tried to sort of fine-tune my dreaming so that when I had dreams on the 22cd [sic] I would be good at remembering them and they would be vivid and worth recording. Or worth sharing with people; or I would get better at writing them down. So that was an extension over that day. I also took photographs, and wrote about them later.
>
> I divided the book into six parts. It was the six parts of the day, as I perceived the day to be. The last part was the time at night when I would go to my desk and write. For the sixth part of the book, that's what I did. I was mostly taking care of babies, entertaining friends. I also made sure to keep copies of the newspapers for that day and whatever other written or visual material happened to pop up by accident. I'd keep track of it so that when I was putting the poem together, I might want to intersperse some of the material. But the only real notes I have are those about the photos. Actually I have extensive notes about dreaming but it would be pointless to begin on that. (100–101)

From this description it would seem as though *Midwinter Day* has as much if not more explicitly in common with Richard Strauss's *Symphonia Domestica* than any of Ashbery's works. Both the symphony and *Midwinter* are arranged into six movements which cover the recounting of dreams, contending with recalcitrant children, a scene at one's desk, meditations on love and sex, and so on. But while Strauss explicitly set out to create "a metaphysical hymn to domestic love," as one commentator put it (Jackson), *Midwinter Day* is more of a testament to the anxiety that such a project can entail for both creator and audience. Hejinian once expressed concern (in a letter to Susan Howe) that Mayer was "trying to make domestic life into a 'romance'" (Vickery, 159), and throughout *Midwinter Day* Mayer worries about this tendency as well, even as she approximates such a goal. Indeed, one of the principal thematic questions underlying the book is how one might live with and write about the vicissitudes of a heterosexual marriage with children without replaying the smugness or romanticization which can at times seem inherent to the so-called nuclear family.[9]

Just as *Midwinter Day* echoes but transfigures the concerns of Strauss's symphony, it also both reflects and tampers with the modernist obsession with charting the path of human consciousness over the time span of a single day—an obsession epitomized not only by Woolf's *Mrs. Dalloway*, but also by Joyce's *Ulysses*. Joyce chose June 16th for Bloomsday; Mayer chose December 22 as her parameter—the shortest day of the year, and nearly the polar opposite of Joyce's date on the Zodiac. *Midwinter* begins with the line "Stately you came to town in my opening dream," while *Ulysses* starts off: "Stately, plump Buck Mulligan came from the stairhead. . . ." There are many such moments of homage and/or intertextual reference, and *Midwinter* ends up staging quite a struggle with its (mostly male) literary forerunners, as is evident in the following ambivalent lines near the book's beginning: "Freud Pound & Joyce / Are fine-feathered youth's fair-weather friends / I take that back, better not to mention them" (19). Later, in *Desires*, as Mayer prepares to teach a course on American writers such as Whitman, Hawthorne, Stein, and Kerouac, this ambivalence veers into angry dismissal (though she retains her characteristic ambivalence): "I like these guys [i.e., the Americans] better than those half-English dolts Joyce and Pound who made such a tight-assed mystery of their love and the horrible head-heart problem, I shouldn't say that, my love is unsettling. I hope I'm like Whitman, exempt" (153). "Tight-assed" is a telling phrase, especially when contrasted with Whitman (the sodomite)—"tight-assed" signifying a distaste for leaking boundaries (a distaste which, as will become apparent, Mayer decidedly does not share).

The first section of *Midwinter*—like Schuyler's "The Morning of the Poem" or O'Hara's "Getting Up Ahead of Someone (Sun)"—chronicles an awakening. It is essentially a celebration of liminal consciousness—of the bardo between sleep and waking: "Eyes open, eyes closed, half-open, one eye open" (7). While much New York School writing—especially that of Koch and Ashbery—is quite preoccupied with dream logic, Mayer's attention to her dreaming mind evidences a looser and yet more explicit interest in the unconscious. (Despite her close affinity with Stein, Mayer also differs from her in this respect, as Stein remained unconvinced that the unconscious exists.) As we shall see, Mayer shares this commitment to working from dreams with Notley, whose poetry poses a variety of questions about the relationship of dreams both to life ("I do think life is a dream. I think we construct reality in a dreamlike way; that we agree to be in the same dream") and to gender ("Did dreams begin when women were first / excluded from public life?," Notley wonders in *Disobedience*, a question which brings to mind Irigaray's comment, "Before seeking to give woman *another* unconscious, it would be necessary to know whether woman *has* an unconscious, and which one?"[10]).

The complex network of dreams Mayer recounts in the first section of *Midwinter* evokes a related set of questions about gender, interpretation, narrative, and authority. By rehearsing for this section—"I tried to sort of fine-tune my dreaming so that when I had dreams on the 22cd I would be good at remembering them and they would be vivid and worth recording. Or worth sharing with people; or I would get better at writing them down" (*DP*, 100)—Mayer exhibits the performance anxiety expected of an analysand grappling with the "imperative to confess" as articulated by Michel Foucault: "Not only will you confess to acts contravening the law, but you will seek to transform your desire, your every desire, into discourse" (63). In fact, Mayer's opening promise—"And for no man or woman I've ever met, / I'll swear to that, / Have there been such dreams as I had today, / The 22cd day of December, / Which, as I can now remember, / I'll tell you all about, if I can" (1–2)—seems to answer to this imperative directly. The section goes on to take all the time and space it wants to translate the meandering particulars of dream logic into poetic line ("I was watching a woman / And something was being done to her tentatively / Then recovered we sat down to eat together / A large flat dull cake like awful life / I broke it into pieces in my adolescent plate" [9]). Throughout it dramatizes the difficulty of taking this freedom by repeatedly asking questions (of herself? of the reader? a beloved? an analyst?) such as "Can I say what I saw?" "Can I say that here?" "Must I go on?" or simply, "Do you see what I mean?" Though at times the telling becomes laborious—"I can't go on / Is there an end / To such love and the duty of dreaming," Mayer asks on page 6 (with twenty more pages of the section to go)—in general the long, unpunctuated lines keep the flow moving. And instead of trickling out, by the section's finish the lines begin to balloon into prose paragraphs.

Upon first glance, this overflow of detail—punctuated by all the questions and anxieties that can mark the psyche's resistances to the confessional imperative—seems to fit nicely with the form of the classic analytic scene. But in the end Mayer's recitation has little to do with the standard goals of analysis, be they catharsis, diagnosis, desublimation, interpretation, and so forth. As discussed earlier vis à vis Ashbery's love of parasitical detail, the surplus of specificity Mayer relates in this section—"Then we climb / A mountain to the Metcalf's house, Nancy's fixing us / The eighteen intricate courses of a Japanese dinner / We sit at a counter curving around the kitchen / Like what they call a kidney-shaped pool / Eating hearts of wet green and red lettuce . . . Then I dreamed / I was ordering pompoms / Not those ornamental tufts on hats and not chrysanthemums / But a kind of rapid-firing machine gun," and so on (3–4)—eventually defies Freud's edict (articulated in the Wolf-Man) that "an explanation must be found for every detail" (Freud, 414).

Instead, Mayer postpones interpretation, perhaps forever, in an attempt to chip away at both her and her reader's compulsion to know where the writing is going. At times she attempts to interpret her dreams—"I was involved in creating a soup with pickles in it, it was the perfect soup, there's no end to these dreams, if only I could remember to solve problems, what does hot pickles connote" (22)—but her efforts usually lead nowhere. Indeed, who knows what "hot pickles" connotes? The fact that the phrase quickly invites a hackneyed phallic interpretation doesn't help but rather furthers the sense of futility. As with Ashbery, the point of the reverie becomes the pleasure she finds in the mind's capacity to produce details, and the undeniable pleasure of offering them up to discourse. Near the end of this section Mayer admits, "I'm refusing to understand what I mean," perhaps tacitly inviting us to do the same. To take up this invitation is to take leave of the writer-as-analyst and/reader-as-analyst metaphor that has come to structure so much of the twentieth-century reading experience, and to make room for other relations. And one of these relations entails challenging the emphasis that both psychoanalysis and literary criticism have laid on desire as opposed to pleasure. As Barthes reminds us in *The Pleasure of the Text*, "we are always being told about Desire, never about Pleasure; Desire has an epistemic dignity, Pleasure does not" (57).

Mayer spins this aversion to interpretation by pairing it explicitly with issues of gender. For the first section of *Midwinter* can also be read as a struggle to find a place for Mayer's role as a sexual, intellectual mother to two young daughters within a Freudian schema which has notoriously treated the female subject (and the mother/daughter relationship) as aporia or afterthought. "In my dream my daughters Sophia and Marie / Are always with me," Mayer writes early on, announcing the inextricability of this relationship from her dreaming mind. She then rehearses the terms of Freud's "Electra complex" (the underbaked equivalent to the male child's Oedipal complex)—"First girls / As infants love their mother who are women, then girls / Learn how to love men unless they become homosexuals . . . / The mothers of men and women / Are always loved more later by sons / Than by daughters who seem to love fathers better / Because that's the way it is / They say." Right after this passage, she adds the simple rebuttal: "There's more to it than that" (10). There is more indeed, and in subsequent sections of *Midwinter* Mayer devotes much of her time to carefully watching, listening, and transcribing the desires and speech of her daughters, noting how and where their behavior overlaps with, or chafes against, psychoanalytic cliché.

To take an obvious example, "penis envy" recurs as a motif—"I think [Marie] thinks about her diaper as a penis and so she doesn't want to lose it" (23); "Marie says she has both a penis and a vagina. She puts a ruler between her legs"(86)—but Mayer presents this moment as only one of the many imaginative scenarios that her daughters invent, not as an über-narrative. In fact, those specific lines illustrate Mayer's (or Marie's) subtle aversion to Freudian and Lacanian schema. Here Marie's ruler doesn't serve to cover up the "nothing" that Marie has. Rather, Marie knows she has a vagina—she names it, and plays with the pleasure of adding another presence to its presence. Just as Mayer's dream sequence emphasizes the pleasure of production over the production of desire, Marie's pleasure has less to do with lack and more to do with abundance. Marie's play with the ruler eventually becomes part of a flow of affects which, as the psychologist Silvan Tomkins has suggested, can be attached to any object (see Tomkins, 49–61). Mayer charts this flow throughout the book, staying remarkably faithful (or so one imagines) to the specificity of the language her children use: "Marie says children have candy my name is Betsy you'll get sticky. She calls Sophia baby brother, it's from a book. She says here's a mountain I made I cut it sharp and thick. Sophia plays with the butter, Marie says Jessica said nar for star and I'm afraid of the light" (84).

Mayer's interest in the language of her daughters persists throughout *Midwinter*, and constitutes a sort of tacit contrario to the assertion made by Wittgenstein that Mayer cites in part 4: "Marie's spilled her milk again, no use crying over spilled milk. Wittgenstein says there is no such thing as a private language. I think it would be worth trying to make one" (68). *Midwinter* is, among other things, an account of the private language that one family shares: "Lewis says I'm not a pillow, then Marie does. They read *The Little Lamb*. He says to her there's a worm in your shirt I'll get it out. She says now say a snail" (85). This play recurs in *Desires*, when Mayer relates more of the private language shared by her daughters: "When one of them says a certain word, like 'tedemone,' then the other one has to say 'Don't say tedemone! Say Dakey-doe!' and that's how the game goes" (167). In this way, Mayer actually fulfills a different Wittgensteinian edict: "Don't, *for heaven's sake*, be afraid of talking nonsense! But you must pay attention to your nonsense" (*Culture and Value*, 56e).

Earlier, in part 2 of *Midwinter*, Mayer's recitation of her account at the local library serves as yet another example of the kind of melding of adult-language and child-language that shapes her linguistic universe: "*Three Little Kittens* / And *There's a Wocket in My Pocket* are overdue . . . We borrow / Pepys' *Diaries* and Drinkwater's book on Pepys, / *Bit Between My Teeth* by Edmund Wilson, *Alone*, / *The Little Lamb* and *Curious George*" (43–44). As is apparent from this list—and from other moments in the book, such as when Mayer notes, "There's jelly on *Borrowed Feathers*"—proper names are the source of an inordinate amount of pleasure for her. (*Proper Name and Other Stories* is in fact the title of a 1996 Mayer book.) The principal progenitor of this pleasure is, of course, Stein. As Koestenbaum has put it: "In Stein the central amusement or beauty is often the name, the proper noun, that arrives, unexplained, uncontextualized" (*Cleavage*, 313). Stein revealed the pleasure of proper names as an essentially infantile one; then, without apology, she claimed it as viable ground for literature. ("Infantile" both is and isn't the right word—it is in the sense that "Stein's paradigm of the writer was the baby: the author as infant," as Koestenbaum notes; it isn't insofar as "infant" derives from the Latin *infans*, meaning "unable to speak." Speaking—or at least generating language—was not a problem for Stein or for Mayer; on the contrary, both could be said to have a predilection toward logorrhea.) Stein's relationship to the infantile differs from Mayer's, however, in that Stein cast *herself* as "Baby Woojums," not as the mother or observer of actual infants.[11] Mayer, on the other hand, directly links her stylistic tics (such as iteration) to the manner in which she has to speak to her children: "We repeat alot because of the children . . . they don't know logic at all" (23).

This point of divergence from Stein becomes explicit in *Desires* when Mayer muses: "I'm not as smart as Gertrude Stein was, she simply lived and died, she seemed to enjoy the feeling of herself, she drove her Ford. . . . She learned everything, she delivered babies but she didn't have one. Was she horrified by them?" (180). Though both *Midwinter* and *Desires* take on notable males ("Wife and mother are general relations hideous Hegel said, individualized desire renders her ethic impure. I only said that so I could throw away the paper it was written on," she declares in *Desires* [135]), her relation to Stein and other female precursors is perhaps more intriguing, and both books spend quite a bit of time contemplating undertheorized questions about female literary influence and ancestry.[12]

One part of this contemplation involves the simple act of naming. Instead of suffering under the weight of great males of the past, Mayer often opts for the by-now-familiar trope of naming women in an attempt to constitute a literary heritage. "Who are the great American women novelists?" she asks in *Desires* (echoing Myles's "Where's the mothers"); at the end of *Midwinter* she provides a list of female precursors and contemporaries, which includes Anne Bradstreet, Tsai Wen Gi, Elizabeth Barrett Browning, Notley, Rich, Plath, Sexton, Elinor Wylie, Louise Bogan, Denise Levertov, Guest, H.D., Harriet Beecher Stowe, Maureen Owen, Nikki Giovanni, Diane di Prima, Murasaki Shikibu, Fanny and Susan Howe, Muriel Rukeyser, Mina Loy, Lorine Niedecker, Gwendolyn Brooks, Marina Tsvetayena, Anna Ahkmatova, Rebecca Wright, and "all the saints" (111). Such lists are prototypical examples of Rich's call for "revision," but in the context of Mayer's work, they also engage more fraught feelings: the yearning and anxiety produced when one compares one's own life or writing with those of others ("I'd like to know / What kind of person I must be to be a poet / I seem to wish to be you" [26]); the difficulty of taking license to write whatever one wants when "each time I write a line / I know someone who won't approve of it" (103); and the struggle to balance a sense of self-reliance (or what Notley will call "disobedience") with an openness to having one's mind changed by interaction with others.

Part 4 of *Midwinter Day* revolves around these questions by way of prose paragraphs which combine descriptions of what Mayer is doing (watching her kids paint with tempera, chopping vegetables for a spaghetti sauce, putting Sophia down for a nap, drinking beer, reading aloud children's books such as *Beady Bear* or *The Tiny Tawny Kitten*) with a rambling meditation on the lives of an enormous number of figures—the short list includes Tolstoy, Wagner, Beethoven, Shackleton, Margaret Fuller Ossoli, Rudy Burckhardt, Margaret Mead, Rudolf Steiner, the Buddha, St. Augustine, Verlaine, Poe, Hawthorne, Milton, Christ, O'Hara, Charles Olson, Henry Miller, Patti Smith, Godard, Ra, Picasso, and Neil Simon. The juxtapositions are sudden but seamless: "I chop onions for the sauce. St. Augustine hated the Greek language"; "I call nursery school to find out when they'll be closed for Christmas and talk to Barbara about Chanukah. Margaret Fuller married an Italian revolutionary named Count Ossoli and had a child when she was thirty-seven"; "Lewis goes into his room to work. Someone said Harriet Beecher Stowe became quite crazy towards the end of her life and pretended she was selling matches on the street." The accumulation of these juxtapositions produces a peculiar effect: instead of measuring her life against the adventures of a Shackleton or a Verlaine, they simply place her "continuous present" alongside theirs. The domestic qua the domestic is thus neither elevated nor denigrated. It is simply included, gracefully but firmly. The section eventually becomes a hymn to the art of paying attention to the details of one's own life as well as to those of others. In this sense, it dramatizes Thoreau's revelation: "The question is not what you look at—but how you look & whether you see" (*Journal*, 146). The kinship with Thoreau runs deeper still, as throughout his writings Thoreau repeatedly conjoins the time span of a day with the injunction to pay attention: "The art of spending a day . . . it behoves us to be attentive. If by watching all day & all night—I may detect some trace of the Ineffable—then will it not be worth the while to watch?" (*Journal*, 206). In a 1988 lecture at the Poetry Project called "The

Poetry of Everyday Life," Mayer echoes this sentiment, but adds some love: "I love you and daily life, what life isn't daily? . . . what poetry isn't everyday" (3).

In his blurb on the back of *Midwinter Day*, Ashbery casts this attentiveness in a slightly different light: "The richness of life and time as they happen to us in tiny explosions all the time are grasped and held up for us to view in this magnificent work of prose and poetry that teaches us at the end why 'no one knows why / Nothing happens.'" By picking out those lines, Ashbery points toward one of the many paradoxes of Mayer's work: the more minutiae of the "richness of life and time" that she recounts—and remember that the desire behind the "Everything" work is to contain as much minutiae as possible—the more we may feel as though "nothing happens." Mayer or Ashbery might happily relate this sensation to the Zen saying popularized by Suzuki (here paraphrased by Cage) that "men are men & mountains are mountains before studying Zen / & men are men & mountains are mountains after studying Zen" (*Silence*, 161), but I doubt such a notion will placate any disgruntled readers hoping for more "action."

The paradox that "nothing happens" in an "Everything" work can in fact be related to two other intriguing conundrums. The first has to do with a paradox produced by the imperative of a confessing society: that wherever there's the presumption that a writer is "telling all," you'll usually find a crabby critic arguing that the writer at hand has nothing to tell. (Think of the criticism leveled at Anne Sexton by the critic Victor Howes, for example, who complained that "the confessional mode reveals that people with nothing to hide usually have little to confess" [17].) The second has to do with the specific character of logorrhea, an affliction in which more often means less, or at least means differently. As Koestenbaum once noted about Stein, "Stein's writing makes the most sense if it is read aloud; and yet hers is the most silent voice I know—silent because, under the guise of including everything in the world, it includes remarkably little" (*Cleavage*, 332).

THIS LATTER PROBLEM leads us to *Desires*, a book which evidences a logorrhea only hinted at in *Midwinter*. Of course I'm not using the word scientifically, but rather in accordance with Koestenbaum's definition in his essay "Logorrhea": "Logorrhea—addiction to talk—is inevitably a matter of solitary binge, or isolation. . . . Logorrhea is not social speech. Logorrhea is the hallmark of contemporary discourse: to be contemporary it must be boundless, it must be fatiguing, it must be manically self-perpetuating" (*Cleavage*, 286). There could be no better way to describe *Desires*. Although the structure of the book is epistolary, the letters are never sent, and thus they form a kind of closed circuit. All the letters are titled, but only some indicate a specific addressee (as in "Dear Ed," or "Dear Rosemary"). Sometimes there is an abstract addressee (as in "Dear Alive"); some are addressed to the dead. More often the titles have nothing to do with a recipient, in which case they serve to distance the letters from an epistolary economy and instead grant them autonomous aesthetic status (as in "Gardening in Containers," "Under My Green Jacket," or "Portrait of a Man Holding a Glove"). Further, though the text of the letters usually addresses a "you," over the 346 pages, the many "you's" tend to blur together, especially as neither the tone nor the style significantly varies from letter to letter. None of this is to say that the speaker of the letters doesn't reach out, often with great anguish or affection, to an "other." But a sense of solitary binge persists throughout, especially as Mayer has left New York City and is writing in a sort of exile—the exile of living in one small town, then of moving to another, about which she writes, "No one writes to us, no one calls . . . we have nobody to talk to. I don't know any women here, the children have no friends. I can't drive the car, I'm scared of it, I can barely eat dinner, there are fights, the food makes me sick" (177).

Thus while *Desires* postulates an audience—indeed, while it may yearn for one—it also insulates itself against one. On the one hand, the letters want to please their readers, and they worry constantly over their capacity to do so: "Writing about moving seems to make for some dullness, I'm sorry," one letter begins; "Are you mad at me?" another ends. On the other, the letters evidence a flagrant disregard for whether they please at all, a disregard that may be the hallmark of a letter never sent, or of any writing written without publication or exchange in mind. Each letter is a block of dense prose composed primarily of run-on sentences, ranging from about one to ten pages. Although the stream-of-consciousness can be enthralling, it is also undeniably rough going. It is not an easy book to ingest in one sitting, and I know many who have preferred to read in or around it instead of straight through. The fact that Mayer finished the book in 1980 but didn't find a publisher for it until 1994 may also reflect its ambivalence about finding readers—as

Vickery has noted, "As with the trouble she had in publishing her journals, Mayer's letters failed to please others, perhaps primarily because they do not attempt to please" (161). (Ashbery's line about Mitchell's painting—that it evidences "a fierce will to communicate and an equally frantic refusal to make this task any easier for the sender and the receiver"—would seem to apply here.)

For those who would prefer that a pregnancy journal testify to the *jouissance* of the pregnant body, Carole Maso's pregnancy journal *A Room Lit by Roses* is more likely to please. Maso writes: "I have never even come close to this much happiness. . . . So much freedom and bliss. I feel completely liberated" (28, 85).[13] In testament to the fact that each pregnancy is as distinct as each pregnant person, Mayer writes: "A lot of women say they prefer being pregnant to afterwards, with the baby being outside, I do not feel that way. I find no relish or what it is in being physically so big and hampered like a covered bridge or gargling with marbles" (174). At the start of her second letter, titled "Public Lice," Mayer announces: "Things have been going horribly, let me just begin by telling you we've been getting hate mail"—thus introducing the crabby mood of many of the letters that follow. What's more, these emotions have formal consequences. On several occasions Mayer suggests that the overwhelming demands of taking care of two children while being pregnant with a third, moving cities and taking on a new teaching job, editing a magazine (*Adventures in Poetry*) and publishing books, sustaining a marriage (to the poet Lewis Warsh), making sure daily needs are met while subsisting at a near-poverty level, and keeping up with one's own writing, have all contributed to pushing her out of poetry and into the more bloated, dirty, even boring realm of prose:

> I'm so tired of poetry I don't want to talk about it . . . I couldn't write a poem now anyway my intentions are less than pure, don't laugh at me, often my own writing seems to me to be having too many cheap ingredients like poor people's food however at least I've never written a salmon mousse. I mean it's like the meats at the delicatessen counter, those awful rolls of chicken and ugly meatloafs, with pimientos in them or onion-flavored American cheese, luncheon meats, full of salt and pepper. (30–31)

This simultaneous disgust with and celebration of the "cheap ingredients" of life has inspired the observation, here made by Elizabeth

Willis, that "here is where Mayer departs from the European polish of Stein: this work is a messier, more worldstained experiment. It's full of dirty American content" (19). One might also note that it is where Mayer departs from the first generation of the New York School, whose class affiliations or aspirations don't usually evoke "ugly meatloafs."[14]

The "impure" and "clogged with matter" earthworks of an artist such as Robert Smithson may come to mind here, and Smithson has described his aesthetics in terms that could easily describe a book like *Desires*: "I'm for a weighty, ponderous art. There is no escape from matter. There is no escape from the physical nor is there any escape from the mind. The two are on a constant collision course. You might say my work is like an artistic disaster. It's a quiet catastrophe of mind and matter" (Lippard, 89). But female matter (*mater*) is different from other matter—female dirt is different from other dirt. Whereas the art of Smithson, Schwitters, Duchamp, Rauschenberg, Ashbery, Joyce, etc., has been celebrated for its sifting through the dirt and detritus of "modern life," whether literally or figuratively, the enterprise differs for women, whose filth has been presumed—across cultures and across centuries—to come both from within and from without.[15] In short, women leak: their filth—inaugurated by Eve's disobedience in the garden—is punitive, dangerous, and redundant. It knows no bounds, and has thus occasioned serious regulatory consequences: "In her natural state, then, woman demands the attention of culture to impose those boundaries, physical and metaphysical, that will guarantee her virtue against transgression and digression," Carson explains in her essay "Dirt and Desire: Essay on the Phenomenology of Female Pollution in Antiquity" (*Men*, 142), cogently summarizing in one sentence the obsession with controlling women's bodies that has spanned millennia, from ancient religious taboos against menstrual blood to *Roe v. Wade*.

As Mayer well knows, a pregnant woman is the very epitome, or exhibition, of this leakage. She is, as Plato might have it, a shape-shifting receptacle—her body says: *I house both the "me" and the "not-me"*; or, more ominously: *Not only have I taken in extraneous matter, but I also promise to expel it*. In *Desires*, Mayer doesn't counter these stereotypes, but rather plows into them at full throttle. *Desires* begins with garbage—its very first line is the imperative "Throw stuff away," a command to the reader (and/or the speaker, if she's talking to herself) to start creating refuse. From the very start, Mayer warns that what follows will be filthy and female—a kind of prole *Symphonia Domestica*, sometimes like "those awful rolls of chicken and ugly meatloafs, with pimientos in them," and markedly devoid of designs on sublimation.

Lest I'm making *Desires* sound like an unpleasant read, I should be clearer about its many pleasures. I noted above that it is not an easy book to read straight through, but the flip side of this dilemma is that it grants the reader a tremendous amount of freedom. Each letter stands on its own as a prose poem of sorts, and thus one can read in and around the book at one's leisure. If read front to back, however, the letters delineate a narrative, eventually adding up to the story of a pregnancy. Also, as Hejinian has noted, *Desires* is full of good advice. One example is the ritual of foretelling the story of Max's birth that Mayer performs near the end of the book. Mayer explains, "People like to write and tell the stories of their babies' births but I like to do mine beforehand" (316). Mayer's description of what to expect in childbirth is both matter-of-fact and moving:

> The best thing is not to fear losing control, not to be forced to lie down if you don't want to. At this point it seems that giving birth to babies might be all that you will ever do in all the rest of your life, however that's not so, and aside from the famous forgetting, imagine all the years you are not involved in this. If you have three children, say, you are actually only giving birth to them about 3 days out of your entire life. OK then it gets more painful and there isn't much time in between contractions so you are one moment feeling like screaming and the next it is gone and you are you, and then every-one hopes this part won't last too long and if the baby's going to come out now, it will start to be coming but you have to push it out, some very hard and for what seems like a long time but actually it isn't, some easier. It's helpful at this time to have another woman around who's already had a baby because she can be loving and convinced. (314–315)

Here the speaker's struggle with self-reliance disappears, and a quiet, unpretentious wisdom and self-knowledge take its place. (This self-knowledge is actually present from the very beginning: after an early trip to the doctor, who tells her she isn't "theoretically and scientifically provably pregnant," Mayer writes: "I had a series of the famous bee-sting dreams. I've had them every time I was pregnant and never when I was not & just fearing it, this time I got stung on the head!" [17]). Mayer definitely pushes for the revaluation of this kind of "feminine intuition," yet as her pregnancy "genders" her more and more as female, she also becomes more adamant about the fluidity of gender roles. As she defiantly puts it in one letter: "I am not just a woman, are you always a man" (58).

The pleasure of defiance is but one of the many "not-nice" pleasures that *Desires* contains. Mayer may envy the image of Stein as a woman essentially at ease with herself in the world ("she seemed to enjoy the feeling of herself, she drove her Ford") but the pleasures of Mayer's not-nice writing may have more in common with Stein's temperament than she thinks. By many accounts, Stein was not always such a ball to be around—she was fussy, opinionated, and notoriously stubborn. (Likewise, Joan Mitchell was famously unhappy and volatile—she drank voluminously, and was known for vicious verbal lashings of her closest friends and lovers.[16]) How pleasure—indeed ecstatic pleasure—gets transmitted alongside such grouchiness and rage is a mystery that shapes the work of Stein, Mitchell, and Mayer (and Notley and Myles, as we shall later see). Such a complicated transmission trades "pure bliss" for a swarm of pleasures and dissatisfactions, a list of which Mayer compiles at the end of a letter in *Desires*:

> how do you like to be high, to be exalted, to be free, to be without
> everything, to be alone, to be full of clarity, to be lost, to be retrieved,
> to be seen again, to see the light, to be resurrected like they say, to
> be devoted, to be all askew and at odds with everything, to be con-
> fused, to be dying, to be lost, to be useless, to be continued, to be
> continuing, to be reincarnated, to be too much, to be left to be alone,
> to be irredeemable, to be hopeless, to be inspired, to be someone, to
> be abandoned, to be surrounded, to be at a loss, to be reconciled, to
> be reunited, to be at one, not to be undone, to be made. (69)

In the end, the paramount pleasure of *Desires* is its affirmation of desires of all kinds: desire for human connection; desire for food; desire for money; desire for beer and cigarettes; desire for sex; desire for babies; onanistic desire; desire for the literature of others; and, above all, desire for words and the act of writing itself. "Am I just this greed speaking outloud all the time," Mayer wonders (23), and the book can indeed be read as one long catalogue of idiosyncratic wants. She wants it to rain "hotdogs and Pampers" (25); she'd give anything to "be lyrical and have good teeth" (21); she wants to eat good cheese; and so on. While Maso's pregnancy journal celebrates the more ascetic pleasure to be found in the way that her pregnancy puts an end to certain desires (the desire to drink alcohol, the desire to focus intensively on one's writing career), Mayer's book does the opposite: it elevates the cravings that can accompany a pregnancy to metaphysical proportions. In this way, the book takes part in an "often overlooked tradition in which desire is productive," as Juliana Spahr has put it (110)—a tradition which understands and demonstrates that "one speaks too much, writes too much, because the mere act of piling up words—apart from their meaning—brings relief or delight," as Koestenbaum puts it in a paraphrase of Barthes (*Cleavage*, 287).

A more skeptical reader might here interject that while the piling up of words may bring "relief or delight" to the piler, it doesn't necessarily bring either to the reader. That is precisely true. As Barthes eloquently explains in *The Pleasure of the Text*:

> Does writing in pleasure guarantee—guarantee me, the writer—my reader's pleasure? Not at all. I must seek out this reader (must "cruise" him) *without knowing where he is*. A site of bliss is then created. It is not the reader's "person" that is necessary to me, it is this site: the possibility of a dialectics of desire, of an *unpredictability* of bliss: the bets are placed, there can still be a game. (4)

I imagine that some readers have loved *Desires*, some have been exasperated by it, and some have never made it through. Others (and I'd put myself in this category) may bounce between these experiences, but in the end deeply appreciate its game, its gamble—its willingness to write without knowing where its audience may be, its willingness to go too far, its willingness to believe that "women can still wind up writing some unheard of things don't you think, I mean things that have never been written yet" (19). The anxiety about "going too far" with verbal profusion is not a new one. What's notable about Mayer's elaboration of it in *Desires* is how she links it to the various anxieties that cluster around experimental poetry, the female body, and reproduction. (The phrase "to bring forth issue"—which is the last line of Mayer's penultimate letter—makes this linkage clear.) The very last letter of *Desires* is titled "A Few Days Later

It's with Pleasure I Write," and it announces the birth of her son; the book's final gesture is thus the merging of the pleasure of birth with the pleasure of writing, the pleasure of issue, the pleasure of the text.

Considered as a whole, the overriding obsession of *Desires* is economy: the economy of personal finance; the economy of time measurement, especially the time it takes to write and the time it takes to gestate; and, overwhelmingly, the economy of language production. At the start of the book, Mayer hopes she isn't pregnant because "if I were pregnant again everybody would feel impatient with me as if I had finally gone too far again" (15). She knows that the problem of having children without much money to support them has both a metaphorical and a literal relation to the problem of producing writing that has no audience to support it. Mayer experiences both types of profusion as natural and takes pleasure in them both—her lament is that others do not: "People seem to wind up calling and they find out we're pregnant but it's not really any fun telling them except for Peggy because, like having friends who think your poetry is silly, nobody can really see any good or joy in it, just problems" (47). In a later letter, Mayer makes this connection even more explicit:

> There are so many people in the world now . . . just like and while some men and women are saying it's too long, I can't read it. I even read they said too much writing was being written, and Lady Montagu saying the tales told never intended to be published had the only truth in them. Well it's simple to see the simple truth in something but is someone doing us a service by not writing something, I can't see that. (124)

In 1999, Anne Carson published a book entitled *Economy of the Unlost*, which considers the "economies of language" of the ancient Greek poet Simonides alongside those of the twentieth-century Romanian poet Paul Celan. Carson opens her book with the following questions: "Humans value economy. Why? . . . What does it mean to save time, or trouble, or face, or breath, or shoe leather? Or words? . . . What exactly is lost to us when words are wasted?" (3). In the above passage from *Desires*, Lady Montagu—the eighteenth-century aristocrat and writer who was also known for her voluminous letters—speaks to this latter notion of economy: that the words that really matter are the ones saved; that words gain in value when scrimped; that if the world is too full of language or literature or children, the responsible thing to do might be to stop producing them altogether.

But Mayer's response to the idea that "someone is doing us a service" by withholding any of the above is simple: "I can't see that." Carson is right that humans value economy. And, traditionally speaking, poetry is by definition an art of measurement—of placing syllables into circulation and of withholding them, of accumulating and excising words. But Mayer's work reminds us that humans also take great pleasure in experiencing time, money, bodily sensations, and/or words that also feel somehow impermeable to measurement. There is deep pleasure in the apprehension, however dim, of a world in which words are neither spent nor saved. At its best, *Desires* intimates such a place. *Desires* may have had to swerve out of poetry and into prose to do so, yet *Midwinter Day* somehow imparts a similar feeling. This latter achievement may have something to do with the fact that *Midwinter* is a time-based experiment, and the great paradox of time-based experiments is that their temporal constraints often produce the dizzying and liberating sensation of unconstrained time.

Recently it has become something of a truism to note that poetry—especially "experimental" poetry—is one of the few activities that does not, indeed cannot, participate in the market. Anyone even peripherally involved with poetry knows it doesn't sell. As Charles Bernstein is fond of saying, a blank piece of paper is worth about two cents or so, but once you write a poem on it, it takes on a negative value. Some find this situation deplorable, an example of everything that's wrong with contemporary culture; some, like O'Hara, have shrugged it off, accepting the fact that poetry probably has about as many serious adherents as bungee-jumping or bonsai-tending, and it has probably always been so, despite what those inclined toward nostalgia might say; some, like Bernstein, argue that poetry's negative market value is precisely the source of its political and aesthetic power and freedom. Mayer's contribution to this discussion is an insistence that we consider how a phobia of "going too far"—of writing too much, of wanting too much, of transgressing the proprieties of an economic system infused with morality—is often inextricably tied up with a paranoia about the voracious desires and the vexing capacities of the female body.

SOME FANS OF Mayer's work have complained that it lacks adequate critical or scholarly attention, though this situation has certainly begun to change. On the other hand, some critics, such as Rifkin, have rightly pointed out the many conflicts inherent in the drive to institutionalize or canonize the work of a writer who has so insistently "not cared" about academic merit-making, who has dedicated so much time and energy to the self-erasing tasks of collaborative and anonymous writing, and whose overriding statement of purpose might be her proclamation: "Work yr ass off to change the language & dont ever get famous."[17] Further, the largesse of Mayer's work so fiercely resists the ideal of the well-wrought urn that it can be difficult to publish, teach, anthologize, or even excerpt from it. The slim, 147-page *Bernadette Mayer Reader* that New Directions issued in 1992 is frustrating for precisely this reason. To shrink the work to a palatable size won't do, for as Willis has smartly noted, "What makes this writing 'work' is (as it was for Stein) its larger gestures" (19). (I await the one-thousand-page-plus collection of all of Mayer's works from *Memory* on—complete with color plates!)

In her chapter on Mayer, Vickery goes so far as to say that "suffering the equivalent of a stroke in 1994, [Mayer] defeated death and became, inadvertently, a literal 'living legend'" (151). There's some truth in this statement, and Mayer's legacy of experimentation has had and continues to have a profound influence on both her peers and younger writers. But I worry a bit that the hagiography of Mayer which Vickery, among others, freely indulges may at times obscure the real exasperations of Mayer's work—its capacity to produce "not-nice" pleasures—which I consider as important as its satisfactions and inspirations.[18] Work that depends on its larger gestures nearly always includes its failures as well as its successes. For this reason, Mayer's work nearly always feels uneven. Sometimes this unevenness carries the charge of excitement; at other times it undeniably feels lazy, dull, or simply impossible. Mayer's work seems to vacillate between "caring" and "not caring" about its status as "good writing" perhaps more wildly than any other writer at issue in this study, but that is part of its point. The specters of failure and carelessness are intrinsic to her project, and the source of both its frustrations and fascinations.

In closing, I must confess that any hesitation I may have about ending this chapter with an unequivocal call for more academic attention to Mayer's work also stems from a more personal source.

Many years ago I participated in one of Mayer's famed "Experiments in Poetry" workshops at the Poetry Project. At the time I was living as a poet and a waitress in New York, feeling a little brain-dead, and considering applying to Ph.D. programs in English. I asked Mayer's advice on the matter, and she sent this written reply: "if i were you i would do a lot of reading on your own and find another way besides phd programs to earn a living. . . . better to be a carpenter or something, I feel." Later in the letter she makes herself clearer: "i don't think you should ever write criticism." I suppose, then, that the present study must be seen as an act of both disobedience and homage. Many people—Mayer, perhaps, included—tend to think of the writing of criticism as an essentially gratuitous activity—far more gratuitous than the writing of poetry, for example, and perhaps even parasitical in nature. At times I am tempted to agree. But if there's one thing Mayer's work has to impart, it is a promotion of the paradoxical value of the gratuitous itself. To allow for this paradox—to pay attention to it, to admire it—is to salute that which is unpaid, uncalled for, unjustifiable, and, in a complex sense of the word, free.

DEAR DARK CONTINENT

ALICE NOTLEY'S DISOBEDIENCES

4

Portrait of Alice Notley by Matt Valentine, 2006. Copyright © 2006 by Matt Valentine. Used by permission of Matt Valentine and Alice Notley.

OF THE THREE WOMEN at issue in this half of my study, Alice Notley is perhaps the most solidly associated with the New York School, as a line from her recurrent bio note suggests (albeit with some subtle qualifications): "For sixteen years, [Notley] was an important force in the eclectic second generation of the so-called New York School of poetry" (*Disobedience*). During these sixteen years—roughly, 1970–1986—Notley lived on the Lower East Side with her husband, the poet Ted Berrigan (who died in 1983), raised two children, ran workshops at the Poetry Project (Myles was one of her students), and published about thirteen volumes of poetry. In a 1988 interview, she describes this period as follows: "We came to New York and lived inside this tiny space, and sometimes Ted worked, and sometimes he didn't, and I hung around and wrote poems, and we were always surrounded by the babies, who grew up" (Foster, 70).

In her introduction to Berrigan's *Selected Poems* (published posthumously in 1994), Notley elaborates on this description, using terms that echo Mayer's penchant for the "Everything" work that would collapse the putative boundaries between "writing" and "living": "My life with Ted Berrigan consisted of a continuous involvement with poetry: It was all we talked about; everything we did or said became part of it, as atmosphere or literally as phrase or fact in a poem" (vii). Berrigan famously took the idea of the "New York School"—its supposed existence and his role in its lineage—both more and less seriously than anyone before or since. "Ted used to tell people that he was in charge of the New York School and that anyone could join it if they paid him five dollars—at some point ten for inflation," Notley explains, adding, "no one ever joined this way" (vii, x). Joke or no, the net effect was to designate the Notley-Berrigan household—and the work that emerged out of it—as a critical node in the circuit of New York School poetics in the seventies and early eighties.

At the same time, since the 1980s, Notley has also put the most distance between herself and the New York School, geographically (she moved from New York to Paris in the early nineties), aesthetically, and one might even say politically. Very few people enjoy the constrictions of a label, and Notley—who has said she wants "to shriek at / any identity / this culture gives me" (*Mysteries*, 38)—is no exception. Indeed, once saddled with a label, one's options appear few: disavowal, reclamation, studious avoidance, and so on. "I don't accept any labels or placements, even for the 'early work,'" Notley insists; about the term "New York School," she says simply: "I've never quite identified with it" (Foster, 84, 83). At times this distancing has been of a benign variety—"I guess I resist thinking of myself as a New York poet," she says, partly because "it's really important to me that I come from the Southwest. . . . I still articulate in a lot of the ways that Southwesterners do and make sentences the way Southwesterners do" (Foster, 64). (Notley is originally from Needles, a small town in the California desert near the Arizona border.) But as the nostalgic interest in the New York School picks up speed, as we ourselves have sped into a new century, Notley's distancing has become more acute: "I just go by what anyone else says about the New York School. Really. They can have it" (email interview, 4 February 2002). On the topic of how women might fit or fail to fit into literary movements, Notley is even more caustic: "How many years does it take for a girl to get recognized as part of a movement? (This could be like a lightbulb joke: five years to certify her and five more to screw her in)" (Foster, 85).

As one might suspect from the above comments, Notley isn't as much of a cheerleader for "girls to get recognized as parts of movements" as she is a trenchant critic of movements qua movements. This stance can be traced in part to her feminist conviction that "the ways in which poetry gets published . . . not to mention the whole idea of a literary movement, the academy, the avant-garde, are all male forms" (Goldman, 8). Notley consistently troubles the impulse to drag women into the history of any of the above by arguing that "our achievement [i.e., that of women writers] has probably been to become ourselves in spite of the movements" (Foster, 85). When I think back on the New York School of the 1950s and the idiosyncratic achievements of Mitchell and Guest, this statement seems to be borne out. In keeping with these tensions, this chapter aims to consider Notley's singular aesthetic journey alongside the question of how her poetry expands and challenges certain aspects of New York School poetics (even, or especially, the assumption that there is such a thing as a "poetics" that can exist outside the act of making a poem), and what these expansions and challenges have to do with gender. For while the vast and ever-changing landscape of Notley's body of work certainly echoes the kind of prolific, dogged experimentation that characterizes the long careers of Ashbery and Kenneth Koch, Notley differs in that she has consistently tethered this experimentation to an explicitly feminist journey, and has cast her rigorous poetic investigations into the possibilities and limitations of speech, personality, community, humor, and narrative as part and parcel of a search for feminist vision.[1]

In trying to get an overview of Notley's career, it is initially tempting to mark a pronounced split between her earlier, more readily identifiable "New York School" style, and her more recent eremitic experiments in feminist epic.[2] Notley began to lay out the terms of this shift in the early nineties, in essays such as "Homer's Art" and in talks such as "Epic and Women Poets" (in which she insists that "*Someone*, at this point, must take in hand the task of being everyone, & no one, as the first poets did. . . . There must be a holy story" [Rasula, 28]). She then put them into action in three book-length poems, *The Descent of Alette* (1996), *Mysteries of Small Houses* (1998), and *Disobedience* (2001).[3] At first glance, these long poems—especially the hallucinatory, shamanistic *Descent of Alette*, Notley's most specific and elaborate attempt to date to tell "a holy story"—would seem to have little to do with the critical maxims about her work that one finds in, say, her online entry in *Contemporary Authors*: "Deeply influenced by the work of William Carlos Williams, Alice Notley is a poet whose verse focuses primarily on her life in New York with her first husband, the poet Ted Berrigan, and their two sons," or even at the home page to her online archives at the University of California at San Diego: "[Notley] believes that she is writing primarily to express her personal tone of voice. She feels that her speech is the voice of 'the new wife, and the new mother' in her own time, but her first aim is to make a poem, rather than present a platform of social reform."[4] Notley's work from the past fifteen years, along with her current uninterest in—indeed disgust with—the so-called daily, seems to stand in stark contrast to these characterizations. For example, when I told Notley that I had been startled by the phrase "the despised daily" on the back cover of *Disobedience*, she told me: "I myself wrote the phrase, despised daily, because . . . I do utterly despise dailiness as it stands. I can't abide what the world has become, the frozen-ness of our product this evil thing that we kiss the ass of every hour. I want a dailiness that is free and beautiful" (email interview, 4 February 2002).

On some level, this stance can and should be read as a repudiation of the celebration of quotidian detail and the collage of communal city life that characterizes much New York School writing, including much of Notley's earlier work. Partly for this reason, some critics and readers have seemed a bit stymied by Notley's turn to epic, and disinclined to consider her lyric and epic impulses together. In his *Parnassus* review of Notley's *Selected Poems* from Talisman (1993), Eric Selinger notes this problem and poses the question: "If the poet judges the world, as Whitman attests, 'not as the judge judges, but as the sun falling around a helpless thing,' why shouldn't we read [Notley] in the same gracious way, not sifting collagist sheep from epic goat?" (Selinger, 324). Selinger admits he isn't the man for the job, but concludes that "Notley deserves a critic who will help her readers find the pleasures in [the epic poems] that I've learned to take in her earlier work" (322). Whether or not any writer deserves a critic is up for grabs, but I think Selinger is on to something in his reluctance to "sift collagist sheep from epic goat." For this sifting elides the fact that many, if not most, of the concerns and tropes of Notley's recent epics have been alive and at play throughout her career. To cast her work from the seventies and eighties simply as New York School poetry with the added content of the "voice of the new wife and new mother" misses the depth of the ways in which Notley has, from the start, consistently recast and deepened the stakes of writing an urban, speech-oriented, personality-driven poetry that inherits and critiques the poetics of her male predecessors, responds to those developed by her various contemporaries, and pitches wildly ahead into the future.

The very first poem in her 1993 *Selected*, "Dear Dark Continent," announces these stakes.[5] The epistolary address to an abstract concept—a relative of Mayer's *Desires*, and of Koch's 2000 apostrophe binge, *New Addresses*—introduces the dialogic mode that Notley will mine throughout the poetry that follows, whether in poems that record overheard conversations from the street, such as "Bus Stop"; poems that record disjunctive conversations with her children, as in "January" ("Mommy what's this fork doing? / What? / It's being Donald Duck"); her nasty/funny postcard pieces ("Dear Fuckface," one begins); her first attempts at channeling the voices of the dead, as in "Jack [Kerouac] Would Speak through the Imperfect Medium of Alice," or her more elaborate attempts at channeling, such as the book-length sequence *Close to me & Closer . . . (The Language of Heaven)*, which stages a conversation with her dead father. "Dear Dark Continent" also introduces us to the particular combination of jaunty humor and dead seriousness Notley maintains throughout her poetry. (The seriousness arrives in the first two lines of the poem: "The quickening of / the palpable coffin.") The phrase "dark continent" is Freud's, of course, from "The Question of Lay Analysis": "We know less about the sexual life of little girls than of boys. But we need not feel ashamed of this distinction; after all, the sexual life of adult women is a 'dark continent' for psychology."[6] To begin a *Selected Poems* with such an epistle is an audacious move, vaguely reminiscent of Anne Sexton's cocky positioning of herself as Oedipus (and the reader as Jocasta) in the epigram that begins her first book.[7] Such beginnings announce that the poet (and by extension, her readers) are free to play with the doxa of Western thought—to mock its terms, to examine them seriously, to refute them, to offer alternatives.

Bold as this announcement may be, it also notes a degree of alienation: what does it feel like, as an adult woman with a sexual life, to address a poem to "the sexual life of adult women," even with a rich sense of irony? (And here I'm using irony not in the sense of postmodern high jinks, but rather in the sense elaborated by the poet Rae Armantrout in her excellent little essay "Irony and Postmodern Poetry," in which she declares, "Irony is the stubborn mark of the divided psyche" [*Moving Borders*, 679].) The text of "Dear Dark Continent" goes on to chart the contours of a divided psyche—or, rather, those of an *un*differentiated psyche:

> but I've ostensibly chosen
>   my, a, *family*
> so early! so early! (as is done always
> as it would seem always) I'm a two
> now three irrevocably
>   I'm wife I'm mother I'm
> myself and him and I'm myself and him and him
>
> But isn't it only I in the real
> whole long universe?
>
> But I and this he (and he) make ghosts of
> I and all the *hes* there would be, won't be
>
> because by not I am he, we are I, I am we.

We're not the completion of myself.

Not the completion of myself but myself!
through the whole long universe. (1)

Though Notley has said that she rejected the models of Plath, Rich, and Sexton quite early on—"when I was dealing with the problems of being a young mother and an aspiring poet . . . I decided the poems of Plath and Sexton were a genuinely negative influence" (Foster, 80)—the pronoun struggle at play here certainly echoes Rich's "I am she: I am he" moment from "Diving into the Wreck,"[8] and, even more strongly, Plath's endless struggle to pull herself out of a vortex of swirling masculine pronouns, as in the end of "Fever 103°": "Not you, nor him // Not him, nor him / (My selves dissolving, old whore petticoats)." As the progression of these three lines from "Fever 103°" demonstrates (and as I explored in relation to Guest in chapter 1), Plath's drama of undifferentiated female identity rarely finds a happy ending. Instead Plath relentlessly revisits a traumatic scene of origin: that of the birth of Eve out of Adam's side. Over and over again, Plath imagines this scene as the simultaneous birth and death of the female subject: "It is Adam's side, / This earth I rise from, and I in agony. / I cannot undo myself, and the train is steaming," she writes in "Getting There"; in "A Birthday Present": "There would be a nobility then, there would be a birthday. / And the knife not carve but enter // Pure and clean as the cry of a baby, / And the universe slide from my side." Part of the dark generosity of Plath's poetry—and probably part of the reason that Notley and so many others cite her as a bad influence—is that she dwells so persistently on the impossibility of finding a self that is "not you, nor him," without simultaneously forecasting its immolation. In her book on Plath, Jacqueline Rose articulates this conundrum as follows: "We do not in fact have a term for identity free of the worst forms of social oppression which does not propel us beyond the bounds of identity in any recognizable form" (149).

Notley's poetry—especially her later poetry—militates against this pronouncement, and attempts to create, or discover, what forms may lie beyond. Instead of fixating on Eden, Notley stages the action of her poetry "at the beginning of the world, before things were male & female in the way that they are now," and to use a mystical sort of poetic vision ("in the most unrestricted sense of that word") to conceive of as yet unrecognizable forms of identity and the images that might embody them (*Disembodied Poetics*, 108). (*The Descent of Alette*, for example, features a fish-human, a headless woman who speaks from her bloodied throat, a woman with the beak and eyes of an owl and a vagina of bone, and so on.) Like Plath, Notley explores the dangerous self-effacements of childbirth and the subsequent process of becoming "a slave, well mildly, to a baby" (*Selected Poems*, 7), but Notley does so in a wider tonal register. In "Dear Dark Continent," for example, the line "I'm / myself and him and I'm myself / and him and him" may feel a little claustrophobic, but there's considerable pride and pleasure in the declaration a few lines later, "we are I, I am we." Yet Notley then complicates this intersubjectivity with the question: "But isn't it only I in the real / whole long universe? Alone to be / in the whole long universe?" This question has preoccupied Notley throughout her career, though her focus has shifted from the links between the living onto the links between the living and the dead. "I'm speaking of a dying person / embedded in certain ways self to self with me: how will we / extricate each other, to exist as separate essences?" she asks in "How We Spent the Last Year of His Life," a poem in *Mysteries* about the death of Berrigan (70). Indeed, how *does* one experience oneself as a "separate essence"—how does one learn to think for oneself, and thus become, in Notley's argot, truly "disobedient" (Emerson might say "self-reliant")—while also coming to grips with how deeply shared our consciousness and bodies can be, and how deeply embedded the living and the dead remain in each other? This is the dialectic that has come to shape so much of the form and content of Notley's poetic inquiries.

By the end of "Dear Dark Continent," Notley seems to have momentarily talked herself away from the potentially devastating effects of postpartum disorientation via a Whitmanic celebration of self—a celebration which famously privileges communion over consolidation: "Not the completion of myself but myself! / through the whole long universe." This invocation of Whitman also signals the depth of Notley's early identifications with male predecessors, an identification which became most explicit in her book-length essay from 1980, *Dr. Williams' Heiresses*. In her interview with Foster, she explains the drive behind that book and its title:

> Well, *Dr. Williams' Heiresses* is about that. It's about my being able to
> relate to him and identify with him out of sexual reversal. I guess my

theory was that it was easier—it was probably easier to be like Williams if you were a woman, because you couldn't be like him if you were a woman—and opposites can be the same in spirit, and you could relate to a person like that in this whole oppositional way—in a battles of the sexes way. I don't know if this makes any sense to you . . . I don't do that anymore. (71)

I can understand why Notley's interest in this "battle of the sexes" reverse identification has evaporated. But her elaboration of it in the seventies and early eighties still marks an important alternative to both the patriarchal anxiety-of-influence model of literary relation and its inverse, the woman-centered call to matriarchal "re-vision" set forth by Rich in her influential 1971 essay "When We Dead Awaken: Writing as Re-Vision." Instead, Notley privileges the play of gender performativity, along with a longstanding belief that cross-gender identification is a central aspect of being a poet: "I used to have this whole girl theory of poets, that all poets are essentially girls, and especially all the ones I related to, and that was what made all male poets different from other men. . . . I think that men who are poets have to be in touch with their girl selves in order to be good poets, and I'm beginning to think it's my responsibility as a woman poet to be in touch with my male aspects in order to work properly" (Foster, 72). One could hear in this idea an echo of Keats's negative capability, or of a humanism that celebrates Shakespeare, for example, as a truly "universal" artist—someone whose imaginative vision extends beyond all polarities, be they sexual or otherwise. But Notley's "girl theory" is a bit more sly, for its androgyny never trumps its feminism. For example, in the poem "World's Bliss," Notley conjures a vision of androgyny—"Why should a maiden lie on a moor / for seven nights and a day? / And he is a maiden, he is & she / on the grass the flower the spray / where they lie" (SP, 64)—but by the end of the poem, this fluidity serves to render the last line of the poem only more forceful and surprising: "oh each poet's a / beautiful human girl who must die." Notley repeats this gesture—moving the "beautiful human girl" from poetic object to poetic source—throughout her lyric poetry, while her narrative projects address slightly distinct but related questions: "Does a woman have a story? . . . What does a woman 'do'?" (DP, 103).[9]

Given the importance of male homosexuality in the first generation of the New York School, it isn't surprising that many of the second-generation writers—a much straighter bunch, for the most part—would inherit and transform (some might say coopt) the queerness of their predecessors. "It's important not / to back out / of the mirror: // You will be great, but / You will be queer // It's a complication," reads a short but intriguing poem ("It's Important") by Berrigan (*SP*, 51). It's fascinating to see how a straight poet like Berrigan works the queerness of his first-generation heroes and Notley's "girl theory" of poets—see, for example, his poem "For You (*for James Schuyler*)," which recounts a trip uptown with "Joe" to Klein's department store: "I go reeling / up First Avenue to Klein's. Christmas / is sexy there. We feel soft sweaters /and plump rumpled skirts we'd like to try" (4). The trip, along with the poem's dedication, bring us back to the scene in Schuyler's "The Morning of the Poem" in which Schuyler and Ashbery stand outside a department store window, contemplating those knitted ribbon dresses.

Perhaps even more interesting, however, is to consider how Notley handled this negotiation, as both an admirer of Whitman and O'Hara and also as the lesser-known wife of an older, driven, opinionated poet who perhaps felt more at ease in donning their poetic mantle. (In a poem from *Mysteries* that converses with the dead Berrigan, Notley looks back on this situation and tries to explain it to him: "Men were a problem then—I see that better / in the future, but you, sometimes you were 'men,' / usually not." To which Berrigan wittily replies, "Then were men men?" [45].) Even though Notley says she sees it better "in the future," her poems from the seventies and eighties waste no time in articulating and railing against any perceived inequalities, as in "But He Says I Misunderstood":

> He & I had a fight in the pub
> 5 scotch on the rocks 1 beer I remember
> only that he said, "No women poets are any
>   good, if you want it
> Straight, because they don't handle money" and
> "Poe greater than Dickinson"
> Well that latter is an outright and fucking untruth (*SP*, 7)

The poem goes on to excoriate the "he" of the poem—presumably Berrigan—for forgetting to put her name on their joint checks, because "He had checks to deposit in his name / Because / He's older & successfuller & teaches because / When you're older you don't want to / scrounge for money besides it gives him / a thrill he doesn't too much acknowledge, / O Power!" The poem—essentially a self-interrupting rant—reaches its climax in the final line: "All I can say is / This poem is in the Mainstream American Tradition." It's a canny finale, as it defiantly asserts its place at the table while hoping to upend the table altogether.

Elsewhere—as in the untitled poem from *At Night the States* (1983) in which Notley pays homage to the O'Hara poem "Joe's Jacket"—Notley muses on the problem of donning the poetic mantle in a quieter fashion:

> I didn't write
> "Joe's Jacket"
> about the way I
> felt today. Luckily
>
> I had "Joe's
> Jacket" to read
> instead. Is it
> my jacket, too?
>
> Yes, as poetry will, still
> protect me from all
> real
> harm.
>   *Nov. 16, 1983* (16)

The poem is short and to-the-point, but like Berrigan's "It's Important," perhaps deceptively so, especially when one goes back to the original O'Hara poem. O'Hara's "Joe's Jacket" is a lovely, dense, and slightly ominous account of a trip to Southampton with Jasper Johns, Joe LeSueur, Kenneth Koch, and Vincent Warren (with whom O'Hara was just beginning an affair), in which Joe's jacket—a seersucker—eventually serves as a symbol of "all enormity and life." At the end of his weekend away from the city, O'Hara puts on the jacket to protect himself against any number of threats named in the poem: melancholy, insomnia, alcoholism, boredom, the risks of falling in love, "anxiety and self distrust," and so on.[10] He borrows the talismanic seersucker from Joe; Notley then borrows it from O'Hara, setting up an intertextual wager about the power of poetry and poetic community. Her "Is it / my jacket, too?" is poignant in its hesitant desire to join the circuit created by O'Hara's poetry, and in its deep hope that poetry itself might be more than a symbolic shield from "real harm."

Notley's poem eventually decides that the jacket can, in fact, be hers too. But the poem also sustains a subtle and unresolved tension, in that O'Hara's poem quietly supplants Notley's—that is, she says she reads his poem instead of writing her own. (Actually, to be exact, she says she didn't write "Joe's Jacket," but she does write the poem at hand, so it's even trickier.) Either way, the attention placed on the problem of wearing a man's jacket brings to mind certain parallel developments in feminist criticism throughout the seventies and eighties—developments which Jane Gallop summarized in 1988 (in *Thinking through the Body*) as follows:

> In 1978, Elaine Showalter saw feminist critics as "Annie Hall," women in "men's ill-fitting hand-me-downs." In 1983, she saw male feminists as "Tootsie," men in women's clothing. But what about the post-structural feminist who is wearing the hand-me-downs of men-in-drag, writing a feminine which has become a male transvestite style? What is double-crossdressing? . . . What is the position of the woman who identifies with men who identify with women? (100)

Though perhaps a bit dated—and a bit deaf to the capacities of lesbian performativity—Gallop's questions are still pertinent here as they draw attention to the ways in which "Joe's jacket" might fail to fit or protect the female poet, even when she's going for butch. Despite Notley's deep affinity with O'Hara (specifically with his commitment to "fast talk," which I'll discuss later), Notley realized early on that her relationship to the quotidian differed dramatically from O'Hara's. As she has explained it, hers lacked serenity. "I wanted to write something like O'Hara's *Lunch Poems*," she says. "They have a serenity to them which seems to emerge from the rather strict borders of his work at the museum: the hours, the suit and tie, the office, etc., as if the fact of being a rather anonymous worker like that was the condition that lit up the poem." But by her early twenties, Notley realized that she "didn't really have anything to put into the form of the I do this I do that, or any other form involving the details of going through the day" (email interview, 9 February 2002). Or, rather, the details that she *did* have to put

into the form couldn't play off of the same mystique of the ordinary
as O'Hara's *Lunch Poems* had. The frustration with this situation
becomes palpable in her long poem "January":

> I didn't lose any weight today
> I had clean hair but I drove
> Ted nuts and spanked Anselm on
> the arm and wouldn't converse
> with him about the letter C. And
> didn't take Edmund out or change
> the way the house smells or not
> drink and take a pill and had to watch
> John Adams on TV
>   and fantasized
> about the powers of ESP when on LSD–
> there is no room for fantasy in
> the head except as she speaks.
> The Holy Ghost is the definitive
> renegade like in the white falling-out
> chair stuffing, 2 chairs
>   asking me if
> I liked my life. I thought she
> meant my life and said
>   how could
> you dislike being a poet? and having
> children is only human
>   but
> she meant my chairs.   (*SP*, 17–18)

"January" goes on to zoom all over the place, demonstrating Notley's gift for getting down the fast-moving sounds of speech, be they
the jumpy juxtapositions of internal monologue ("My armpits smell
like chicken soup. But really I hate them / because of their tacky and
unchanging book collection") or the patterns of another's utterance
("Daddy tomorrow we'll have donuts and chocolate soda / and my
birthday party and eat snow and throw snow and / make snowmen
// He'll take off your wart tomorrow and you won't be sick"). Her
penchant for abrupt and often inscrutable juxtapositions is especially
apparent near the end of the poem: "well if the cape is all wet it
won't / blow in the wind / but I have to check / something / You're

still in no condition / to fight a bull / But he found his own . . . / What a glistening golden / baby!" Such progression reflects the surrealism of, say, O'Hara's "Second Avenue," or the elliptical composition of an early Ashbery experiment like "Idaho," but "January" intentionally shuns the flow of the former and contains far more personal pathos than the latter. The scattered lunacy of "January" pushes at the limits of the kinds of emotions and speech patterns a "daily" poem can contain. As discussed earlier, Mayer's *Midwinter Day* contends with a similar problem, but whereas Mayer opts for narcotic flow, Notley goes for syncopated agitation, as in the beginning of the poem "As You Like It": "Hi. You going out today? / You tell Mommy buy you ice cream. / You tell Mommy go fuck self. / Hi. / Okay" (*Margaret & Dusty*, 21). And though Notley includes and celebrates the language of her children just as insistently as does Mayer, Notley's exhaustion from their endless speech occasionally becomes acute, as in the end of "Waltzing Matilda": "Mom / why don't / people read in the dark? They can't see the words in the / dark. I can. Please go to sleep now. Please, honey" (*SP*, 67). These concluding lines feel especially bittersweet coming from a poet so in love with the ongoing patter of human dialogue, and so enraptured by the mystical ideal of going into the darkness to find words.

Notley's ambivalence about a poetry focused on the details of so-called everyday life may have deepened over the years, but the ambivalence can be found alive and kicking in her earliest poetry. The second poem in Notley's *Selected* is a piece from the early 1970s that addresses the issue quite literally:

Your Dailiness,

     I guess I must address you
begin and progress somewhat peculiarly, wanting
not to be afraid to be anonymous, to love what's at hand
I put out a hand, it's sewn & pasted hingewise &
enclosed in a cover. I'm 27 and booked, and my
grandfather

My grandfather, I begin with, played dominoes
called them "bones." Bones is a doctor on Star Trek.
Black, intensive, rectangular solids starred
with white dots, and laid from end to end. (2)

The task of addressing "dailiness" quickly reveals itself to be more of an imperative than an experiment, perhaps reflecting the fact that Notley was finding the quotidian "a little too fetishized by the time it was [her] turn to write it" (email interview, 9 February 2002). Her epistle instead begins with hesitancy and "peculiarity." The fear of being anonymous is far more intense than in the poetry of her New York School predecessors—and even than in Mayer's—and the sensation of being "booked"—either in the sense of being overly busy or deeply involved with reading or writing—produces as much anxiety and suspicion as it does pleasure. As in her poem about "Joe's Jacket," there is also an understated drama about the process of coming-to-writing, in that "putting out a hand" here doesn't necessarily mean picking up a pen and becoming an *auteur*, but may also involve getting trapped, "sewn and pasted hingewise & / enclosed in a cover."

Notley wants to "love what's at hand," but she doesn't want to feel coerced to do so. Experiencing it as a pressure, she quickly wriggles into a different kind of poem. The first stanza break of "Your Dailiness" marks this move, after which she begins again, this time with her grandfather. The poem continues: "That night I dreamed of my grandfather, playing / dominoes, and my mother my aunts—dreams are not / brightly lit—a brownish dream," introducing the preoccupation with dead men and dreams that will characterize so much of her later work. Like *Disobedience*, which combines daily commentary with fantasy and dreams, "Your Dailiness" also glides between these modes, albeit on a smaller scale:

> Several months before I met my husband
> I began to concentrate on ghosts, that they were there,
> there here, and I, I might see one, if anyone why
> not as with anything, I? I waited every night. I
> went to bed and turned out the light, though no longer
> lovingly hugged the dark, to see if it would appear,
> the ghost. For three months. Nervously fell asleep.
> I told my friend Mary she said Why not just see it?
> I didn't want to be one who saw ghosts. I waited
> waited. Then I dreamed
>
>   a woman a poet spoke to me
> out of a drawing on my wall spoke what? Spoke.
> The ghost would appear, and in a shower of gold, he

appeared and he was Rory Calhoun in his corniest
grin and loudest plaidest with shoulders sportscoat.
We embraced. (4)

Becoming "one who sees ghosts" and who then writes about
the encounters differs a bit from the Surrealist or New York
School embrace of dream-logic-as-compositional-principle. Instead
it marks Notley as a "whacher," as described by Anne Carson—also
a "whacher"—in her long poem "The Glass Essay" from *Glass, Irony,
and God*. Referring to Emily Brontë's habitual misspelling of the
word "watcher," Carson explains that a whacher is one who whaches
"God and humans and moor wind and open night . . . eyes, stars,
inside, outside, actual weather . . . the bars of time . . . the poor core
of the world / wide open" (4). Carson explains that "to be a whacher
is not a choice." A whacher cannot turn away from her visions, for
"there is nowhere else to go, / no ledge to climb up to." (In Notley's
lingo, this "whaching" might be described as "walking straight into
the dark and staying there awhile," as she has described her process
elsewhere [McCabe, 274].) In "The Glass Essay," Carson's psy-
chotherapist repeatedly asks her, "Why keep watching?" to which
Carson answers, "Some people watch, that's all I can say." In "Your
Dailiness," Notley's friend Mary steers in the opposite direction from
the therapist, and instead asks Notley, "Why not just see it?" The latter approach seems to work: when Notley stops worrying about
becoming someone who sees dead people, the dead appear, often as
unthreatening friends or celebrities. The arrival of the gaudily
dressed Rory Calhoun (a cowboy star of Wild West flicks) marks the
first of many ghostly visitations that Notley will record in her poetry,
many of which retain a similar sense of humor, even when they contend with agonizing losses. (See the beginning of *Close to me &
Closer*, for example, where Notley's father tries to describe life in
heaven: "Being dead is like *one fun* . . . that's a Chinese joke" [9].)
    Humor has always played an important role in Notley's poetry, as
it has in most poetry associated with the New York School.
("'Humor" "is closer" "to the / divine than" "you might think,'"
she writes in *The Descent of Alette* [76].[11]) But Notley's use of
humor has consistently chafed against any simplistic opposition of
insouciance and seriousness, especially political seriousness. As she
explains:

New York School in particular was against anguish and in favor of humor and the general light of day. This could be very liberating, but got to be a problem if one encountered anguish in one's life and wanted to write about it. You can see towards the end of *Phoebe Light* a little darkness seeping in, and a sense of woman's problems and feminist concerns. These felt a little forbidden, unless handled inside a certain tonal range. The message seemed to be Don't have those feelings and thoughts, because our poetics doesn't include them. But all poetics, all poetry schools do this—rule out something or other—so they're all suspect. Which doesn't mean they can't be useful at some point or other. But a poetics is a lot more transitory than a poem is. (Foster, 79)

Notley makes several important distinctions here. The first recognizes that while a poetic stance in favor of "humor and the general light of day" may have stood in useful opposition to the more world-weary, depressive attitude of much American poetry in the 1950s, any ideology—even one that advocates joy—can eventually become restrictive and confining. Notley reminds us again that this restrictiveness has more to do with the critical delineation of poetic schools than with the action of the poems themselves: to make distinctions between one type of writing and another is to court generalizations; in doing so, one immediately risks flattening the range of the poetry at hand. Notley also here acknowledges that poetic stances have to change with the *bhav*, a yogic term Myles has used to talk about "the quality of the room when people are there." "The poet has to address the *bhav*, not only in herself, but within the room of the culture," Myles explains. "O'Hara didn't have to watch his friends die around him [of AIDS]. It's a different *bhav*" (Richard, 25–26). In considering Notley's *bhav*, it's not hard to imagine how a woman poet developing a feminist consciousness in the seventies could experience an insistence on a poetry of apolitical frivolity as confining, especially as it was contemporaneous with the development of the stereotype of a "women's libber" as someone who lacks a sense of humor. It's important, I think, to find a way to celebrate the humor of the New York School without making recourse to this stereotype, and Notley's unwillingness to pit her sense of humor against her political convictions or her feminism provides a very good example of how one might do so.[12]

In discussing the particular kind of "avant-garde" that the first generation of the New York School constituted, Lehman says that "they experimented not for experimentation's sake but for the sake of writing great poems" (9). I'm not sure whether I agree, or if such a retrospective distinction bears up under scrutiny, but the statement is useful insofar as it points toward another aspect of Notley's difference. Notley has repeatedly said that her poetic experiments do not pursue beauty, novelty, or aesthetic greatness; rather, they search for truth. "Truth" hasn't enjoyed much popularity as a concept in any field, poetic or otherwise, for quite some time now, and Notley's unembarrassed use of it differentiates her—sometimes vociferously—from a whole host of fellow poets and thinkers. This search goes hand in hand with Notley's deep, unironic investment in poetry as an "honorable, exacting, necessary occupation," which has nothing to do with "who's the best poet" and everything to do with "continuing the tradition of poetry, making sure its 'services'— spiritual, intellectual—remain available to people" (Goldman, 8). For this reason among others, Notley doesn't think of herself as an experimental poet: "I write usually what it seems to me poetry needs next; I suppose that's why all my works look different from each other and I suppose that's what lands me in the experimental category" (Goldman, 28).[13]

And the last thing Notley apparently thinks poetry needs next is another well-wrought urn. "Now I have to improve this / poem by making it longer & a / mess," she writes in the poem "Homage to Marianne Moore" (*Margaret & Dusty*, 54), articulating a sentiment that could be taken as the modus operandi of her book-length poems to come, such as *The Descent of Alette*. At the beginning of *Alette*, Notley includes a note that explains her eccentric use of quotation marks therein. In addition to measuring the poem's poetic feet, she explains that "they should also remind the reader that each phrase is a thing said by a voice: this is not a thought, or a record of a thought-process; this is a story, told." The point is an important one, and not just because it aids our understanding of *Alette*. Notley is here pointing out the vital link between her "feminine epic" and her earlier work: both are deeply invested in speech, and together they constitute a deepening wager about the power of personality that resides in vocalized words and rhythms. And here is where Notley's mystical search for truth meets up again with the New York School, as the New

York School may eventually go down in poetic history as one long celebration of "fast talk." As Myles has put it, "Talk is the throughline in all this work. . . . The talk narrated the New York pace of life, the talk walked you through the party, the hangover" (*Mississippi*, 228). Notley echoes this idea when she says, "That's what O'Hara's all about. It's all about talking fast to someone. That's what we do. We talk fast to someone" (Foster, 71). But poetry in this vein does more than present written approximations of "fast talk." It also recognizes that gushing, rapid speech is a deep pleasure, and that this pleasure can be placed at the heart of a poetics.[14]

Notley's particular contribution to this tradition has to do with her unabashedly spiritual conviction that personality is primordial—that the sounds we generate or "channel" from others speak of something sacred, something boundless. "Poetry is about personality. It's the writer or the poet giving her whole self, and a self is personality," she says, in explicit counter to Eliot's famous edict that poetry is an escape from personality. In lieu of this escape, Notley gets metaphysical by listening to and recording the particular verbal rhythms of others, especially dead others. This task is logorrheic by nature, and agitates against the notion often floated in poetic circles that the words that matter most are the ones that *don't* get said. Most of the dead that she speaks with are men—"the dead in my life are men, and I need to talk to them," she explains (email interview, 4 February 2002)—yet her poetic dialogues with them stand apart from the macho, minimalist models of male speech represented by everything from the laconic prose of Hemingway or Raymond Carver (Carver even has a book of stories entitled *Will You Please Be Quiet, Please?*) to the lovely, if anguished, poetic condensations of George Oppen or Robert Creeley.

We have seen the seeds of this dialogic mode in Notley's early work, but the death of Berrigan in 1983 seemed to bring an urgency to the process, as the following teeny poems from *At Night the States*, written shortly after Berrigan's death, suggest:

grace him my heart there grown pale
joy to hear and see him kind
but now I speak only to air
yet how like my mind he is to me
                    9/2/83 (4)

Aside: Voice

I love your voice.
And when they die
their voices will still
live together.
                12/84 (65)

By all accounts, Berrigan was a loquacious man, and in these poems one can hear the deep pain of losing an intimate and captivating conversationalist. But the pain is mitigated, or at least accompanied, by the hope that there's something unfathomable or eternal about voice, that voice is in fact some kind of immortal essence. And here I don't mean "voice" in its customary lit-crit sense, as in "point of view," creation of a character, or the approximation of a dialect. I mean the idiosyncratic way that personality, or "soul," collaborates with physiology and culture to create the actual rhythm and sound of an individual's speech. After *At Night*, Notley embarked on a number of pieces that attempt to bring dead men to speech, be they Berrigan, her brother, her father, or the Surrealist French poet Robert Desnos (a poet also known for writing in trances and his sleep, and who died tragically as a result of his internment in a Nazi concentration camp).

This channeling isn't always an easy task, and often Notley records its tribulations. Listen, for example, to the beginning of the poem "I Must Have Called and So He Comes" (from *Mysteries*):

"You're accusing me of something in these poems."
"No, Ted, I'm not accusing you—can't catch your voice though."
"Through dead curtains," he says. Gives me the disgusted
Berrigan moue, casts match aside lighting cigarette
"So what are you doing?" he says. I say, "As the giant lasagna
on Star Trek—remember, Spock mindmelds with her
and screams, Pain." "So this is pain?" he says.
"I suppose it is. Was. But not from you," I say.
"We don't say pain we say fucked-up," he says, "Or
Kill the motherraper. Inside yourself . . ." (he fades)
"I can't catch your voice . . ." (I say)
". . . there's a place inside you," he says, "a poetry self, made by
        pain but not

> violated—oh I don't say violated,
> you're not getting my dialogue right, you can't remember
>   my style."
> "Would you say touched, instead?" I say.
> "There's this place in us," he says, "the so-called pain can't
>   get to
> like a shelter behind those spices—coffee and sugar, spices,
> matches, cockroach doodoo on the kitchen shelf." (45)

The passage manages to impart a sense of Berrigan's character and presence while also giving voice to a lonely speaker facing all kinds of complications about grief, remembrance, and communication. Further, the "mindmelding" of Spock and the "cockroach doodoo" evidence the same *"one fun"* sense of humor that keeps Notley's very serious channeling procedures from seeming unbearably so. For anyone who is wondering how seriously Notley takes them—to what extent she believes that the dead actually speak to her—her introduction to *Close to me & Closer* sheds some light on the subject:

> I wrote *Close to me* . . . in '91 and '92, beginning around Christmas-time and concluding in February. I remember feeling very happy writing it, waking up mornings with my dead father's voice in my head. In order to write his speeches properly I had to have faith that that was his literal voice I heard. . . . I hadn't heard my father speak in fifteen, sixteen years, but one never forgets a parent's voice, and he just took over. . . . I'm loathe to say he didn't *really* write his part of the poem; and I feel the daughter's parts of the dialogue are nowhere near as good as the father's. He bested me. He should have, he had the knowledge of the dead. (3)

The emphasis here is on faith, without which it's virtually impossible to pursue any ambitious artistic project—ghosts or no ghosts—to its completion. With this kind of project, the question of whether or not the finished product ends up an aesthetic masterpiece becomes less and less the point.[15] Caring about aesthetic mastery takes back seat to the challenge of writing "unheard of things, I mean things that have never been written yet," as Mayer put it.

For Notley, this task has often entailed finding new ways to notate speech patterns, and the result has been some pretty freaky-looking poetry—poetry almost guaranteed to alienate the more casual reader (though she insists that she has "*always* want[ed] to write poems anyone can understand" [Goldman, 6]).[16] Her books have increasingly come with explanations or warnings about their unusual markings, as in the explanatory note about the quotation marks in *The Descent of Alette*, or the preface to *Close to me*, in which Notley writes: "I warn the reader that the daughter's parts may be initially hard to catch prosodically. They are characterized by mid-line capital letters which signal, quickly (other punctuation's too slowing), the beginning of a new foot or sub-line. This device, as well as the use of underline and ellipsis in the father's parts (though they're in prose), are an attempt to make a more sonically nuanced line." (On the page, the father's lines appear as follows: "The god / fetus / drawing, thing, knows. It knows about . . . what they call the uncreated . . . the big happy dark . . . And the very bad, world"; the daughter's: "The wind is sober Blown through me / I have outlines And an eye" [21].)

Given the profundity of Notley's investment in the relation between speech and "pure self," or "soul" ("I loathe the word 'self,'" she said in a recent interview, before explaining that she now prefers to use the word "soul" instead [Dick]), one can imagine the rift that began to develop between her poetics and those of the Language poets, many of whom labored throughout the late seventies and the eighties (along with structuralists and then poststructuralists at large) to denaturalize and destabilize precisely these concepts. In one of Notley's "Dear Advisor" poems (the one dated "Dec. 5, 1980"), you can hear the beginnings of this rift, though it starts off with humor. She writes her Advisor: "I am having trouble with my writing because the words aren't jostling each other glitteringly in a certain way & they all have referents I think if that is a trouble . . . you see it's all about usage of words & to say what you intend to & [my husband] has always in the past been excessively careful with words, we both read L=A=N=G=U=A=G=E magazine" (*SP*, 71).

In a later response in the same series, her Advisor writes back: "Dear Anonymous . . . I see little difference between you and your husband—you're both big and awkward sentimental truthtelling fuckups though you each have a different cover story" (82). Characterizing oneself as a "big and awkward sentimental truthtelling fuckup" marks a considerable distance from the more sober, theoretical poetic stances developing in Language quarters, exemplified by Bruce Andrews's "author dies, writing begins" slogan (derived from

Barthes and Foucault, among others); Ron Silliman's neo-Marxist critique of the so-called referential fetish; or Charles Bernstein's conviction that consciousness itself is essentially a "syntacticalization" (see *The Language Book*, 54, 131, 43); and so on. This last idea is essentially a paraphrase of the French linguist Emile Benveniste, who asserted: "It is in and through language that man constitutes himself as a *subject*. . . . It is literally true that the basis of subjectivity is in the exercise of language" (see Silverman, 1, 44). This isn't the place to sound the depths of the influence that this idea has had on semiotics, psychoanalysis, linguistics, literary theory, and feminism over the past century; suffice it to say that Notley's resistance to the idea reminds us that it is just that—an idea—not a literal truth to which everyone must eventually submit. "Like many writers I feel ambivalent about words, I know they don't work, I know they aren't it. I don't in the least feel that everything is language," Notley has said, laying bare at least one of the reasons why she has never written "language-based poetry as such" (Goldman, 6).

The divergence is real and significant. At the same time, it should not be understood as yet another conservative, reactionary response to poststructuralist theory and its "radical" ramifications. Notley's investigations into the sounds of the social self have made her work interesting to many writers associated with Language, including Leslie Scalapino, who discusses the collection *Margaret & Dusty* in a heady essay entitled "Pattern—and the 'Simulacral'" from the collection *Artifice and Indeterminacy*. This essay treats the poems of *Margaret & Dusty* as "an interwoven pattern of voices and characters," and the authorial voice as "a social surface, or a constructed personality" (137). Scalapino observes: "The creation of voices in *Margaret & Dusty* apes projections [of] what we think 'life' is or what we think ourselves are. People are mimicked to be seen as social configurations and also as 'talk,' the conversations in the book that are the abstraction the only existence of the person . . . the conversation of all those people in the writing becomes the only stuff there is" (138).

Scalapino rightly grasps that Notley's "fast talking" speech/music collages construct or reflect the social configurations of subjectivity. But a reading that leaves off there, and that concludes that talk is "the only stuff there is," seems to take what it wants from Notley's vision while leaving the rest behind. Some moments in *Margaret & Dusty* give this impression, but there are many others which express a profound dissatisfaction with skimming the surface of social speech. The book closes with the following lines from the poem "Sweetheart":

> I would like not to think, it
> makes me foreigner of myself I'd like
>
> this strange enrichment of the
> spirit I feel though bereft
> but I'd like this lovely inadequate
> apartment
> but I'd like my music
> my mental music not to
> suddenly render me rawly sad
> "You have empty honey" "Yes, I have"
>
> this person who sleeps in my bed
> she's slept there forever and yet
> there was another
> when it was another
> bed looking so same so recently
> but that I would have to remember
> (strangely an involuntary measure)
>
> O Poem really addressed
> to me, it's you are found indulgent
> fit of comfort, lustre, real light
> I praise you, thank you
> for being what I have tonight
> 1/18/84 (75)

Notley here feels out not just the contours of the social self, but also the possibilities of other selves—a split audible in the very first line: "I would like not to think, it / makes me foreigner of myself," then repeated in the image of another self—a twin self, as it were—sleeping in her bed. The collection of poems may showcase a wide variety of her "mental music," but in poems such as this, one also gets a sense of her fatigue with it. Scalapino argues that the book is postmodern in that it recognizes social definitions "as not intrinsic to reality or oneself." Notley couldn't agree more about the nature of these "social definitions," but she does not accept a display of any consequent alienation as an adequate basis for her poetic inquiries.

After *Margaret & Dusty*, this sense of impatience or shame seemed to deepen, and Notley turned further away from both the cacophany of social speech and the vicissitudes of one's own "mental music." She also moved from New York to Paris, which she found a much less open city. "[New York] has a life of its own that is itself as community, as everything out in the open, all the immigrants, the street people, the density of it," she observes. "The French are a private, family-oriented people, though I am told this is less so in the south. . . . Parisians go inside their apartments, shut the door and join their families" (email interview, 9 February 2002). In the introduction to *The Scarlet Cabinet* (1992), the compendium of books that includes *Close to me* and *Désamère*, Notley asserts this change of mind: "One is no longer entitled to write down every thought, rush it straight into print. . . . The mannered tracing of a mind which, by constantly denying its own existence as 'someone,' becomes of interest only to translators of difficult discourse, to critics." In her talk "Epic and Women Poets," Notley's irritation with available forms of speech-based poetry becomes even more palpable: "Think of the typical cadences of the various kinds of modern poetry—Language poetry, New York School, New Yorker–type poetry, etc. . . . The modern trend is to sound very much like a person speaking. Language poetry, on the other hand, often sounds like a mind or voice reading printed matter. But there is the possibility of pushing harder at cadence . . ." (*DP*, 107). For Notley, this "pushing harder at cadence" means finding "a new measure," and then using it to tell a "holy story." Seeing academic feminism as hopelessly invested in the kind of scientized poststructuralist theory that insists that there is no true self or soul outside of linguistic and/or social construction, Notley throws her bag in with an idiosyncratic feminist mysticism that privileges "vision" over "language": "We don't need new words, new languages, new syntax, we need a whole new flesh, new beings to look at, literally, a new universe. The key is not in language, but in vision" (*DP*, 108–109).[17]

Hence, *The Descent of Alette*, Notley's first attempt to construct a narrative poetic epic with a female protagonist—Alette, whose name came to her in a dream. Notley had used a similar form—quotation marks marking poetic feet—to address epic themes (war, quest, death, rebirth, etc.) in an earlier six-page poem, "White Phosphorous," in which a dead soldier talks to his sister (a dialogue presumably derived from conversations with her late brother, who had been a tormented Vietnam vet). But Notley grew impatient with the woman's role as "essentially passive: sufferer, survivor." After much meditating on the question of whether or not a woman has any kind of active story that could be the basis of an epic, Notley came up with the following answer: "Insomuch as women dream, they participate in stories every night of their lives. Profound stories which may involve sex, death, violence, journeys, quests, all the stuff of epic & much of narrative" (*DP*, 103). Thus the importance of dreams in the creation of *Alette*, the writing of which consolidated Notley's belief that "life is a dream; that we construct reality in a dreamlike way; that we agree to be in the same dream; and that the only way to change reality is to recognize its dreamlike qualities and act as if it is malleable" (email interview, 4 February 2002).

This political spin on the power of dreaming differs quite a bit from the work of O'Hara, Koch, and Ashbery, who generally used dream logic and surrealist techniques to generate an atmosphere of limitless invention or instances of giddy beauty rather than to change an unjust reality. Like Mayer in the opening section of *Midwinter Day*, Notley makes little or no attempt to organize or prettify the details of her dreams; the emphasis remains on their prolificacy and their essentially feral nature. This method becomes particularly intense in *The Descent of Alette*, which takes its images from dreams Notley had at night, dreams she had during brief spells of sleep during the day, and visions from self-induced trances. Generally speaking, while she was writing *Alette* her rule was to write down the first thing she saw, or whatever images kept coming back, while trying to eliminate what other people had already used. "Dreams are really bizarre," she explains, "but when people write something dreamlike they often don't include the bizarre, they don't trust it. And the tradition of the dream vision excludes the bizarre in favor of the beautiful" (email interview, 29 October 2002). Notley clearly meant *Alette* to counter this tradition.

The result is remarkable, and, paradoxically enough, quite beautiful. Though its opening line, "'One day, I awoke" "& found myself on" "a subway, endlessly,'" is clearly reminiscent of the *Inferno*'s "Nel mezzo del cammin di nostra vita," the universe of subways, caves, black lakes, snakes, and display cases that Alette journeys through creates a cosmology all its own. One can start down the road of comparing *Alette* with other big epics, but the road quickly turns out to be a dead end, as Fred Chappell discovers as he struggles to make sense of the poem in *The Georgia Review*: "It is unfair to hold a contemporary poet to the standard of Dante, but it is also impossible to keep the comparison at bay. . . . Her story is nearly as nightmarish as Dante's . . . but its logic is not so inexorable—in fact, usually the logic is not even discoverable, seeming such a product of arbitrary fancy that it lacks the stern inevitability that chastens and convinces readers simultaneously" (151).

Following this logic, Chappell is forced to conclude, "I do not pretend to understand *The Descent of Alette*. In fact, I will even surmise that it is not meant to be understood in the way that *The Divine Comedy* can be understood" (153). Exactly so—for instead of systematizing the book into an allegorical or symbolic universe, Notley's dream logic combines a tireless investigation into her unconscious with a Cageian randomness, and a feminist ethos not particularly interested in "chastening or convincing" the reader. The combination is a fruitful one: it disrupts the Freudian drive toward fixed interpretation that Mayer also averts in *Midwinter*, and which Gilles Deleuze and others have railed against (i.e., the drive that would reduce the six or seven wolves in the Wolf Man's dream to one wolf: the father). Instead *Alette* offers a kaleidoscope of shifting symbols, and a world in which any affect can become attached to any object.[18] In this world, distinguishing between "logic" and "arbitrary fancy" is not so important; much more important is to "whach," to stay alert to and scrutinize whatever happens to appear, as when Alette encounters a funny eyeball scurrying around the subway floor in book 1: "'This eyeball's funny' 'on the gray floor'' / "among round stains" "& ashes" . . . "I guess it's blue-eyed" "dark blue" "No eyebrows, of / course" "Doesn't blink much" "Intent" "intent on looking" / "What's it looking for?" "I guess, whatever'" (*Alette*, 31). Staying "intent on looking" is what matters, even if the scrutiny must end in bafflement or indifference: "I guess, whatever."

Alette denies autobiographical resonance from the start—its introductory note insists that "Alice" is not "Alette." Shortly after *Alette*, however, Notley reversed course, and published a chronological series of explicitly autobiographical poems, *Mysteries of Small Houses*. The two projects are intimately linked, however, in that both address the question "Does a woman have a story?" The poems of *Mysteries* track Notley's life from around age four to the present, moving through (as the back of the book has it) "the stages of her life and . . . the identities she has assumed—child, youth, lover, poet, wife, mother, friend, and widow." In reaction to the distaste for the "I" that had come to characterize some literary theory and poetic practice, Notley intended *Mysteries* to "re-center the I." As she explains:

> Basic I is terrifying, of course. It really exists, but we seem to construct everything—our world, our social forms, our narratives, and our anti-narratives—in order to keep it hidden. I wanted to find "my self," as the only self I could investigate—in the context of my past in order to determine its constancy, or lack of it, across the years. I thus had to "re-see" my life. I tried for a scary honesty; I wanted to be frightened by my own existence. Be as alive as I am and not be in other people's ideas of life-shapes or other people's theories about the non-existence of the self. (Goldman, 5)

For Notley, understanding one's self as a "signifying practice" (or perhaps, by extension, one's death as a "linguistic predicament," as de Man put it in his essay "Autobiography as Defacement" [930]) is not nearly scary or rigorous enough.[19]

The first poem in *Mysteries*, "Would Want to Be in My Wildlife," dramatizes the descent into this fear. Notley has said that this poem can be read as an introduction to the process of the book, since she went into a hypnotic trance to write it as she did for most of the other poems. In it she tries "to find my four-year-old self and to re-enter the house where I lived when I was four, because it seemed that when I was that age I was both most natural and most good" (Goldman, 6). The opening lines of *Mysteries* place us, *en media res*, in the drama of the body and mind coming to language:

> hold pen improperly against 4th finger not 3rd like when I was six why won't I
> hold it right
> if I'm even younger four I walk more solemnly walking's relatively new but
> talking's even more natural and I can see you really while we talk
> if words are in a sense in motion the universe has always had it
> I'm not sounding young
> though holding the pen wrong
> I don't have to sound young but I couldn't say "oil well" right

erase all that it's not right. You have to erase whatever it is and erase before
that and before that to be perfect

no   perfect's here from ever all along and if it doesn't say it right it's right and I
am it from then now Alley House I am   (1)

The variety of voices that appear throughout *Mysteries* are all at
play here: the childlike self, with its rushing syntax; the adult voice
of metaphysical wisdom ("if words are in a sense in motion the universe always has it"); the self-conscious voice that never loses sight
of her project's vector ("I'm not sounding young"); the rebellious
voice committed to rejecting other people's "life-shapes" ("if it
doesn't say it right it's right and I / am it"); and so on. As she goes
deeper into memory, she moves into fear, and comes out in a different place: "and get scared till I am I / scareder and scareder / then
calm and enter where oil of I does flow. . . ."

As *Mysteries* proceeds, Notley's meditation on the "stripped-down"
self becomes more and more harrowing, and comes to crisis in the
poems that contend explicitly with the deaths of loved ones. One of the
most agonizing of these may be "I–Toward a Definition." When I first
read this poem, I misunderstood the title. The "I" is a Roman numeral,
as the poem after it is entitled "II–The Person You Were Will Be
Replaced." But I took it to mean the first-person "I." Whether or not
the double meaning was intentional, the poem is pivotal to Notley's
movement toward "basic I." As such, I want to reproduce it in full:

I–Toward a Definition

Grief isn't empty it's black and material I've seen it
It's a force, independent, and eats you while you're sleeping
The spring after Ted died I once saw it in pieces
in the air of the apartment tatters
whirled around me like burnt paper

I know I didn't make it what made it
Could hardly stand up some days that year because of it
No luxuriance in this process no dolorous
sea of grief it's a battle
Pieces of myself are hacked away my adulthood is
art a lost story

What's left of me really is a young girl
and to accept her after such a war, after the tears of
myself as a general have hardened into semiprecious
ivory or coral, is sad and
defeating no victory
Oh yes this is who I always am
beginning child literal I
I'm myself so, knowing a new thing, that
the universe is ruled by love and countervalent sorrow
Grief's not a social invention
Grief is visible, substantial, I've literally seen it (77)

It is precisely here, face to face with the substantial and traumatic presence of grief, that the speaker comes to revelation: "Oh yes this is who I always am." Because of its power to strip us down to this state of "beginning child literal I," grief is also the one thing Notley flat-out deems "not a social invention." As Kim Lyons has written about this poem (in terms reminiscent of O'Hara's "Personism," but with a mystical twist): "There's revelation here, a hope and belief that the poem on the page might be a soul-to-soul encounter" (24). The word "revelation" is key: it is at this moment that Notley's poetic narrative begins to become a "holy story."

In the next poem, "II—The Person That You Were Will Be Replaced" she continues with this theme, noting that grief is "god-like / as in possession." The poem continues:

This was the night I was craziest: near my birthday,
four months after Ted's death, walking
on Second Avenue I thought "It's possible
he didn't really die." I felt a maniacal joy
and then became sickened and distressed
I knew a depth of me had, up to then, believed he was alive.
That depth was now emptied of him and filled with grief. (78)

"It's possible / he didn't really die": that kind of moment, that "kind of maniacal joy" which ends with a sickening return to reality, marks the terrifying move from a state of shock to seeing what truly is.

Writing about this moment years later, she is able to move from it into a set of reflective lines that become the silent mantra of the latter half of the book:

> If a self can
> contain the deaths of others, it's very large;
> it's certainly larger than my body
> If the other who dies is partly me,
> and that me dies and another grows, the medium it grows in
> is grief. (78)

Size matters here: Notley's paradoxical, principal charge against most narratives of the self is that they "make it too small and not precisely unique enough" (Goldman, 5). The deaths of others replace, expand, and reconstruct the selves of the living left behind; without this transformation, grief eats mercilessly, leaving the self "hacked away . . . a lost story." To understand how a particular self contains the deaths of particular others is to engage the most frightening and extreme aspects of the "delineation of identity by the way of alterity," as Nancy Miller has put it in a different context (4).

This delineation becomes clear in the title poem, "Mysteries of Small Houses," the penultimate poem of the book. It begins:

> Poverty much maligned but beautiful
> has resulted in smaller houses replete with mysteries
> How can something so finite
> so petite and shallow have
> the infinite center I sense there?
> . . .
> 'cause inside its center I'm, or is it we're
> It's I'm that I won't ever know
> completely unless I do when I die
> How
> do
> we manage to base ourselves on dark ignorance so
> house of pressed-down pushed-in
> origin, is such poverty; or
> apartments where people die, again the strange dense
> center of the four tiny rooms on St. Mark's Place may be that
> Ted died there and so left a mystery vortex inside that fragile
> apartment on stilts–Doug, do you think so? (136)

Poverty has literally forced her to live in small spaces, and it is the smallness of these places that renders extraordinary the discovery of "the infinite center" she senses there. Once again, as in "Dear Dark Continent," in this closeness the pronouns have trouble disentangling from each other: "I'm, or is it we're / It's I'm that I won't ever know / completely unless I do when I die." The slide into the apartment at St. Mark's Place is critical, for these unanswerable questions about origin bring us back to a deathbed, the site of passing consciousness, the "mystery vortex." All this musing brings her to a direct address (to her second husband, Douglas Oliver): "Doug, do you think so?" The question brings her no answer, but into conversation, into relation, with another.

In her feminist meditation on autobiography, Miller proposes that "rather than models, we would do better to imagine more perplexing figures whose intimate and violent dialogues with the living and dead others perform the bedrock of self-construction itself" (19). I can't think of a better way to describe the self that emerges in *Mysteries*—and, perhaps, in Notley's *oeuvre* taken as a whole. Yet it might interest the reader to know that Notley herself rejects this interpretation. When I asked her about the intense intersubjectivity imagined at the end of "Lady Poverty," she responded: "Even if the self is very large, it shouldn't have to contain the deaths of so many others, should it? Why should one have to grow new (social) selves in the medium of grief? I'm describing something I don't necessarily think should be the case" (email interview, 9 February 2002). And so it goes: interpretation, meet authorial intent. But I wonder if this discrepancy actually highlights a provocative tension in *Mysteries*: that while Notley sets out to discover the possibility of a pure, untainted self, the book performs almost everything but. In saying that, I don't mean to conclude smugly that there's no such thing as "pure self"—not only does the term require a great deal more clarification, but I don't think I would want to live in a world that had decided the case. As the poem "Mysteries of Small Houses" puts it, "I won't ever know / completely unless I do when I die." It's precisely here that the meaning of the book's title begins to come clear, in its suggestion that our bodies, minds, and poems might all be seen as "small houses," mysterious to the core.

I'm also inclined to believe that Notley's disagreement with the above reading stems from her absorption in an increasingly hermetic poetry practice, a practice she has described as "a poetics of disobedience," and which she has elaborated at length in her 284-page book, *Disobedience*. In "The Poetics of Disobedience," Notley says that she realized while writing the book the extent to which she "couldn't go along with the government or governments, with radicals and certainly not with conservatives or centrists, with radical poetics and certainly not with other poetics, with other women's feminisms, with any fucking thing at all." It's her most extreme position to date, especially in its argument that the only possible position for her, as a woman, is to "try to know everything from [herself]," as "all thinking from outside seems tainted by the male" (email interview, 4 February 2002). This conviction leaves little to no room for a "we." In its place, it promotes a fundamentally solitary religion of "meditating alone in one's closet." Notley has come to believe that "one can only by oneself have a religion that doesn't impose on others or do harm. The minute, actually, there is more than one person involved in any assertion, truth is lost and aggression becomes possible" (4 February 2002). Whatever one thinks of her current position, the aesthetic question remains, what kind of poetry has Notley produced in its sway?[20]

Disobedience is a long, exciting mess of a book—a loose, baggy monster offering unprecedented pleasures and exasperations. It maintains a "daily" time-based structure of sorts—it consists of five sections of interconnected poems that map out a thirteen-month period from 1995 to 1996—but it also includes a plethora of dreams and fantasies that feel somehow outside time. Paramount among these is a longstanding dialogue with a male detective, Hardwood, who "resembles Robert Mitchum on a bad day." The project of *Disobedience* was to combine the dreamscapes of *Alette* with the chronological, first-person investigations of *Mysteries*, in an attempt to break down "the barriers that separate waking consciousness and dream consciousness, the barriers that separate narratives of real life, fictional narratives, and dream accounts as genres," as she explains in an interview with Brian Kim-Stefans (*Jacket* 15). Or, as she puts it in *Disobedience* itself: "I want real and dreamed to be fused into the real / rip off this shroud of division of my poem from my life" (24). The barriers do break down, but not seamlessly—not only is the poem more anxious and self-conscious about its method than previous works ("Hypnotize self into a fantasy world / a world of caves. [Yes I *do* this, I can]," Notley prods herself near the beginning), but the lines of the poem themselves are also separated by "shrouds of division" in the form of bars, as in:

These lacunae are most great, most restful.

Do I really want to fill them in with suppressions?

The Choros of the future howls quietly.
_____ (23)

Whatever "dailiness" the poem contains has more to do with contemporary political happenings than the details of Notley's personal life. Or, better put, the poems repeatedly act out the slippage between private and public realms. Political events mutate into psychic matter, and vice versa:

29 people were injured by Tuesday's bomb,
four seriously,
who suffered amputations.

I dream that
a bomb might injure me
because some Muslims hate me. I mean
isn't that real possibility a dream,
wouldn't its happening be dreamlike?

. . . if hatred's a vicious phantasm,
waking reality's a dream. (70)

As the above lines suggest, *Disobedience* is in many ways a book about despair—despair about geopolitical conflicts, despair about endemic violence and injustice, about misogyny, about literature, about environmental destruction. But its despair is not of a lyrical or wistful variety. It's angry, combative, and often sounds like a fight for one's life. It's an abrasive reading experience, a veritable hothouse of "not-nice" pleasures. This effect is intentional: as she explains, "my rule for this poem / is honesty, my other rule is Fuck You" (158). Fuck You the reader, fuck mainstream poetry, fuck avant-garde poetry, fuck France, fuck America, fuck daily life, fuck death, and so on. ("My middle finger's sore from too much up-pointing," she says at one point.) You could say that *Disobedience* develops a poetics of pure grouchiness—an audacious endeavor with few or no precursors. What's more, it names names: whether it's Bob Dole or Seamus Heaney or Buddha, no one is spared. "BUD-DHA PRACTICES AUTOFELLATIO / MOHAMMED IS A MUG-GER" are but two of the sacrilegious messages Notley finds on the walls of one of her imagined caves. "I'm enjoying making mean remarks about everyone," she asserts at one point, in a particularly self-righteous mood, "because I am the Soul, misunderstood / I'm pure, wise, and bitchy: that's not / contradictory. I intend to be grouchy throughout my eternity" (92).

Sometimes this grouchiness is exhausting; often it is very funny. I particularly enjoy her rants about dolls. Early on in the book, she writes: "The bitterest part of being a doll / is how to tell you / I hate how you make me this doll / sitting propped up at dinner party or poetry panel // 'You're such a hostile doll.'" (62) "Hostile doll" is fol-lowed by Pocahontas Doll ("the little Whore") and then "Slut Doll," whom she imagines in "tarty short dress and blatant stocking tops / some bullshit in her hair, some glitterbit jewelry there—Her name is Ewe or OO" (105). Slut Doll comes to life in the following passage:

Slut Doll, besides being "Compassion,"
a stiff clit and the question of who strokes it,
is also Psychology, that wornout ancient game.
I've dreamed of her before, in a red dress at the sock hop:
"I'm unable to grieve for Burgess!" she said to me melodramatically
I hovered between caring and not caring, then chose not caring. (107)

Notley's "not caring" is much harsher than either O'Hara's or Mayer's, in that she explicitly extends it out to her readers. "I con-ceive of myself as disobeying my readership a lot. I began the new work denying [my readers'] existence," she says in "The Poetics of Disobedience," echoing Koestenbaum's comments about Stein, that "she wrote without an audience, and she wrote against the idea of an audience." As Notley's interest in mystical truth grows, her car-ing about "good writing" steadily decreases. As the lacuna of one section of *Disobedience* comically demonstrates, in a subtle slam on MFA programs everywhere:

Let's have a page of good writing here.

(Lack of interest)

_____ (82)

But the caring/not caring dichotomy, especially when it comes to matters of audience, is never simple—especially for female writers, or female avant-garde writers, for whom Mayer's "work yr ass off and don't ever get famous" may seem more business-as-usual than radical or inspirational. Notley explains the paradox as follows:

> If you are a woman, no one cares about you, who you are or what you think. You are a perfect observer, you are almost a voyeur. Unfortunately you are finally a part of it all, and at a certain age you are struck quite forcibly by what you have been denied: a voice in politics, for example; or a voice in the dominant literary conversation of your lifetime. Then you don't want to be anonymous anymore; you are older and you have done all this work, you want it published, you want your voice to be as important as a man's. (email interview, 4 February 2002)

Marjorie Perloff's point about O'Hara was that he refused to care "because he knew, all along, that we would indeed be looking." Notley has never felt such assurances. For this reason among others, she has been glad to have her last three books published by Penguin, a large trade publisher. There is a form of irony here: the more "Fuck You" and explicitly insulting to mainstream poetry-publishing and prize-culture her work becomes, the more it has been distributed, reviewed, and awarded prizes: *Mysteries* was a finalist for the Pulitzer Prize and the winner of the *Los Angeles Times* Book Prize in 1998; *Disobedience* won the Griffin Prize in 2002; in recent years Notley has also been awarded the Shelley Award from the Poetry Society of America and a fellowship from the Academy of American Poets. Perhaps there exists some grumpy avant-garde purist out there who would express disdain for such forms of attention, but given the general lack of remuneration and audience in the poetry world—not to mention Notley's substantial difference from the usual suspects in the field, and the undeniable ferocity of her recent work—such disdain really couldn't make much sense. Personally I look forward to seeing how Notley wields this well-earned attention, which I hope only grows in scale.

Once I asked Notley whether she had planned out the narrative arc of *The Descent of Alette* before she wrote it; in response she told me: "I never knew what was going to happen while I was writing the book. I was always surprised by what happened" (email interview, 29 October 2002). I suspect her audience will remain equally surprised by whatever comes next from such a restless, dedicated, and prolific career. Notley's "continuous involvement" with poetry imparts the distinct impression that writing a long poem is not just a literary adventure, but a way of living a life. Notley's investment in this practice has grown steadily; as she says in *Disobedience*, "I don't want out of this poem, / the way I often Want Out" (188). The image of Notley meditating alone in her closet may initially appear the inverse of O'Hara playing the typewriter in a room full of people, but in the end, the scenes may not be so dissimilar. Both remind us that making a poem can be a means of "living a second life in the midst of this one," as Notley has put it. The paradox of this "second life" is that however private, it can also move out to encompass and even shape the energy of the greater room, be it the room of the party, an era, or the culture at large. Notley has pushed hard at the transformative possibilities of this second life, and her body of work thus stands as a constant reminder that making poems can be "a large act, hugely real and involving," while "having piddly conversations with so-and-so about what poetry Ought to be doing, or what those guys over there think, is just, nothing" (Foster, 85).

5 WHEN WE'RE ALONE IN PUBLIC

THE METABOLIC WORK
OF EILEEN MYLES

Eileen Myles *by Robert Mapplethorpe, 1980. © Copyright The Robert Mapplethorpe Foundation. Courtesy Art + Commerce and Eileen Myles.*

OVER TWENTY YEARS AGO, Ted Berrigan called his friend and fellow poet Eileen Myles "the last of the New York School poets," and the label stuck. Unlike Notley, however, Myles has never really chafed against it. When asked in a 2000 interview if the appellation still resonated with her, Myles responded:

> It depends on who asks. Once I was introduced at a reading by someone whom I thought of as a Language poet, and when they described me as "New York School" I experienced it as a critique—like I was retro. But, yes, those were the writers (O'Hara, Ashbery, Koch, Guest) who woke me up, who gave me a sense of what an adventure being a poet could be. . . . Ultimately, though, "New York School" just means I learned to be a poet in New York. As an aesthetic it means putting yourself in the middle of a place and being excited and stunned by it, and trying to make sense of it in your work. (Richard, 25)

Myles here points out how the dimensions of a label are necessarily defined by a host of social contingencies: particular mentors, friendships, and other personal relations; specific aspects of a specific city; the contexts in which a term gets circulated—literally, who speaks it—and so on. Her ease with the label thus has much to do with her longstanding interest in the formation and power of aesthetic and social communities: "I move in groups," she explains. "My feeling for literature is communal" (Richard, 25). "The last of the New York School poets" is indeed a catchy phrase—not to mention a convenient frame for a final chapter—but what does it mean? Beyond the semantics of age or generational distinction (O'Hara was born in 1926; Berrigan, in 1934; Mayer and Notley, in 1945; Myles, in 1949), the phrase clearly places Myles within a certain lineage while also positing her as a liminal figure—a vector rooted in one particular cultural moment or milieu but shooting off into others. It's a useful image to keep in mind, I think, as we begin to consider how Myles's career has radically expanded the social and political capacities of O'Hara's "Personism."

For while the previous two chapters discuss the skewing that motherhood and female "dailiness" have provoked in the context of New York School poetry, Myles's poetic career represents a different trajectory: that of a lesbian whose work self-consciously and repeatedly dramatizes the disruptive appearance of the "female personal" in the predominately masculine "public sector." This path may initially seem a reiteration of feminism's "the personal is political" mantra, but a more sustained inquiry elucidates the substantial alteration and amplification of this equation that Myles has performed over the past three decades. And whereas chapter 2 focused on the importance of homosexuality and gender trouble in the works of Ashbery, Schuyler, and O'Hara, it is largely due to Myles's presence on the scene that the queerness of the New York School does not surreptitiously slip into signifying only male homosexuality.[1] Myles has audaciously championed the queerness of her predecessors and contemporaries, and labored tirelessly to record the "vivid and close-knit way of life" she has shared since the late 1970s "with a number of dykes and fags, mostly artists."[2] And while many critics interested in the New York School seem content to chart its lineage through the great but mostly straight cadre of writers such as Ted Berrigan, Charles North, Ron Padgett, David Shapiro, Tony Towle, Paul Violi, and others, Myles's interpretation summons a different, more anarchic roster—one that might also accommodate Kathy Acker, Dennis Cooper, Tim Dlugos, David Trinidad, and David Wojnarowicz, among others. ("Tim was part of the New York School," Myles writes in a review of Dlugos's work, before adding, "If Dennis [Cooper] agrees to be in it, too, then I totally accept the term" [*Mississippi*, 228].) Myles also consistently disallows the lethal breed of amnesia that ghosts the lesbian, especially the butch, body (whatever that might mean) by articulating (on the page) and actualizing (in performance) a poetry rooted in bodily presence, in the force and rhythm of her own particular body. "I think we all write our poems with our metabolism, our sexuality," she explains in "The Lesbian Poet." "For me a poem has always been an imagined body of a sort, getting that down in time" (124).

At first glance this latter image may seem to echo the poetic doctrine espoused by Robert Pinsky in his 1998 handbook *The Sounds of Poetry: A Brief Guide*: "The theory of this guide is that poetry is a vocal, which is to say bodily, art," Pinsky asserts. "The medium of poetry is a human body: a column of air inside the chest, shaped into signifying sounds in the larynx and the mouth" (8). But Myles's elaboration of a "metabolic" poetry—or a "proprioceptive" poetry, as she has termed it elsewhere ("proprioceptive" meaning "receiving of stimuli arising from within the organism" [*American Heritage Dictionary*, 994])—differs decidedly from Pinsky's theory.[3] In Pinsky's formulation, all of the body's various chemical processes and rhythms get narrowed down into "a column of air inside the chest." The energy that Pinsky and others have relentlessly focused on orality may aim to privilege the performative history of poetry that claims Homer as its source, but it can also effectively displace or sublimate messier, perhaps more voracious bodily processes, such as the anal, the digestive, the hormonal (including the menstrual, the menopausal, and so on), the orgasmic, and the cellular.[4] For while Pinsky is in some sense speaking literally—the enunciation of words aloud does necessitate the use of one's "column"—he is also speaking metaphorically, insofar as not all poetry is composed aloud or meant to be read aloud. Its relation to the body is more mysterious, protean, and unpredictable, as the roots of the word "metabolism" itself suggest: *meta* (change) + *ballein* (throw).

Indeed, in imagining the body as poetic source, Pinsky quickly slips into a telling metaphor: "Poetry is a centaur. That is, in prose, one aims an arrow at a target. In a poem, one does the same thing, while also riding a horse. The horse I take to be the human body" (8). This metaphor may make some sense in relation to, say, Plath's poem "Ariel," which famously offers a fierce and complicated take on mounting and riding this "horse" of poetry when the composer/rider is female, but it does not easily mesh with the body that concerns Myles. Compare Pinsky's centaur, for example, with the following passage from "The Lesbian Poet":

> My poem rumbles through it all, unbelievable, and as the month
> turns the poems get manic, crazy, weird, sullen and bloody, stay at
> home, the words I use narrate a female cycle, probably much more
> than a female orgasm. . . . It's my poetic dilemma, it seems. To
> include the body, the woman's as I see it, to approach this blood as
> part of the score. It should show up regularly in the culture's poems,
> this female conversation, because most of the poets who write bleed
> every month until they pass childbearing years. I'm waiting to watch
> the room change. (130)

This "female conversation" may sound like *écriture féminine*, but Myles's proprioceptive poetry has less to do with finding an essential mode of female expression than with scribing "an economy, a metabolism or energy flow" that is particularly hers. "If anything, my work is about being inside your body and taking your time and taking your space and telling it your own way," she says in an interview with Liz Galst in *The Boston Phoenix*, in reference to her book of autobiographical stories, *Chelsea Girls*. "And that's . . . important in terms of being a female and a lesbian—that you can take that time."

LIKE THE "VISUAL DIARY" created by Nan Goldin's photographs, a major facet of Myles's work has been its construction of an ongoing "poetic documentary" of her life—a documentary in which certain primal scenes recur and get transformed via performance and repetition. One of these scenes is a reading she gave at St. Mark's in 1977, in which she "came out as a poet and a dyke maybe all in one reading." As she explains in "The Lesbian Poet," "It wasn't that I wasn't a poet before that [reading], but I'm addressing some kind of surge, a moving forward that happens at some points in a poet's life, so I mean I was all there, body and soul, after that" (123–124). Myles moved from Boston to New York in 1974, and she describes her first few years in New York as follows: "I was basically a cute girl in her twenties wanting to be a poet that all the guys would then try to fuck. I mean that was just the lay of the land. And be advised not to be a feminist, you know. And so I just sort of caroused around, and I drank a lot, too" (Foster, 54). In the Richard interview, she elaborates further on this period:

> When I came to New York in the 70s, I didn't know I was a lesbian. I
> didn't want to come out. I was homophobic, or scared—I just didn't
> want to be a dyke. There wasn't a woman in that circle of poets, either,
> who could receive me and let me know I was heard. Alice Notley, who
> was married to Ted Berrigan, was there, and we were, and are, great
> friends, but she was a married woman and a mother and she was
> going to have a different life. . . . I made the model of what I needed
> there to be. I put lesbian content in the New York School poem
> because I wanted the poem to be there to receive me. (26)

Here Myles draws crucial distinctions between herself and Notley (and Mayer, though she doesn't mention her here). Yet Myles's wish that the New York School poem would "be there to receive her" echoes Notley's sentiment in her poem about "Joe's Jacket," in which she hopes that O'Hara's poem will fit her, too. (Myles also gestures toward the paradoxical reciprocity of this process: the poem is there to receive you, yet you have to create the poem so that it can receive you.) Notably, in both cases, the emphasis is on aesthetics, on style. The leap of faith, so to speak, that these women made in the seventies had more to do with finding and joining an aesthetic community than an explicitly feminist and/or political one. ("Everybody told me something different, so finally when I went to St. Mark's and met Paul [Violi] and was in his workshop, I mean I just decided to believe this guy," Myles explains, in reference to how she ended up getting "educated" in a New York School milieu [Foster, 54].) Myles's "lesbian content"—like Notley's voice of a so-called new wife and new mother—thus forms an intricate weave with the aesthetic impulses and experiments that preoccupied O'Hara, Schuyler, Ashbery and others throughout the fifties and sixties. And apart from Guest and the female painters, most of the local forerunners at that time were men. As Myles explains in "The Lesbian Poet," "When I teach workshops I've always brought in both men and women, poetic models, but actually I've got many more fathers. I was writing poems, like I said, before I came out and wanted to get ahead, to know what you had to know to be in the conversation. It was mostly men who were doing the talking" (126–127).

On the one hand, Myles's situation is familiar to almost every woman (and man) in almost every art form, as "having many more fathers" is the natural effect of a male-dominated canon. But her description deepens in resonance when placed in the context of a butch lesbian for whom masculine identification—and working-class affiliation—is paramount. (As Myles writes in "Bath, Maine," the opening piece of *Chelsea Girls*: "This is baseball hat and truck country. I loved it. The men were all men, and we were all lesbians, and everyone loved to get smashed" [12].) In terms reminiscent of Notley's aversion to Rich, Myles explains (in a piece called "My Intergeneration," in the *Village Voice*) that even though she came out in the late seventies, "Lesbian feminism left me feeling like I didn't cut the mustard, like I'd gone to the wrong non-Ivy League school and liked punk rock and amphetamines too much and Aphra Behn too little. Generally I hung out with the boys and often I was alone. With poetry." She explains further:

> When I did connect with a girl (I could drink with), we were at war with the lesbian culture around us. I remember throwing beer cans off the balcony at an Alive concert. They were these dykes in leisure suits playing fusion jazz to a roomful of women with dangly earrings.

"Ugh," we yelled up the street. . . . For dykes, generations are less
about age than attitude. Try standing with a clump of your lesbian
contemporaries. The dividing lines of race and class, shoes and musi-
cal taste, will predictably send us flying to our corners quicker than
you can say *butch/femme*. (75)

In "The Lesbian Poet," Myles returns to this insistence on the aesthetic as it relates to the political: "A lesbian is just an idea. An aesthetic one, perhaps," she says, offering another spin on the notion
of a true abstraction. In some ways this comment is an extension of
Judith Butler's declaration (from "Imitation and Gender Insubordination") that "it is always finally unclear what is meant by invoking
the lesbian-signifier" (309), but Myles's line is less interested in this
unclarity and more in offering up a manifesto of sexual and artistic
liberation, in which the "lesbian-signifier" (or "lesbian content")
means something very clear and powerful, but also remains inextricable from the vicissitudes of form and attitude.

The investigations that Butler, Sedgwick, and other theorists have
done into queer performativity are obviously relevant here, especially
in their shared insistence that sexuality always remains in excess of its
performance. Wayne Koestenbaum describes this phenomenon eloquently in his book *The Queen's Throat: Opera, Homosexuality, and
the Mystery of Desire*, and usefully links it up with the body:

Sexuality, whether homo or hetero, does not arrive only once, in that
moment of revelation and proclamation that we call "coming out."
Our body is always coming out. Every time is the first time. Every performance is a debut. Every arousal is a repetition of the first arousal.
Every time you speak, you are coming out. Every time air makes the
trip upstairs from lungs to larynx to mask, every time your body plays
that old transcendental number, you are coming out. You *are* the OUT
into which sexuality comes. Coming out is way of telling a coherent
story about one's sexuality, and it has worked political wonders, and it
is a morally and psychologically cleansing process. But coming out is
only one version of the vocalization underlying sexuality itself. (174)

Just as vocalization is but one aspect of the bodily, coming out is
but one version of vocalization, one means of expressing sexuality.
Myles's 1977 "coming out as a poet and a dyke all in one reading"
marks a beginning of a long and restless poetic journey, in which her

stream of writing becomes the "OUT" into which sexuality—and bodily rhythms by other names—endlessly come. Her poems often play with the ceaselessness, variability, and comedy of this performance, as in the following section of the poem "A Blue Jay" (from *Not Me*):

> . . . Let's
> say I'm
> clothed
> in Nature
> w/ an
> open ear.
> Any more
> riddles for
> the human
> race while
> I've got
> you here.
> There's
> a hollow
> in the
> trees. A
> bush I
> could crawl
> in and
> pee. The
> trees are
> my friends.
> Hello Tree.
> Can I come
> out to a
> tree. I know
> you'd hardly
> know it
> to look at
> me, but
> would you
> believe I'm
> a Lesbian. But
> Nature is
> no stage. (65–66)

The poem is typically fluid and forthright, punctuated by surprising turns and lascivious wit (I especially appreciate the part about peeing on a bush). With skinny lines like these, surprise is paramount: for example, one might not expect "pee" after "crawl / in and," but it brings sudden satisfaction (especially to the ear, as it picks up the "trees" from seven syllables before). Something stimulating can't happen at every line-break—there are too many—but Myles keeps the poem flickering by scoring the enjambment with occasionally startling pauses: "Hello Tree." Otherwise the eye follows the river of words down the page—for Myles, often down many pages—never knowing when the sentences, protracted by enjambment, are going to end. When they do, they often go out with a bang: "I know / you'd hardly / know it / to look at / me, but / would you / believe I'm / a Lesbian." The whole poem invokes Whitman, especially its earlier lines, "it's hard / to be / at peace. / This is / a song / to that." Indeed, if Whitman were writing a century later, I can easily imagine him wondering if he, too, could come out to a tree. In the end Myles decides that "Nature is / no stage." But it both is and isn't: the poem uses it as a stage, while it also has fun with the ways in which human terms of sexuality and identity fail to have substantive meaning in its context.

This musing recurs in a later poem, "Tulip," from *On My Way* (2001):

The incandescence
of poetry
is a result
of the
moment of
being alive

so to be
afraid
that the
body that
emitted
the light
was consciously
a lesbian
does not

have a
huge bearing
on the
work but
is it
a lesbian
moment
truly no
I don't
think so
I was
alone. (28–29)

The poem starts off with clarity and beauty, pools out into the disorienting syntax of the second stanza, then lands firmly with understated humor in the final lines: "is it / a lesbian / moment / truly no / I don't / think so / I was / alone." (Teresa de Lauretis's so-called catchphrase from "Toward a Theory of Lesbian Sexuality"– "It takes two women, not one, to make a lesbian"–feels toyed with here.) But as immediately gratifying as the poem is, its rhetorical questions linger. "Tulip" brings us back to asking, with Butler, what the "lesbian-signifier" can mean or fail to mean: if it means desire for another woman, what does it mean when one is alone? Not that one doesn't desire in solitude (some might argue that solitude renders desire most acute), but what about the state of non-desiring? Who are we, apart from the shifting field of our desires, especially if "to be a person is to be asking for something," as psychologist Adam Phillips has put it (*Terrors and Experts*, 3)? Though Notley's poetry does not revolve as explicitly around sexuality, her pursuit of "Basic I" is kindred in spirit. The issue, once again, is female transcendence, and the terms in which it can be experienced or thought. In "Tulip," Myles performs it by means of the image of a body emitting light, an image that recurs throughout her poetry, as in the final lines of "An Explanation" (from *School of Fish*): "I have nothing more / to offer you but stripes of light" (147). "Light" functions for Myles as "air" does for Guest: the lacunae and spaciousness of Guest's poems hope to offer the transcendent experience of "seeking air," while Myles's choppy, incandescent lines offer themselves up as "stripes of light"–pulsating waves which make their mark on space, but in an ephemeral form.

Sedgwick's thinking about queer performativity makes heavy use of the linguistic philosophy of J. L. Austin—specifically, Austin's notion of the "performative utterance." Sedgwick is interested in "the implications for gender and sexuality of a tradition of philosophical thought concerning certain utterances that do not merely describe, but actually perform the actions they name: '*J'accuse*'; 'Be it resolved . . .'; 'I thee wed'; 'I apologize'; 'I dare you.'" Sedgwick sees this site of linguistic performativity as particularly rich and provocative because it represents "a place to reflect on ways in which language really can be said to produce effects: effects of identity, enforcement, seduction, challenge" (*Tendencies*, 11). I can think of no other contemporary American poet who has wielded the power of the performative utterance as astutely and exhaustively as Myles. As I've already discussed at some length, New York School poetry in general (save Guest's, perhaps) is known for its investment in speech. But Myles's exploration of the possibilities of linguistic utterance is of a different nature, as it has been shaped by her involvement with performance art and political activism. Though performative utterances can clearly take place in private ("I'm sorry," "I forgive you"), they proliferate in the public sphere. You can fight forever about whether or not your lover is really sorry, or whether or not you really forgive your parents, but to argue that a minister didn't really marry you, or that a judge didn't really sentence you, etc., opens up a whole different can of worms. That is to say: it brings in the question of social power, and of authorization.

Myles's public disclosures have obvious ties to the confessional poetry of the 1950s—perhaps to Sexton most specifically, who was known for her theatrical readings—but the terms explored by Sedgwick and Butler, not to mention by feminist performance artists of the seventies and eighties such as Carolee Schneeman, Diamanda Galás, Kathy Acker, Sapphire, Holly Hughes, Karen Finley, and others strike me as a more fruitful context; in part this is because of their emphasis on queer sexuality, but also because they draw our attention away from the more intimate, partitioned confessional scene and into the realm of public proclamation and controversy, which reached a point of actual confrontation with the state during the NEA art-funding scandals of 1989–90. Like Stein, who famously set out to write "everybody's autobiography," or like Notley, who insists that "*someone*, at this point, must take in hand the task of being everyone, & no one, as the first poets did," Myles habitually asserts an ambitious, all-encompassing, public role for herself as poet. "I would like to replace the poet with the whole human race," she recently wrote in her contributor's note to *The Best American Poetry 2002* (210). In an essay entitled "How I Wrote Certain of My Poems," Myles explains that she wants to address her culture—"some new, larger [culture] out there which I suspect exists"—by "making work which violates the hermetic nature of my own museum—as a friendly gesture towards the people who might recognize me. I mean exhibitionistic work, really" (*Not Me*, 202).[5]

"Exhibitionism" is a particularly interesting concept when applied to or used by a woman, as its clinical meaning is "compulsive exposure of the sexual organs in public" (*AHD*, 475). Given that psychoanalytic schema typically figures the vagina as lack, the question of what, exactly, women can exhibit or "flash" necessarily invokes the spectacle of phallic appropriation. And it is precisely at this point of tension that Myles situates so much of her work, as to broadcast the "female personal in the public sector" is necessarily to impinge on male territory. In her interview with Foster, Myles explains the complexities of this impinging as follows:

> There's a privacy in public [that men have] that women do not
> have. . . . I'm really interested in public poetry and a private person's
> public nature. And I haven't found that a lot in women's work
> because it's not in women's lives. I mean it's kind of a fool's journey
> in a way, too, because I have the fate of a woman, that destiny. And
> so, much as I might like to move it over there, a lot of the reason my
> privacy will always be disturbed is that I am female. (60)

A "fool's journey" it may be, but Myles has used it to transform the boundaries of what kinds of claims on public space a female poet can make. "Although women are very visible as sexual beings, as social beings they are totally invisible, and as such must appear as little as possible, and always with some kind of excuse if they do so," Monique Wittig observes in *The Straight Mind*. "One only has to read interviews with outstanding women to hear them apologizing" (8). Myles's poems expressly avoid any such excuses or apologies. They also reject and transform any erasure of female anatomy and specificity by performing pussy-as-presence in both the private and public realms, as in her incantatory anthem that begins, "I always put my pussy / in the middle of trees," and goes on to assert: "I always put my lover's cunt / on the crest / of a wave / like a flag / that I can / pledge my / allegiance / to. This is my / country. Here, / when we're alone / in public" (*MP*, 48).

In an essay that discusses Baudelaire's reaction to the French "poetess" Marceline Desborde-Valmore, Barbara Johnson notes that Baudelaire celebrated Desbordes-Valmore for her "avoidance of monstrosity or masculinity"—that is, for a femininity so innate and natural that it represented "the total absence of pose." Myles's aesthetic steers in precisely the opposite direction. As she writes in her autobiographical novel *Cool for You*:

> There is hardly any femininity in my family. We are weak people, we are not striving people, we are not brave people, but we are posturing people, and we are masculine. We like the weapons of our time: the clothes, the belts, the boots, the hats, the lifted legs, leaning on cars. We like to look great. When we do, we know "I am." It's an adolescent kind of power—it reigns in the world of photographs, of moments triumphed over in a flash of appeal. (95)

As this passage suggests, Myles is the first to admit that the exhibitionist pose stems from a lack of power—a lack of power that has as much to do with class as gender. This idea becomes vivid elsewhere in *Cool for You*, when Myles describes the day when all the Harvard alums come back to town: "Everyone was so happy and sometimes they had a golden son with them, and even outside you could hear the goony Harvard Band marching around the Square and when you rode along Memorial Drive they would be out there sculling and you could see it was their river and you were entirely fucked. Slam" (10). Myles often talks about how her Catholic-school education worked together with her working-class background to drill into her the sense that she wasn't "something special." When she got to New York, she says she was consequently just "glad to be in the phone book" (Foster, 55). "There's a lot of class stuff in the internal voice that says, 'Don't think you're so special,'" she explains. "In some ways my whole art impulse derives from saying 'I know I'm not special'" (Richard, 29).

This impulse is complex. On the one hand, it has spurred Myles to a kind of self-mythologizing that stands in belligerent protest of this rebuke. On the other, it has led Myles to use this self-mythologizing to push beyond individual "specialness" and toward "replacing the poet with the whole human race" (another fool's journey, without a doubt). The title of the collection *Not Me* provides a condensed example of this paradox, as the phrase "not me" could be read as an intentionally unconvincing disavowal of the personal, or as the assertion of something patently true—that the collection is "not her," as representation is always incomplete, identity always in excess of its performance, and self always larger than language, no matter how "personal" the work. This paradox is also on display in Myles's many experiments with "mock-exaltation," as Durgin has put it: in "The Windsor Trail," she invents a "Lady Eileen"; in "Immanence," she aligns herself with God; in "The Poet," she is "the only saintly man in town"; in the opening poem of *School of Fish*, she is "The Troubadour"; elsewhere she casts herself as road warrior, shepherd, hunter, captain, and so on. These characterizations are not static dramatic personae, but rather momentary flashes of identification, mostly masculine, that glimmer throughout her work.

One of her best-known poems in this vein is "An American Poem," which cannily performs being "somebody" and "nobody" at the same time. It begins:

I was born in Boston in
1949. I never wanted
this fact to be known, in
fact I've spent the better
half of my adult life
trying to sweep my early
years under the carpet
and have a life that
was clearly just mine
and independent of
the historic fate of
my family. Can you
imagine what it was
like to be one of them,
to be built like them,
to talk like them
to have the benefits
of being born into such
a wealthy and powerful
American family. (13)

Autobiographical detail bleeds seamlessly into fictive conceit: Myles *was* born in Boston in 1949; it isn't until the line "a wealthy and powerful family," that one begins to catch on to the poem's ruse. The poem continues:

> I hopped
> on an Amtrak to New
> York in the early
> '70s and I guess
> you could say
> my hidden years
> began. I thought
> Well I'll be a poet.
> What could be more
> foolish and obscure.
> I became a lesbian.
> Every woman in my
> family looks like
> a dyke but it's really
> stepping off the flag
> when you become one.
> While holding this ignominious
> pose I have seen and
> I have learned and
> I am beginning to think
> there is no escaping
> history. A woman I
> am currently having
> an affair with said
> you know you look
> like a Kennedy. I felt
> the blood rising in my
> cheeks. People have
> always laughed at
> my Boston accent
> confusing "large" for
> "lodge," "party"
> for "potty." But
> when this unsuspecting
> woman invoked for

the first time my
family name
I knew the jig
was up. Yes, I am,
I am a Kennedy. (14–15)

The line "I am beginning to think / there is no escaping / history" takes on a particularly complex meaning here, in that the poem dramatizes a means of escape from her own personal history while it also fuses her story with the "historic fate" of the Kennedys, thus refusing to allow her "foolish and obscure" roots to be relegated to history's sidelines. As the poem goes on, its complexity thickens, as the speaker continues to posit herself as near-royalty slumming it as a poor poet and dyke, while she also *is* that poet and dyke, boldly asking her audience: "Am I the only / homosexual in this room / tonight. Am I the only / one whose friends have / died, are dying now." The oratorical grandiosity of the poem grows as it heads toward its final, climactic lines: "It is not normal for / me to be a Kennedy. / But I am no longer / ashamed, no longer / alone. I am not / alone tonight because / we are all Kennedys. / And I am your President" (17).

The term "mock-exaltation" begins to seem inaccurate in light of such brazenness, as one of the most compelling aspects of Myles's posturing is how it eventually becomes indistinguishable from exaltation itself. The performative utterance "I am your President" is technically "infelicitous," to use Austin's term, in that Myles lacks the authorization or social power to make herself the president. But as Butler makes clear in *Excitable Speech*, not only is it "clearly possible to speak with authority *without* being authorized to speak," but also it is precisely this kind of "insurrectionary speech" that often brings about social transformation (157). (For a nonverbal example of this phenomenon, Butler uses Rosa Parks: Parks had no authorization to hold her seat in the bus, but her assumption of the authority to do so sparked meaningful change.) Butler explains this idea further by means of comparison with Pierre Bourdieu:

> For Bourdieu, then, the distinction between performatives that work and those that fail has everything to do with the social power of the one who speaks: the one who is invested with the legitimate power makes language act; the one who is not invested may recite the same

formula, but produces no effect. The former is legitimate, and the latter, an imposter.

But is there a sure way of distinguishing between the imposter and the real authority? And are there moments in which the utterance forces a blurring between the two, where the utterance calls into question the established grounds of legitimacy, where the utterance, in fact, performatively produces a shift in the terms of the legitimacy as an *effect* of the utterance itself? (146–147)

Myles's performance in "An American Poem" sets out to blur the boundaries between "imposter" and "real authority," for while she is indeed a Kennedy imposter, the authority claimed by the poem ends up no sham. Further, this authority is more than poetical, and more than her own. "Shouldn't we all be Kennedys?" she asks her audience, before concluding triumphantly: "we are all Kennedys."

The opening of the short piece "Light Warrior" (in *Chelsea Girls*) makes related claims: "My name means Light Warrior when you bring it home to the present day through Latin and Gaelic. I am a significant person, maybe a saint, or larger than life. I hear that you judge a saint by her whole personality, not just her work. I'm beginning to see my work as my shadows, less and less necessary, done with less and less care" (35). And here we have yet another affirmation of "not caring," perhaps to be placed alongside Notley's "Let's have a page of good writing here . . . (Lack of interest)." "Light Warrior" appears, however, just stories away from "Popponesset," Myles's chilling four-page account of getting gang-raped at a party at a beach house in Cape Cod while nearly unconscious from drinking. "A bunch of good-looking suburban guys, 18 or 19, same as me, who all owned cars, trashed me for two reasons: I was drunk, they didn't know me," she writes. The morning after, she wakes up alone, sick and "painfully numb." She walks down to the beach, where she writes her name in the sand with her toe. "EILEEN MYLES. Yes, that's who I am. I rubbed it out with my foot" (190). The "larger than life" celebration of her name in "Light Warrior" cannot be disentangled from the name written in the sand in a solitary act of survival and protest. Myles's developing role as a "cult figure to generations of young, post-punk female writer-performers," as Holland Cotter put it in a 2001 profile of Myles in the *New York Times*, stems in part from this dialectic, which balances a Stein-like conviction of her own genius and significance with a startling—indeed shameless—exploration of her powerlessness and shame.

"I think the form of the novel gives dignity to my shame," she says in *Narrativity*, in reference to *Cool for You*. "Sometimes I'm just ashamed to block the sun." A poem from *Skies*, "Inauguration Day," which corresponds to the controversial inauguration of George W. Bush in 2001, brings this shame into the public sphere, and transforms it with defiance: "you cannot insult / Me," the poem concludes. "I hold this sense of awe" (204). The sense of awe is hers inalienably, so to speak—the speaker holds it, contains it, a priori. But she also has to hold onto it, grasp it, protect it from that which might insult it. The poem thus becomes the container which the poet holds out to the *bhav* as spectacle, offering, declaration, and potential agent of change.

"An American Poem" is but one of many of Myles's poems that rhetorically address a civic audience. Others, such as "To the Class of '92" (in *Maxfield Parrish*) take the form of actual addresses written for public occasions or ceremonies. These poems differ from other "publicly minded" poems (the kind you might read on the Op-Ed page of the *New York Times*, or hear recited at a funeral, inauguration, or other ceremony) in that Myles customarily engages the protocol of these platforms in order to violate it. As she tells the "class of '92":

> The time you spent
> here, 4 years goes very
> fast so perhaps what you'll
> be saying goodbye to when
> you leave here is slow
> time. (Long silence.) Wasn't
> that hell? Something in
> me gets de-railed mentally,
> it's always been so. I
> make most of my living
> as a public speaker, this
> is what I do & yet I
> freeze up like a deer
> in the light of your attention &
> like something that's bound
> to be killed by the swerve
> of your attention I've
> begun to relish it. Because
> it's so slow before you

die. Think of it this
way—you're dying now.
I just knew I'd say the
wrong thing. (113–114)

The poem goes on to tell its audience that it's too late to change the world, that "graduation day is / meaningless," "you don't believe in those gowns," and "I'd like my check." Throughout, Myles explores the strangeness and precariousness of being "in the light" of the audience's attention. Indeed, the condition that lights up the poem is the intimate reciprocity necessary for speech acts to occur, even, or especially, in public forums: "You have invited me / to speak today because I / love you." The poem sustains the promise of O'Hara's "Personism," in which O'Hara realizes "that if I wanted to I could use the telephone instead of writing the poem," but whereas O'Hara's occasional poems tend to correspond to more-intimate coterie events ("Poem Read at Joan Mitchell's," for example), Myles's often take on the largest, most formidable of cultural settings. "I've always thought a poet should think big, not small," she says (Richard, 26).

And in the United States, what could be bigger than the presidency? In a blurring of art and activism which Allen Ginsberg pioneered in the fifties and sixties, and which feminist and conceptual artists hammered away at throughout the seventies, eighties, and early nineties, in 1992 Myles ran as an "openly female" write-in candidate for president. In this context, the conceit of "An American Poem" collapses: the poem no longer just resembles or apes a presidential campaign; it became a part of one. By this point in her career, Myles had published several books of poems, including *The Irony of the Leash* (1978), *A Fresh Young Voice from the Plains* (1981), and *Sappho's Boat* (1982). She had also written several plays and two books of prose, *Bread and Water* (1987) and *1969* (1989); edited the poetry magazine *dodgems* (1977–79); served for two years (1984–86) as the director of the Poetry Project; and performed extensively. ("In the 80s I remember a friend telling me he thought I was 'bringing Personism to performance,'" [Richard, 26].) In 1990, she began touring a stage show called "Leaving New York." As the title suggests, around the time she turned forty she was feeling "fed up" and ready to leave New York altogether. While touring, she was constantly "thinking of where I was performing and who I was performing for. Just regarding the public space as a political one, thinking what would be political for this particular group of people" (Durgin). In the end, the experience brought her "to a whole new place with my art and my dealing with community." Instead of leaving the city, she had "one of those lightbulb experiences . . . I thought, I'm 40, I can run for president. I'm female, but I can run. I went down to the board of elections and looked into it and I found out the regulations for being a write-in candidate, so I did that for about a year and a half" (Durgin).

Myles's run for president wildly amplified the personal-is-political formula. She describes the campaign experience (in an online interview with Michelle Alb at Naropa) as follows:

> I toured 29 states, I fund-raised to continue the campaign. I was on MTV, *Interview* did a piece on me. If the point was to get attention, I could have gotten more. But I was sort of treating it like a performance artist doing duration, and my idea was, no matter what, I was going to run to the election. And I was going to run according to how I felt. Because a candidate never really tells you how they're feeling. And I thought I would be the candidate who did do that. My campaign was total disclosure, and I would endlessly disclose details about my life. It also enabled me to politicize personal poetry. Because it was all political, it was all personal. It was exhausting. It invaded every part of my life. You know, I'd go to a party, people would say, how's the campaign. I just could not get away from it. So I got a sense of how much, when you put something out there, it's really beyond your control. . . . Every public appearance I had, I would turn into a political opportunity. Every reading was a campaign opp, every performance, every panel. So I already had some [recognition] and it gave me more. Of course, interestingly, I did get more attention as a presidential candidate than I ever did as a poet. But the fact of the matter was, it was a poetic experience. (n.p.)

Her candidacy didn't just politicize personal poetry; it also revealed something about the poetics of politics. What made it "a poetic experience" was the revelation that "when you put something out there, it's really beyond your control." In politics as in literature, rhetorical effects always exceed intention; they cannot be fully governed. This is the scandal of the speaking body, that "speech is always in some ways out of our control" (see Butler, *Excitable*, 155). And the unpredictability of both poetry and politics designates them both as sites of potential transformation. That Myles wouldn't win the election was a foregone conclusion. But her candidacy was scandalous, not only in its spectacle of a broke, avant-garde, lesbian poet making a claim on phallic power, but also in her willingness to dedicate a period of her life to the production of unforeseeable effects.

NOT ALL OF MYLES's claims on public space have been as explicitly political as her civic addresses or presidential candidacy. Many of Myles's poems operate in the tradition of poet-as-*flâneur*, a tradition with its roots in nineteenth-century France, and refashioned in midcentury New York by O'Hara. But as the word alone makes clear, when a woman poet takes on the role of street-walker, the terms of the tradition immediately transmute. In 1949 (the year Myles was born), Plath famously wrote in her journal, "I want, I think, to be omniscient. . . . I think I would like to call myself, 'The girl who wanted to be God.'" A year or so later, Plath returned to this sentiment, but with a defeated spirit: "My consuming desire to mingle with road crews, sailors and soldiers, barroom regulars— to be part of a scene, anonymous, listening, recording—all is spoiled by the fact I am a girl, a female always in danger of assault and battery."[6] Plath's cocky lust for "omniscience"—along with her anger and depression at the limitations of her gender—give voice to how compelling and frustrating the fantasy of a powerful, roving female can be. And while the culture has transformed dramatically since Plath's time, the danger of assault and battery that Plath refers to— and, by extension, the general policing of the public activities of women by means of the threat of rape and a persistent blame- the-victim ideology—continue to affect women everywhere.[7] Thus, regardless of whether or not its political content is explicit, Myles's "street haunting" (as Woolf once elaborated in an essay by that name) or "street hunting" (as Myles herself puts it) represents yet another expansion of the public possibilities for the female poet.

The poem "Hot Night" (from *Not Me*) is a classic instance. It begins: "Hot night, wet night / you've seen me before. / When the streets are / drenched and shimmering / with themself, the / mangy souls that wan- / der & fascinate its / puddles, piles of trash. Imper- sonal / street is a lover / to me" (51). Continuing in a kind of rhap- sodic fever, the poem roams through the scabrous, trash-filled, shimmering East Village landscape on a hot, rainy evening in July.

"It could / be another city / but it's this / city where / I start / being alone / & alive bringing / my candles / in while / I go walking / in the rain," Myles writes, echoing Ashbery's claim that New York is "really an anti-place, an abstract climate" (Lehman, 26). As do O'Hara's lunch poems, or as does Apollinaire's great 1917 pedestrian poem "Zone," "Hot Night" creates the illusion of being written while actually walking. Myles explains the actual writing of the poem as follows: "I literally stepped out of my house that night, feeling a poem coming on . . . I've had this feeling before—of going out to get a poem like hunting . . . I felt '. . . erotic, oddly / magnetic . . .' like photographic paper. As I walked I was recording the details, I was the details, I was the poem." After the walk, she says she went directly to Yaffa (a café on St. Mark's Place) and wrote the poem down. "I haven't changed a thing," she says. "Naturally I left a big tip" (*Not Me*, 202, 201). The writing of the poem becomes analogous to developing a roll of film, after the shocks, as Walter Benjamin might put it, have registered in the poet's consciousness.

In an essay entitled "Walking in the City," Michel de Certeau describes what he calls "practicing space" in an urban milieu. He suggests that a walker moves through urban space not as its author, but rather as one "turned and returned according to anonymous law" (152). "[Walkers' bodies] follow the thicks and thins of an 'urban text' they write without being able to read it," he says (152). "Hot Night"—which is, if we take Myles's word for it, essentially a one-draft performance—collapses the metaphorical dimension of de Certeau's "urban text." The poem itself follows the thicks and thins, gets turned and returned, and feels driven by unknowable forces: "who's driving? God? / I don't believe in / God. New notebook / I'm scared. My / hand tries to fly / free, but it's my / life, not my / death." More recently Myles has testified to the mystery of this process as follows:

> I have a strong experience of dictation. I've always felt that writing the poem is listening. . . . I feel like I'm drawing. I'm paying attention to something, and some part of me someplace is doodling, but it's not a real place and the only thing that's really getting done is this nice kind of printing that I love. I'm always very into my materials, and I usually use a little notebook. The size of the notebook often dictates the size of the lines. I get these at a stationery store on Avenue A. Mostly I feel I'm experiencing a kind of tension release that feels curt and tough. (Richard, 28)

Here Myles explicitly links her "materials"—the small notebooks that hem in the line length of her poems—to her peripatetic habit. Though not all of her poems are skinny, the majority of them are—enough to incite Dennis Cooper to write in *Artforum*, "Myles basically talks shit in skinny columns and calls them poems."[8] (Cooper doesn't mean "talking shit" as an insult, as the rest of his review makes clear: "Thing is, hers is one of the savviest voices and most restless intellects in contemporary literature—honest, jokey, paranoid, sentimental, mean, lyrical, tough, you name it.") Myles has characterized her writing similarly: the back cover of *A Fresh Young Voice from the Plains*, for example, reads: "[Myles] describes her poems as 'cheap talk' and most critics agree." The New York School's love of "fast talk" here meets up once again with deflation: as with Mayer's "ugly meatloafs," the talk has now become cheap.

This vacillation between skinniness and fatness returns us to Myles's notion of a metabolic, or proprioceptive, poetry. In considering such, it's important to note that Myles has been a famous dieter, as was Schuyler before her.[9] *Cool for You* extensively chronicles her early experiences with binge eating and dieting: "I had never experimented with this kind of eating as much as you could. I was just out to smash something as hard as possible. . . . You know what it's like to eat seven candy bars, one after another" (62). The *Chelsea Girls* story "Merry Christmas, Dr. Beagle," which deals with buying speed from a "diet doctor" in Queens, puts a comic spin on this subject. "Watch the breads," the corrupt doctor tells her, "and I'm sure we'll see some *progress*." "What a cynical bastard I thought to myself, dropping the tinkling container of pills into my bag," Myles thinks, before stopping in the local pub to wash them down (31).

The relationship between the length of a poetic line and the management of one's desire for food can be profound. "One day sitting in [David Rattray's] house I told him when I was a dieting nineteen-year-old in Boston I would close my eyes and see the day as an empty page with horizontal stripes which represented meals," Myles says in "The Lesbian Poet." "David said that's interesting because the first writing occurred in Egypt, and the parchment represented the Nile and its first use was to indicate future shipments of food and how much. Rafts and rafts of the stuff. Poetry, not prose. It indicates desire. My poem is a menu" (124). Myles later acknowledges that this story about the Nile may not be historically precise, but she doesn't care. It provides a foundational image for a poetry whose primary task is to take inventory of transient goods and desires. The poem-as-menu image also places the action of desire at center stage: a menu aims to tempt a hungry audience. But this isn't to say that the poem speaks only to unquenchable yearning. Myles also hears in it the promise of satisfaction. As she writes in *Cool for You*, "These little marks tell us about the things that are coming down the river in the future. That we will be okay, that we will be fed" (192). In a letter to the editor that Myles recently sent to the *New York Times Book Review*, in response to a piece by Judith Shulevitz entitled "Sing Muse . . . Or Maybe Not," in which Shulevitz argues that recorded poetry is better than live poetry because one can always turn the former off, Myles further articulates her sense of the voracity, and of the potential satisfaction, of an audience's desires:

> The human need to hear *any* speech live, but particularly rhythmic speech, is unstoppable. Judith, people just like it. They really do. They like to sit communally and hear messages that aren't tinkered with by the government, or intended to sell a product, or gauged to spin some denatured piece of information that's already been stripped of its dangerous content. Poetry is and has been for a while where lots of citizens get the real and irregular news of how others around them think and feel. What's so discomforting about that? (n.p.)

The *Times* may have found something discomforting about her letter, as they did not publish it. So Myles published it herself as a pamphlet entitled *We, the Poets*, with the help of feminist publisher belladonna* books.

In "Walking in the City," de Certeau characterizes the process of "practicing space" in an urban setting as "being other and moving toward other" (180). A walking poem such as "Hot Night" inhabits both modes, in yet another instance of making a claim on being both "somebody" and "nobody." "Let me be lost / in the lonesome / place, the human / sea of no one," Myles writes, then states, "You know a / genius when you've / seen one, don't / you. I am one. / Take a good look, / you've seen me / before. Don't / turn back." The poem performs its alienation—its state of "being other"—while it also moves "toward other." *Let me be no one*, it pleads, alongside the equally potent imperative, *Recognize me as someone*. The British psychoanalyst D. W. Winnicott might hear in these lines evidence of his theory that artists of all kinds find themselves in an "urgent dilemma" which is characterized by the coexistence of two needs: "the urgent need to communicate and the still more urgent need not to be found" (Phillips, *Winnicott*, 151). This predicament is also, of course, a classic recipe for cruising. As the title "Hot Night" indicates, the speaker is out hunting for sex as well as a poem, and the poem concludes accordingly: "I need / whiskey sex / and I get / it."

The rote way of gendering the terms here would be to designate the "somebody" as the embodied, differentiated female, and the "nobody" as the anonymous, universal male subject. But in "Hot Night" and elsewhere, Myles creates a great deal of slippage between such distinctions, by creating a space in which an "undeniably female" speaker slips into being "nobody, this human, a man," and vice versa. As she concludes another "scribing" poem (this one from *On My Way*, and called, appropriately enough, "Scribner's"): "I do this. / Appear to / be a bum / in my hiking / boots & hairy / legs I'm no / longer a dyke / just a man" (58–59). In "The Lesbian Poet," Myles tells a related anecdote: "Last summer I was standing alone on a hill with my dog and a car as an amazing shower of meteorites *flash flash* had stained the sky orange. It was so sensational and I was utterly alone with my animal. I knew I was a man. It was utterly clear, there was no thing of woman at all. I was standing in nature alone, this guy. It was a terrifically human feeling. Alone. Completely full" (125).

Myles's work is rife with ambivalence about, if not downright loathing of, being a woman. "I used to pray to be a boy. I used to pray to God to make me be a boy. And I don't know if that was because I thought I was masculine or because I liked what masculine people got or that I wanted women," she explains to Foster (59). Indeed, one of the most powerful segments of *Cool for You*—the piece that tells the story of her getting her period, among other things—begins with the blunt declaration: "I hate being a woman" (87). A poem called "Misogyny" from Myles's first book, *The Irony of the Leash* (collected later in *Maxfield Parrish*), humorously extends the theme: "'My new tack will be to hate women,' / I uttered to Ann, / my voice quivering with discovery. / 'But, Eileen . . . you *are* a woman,' / my sister Ann uttered back, / the usual disdain creaking through the air. / 'That's the only hitch . . .' I slowly sighed // and another near adventure was bypassed" (214). Yet Myles consistently tethers these sentiments to an insistent focus on the rhythms, specificity, and attractions of the female body. "I like the smell and taste of women's bodies," she writes in *Chelsea Girls*. "Sometimes I'm sure that's what I'm living for" (80). Indeed, the aforementioned segment of *Cool for You* plows straight into hating being a woman, hating one's period, and comes out somewhere else:

> All that blood like some kind of sex with yourself. Is it clotty. Is it red, brown; does it look too bright. Don't you think better when you're bleeding, don't you want to stay home and smoke and read and write. Don't you feel tremendously sexy. Have you spent years hiding it, arming yourself against revelation, the stains and the bloody smell. Do you want to fuck. I remember my friend describing his face when he described eating the pussy of a bleeding woman. That he had red wings. (88–89)

Passages like the above practice a sort of alchemy—they venture into hatred and ambivalence and come out with desire, with all its wild markings. In doing so, they avoid a polar situation, and Myles's masculine and feminine identifications are nothing if not fluid. They are, in fact, almost as simultaneous as syntax will allow, as is evident in the following lines from her prose poem "The Poet": "we are the women we are the women I am full of holes because you are. I am the only saintly man in town" (*MP*, 110).

These shifting gender identifications are but part and parcel of Myles's exploration of "identity" at large. In fact, in the *Dictionary of Literary Biography*, Durgin cites as one of Myles's principal achievements her "thoroughly postmodern, if not somewhat confrontational, view to the problem of identity in twentieth-century American poetry." Identity is an enormous and amorphous topic, and Myles's poetic experiments with it are accordingly expansive. The word itself has two back-to-back, nearly opposite meanings: "the quality or condition of being the same as something else" (i.e., the collective identity that enables the formation of groups), and "the distinct personality of an individual regarded as a persisting entity" (i.e., the conglomerate of traits that forms a specific, recognizable individual [*AHD*, 639]). By creating a poetry that is simultaneously extravagantly communal and deeply personal, Myles thoroughly engages both models.[10] In "Tradition and the Individual Talent," Eliot famously says that poetry ought to be an escape from personality and emotions. Less famous, however, is his next line: "But, of course, only those who have personality and emotions know what it means to want to escape from those things" (43). In a weird echo of Eliot, Myles freely admits that she is "plagued with personal identity." But whereas Eliot advocates escape, Myles wants to venture into the heart of the storm, with all its attendant risks and shames. "The body always seems like the shame," she says. "The camera must cut away to the trees, the animal is telling too much" (*Narrativity*). But Myles's camera will not cut away to the trees. The animal will not stop talking.

The Antonin Artaud epigraph that begins *Cool for You*—"*Jamais real, toujours vrai*"—sheds more light on Myles's particular approach to this first-person, talking body. The epigraph recalls the line that prefaces *Roland Barthes by Roland Barthes*: "*It must all be considered as if spoken by a character in a novel.*"[11] Myles's stance is similar, but more Pop: she likens her "I" to a character in a comic strip—a comic strip in which the figure "Eileen Myles" is necessary to carry the action from frame to frame, speaking in word-bubbles. "It's just that, for me, the pictures are invisible—the poem is purely the balloons, and the balloons are infinite." In creating this character, however, Myles does not fall back on any self-protective platitudes that hope to wedge a safe distance between speaker and self.[12] And here we might recall the distinction Myles draws between her work and that of the first-generation New York School poets: "They would all assert that the poetry was not about them. It's about skimming the surface of the self. Using that facility to shape the poem. My dirty secret has always been that it's of course all about me" (*Narrativity*).[13] Not only is Myles unafraid of collapsing into the "dirty" realm of the overtly personal, but like Mayer, Ashbery, and Warhol, she is also unafraid of collapsing into boredom. "My vehicle, my cartoon, coincided with say, Warhol and the soup can, or *Interview* magazine, these really boring interviews with people saying, 'Um.' I thought, 'Wow, boring. Great!' Warhol's movies, people just talking—pouring all that detail into poetry" (Richard, 29).

In addition to Warhol's movies, another influence Myles cites is the Alfred Leslie film *The Last Clean Shirt* (1964), with subtitles by Frank O'Hara. *The Last Clean Shirt* consists of the same footage shown three times—once in silence, then twice with a different set of subtitles. The footage shows two people—a dark-skinned man and a white woman—getting into a convertible with a prominent clock on the dashboard, then driving in circles around Astor Place and the Bowery. Throughout, the woman talks excitedly to the man in an indecipherable blur (Finnish, I've heard) while he drives in silence. The first set of O'Hara's subtitles supposedly corresponds to the woman's speech; the second, to the silent man's thought. O'Hara's titles, like his poetry in general, range from the non sequitur to the hilarious to the philosophically profound. As in Leslie's more famous Beat movie *Pull My Daisy*, in which Kerouac's voiceover purports to correspond to what the characters are saying but quite obviously does not, much of the humor in *The Last Clean Shirt* stems from the suspected discrepancy between O'Hara's lines and what the woman is really saying, and then what the man is really thinking. O'Hara's subtitles are the word-bubbles which constitute the poem; the footage is the cartoon, the vehicle that makes it possible.

When it was originally screened, people booed *The Last Clean Shirt* because it was so boring. It's still boring, as it loops the same real-time footage for forty minutes. But the boredom coexists with tremendous excitements—the excitement of O'Hara's witty lines; the woman's excitement in verbalizing; the excitement of driving around in a big car in downtown New York City at midcentury; and, perhaps, the excitement of a dark-skinned man and a white woman driving together in 1964, appearing together in private and public simultaneously (i.e., in a car, but with the top down). As is often the case with "boring" art—as beautifully demonstrated in Warhol's *Screen Tests*—the action lies in how the boring can miraculously morph into the riveting and vice versa over time. Myles characterizes the tone and import of *The Last Clean Shirt* as follows:

> It was kind of like yippee! and kind of like sorrow, and it was profound and excited in the way O'Hara's voice just shifts and shifts and shifts and keeps taking in everything and letting it out. When I saw the movie I thought, "That's it." That is, in the most classic sense, who O'Hara was, even what the New York School was. The poet was like this open car in the middle of the century, at some peak moments just saying, "Yes!" and catching the shape—moving through it all in a very excited way. People who romanticize and imitate O'Hara's moment mistakenly think that abundance gets to be what it's about—that mid-century excess and heroism and triumph, which it isn't. (Richard, 28)

Later in this interview Myles connects the openness of this convertible and cultural moment with the metonymic quality of the New York School. For Myles, metonymy is "about proximity—an open universe, not a closed one. In O'Hara's movie, it's the car" (Richard,

28). Myles even sees the creation of the character "Eileen Myles" as a metonymic move, because, as she says, "instead of inventing some symbolic name for my narrator, I use a real piece of me."

Myles thinks of metonymy as a "filmmaker's term," and her embrace of it corresponds to her desire to move away from the "literariness" of poetry. "I experience writing poems as the chance to make a little movie," she says (*The Best American Poetry 2002*, 210). Her interest in meshing filmic devices with poetic tropes recalls the kinship that the first-generation New York School poets felt with Abstract Expressionist art. As Schuyler once said to Myles, "I think anything that's all poetry is pretty boring, don't you babe?" (Richard, 28). Myles regularly posits her speaker as a camera and the poem itself as a snapshot or collection of snapshots, complete with recurring "clicks": "used magazines, / poetry books on a blanket, click" ("Hot Night," *Not Me*); "I'm not a fool (click)" ("My Light," *Skies*); "this is a relationship / click / this is a relationship" ("Scribner's," *On My Way*). This photography-poetry parallel saturates the collection *Skies*, as exemplified in the poem "Where's ya camera," which opens: "That's so beautiful // framed by the wood stain / the sky stained palest orange / for only one moment // I must be precise / the tree is pure silhouette / pure black" (139). The poet's job here is to turn the camera outward to the world and start shooting.

In describing what she sees, Myles often uses extremely plain language, and lets the principal artifice lie in the art of juxtaposition. Juxtaposition as a structuring principle was plumbed throughout the twentieth century in the development of collage and montage aesthetics; Myles's contribution is an unprecious, increasingly abstract minimalism, propelled by a politicized nerve and relentlessly in pursuit of beauty, in all its simplicity and strangeness. As its title suggests, the poem "Writing" (from *Skies*) could be taken as a sort of manifesto for this technique:

I can
connect

any two
things

that's
god

teeny piece
of bandaid

little folded
piece
of bandaid

I ran
to the
bathroom

to see
my face

sometimes
I don't
want to

see my
face in

the mirror

sometimes
I can't
bear
my thoughts

sometimes
I can't
do anything

but that's
okay

bandaid
book
god

that's
right (80–81)

The nerve appears right from the start, as the female poet feels, or flexes, her power—indeed, her godlike power—to "connect any two things." But just after proclaiming this power, a trip to the bathroom derails it. The shame of the body—here, of the face and the thoughts it reflects—is never far behind: "sometimes / I don't / want to / see my / face in // the mirror. // sometimes / I can't / bear / my thoughts." The poet talks herself away from this shame-spasm by remembering, or by performing, her poetic powers: "bandaid / book / god." The concluding remark, "that's / right," is tonally multivalent: it sounds reassuring and self-confident but also vaguely panicked, like an internalized parent or teacher trying to calm the speaker down.

The movement of the poem—its swing from the power and pleasure of writing to an intense flash of self-contempt then back to power and pleasure—makes palpable the intimate relation that can exist between speech-making (particularly logorrheic speech, though not only that) and shame. Throughout this study I have noted how all kinds of "fast talk" can bring deep and voluptuous pleasures. But as Silvan Tomkins has made clear, whenever one experiences a positive affect, such as interest, excitement, desire, or enjoyment, shame is almost always nearby, ready to jump in to reduce or inhibit the positive feeling. Sedgwick and Adam Frank explain this relationship succinctly in the introduction to their Tomkins reader, *Shame and Its Sisters*: "Without positive affect, there can be no shame: only a scene that offers you enjoyment or engages your interest can make you blush" (22). Thus the more deeply one invests in the pleasure of "fast talk"—the woman babbling excitedly in the front seat of the convertible, O'Hara writing not one but two sets of subtitles—the more intense the accompanying shame may be. "The pluralism of excitement and enjoyment is without limit," Tomkins writes, "and hence shame, too, knows no bounds" (150).

For a writer, the stakes of this boundless excitement and boundless shame run especially high, as shame threatens to curtail speech. But even this curtailment need not shut the writer down entirely. "Shame is both an interruption and a further impediment to communication, which is itself communicated," Tomkins observes (135), and in a sense Myles's prolific career relies on the latter part of this cycle. ("I find self-hate extremely motivating," she writes in an early poem from *Sappho's Boat* [MP, 142].) Often Myles places herself in the very center of shame's sickening swirl and charts the action from its inside, as in this description of PMS in *Cool for You*:

> The whole world becomes my enemy. You start to go crazy. I know I do. I cry for myself. All alone. A life ruined. Tragic mistakes, things I repeat again and again in my head, trying to get right. Sometimes I can taste the thought of the thing I should have said, should have done. I'm so ashamed of myself. Bragging, raging, remaining quiet. Everyone I talk to has that edge in their voice. They pity me. I'm over. You can see it in my eyes. And you must leave me forever. I can never forget what you've done. I didn't deserve this. I don't love you anymore. You had my body. I was completely open to you. It's taken me years to get this way. No one could touch me. They couldn't get through. I gave you such a gift. My cunt. And now we're through. And then I bleed. (89)

The blood breaks the spell, but for better or worse, the cycle will continue. In fact, this passage itself recycles sentiments expressed over a decade earlier in the poem "Exploding the Spring Mystique." "I go home to my lover, who's of course / in her early 20s / A Younger Poet. There's a note on my pillow / *Sorry, Honey, you peaked.* / Arrrgh! I shriek at the heavens. . . . I collapse on my bed, a sexual and artistic homicide. / Though still breathing, and it is Spring" (*MP*, 144).

As anyone who has lain awake at night replaying a botched scene over and over again well knows, repetition is one of shame's closest allies. "Once shame has been activated, the original excitement or joy may be increased again and inhibit the shame or the shame may further inhibit and reduce excitement or joy," Tomkins explains (135). Unafraid of repeating herself ("I know I've told you this before but I'm lonely tonight and it's raining out," she says on page 1 of *Cool for You*), Myles retells certain shameful stories throughout her poetry and prose. The effect is somewhat similar to the looping reels of *The Last Clean Shirt*—it may be the same story, but the subtitles, or the word-bubbles, keep shifting, ever expanding the dimensions of self and memory. Some of her toughest stories revolve around her father, an alcoholic who died in front of Myles when she was eleven. In "The Kid," a story from *Chelsea Girls*, Myles relays a brief but astonishingly painful anecdote: Her father is lying sick with one of his "awful headaches," and he makes a gesture to her—two fingers to his lips. Thinking he wants a kiss, Myles kneels down and kisses him, only to have him growl: "No, God damn it, a cigarette." Desire is a tremendously exciting and vital force, but when desires are misunderstood, when they do not match up, when they are rejected, ignored, or ridiculed, the result can be a stunning shame. "I know you got angry because of your headache, Dad," Myles writes to the dead man, years after the fact, "but I felt like such an asshole" (25).

"The Kid" goes on to tell the story of his death, a scene Myles revisits again at the close of *Cool for You*. In both cases, Myles's narrative contends with a staggeringly complex happenstance: when her father died, Myles was in the room with him, writing "*I will not talk in the corridors*" five hundred times—a punishment which had been given to her by a nun at school. The end of *Cool for You* describes the scene in detail:

> Around the two hundredth repetition of *I will not talk* I could see all the "wills" crookedly lining up and the talk, talk, talk, talk, talk with all the messy *k*'s. I stopped for a moment. I was trying to decide if a public school standing I, a big capital letter, was easier than the fat loopy I of Ignatius Loyola which we had been taught. . . . Yes. It would definitely go smoother and look better once my hand got crampy . . . and then it began. My father's blue notes. Sometimes I wake up in the middle of the night and my breathing is short and I fling myself up to save me. I look around and the thing that frightens me in that wakening moment is that I am dying and I am alone. It would be the worst thing in the world to leave your life that way, and I suppose this fear is printed on my breath, breaths can suddenly go false and shallow and the bowl of you can be perched, still, and then shatter from everything that doesn't return—air, life. I took notes. I heard my father die. I saw him die, but it was the sound. Believe me. Words are empty. It's the squawking of the animal, the wheezing, the desperate wind of a life rattling through the body, I heard him, he was not alone. This man who tried to hear me. I became possible. Now the message is complete.

> I am not alone, I wrote. Words are nothing. The empty repetition of language, that holds me like a friend, a pattern, a net. I will not talk, I will not talk, I will not talk, my rattle, sash. I must not die alone. I heard his blue notes as he slipped away. I yelled, Mom. (194–195)

It's difficult to do justice to this section of the book, partly because of its brutal emotional impact, and partly because there are simply so many elements of the story that compete for attention. Like most pivotal moments in a life, its import necessarily changes with time and representation. Myles's written vow is itself paradoxical, for while its content blunts her verbal expression, its form affirms that she will write—that she *must* write—and voluminously. The punishment thus intended to make her ashamed of her inappropriate speech ends up setting the stage for her to "become possible." Further, she "becomes possible" via witnessing the death of another—and not just any other, but her father. His death spurs her to speech—indeed, to a yell: "Mom." Needless to say, this perceived trade-off—a father dies, a daughter speaks (and calls out "Mom")—is an incredibly vexed site for a girl, especially one who will become an outspoken feminist and lesbian writer and performer.

Myles's dying father—with his squawking, his wheezing, his "desperate wind of a life rattling through the body"—also stands in marked contrast to Pinsky's heroic poet-orator, who uses his "column of air," then his larynx and mouth, to shape breath into the signifying "sounds of poetry." Here the father fails to make words, he fails to shape breath, eventually he fails to breathe. The animal dies, its inarticulate death rattle the underbelly of poetic expression.[14] The "blue notes" are still the poetry of a metabolism, but of a metabolism shutting down. Yet Myles's "coming to writing" isn't just the story of a daughter supplanting a father with her own breath and words. Hearing him die, not letting him die alone (even if by revisiting his death in print years later) is what "completes the message." Words may be nothing, but the squawking of the animal counts, along with our capacity to bear witness to each other's sounds, or to turn away from them in anguish, disgust, or indifference.[15]

Myles's telling of her father's death also underscores her sense that writing is "just making a mark. It's your mortality, your need to exist. It is probably totally linked to feeling endangered" (Richard, 29). Myles reiterates this idea in her *New York Times* profile: "There was something about my particular life—as a female, as a person prone to drug and alcohol abuse, as a lesbian—that I sensed was endangered. I had a feeling nobody would know what it was like if I didn't tell it." Her working-class background clearly contributes to this feeling, and Myles's metabolic poetry often meditates on the various links between one's class, one's speech, and one's body. "You know so much about people from the second they open their mouths," she explains. "Right away you might know you want to keep them out" (Cotter). Her most explicit meditation on the subject to date is the short essay "The End of New England" (from *On My Way*) which discusses speech patterns of the white working class in Massachusetts. Myles begins the essay by exposing the assumption—an assumption written "up there on the wall where all the secret thoughts of our culture are written in invisible ink"—that "people who work with their bodies, I don't mean artists, but people who lift things, people who say move the huge sculpture from there to there, I'm talking about the working class, that these people are stupid. Those people are dumb. They speak in short hand these people, they say: hey behind you. They say, on your left" (62). Though Myles can be brilliant at articulating the economy, rhythm, and phonetics of language from this environment, her main concern isn't nailing down any one particular dialect. Instead her curiosity about speech forms of all kinds draws her into wide, speculative circles. "The End of New England," for example, touches on the speech-sounds of a sarcastic parrot, a Russian woman named Alla, an Irish immigrant wailing over the dead, John Cage's silences, a lecture by Avital Ronell, along with much else.

The point is the wild movement between all these forms of speech, and, by extension, forms of class identity, that we consciously or unconsciously hear and perform on a daily basis:

Those of us who write about it—class, and/or utilize the dialects that link one class with another . . . are *typically* moving between one language and another, for instance—shuttling between the literary language which is written and more affiliated with the middle class and up, and the working and lower classes whose story is generally spoken: it's a language of pleasure, adjustment and use. By its very nature it's a language of repetition, shorthand, working class speech is incomplete. *Heads up!* Whatcha gonna do means something vastly different from What are you going to do? The first is a shrug, expects no answer except its own echo in a culture that knows exactly what it means. What are you going to do is a guidance counselor, a human being demanding a reply from another, not a human looking at another human looking at a machine, the job, or the bigger machine, which is life. (64)

Myles sharpens our ability to discern and name the distinction between "whatcha gonna do" and "what are you going to do," but the broader point is the revelation of the extent to which class identity can be as ambiguous and fluctuating as any other category of identity. "Frankly I don't know what class I am today," she says. "I can tell endlessly all about my family and how much money we had and education and what were the things inside our home. But class I think is utterly not about content" (66). What class may ultimately be about—at least in this context—is sound. Just as the "blue notes" of her dying father emptied words of their meaning, class's content—"how much money we had and education and what were the things inside our home"—begins to fade as its timbre takes center stage.[16] "The End of New England" concludes:

> my mother that wonderful secretary the queen of language tried very hard to get us to speak correctly so that we would fit into America and advance but my neighbors spoke pretty poorly or I loved the way they spoke "bare naked" taping words together, really making the point, *hiney*, a million ways to be dirty and there were eight of them so you heard it again and again, I guess you call it an idiolect. My sister said "nakin" she adamantly dropped the p, I miss her, I miss my family, it was another way to say us. Nakin. (69)

Standing alone as a final sentence, "Nakin" expresses a love which is somehow both ambivalent and pure, its two syllables sounding out lament, tribute, defiance, and, perhaps above all, reclamation.

Reclamation is a recurrent and far-reaching gesture in Myles's work, as the following excerpt from her interview with Richard suggests:

> FR: So how do you address yourself to a contemporary avant-garde?
> EM: I like the term. It's a little pedantic, but if I'm not that, what am I? "Experimental" has a much more tentative sound to me than "avant-garde." I always think of Bob Perelman saying that "experimental" sounded to him like you have some test tubes and a white lab coat and you might just blow up the science building. Bernadette Mayer always liked the word and used it.
> FR: "Avant-garde" has that military connotation. You *meant* to blow up the science building.

EM: Yeah. You had to! It's like "queer." It's taking on a term of contempt and saying, "No, I'm proud to be avant-garde." I might feel the same way about the name "New York School." (27)

Myles is not willing to cede any of these terms in the way that Notley is, for example, when Notley says, "I just go by whatever anyone else says about the New York School. Really. They can have it." Myles has too much riding on the power of the performative utterance—and on the role she has played in creating possibilities for it in poetry—to excuse herself from the conversation. For Myles knows that there exist no objective criteria for what constitutes a "real" avant-garde and what doesn't; she knows that imagining or articulating the possibilities of a movement, be it artistic or political, often goes a long way toward consolidating one.[17]

When Myles came to New York in the seventies and "put the lesbian content in the New York School poem because [she] wanted the poem to be there to receive [her]," she didn't know who or what would be there to receive her vision. But as she explains in "My Intergeneration" (here in reference to Sister Spit, the all-girl spoken-word group from San Francisco with whom Myles toured nationally in the mid-nineties and again in 2007): "What was so great about meeting this bunch of punky girls twenty years later was that I was received. But I was received *later*. It was like I had been talking to an imaginary tribe that then appeared, and that weirdly I even invented. Because when they saw my work they thought, 'Oh, I can do this.' I sort of created my own audience." She explains further:

> There's a teeming society of women who identify the postpunk third
> wave of feminism as the beat we're listening to, because unlike the
> taboo-laden feminism of my youth, the new lesbian mise-en-scène is
> a fierce, wildly infectious, and inclusive cultural force. It's a dyke
> world where straight girls can come too, and maybe even men. Who
> needs separatism if you're the boss? . . . Lots of the Sister Spit girls
> are working-class like me, and to shoot our wry and explosive wad of
> lyric culture here on a Cambridge stage was the sweetest success. I
> have never been so proud in my life, standing about a block away
> from where my mother was born, being a member at last of a
> utopian cadre of female outlaw optimists, teeming butch/femme tal-
> ent, total tattoos and fearlessness, gaudiness, booziness, and flaunting

a complex sexuality that would embarrass anyone's mother. . . . I was 46 on that tour. I'm 50 now. I just had to wait to be young. ("My Intergeneration," 75)

The word "girl" is pivotal here, as it indicates an abiding care for the next generation, and another important site of reclamation. "There's this huge girls' art movement going on, straight girls and gay girls together," Myles explains to the *Times*. "The energy has been building for years. It reminds me of the explosion of rock n' roll in the '60s."[18] In her *Index* review of *Cool for You*, Laurie Weeks eloquently summarizes the stakes of Myles's Bildungsroman as follows: "I don't know if anyone's ever so utterly captured the weirdness of being a girl, and by extension, the weirdness of being." On the one hand, Weeks is simply making a critical observation; on the other, she is making a revolutionary claim—one that serves the same purpose as the female Abstract Expressionists' fight for a "feminine abstract," the male New York School poets' embrace of girliness, Mayer's attention to the speech of her daughters, and Notley's "girl theory" of poets. Weeks is here claiming girlhood—in all its weirdness, pleasure, danger, agony, ferocity, lasciviousness, and fantasy— as a rich and fundamental site of human experience.

Myles's teaching has further extended her contribution to this movement. In addition to her many stints at a variety of colleges and institutions, throughout the nineties Myles also regularly organized and led informal, unaffiliated writing workshops throughout New York City, usually taught out of an apartment or loft and advertised via word of mouth and flyers. These workshops—several of which I participated in—constructed a loose community of people (mostly women, but not all) who were combining experimental writing practices with personal and political convictions. These workshops were not populated solely by poets, but rather by artists of all kinds, and provided a place for a younger generation of women, often newly arrived in the city, to meet and learn from slightly or significantly older artists who had already been working in New York for some time.[19] Such an environment provided the grounds for a casual form of *affidamento*, a term Italian feminists use to describe "a relationship of trust between two women, in which the younger asks the elder to help her obtain something she desires," as Myles puts it in "The Lesbian Poet" (130).[20] Certainly the time I spent in these workshops taught me, and continues to teach me, in retrospect, a tremendous amount about poetry, *affida-mento*, and the power and potential of artistic communities that exist apart from any institution.

In a review of *Skies* in the *Village Voice*, Cathy Hong wrote that Myles has an "anarchic post-feminist energy that has inspired legions of baby dykes to vent in front of the mic" (53). I'm pretty sure Hong means this as a compliment, but I want to resist any shadow of distaste for these "venting baby dykes," even if it's just a natural side effect of journalistic punch. It's easy to get blasé about social change, and harder to remember that "baby dykes" making a claim on public speech—what Myles describes as "a utopian cadre of female outlaw optimists, teeming butch/femme talent, total tattoos and fearlessness, gaudiness, booziness, and flaunting a complex sexuality that would embarrass anyone's mother"—would have been unthinkable just a short time ago, as would high schools and community centers specifically designed for gay, lesbian, transgender, or transsexual youth. Likewise, when faced with a flood of open mikes and poetry slams, it's understandable that some might feel annoyed by the "venting" of poetic speech. In the hours and hours I've personally spent hosting open-mike nights at the Poetry Project at St. Mark's Church, I fell prey to this annoyance at times myself. But Myles's career reminds us of a different path—one that continually embraces the flood, with all its irritants, amusements, boredoms, and provocations. "The pleasure of meeting all this wealth of live speech simply requires a fearless listener," Myles says in her response to Judith Shulevitz. "It invites some kind of aesthetic citizenry. Who will take the bumps as they go" (*We, the Poets*, 4).

In her *Times* piece, Shulevitz also expresses her irritation with the phenomenon of "poetry voice"—the monotonous, plodding iambic measure in which many poets inexplicably read their work aloud. Myles has this to say in response: "Poetry is like jazz, in that you go to watch it happen. The more it's predictable the more you do get 'poetry voice,' as Judith describes it. It's a poet putting a predictable rhythm on unpredictable speech. . . . It's something in between that you're hearing, Judith, it's aesthetic failure. It happens. When you hear poetry voice you're hearing the poet's fear, and I agree with you, Judith, but, ugh, *move on*" (5). *Ugh, move on* may be one of the New York School's most abiding messages. In the face of aesthetic failure, it shrugs. "It happens." Instead of fixating on obstacles, it advocates "putting yourself in the middle of a place and being excited and stunned by it." In the face of thwarted desire or crippling shame, it says, *Get back in the convertible and start looking around. Feel free to babble to your copilot. Don't be afraid of speech, be it your own or that of others.* To the poem on the page, it says *Keep moving,* but unlike Olson's demand that "one perception must must must MOVE, INSTANTER, ON ANOTHER!" (Allen, 388), it isn't bossy. Instead it counsels, *It's OK to move in a circle, to drive around the block, to cruise. It's OK just to chart what's coming down the river.* And, as Myles crucially adds in "The Poet": *Don't be afraid to be feminine* (*MP*, 110).

It would have been possible to write a book that studiously repudiated the matrix of terms that Myles has worked to reclaim—"queer," "avant-garde," "girls," "the New York School," and so on. Instead I've taken my cue from her tenacity, and tried to consider them together at the point of tension that each deserves. Like "lesbian," "women," "feminism," or "poetry" itself, what each term signifies will necessarily remain subject to endless debate and expansion, while also retaining undeniable power. The best of the New York School, as I choose to understand it, feeds on this play and perversity. "Poetry is complexity—seeing the world in the terms it's arriving in," Myles insists (Richard, 25), and I can think of no better journey. As Myles concludes one of the poems from *Not Me* that first inspired me to come along: "I / wink. I / take the ride" (72).

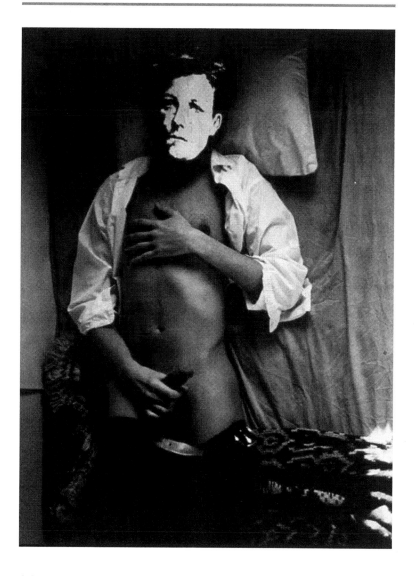

AFTERWORD

Arthur Rimbaud in New York 1978–79 (masturbating), *gelatin silver print by David Wojnarowicz. Courtesy of the estate of David Wojnarowicz and P.P.O.W. Gallery, New York.*

Tʜᴇ ᴡʀɪᴛɪɴɢ ᴏғ ᴛʜɪs ʙᴏᴏᴋ—which was, for the most part, a joyous adventure—was also bracketed by violence. I began it in the fall of 2001, right after the terrorist attacks that destroyed the World Trade Center, and finished it in the spring of 2003, in the middle of the "shock-and-awe" phase of the war on Iraq—a war which, as I write today, has no end in sight. Writing from New York City within this window, I often found the commonplace that Abstract Expressionism marked the moment at which New York overtook Paris as "the art capital of the world" (as dramatized in the title of Serge Guilbaut's book, *How New York Stole the Idea of Modern Art: Abstract Expressionism, Freedom, and the Cold War*), along with the fact that this "takeover" was part and parcel of the postwar rise of the United States as a military and economic superpower, not so easy to celebrate. In an email conversation with Notley in early 2002, she asked me: "Somehow people don't connect the New York in the New York School with the city itself, why is that?" (4 February 2002). Originally I thought I might make more of this connection, and pay some kind of tribute to the teeming specificity of New York along the lines of what Walter Benjamin once did for Paris. I hope I have gestured in that direction, but, truth be told, writing about the excitements of the New York School and New York City itself while trying to keep the smell of the dead out of my apartment often felt quite strange, not to mention immeasurably sad. Likewise, when placed alongside the destruction of cities such as Baghdad and Fallujah, New York City's happy brag of being "the greatest city in the world" at times struck me as not only provincial but also potentially lethal, when made to work in tandem with the presumption that American cities and lives are the ones that matter most.

Under these circumstances, the conclusion Schor comes to in her meditation on the feminine and the detail began to take on particular poignancy and urgency for me (especially given Schor's own untimely and sudden death in December 2001). Schor writes:

> Despite the extensive and highly sophisticated work carried out in recent years by feminist critics committed to uncovering the specificities of women's artistic productions, there exists no reliable body of evidence to show that women's art is either more or less particularistic than men's. Indeed, further investigation of this question may lead us to formulate a surprising hypothesis, namely that feminine

specificity lies in the direction of a specifically feminine form of idealism, one that seeks not to transcend the sticky feminine world of
prosaic details, but rather the deadly asperities of male violence and
destruction. (97)

In reading, thinking, and writing about women associated with the
New York School, I have tried to avoid looking for or claiming any
"specificities of their artistic productions." Instead I have tried to
enact a certain kind of feminist reception—one which DuPlessis has
described as "a reading strategy that puts no limits on the nature of
the work, is agnostic as to whether it conforms to this or that version
of womanhood, nor even cares whether the writer can be assimilated
to (available, contemporaneous, consistent, or currently approved)
feminist positions" (*Scene*, 189). Such a strategy doesn't look for the
return of the repressed as much as it aims to pay close attention to
art made by women. As Louise Bourgeois once said (in terms that
even Mitchell might have found palatable): "My feminism expresses
itself in an intense interest in what women do" (*Theories*, 40).

But I must admit, Schor's "surprising hypothesis"—that is, her
sense of a "specifically feminine form of idealism"—only gained in
force as I went along. The relationship of women to war is an
immensely complicated one, and not my primary subject here.[1] But
it's worth noting that recent works by Mayer, Notley, and Myles all
make powerful, outraged protests against "the deadly asperities of
male violence and destruction." Notley has devoted herself to the
subject at least since the long poem "White Phosphorous." Like
Simone Weil before her, she has been thinking and writing about
bodily suffering, war, and the *Iliad* for some time now. In the conclusion of her experimental essay "Homer and Postmodern War," Notley unites her sense of the poet's duty with antiwar defiance: "The
poet's job is to unsay Fate . . . / I refuse to live in the ancient world."
And Notley's most recent epic—*Alma, or the Dead Women*, which
appeared just as this book was going to print in 2006—directly
addresses the events of 9/11 and the Iraq War, and is arguably her
most political book to date.[2] Myles is the recent author of a surreal,
caustic libretto for *Hell*, a multimedia opera with a score by Michael
Webster that has been touring the U.S. and Mexico since the 2004
presidential election season. *Hell* involves "a presidential character"
who rules "what used to be called Hell and is now called Constant";
the final line of the opera is: "Get ready for World War III"—to which

the chorus "ALL" responds: "Ow!" And Mayer's most recent collection, *Scarlet Tanager* (2005), contains this wild excoriation, entitled "To a Politician," which uses the ancient form of the insult poem to register fury at our current state of affairs:

Your penis is homeless

You are covered with as many warts as the lies you've told

Your syphilitic mouth sucks the slugs from the irradiated cocks of your cohorts

This gives a bad name to syphilis, if I mention it in relation to you

Your asshole farts from overeating of civilian casualties

The toxic fingernails of your leprous hands

Flip through the reports of your medievally botulistic bubonic policies

Your brain is full of lice, tickling it with greed for pesticide-ish powder

Cockroaches fill your pancreas with their eggs

But this is an insult to cockroaches

Your lungs fill with the blood of the dead

Poisonous snakes of freedom crawl into your every orifice, but to no avail

Spiders come out of your nose

Your heart is being pinched by Lyme-diseased tics, stung by killer bees, bitten by the

    rattlesnakes of prevarication

First thing every morning your gangrenous arms embrace the rabid turds of your generals

Your penis is the size of a junkie's needle

Your nostrils resemble the assholes of cops

It seems to us you convert your farts into speeches

Your disease-ridden mouth is full of the incurable sores of your lies

Your petrified eyes eat the bulimic vomit of your violent words

All words, all humans, insulted, disgusted, by your depraved existence. (41)

In the face of the so-called war on terror's sanctioning of a present and future defined by endless, preemptive warfare abroad and an increasingly inhumane and undemocratic administration here at home, I am at least grateful that such outspoken and inventive female voices are here to accompany us on this ride into the twenty-first century.

THIS "POST–NEW YORK SCHOOL" turn toward the political or the deadly serious is not exactly new, however. Not only did the feminist concerns charted in this study alter the idiom, but by the mid-eighties, the AIDS epidemic had profoundly transformed the frivolity of midcentury gay life and culture. As Myles says, "Post–New York School, when I think about it, comes pretty close to meaning the generation of writers who stopped drinking, and, in Tim Dlugos's case, died of AIDS" (*Mississippi*, 230). Carr describes the height of the AIDS epidemic in New York as follows:

> Those were the days when forty-year-olds suddenly looked sixty, when people came down with diseases once seen only in pigeons or sheep, and the best doctors were just baffled. Each new symptom was another nail in your coffin, because you knew you might never get rid of it: night sweats or rashes or constipation or diarrhea or spike-in-the-brain headache or shortness of breath or pain in every joint. So you did anything and traveled anyplace where help might be found. When someone came up with an egg-white cure, when some-one recommended drinking your own piss, when some new untested illegal drug came out of Mexico, there were always people not just ready but desperate to try it. (87)

Needless to say, this period produced a different sort of poem, such as Dlugos's classic "G-9," a chatty, Schuyler-esque meditation on memory, loss, desire, illness, and death written in the AIDS ward (G-9) of the hospital where Dlugos was dying. "G-9" spends much of its time charting the shift from more carefree times to the frightening and sorrowful present: "Who'd have thought when we / dressed up in ladies' / clothes for a night for a hoot / in Brad ('June Buntt') and / Howard ('Lili La Lean')'s suite / at the Chelsea that things / would have turned out this way: / Howard dead at 35, Chris Cox / ('Kay Sera Sera')'s friend Bill / gone, too, 'Bernadette of Lourdes' / (guess who) with AIDS, / God knows how many positive" (91–92). But part of what makes "G-9" so moving is that it goes beyond paying tribute to "good times past" and into a thorough celebration of the care and community now being provided by his friends: "What we have / to cherish is not only / what we can recall of how / things were before the plague, / but how we each responded / once it started" (91), Dlu-gos writes, before going on to chronicle the "avalanche of love" that has come his way. The poem's closing lines bravely extend the New York School's embrace of the present moment into uncharted waters: "Joe O'Hare flew in last week, / he asked what were the best / times of my New York years; / I said 'Today,' and meant it" (100–101).

The avalanche of love provided by Dlugos's queer community stands, of course, in sharp contrast to the profound lack of care the state offered to those sick and dying of AIDS—an abandonment which utterly transformed both the nonchalant "not-caring" stance associated with the poets and the inward, metaphysical probing associated with the painters of the New York School. In the case of artists such as David Wojnarowicz, who died of AIDS in 1992, this transformation resulted in a ferociously committed and politicized form of art-making, one which made use of certain New York School and Pop forms—playing with cartoons and capitalist detritus, including advertising posters, bills of money, newspapers, garbage, or the wastelands of the city itself, as in the wreckage of the Hudson piers— only to catapult them far beyond playfulness and gentility and into enraged, apocalyptic territory. As his classic fragmented autobiography *Close to the Knives: A Memoir of Disintegration* makes clear, the "art of being" was replaced with "the art of survival"—or, when survival is no longer an option, with the art of dying—but not quietly. Whether having a friend pose with his cartoonish Rimbaud mask on while jerking off, shooting up, or riding the subway (as in his *Arthur Rimbaud in New York* series [1978–79]), or placing insets of graphic gay sex scenes into landscape photographs (as in *Sex Series [for Marion Scemama]* [1988–89]), or collaging Jesse Helms's face onto a Cibachrome spider wearing a swastika (*Subspecies Helms Senatorius* [1990]), Wojnarowicz did not just chip away at the partitions between the aesthetic and the political; he rendered them nonsensical. He showed no concern for the boundaries of medium or genre: he worked as a writer, a painter, a photographer, a sculptor, a muralist, a video artist, a filmmaker, and much more—in short, whatever form was available, of interest, or best suited to the urgency of the task at hand.[3]

Further, Wojnarowicz's multimedia writing projects, such as *Memories That Smell Like Gasoline* (1992)—a collection of cartoon drawings of remembered sexual encounters and men dying of AIDS, ink paintings of public sex at the Third Avenue movie houses, written accounts of sexual episodes from his past, and notes on the present state of his illness—stand in important relation not only to the work of O'Hara and Brainard, but also to the multimedia "memory" experiments of Mayer, the shamanistic, sometimes nightmarish journeys undertaken by Notley, and the activist poetry and performance of Myles.

In all of these cases, the urgency to find new forms—to "unsay Fate"—trumps worrying over medium or genre boundaries, or sometimes even over aesthetic arguments about boundaries or styles. As Notley has put it, "When I read the facts about global warming or overpopulation I really don't care how one's *supposed* to write the poem. . . . If a whole world is being destroyed, I don't think it matters as to whether it's correct to 'imagine' that destruction or to attack it from a vantage of realistic depiction and overt reaction. Either will do, as long as we're talking about the problem" (Goldman, 28–29). In an interview in *Time Out,* Myles offers her take on the topic of genre in relation to *Cool for You*: "This is not a quote-unquote real novel. It's my kind of novel—pasted together and funky. While writing this book I thought, It's going to explain more than novels are supposed to; it's just going to do any fucking thing it wants to do, and then I'm still going to say it's a novel when I'm done." For Myles, active disobedience to categories in a publishing world increasingly obsessed with explanatory delimitations is another form of resistance: "I think literary categories are false," she explains to Laurie Weeks in *Index* magazine. "They belong to the marketplace and the academy. It's the obedience issue that I'm saying fuck you to, the scholar or the editor trying to trap the writer like a little bug under the cup of 'poetry' or 'prose.'"

This resistance to categories has in fact come to characterize some of the most exciting work by women poets in recent years, even when it's not as "fuck you" in sentiment. I'm thinking, for example, of Anne Carson's spectacular melding of literary criticism, scholarship, poetry, and prose, which extends a "not-caring" attitude out to the categories of "poet" or "poetry" themselves.[4] "I never did think of myself as a writer," Carson said in a 2000 interview with Stephen Burt. "I know that I have to make things. And it's a convenient form we have in our culture, the book, in which you can make stuff, but it's becoming less and less satisfying. And I've never felt that it exhausts any idea I've had. . . . I don't know that we have poetry anymore. You have writing of lots of undefined kinds. . . . Homer was a poet, I'm not sure if anyone else—Sappho, maybe." This indifference to recent poetic history (i.e., the past two millennia) reminds me of Stein's definition of a genius in *Everybody's Autobiography*: "A genius is someone who does not have to remember the two hundred years that everybody else has to remember" (121). This amnesia might outrage some, but its refusal to get worked up over ultraserious notions of literary value, along with its abstention from the anxiety-of-influence model of authorship, has given writers such as Carson an enormous liberated space from which to work. In Carson's case, the result has been a glorious paradox, articulated by Bruce Hainley in his review of Carson's "novel in verse" *Autobiography of Red* (1998) in terms quite intimate to the study at hand: "[Carson] has written a brilliant novel because she doesn't care about the novel, and some of the most important poetry of our time because she doesn't care about verse" (32).

Another genre-defying, politically crucial piece of work to appear in recent years is Claudia Rankine's *Don't Let Me Be Lonely: An American Lyric* (2004), whose title presumes that a "lyric" should or can be big enough to house a disjunctive prose meditation which incorporates photographs, elaborate footnotes, and plenty of white space, and which weighs in on everything from mortality, race relations, terrorism, TV, grief, the pharmaceutical business, forgiveness, loneliness, police brutality, violence in Hollywood movies, and literary figures from Derrida to Hegel to Cornell West to Paul Celan to J. M. Coetzee to Emily Dickinson to Myung Mi Kim to Fanny Howe. Rankine's 155-page lyric, whose speaker is a sort of collaged, nobody/everybody first person, speaking in a language which is somehow informational, limpid, despairing, and consoling all at once, seriously challenges all three definitions of "lyric" offered by Ron Padgett in his *Handbook of Poetic Forms*: "1) [lyrics] are shorter than dramatic or epic poems; 2) they tend to express the personal feelings of one speaker, often the poet; 3) they give you the feeling that they could be sung" (105). Further, Rankine's designation of her lyric as "American" refuses to cede the term even as her book excoriates the fallout of American exceptionalism and jingoism, not to mention its racist and consumption-obsessed past and present. The effect is complicated and moving, and related to that of Notley's pronouncement: "All I can say is / This poem is in the Mainstream American Tradition," Mayer's alignment of herself with Thoreau, Whitman, and Kerouac in *Midwinter Day*, and Myles's claim to be a Kennedy in "An American Poem." Rankine's book is remarkable for globalizing the stakes of this claim, and for managing, within its terse and deceptively private idiom, to grapple with the Iraq war, Al Qaeda, the Holocaust, South Africa's distribution of AIDS drugs, the Israeli-Palestinian conflict, and much, much more.

Both Carson and Rankine bring economics to the fore in their work—Carson primarily in *Economy of the Unlost*, in which she reminds us of poetry's ancient relationship with money via an examination of the Greek poet Simonides, "the first poet who introduced meticulous calculation into songmaking and composed poems for a price" (15); Rankine by cogitating on the problem of economic compensation for suffering, as in Abner Louima's lawsuit against the city of New York and the police union, or an insurance company's practice of assigning numerical value to a life. But as Myles's "fuck you" to the marketplace suggests, much post–New York School writing makes a more personal, blistering insistence on financial matters in the poetry. Mayer, Notley, and Myles never let their readers forget the somewhat inglorious fact that in the U.S., barring patronage or independent funds, a life dedicated exclusively to poetry is also a life dedicated to a form of poverty. The work of all three explicitly and continually addresses the problem of finding affordable food, shelter, healthcare, and time and money for artmaking. "Am I / the only one with bleeding gums / tonight," Myles asks in "An American Poem." "Am I the only / one whose friends have / died, are dying now. / And my art can't / be supported until it is / gigantic, bigger than / everyone else's, confirming / the audience's feeling that they are / alone. That they alone / are good, deserved / to buy the tickets / to see this Art. / Are working, are healthy, should / survive, and are normal" (*Not Me*, 16–17).

The tonal range within which the poets treat the subject is quite wide: sometimes lack of money is a badge of honor, sometimes a source of humor, and often cause for tremendous anger. Mayer, whose short poems are often in conversation with the forms and tropes of ancient Greek and Latin poetry, often jokes about the relation (or lack thereof) between writing poetry and making money, as in "Thanksgiving": "I'd better count my money before I call you, muse / ($166 for 19 days) . . . / I need more money than I have / There must be something to sell / So you get started, / new stanza" (*Pinecone*, 25) or "Sonnet Welcome" from *Scarlet Tanager*, which introduces the poems that follow with the line: "Let's get on with our non-paying work as always" (1). In poems such as "Failures in Infinitives," Mayer takes a more rueful approach: "Why am I doing this?" she asks at the start, then goes on to chronicle her many failures: "[failure] to earn enough money to live on . . . [failure] to not need money so as / to be able to write all the time / to not have to pay rent, con ed or telephone bills / to forget parents' and uncle's early deaths so as / to be free of expecting care" (*Reader*,

139). Elsewhere Mayer lashes out at the economics that continue to push so many artists and writers out of New York City, thus thwarting the chances of a "New York School" of any kind:

> if we flee to the various corridors
> we're expected to flee to
> for jobs & places to live
> we will become a part of
> the grand real estate plan
> already written in some offices
> & only rich people will remain
> living in the new manhattan layers
> which wouldn't be so bad if the bomb dropped
> but in that case
> it probably wouldn't fall here
> all the symphonies & ballets
> & academic poetry readings
> will be attended by those privileged ones
> those few young people left
> in the city
> will create a beautiful neo-fascist art
> which will be fashionable
> even among the naïve
> & all will struggle
> for their incomes
> to pay the landlords
> or else suck their cocks
> once again
> for the rent (*Pinecone*, 34)

Notley has also returned continually to the subject; her treatment of it has ranged from the allegorical (as in the creation of a "Lady Poverty" in *Mysteries*) to the borderline religious ("When I was young I attached great importance to certain ethical statements as received, viz. blessed are the poor in spirit for theirs is the kingdom of heaven" [*Interim*, 117]), to the purely enraged: "I can't get to the poem of this . . . / the rage of unremunerated work— / can't you hear the voice in my head / can't you hear this fucking voice in my head / of course I'm not right I'm never right / I'm fucking lazy unskilled and you deserve your money" (*Mysteries*, 67). In a recent interview with Claudia Keelan, Notley explains: "Poet is the world's most underpaid job, but it was years before I caught on that no one respected it any more either and that hardly anyone cared if there was poetry in the world or not and that was why it was underpaid. . . . I feel clearer not having much; I don't feel part of the infernal and illusory machine which churns out jobs, objects, and the walls of the visible world" (*Interim*, 118).

This focus on economics relentlessly delivers news that some readers would prefer to ignore, or would at least prefer remained *outside* of the poetry itself—as if to bring it in is somehow in bad taste ("those awful rolls of chicken and ugly meatloafs"). In my own teaching, I've sometimes been surprised to hear young aspiring artists or graduate students in poetry respond to this aspect of the work with a "get a job already" brand of impatience—an impatience which, I might add, often coexists with an admiration for the unremitting commitment each writer has made to her work. ("She has never tried to be anything but a poet, and all her ancillary activities have been directed to that end," Notley's bio note reads in the back of *Disobedience*, with characteristic intransigence.) I tend to read this "get a job" impatience as a natural response to writing that intends to be abrasive, or as a sublimated protest against the very real social and economic challenges the poetry decries (challenges which my students know that they, too, will most likely have to face, if they aren't already). On the other hand, I sometimes worry that their impatience may also signal that the absurdity, beauty, and necessity of a life devoted to poetry—at whatever the "cost"—may be becoming less captivating, and perhaps even somewhat shameful, in a literary and artistic world increasingly obsessed with professionalization and commodity.[5]

Often I've heard it said that there is so much squabbling in the poetry world over prizes or grants or publication because the stakes are so low—a truism which I think misses the greater and more interesting point: namely, that all literature exists in a symbolic economy, one in which "the goods themselves are physically worthless," as Louis Menand recently put it in an essay about the prize industry. Menand goes on to describe how in a symbolic economy, "what makes [literary works] valuable is the recognition that they are valuable," and that to accrue this recognition—this cultural capital—a work of art "has to circulate through a sub-economy of exchange operated by a large and growing class of middlemen: publishers, curators, producers, publicists, philanthropists, foundation officers, critics, professors, and so on" (137). The fact that this "sub-economy of exchange" never (or extremely rarely) grants the work of poetry significant financial remuneration doesn't make its stakes "low"; rather, it makes the importance of cultural capital, or the lack thereof, all the more clear, and brings the machinations that confer such capital into starker relief. Given this situation, the focus on these machinations within the poetry of Mayer, Notley, and Myles remains scandalous, insofar as it both rages against these economies and sub-economies while also refusing to pretend that they don't exist, that they haven't already shaped the work you are now holding in your hand.[6]

As Menand suggests above, one way to confer cultural capital on a literary work is to write criticism about it—which brings us to the charge of the present study. In her 1994 talk "The Lesbian Poet," Myles observes: "The awesome mortality AIDS conjures up leaves fags ever more protective of their lineage. Melvin Dixon pleading at the 1992 Outwrite conference in Boston, 'Who will call my name when I'm gone.' We will, I whisper but I've never been so aware of the conversation between lesbians and gay men, not going on" (*Fish*, 126). This comment speaks eloquently not only to the fissures that can exist between gay men and lesbians, but also to larger questions about literary value itself—what it consists of, how it gets made, who speaks it, the raw desire that writers can feel for it, and the frightening specter of invisibility which threatens to erase a life or career lived without it. ("Say Goodbye to Legacy," Mayer jauntily titles one of her poems.) It is my hope that this study has called out some names, and perhaps even conferred some value, without ever losing sight of the complexities of such an endeavor, and, more important, of the vast possibilities that lie beyond it.

And one of these possibilities may involve the destruction or unsettling of—or maybe just the "not caring" or caring less about—a certain knee-jerk belief held dear by critics and writers alike throughout time, a belief which Aaron Kunin has usefully termed the "preservation fantasy"—the "humanist value shared by film, literature, and academic culture: if it exists, it must be preserved—every Shirley Temple movie, every Barney Google comic strip, every strain of the smallpox virus" (7). In his introduction to his guest-edited edition of *The Best American Poetry 2003*, Yusef Komunyakaa weaves this belief in with a generalized diatribe against the "overexperimentation" of something he calls the "exploratory movement"—two terms which, no matter how hard I try, I can't get myself to read as pejoratives. Komunyakaa then concludes: "As poets, as artists, we do want meaning to remain in our works, and not have the essence of our lives and visions become like that moment when Robert Rauschenberg erases the de Kooning drawing and says that the erasure is art" (21). Women artists and writers—and not just the "exploratory" ones I've considered here—do not need to be reminded of the risks of erasure. It is all the more inspiring, then, when they face these risks squarely while also staying open and alive to the beauty, freedom, critique, humor, disobedience, and even divinity that also reside in Rauschenberg's disappearing gesture.

NOTES

1. The list could go on and on: Ed Sanders, Lewis Warsh, John Giorno, Andrei Codrescu, John Godfrey, Jim Brodey, Tom Clark, Tim Dlugos, Charles North, Robert Hershon. See also *An Anthology of New York Poets* (1970), eds. Padgett and Shapiro.

2. See also the anthology *Angel Hair Sleeps with a Boy in My Head* (eds. Waldman, Warsh, and Coolidge), the *Out of This World* anthology (ed. Waldman), the 2003 issue of the *Mississippi Review* called "Poets of the New York School," Myles's list of women writers-artists in "The Lesbian Poet" (*School of Fish*, 127), and so on. . . . By the time one gets to talking about third- or fourth-generation poets, the list gets too endless, the influence too diffuse, to be of much use, but I suppose a short list might include poets such as Lee Ann Brown, Brenda Coultas, Olena Klytiak Davis, Elaine Equi, Joanna Fuhrman, Amy Gerstler, Noelle Kocot, Lisa Jarnot, Sharon Mesmer, Ange Mlinko, Tracie Morris, Cynthia Nelson, Jeni Olin, Prageeta Sharma, and Jacqueline Waters, among others.

3. For Kraus, see "Ecceity, Smash, and Grub," in *French Theory in America* (ed. Lotringer and Cohen); for Fraser, see "The Tradition of Marginality," in *Frontiers* 10, no. 3 (1988); for Vickery, see *Leaving Lines of Gender*; for DuPlessis, Rosenbaum, Keller, Kinnihan, and Lundquist, see *The Scene of My Selves*. See also Notley's *Coming After: Essays on Poetry*, and Phillips and Clay's *A Secret Location on the Lower East Side*, as well as Kane's discussion of the many women poets on the scene in the mid-1960s, including Diane Wakoski, Kathleen Fraser, Carol Bergé, Barbara Moraff, and Leonore Kandell, and of the central positions assumed by younger women poets such as Anne Waldman, Marilyn Hacker, Ruth Krauss, Notley, Mayer, Joanne Kyger, Hannah Weiner, and many others (20, 141). Despite the incipient sexual revolution, however, Kane also notes the insidious sexism of the "progressive" male literati of the period. See his discussion of George Montgomery's magazine *FEMORA*, and of Paul Blackburn's comments that women should use "proper speech" in poetry, instead of the "common speech" that was becoming a "fair and valid medium" for male poets (20–21).

4. In art history, however, much "revisionary" work of the New York School of painting has been done in recent years—see Michael Leja's

Reframing Abstract Expressionism: Subjectivity and Painting in the 1940s,
Ann Eden Gibson's *Abstract Expressionism: Other Politics,* and the anthology
Reading Abstract Expressionism: Context and Critique (ed. Ellen G. Landau),
all published by Yale University Press (in 1993, 1997, and 2005, respectively).

5. For Lehman's discussion of women and the New York School, see p.
12; for Ward's, see his 2001 "Post-Postscript," *Statutes,* 192, 196–197 (the
1993 version of Ward's *Statutes of Liberty* does not mention Guest at all).

I don't wish to rehearse here all the reasons why the label "New
York School" does or doesn't make sense—as Lehman explains, the name
was always a joke of sorts, and one which the poets themselves generally
rejected (see Lehman, 26). Clearly such groupings are used mostly as critical conveniences, marketing devices, a means of placing oneself or others
socially, and so on, and their applications always risk paving over important contradictions and aesthetic differences between artists that most
inquiring minds would prefer to highlight and explore. Nonetheless, the
critical urge to consolidate a "school"—even, or especially, an "avant-
garde"—out of an otherwise amorphous amalgam of friendship and happenstance can be an act of power as much as simple advocacy: by creating
a team and designating its major players, one determines who gets to play
the game—not to mention what game is being played. As Michael Davidson
and others have pointed out, the field of midcentury avant-garde poetics in
the United States—from coast to coast, as it were—is overwhelmingly dominated by "boys' club" metaphors, be it the "baseball team" of the New York
School, Charles Olson's tribal fraternity, Robert Duncan's mystical brotherhood, and so on. Given such mythic forms, it doesn't come as a surprise
that oppositional writing by women throughout the twentieth (and now the
twenty-first) century has often worked in tension (if not out-and-out conflict) with the masculinist ideology that underpins prototypical notions of
what constitutes an avant-garde.

It might also be worth noting here that women have a historically
different relationship to collective groupings than men, be it in literature
or otherwise. As Davidson explains, "male bonding often leads to material
enrichment [whereas] the same experience among women has no such
material base" ("Compulsory Homosociality," 201). Though material enrichment may seem to have little to do with poetry, Davidson's point can certainly be understood metaphorically, if one takes literary reputation as a
form of currency (see the end of this study's afterword). For example, in the
fields of art and/or literature, when men get together, the grouping is often
seen as an aesthetic force; when women join together, the fact of their gender usually overshadows any aesthetic inclination.

6. Claudia Rankine and Alison Cummings, "Afterword and Conception," published in *Fence Magazine,* Spring–Summer 2000, 125–126. They
also here note several exceptions—i.e., women poets who are *not* adverse to

talking about their poetics, such as Lyn Hejinian, Rae Armantrout, Annie Finch, Alice Fulton, Joan Retallack, and Rachel Blau DuPlessis.

7. See Myles, interview with Richard, 26. I'm thinking of Lehman's attempt to distance Ashbery from Warhol and Pop (see chapter 2 of this book, note 28) and Ward's attempts to isolate New York School work from "identity-based" poetry by "marginalized groups" (193).

8. Ward makes a similar point (for somewhat different reasons) on p. 197 of his "Post-Postscript." Guest's writing has indeed occupied a central, albeit slippery position in both realms; see also the chapter on Mayer in Anne Vickery's *Leaving Lines of Gender: A Feminist Genealogy of Language Writing*. See also the email exchanges between Scalapino, Hejinian, and Notley in the 2005 issue of *Interim* dedicated to Notley's work (23, nos. 1–2). Further, the ideological demarcations of "Language writing" itself are nowhere near as cut-and-dried as its critics often suppose: see Rae Armantrout's statement for the Barnard conference "Cheshire Poetics" (in *Fence*, Spring–Summer 2000, 92–98), which begins: "Most of you know [that I am associated with Language writing]—but when you know that, what do you know? This group is as varied, as diverse as any poetic school you can think of" (92).

9. See Notley's interview with Jennifer Dick, in which Notley goes on to name Waldman, Mayer, Susan Howe, Fanny Howe, Carla Harryman, Lyn Hejinian, Leslie Scalapino, and Jorie Graham as "women [her] age who are very strong."

10. Douglas Oliver, "Poetry's Subject," 52; originally given as the Judith E. Wilson Annual Lecture on Poetry in the University of Cambridge, 1995.

11. Though it's not a connection I'm prepared to take up here, Marx's conceptualization of money as a "real abstraction" is also relevant here. For more on how this concept might relate to poetic issues and history, see Carson's *Economy of the Unlost*, 45.

12. As for feminist problems with the category "women," see Monique Wittig's 1980 essay "The Straight Mind" (in *The Straight Mind*) in which she famously asserts: "'Woman' has meaning only in heterosexual systems of thought and heterosexual economies. Lesbians are not women" (32). See also "Questions" in Luce Irigaray's *This Sex Which Is Not One*, in which she refuses to answer the question "Are you a woman?" (120–122). For a historical consideration of the conflict, see Denise Riley's book *"Am I That Name?" Feminism and the Category of Women in History*. Judith Butler's *Bodies That Matter* may also bear some relevance here, as in it she does for the category "body" something of what Riley does for "women."

13. Given how little work has actually been done on the subject to date, a premature aversion to the topic brings to mind the passage from Sedgwick's *Epistemology of the Closet* in which she adeptly summarizes the many discouragements that aim (consciously or not) to preempt inquiry

into queer issues in the literary arena: "Stop asking here, stop asking just now; we know in advance the kind of difference that would be made by the invocation of *this* difference; it makes no difference; it doesn't mean" (see Richter, 1485).

14. For example, while Lehman grants that "a critic could make the plausible claim that what I have been calling the pursuit of happiness is code for a celebration of a gay sensibility," one has to wonder what such a claim could really *mean*. The either/or formulation implies that (a) there exists such a thing as a specific, singular gay sensibility, which one could elaborate with, say, a cluster of adjectives, and then map back onto the poets, and/or (b) that a reader or critic could—or should—eventually determine which interpretation is "code" and which one "real." (John Shoptaw's *On the Outside Looking Out* smartly focuses on the intransigence of this problem in Ashbery's drafts and many published works.) The first option prescribes and contains both the sexuality of each writer and its relationship to his or her writing; the second only makes sense in the "epistemology of the closet," and thus brings us face to face with how "outing" functions as "the promise of a disclosure that can, by definition, never come," as Butler puts it ("Imitation and Gender Insubordination," 309).

15. Here I'm simply repeating and condensing the many different feminist critiques of deconstruction, made by everyone from Gayatri Spivak to Barbara Johnson. Johnson is especially trenchant on the issue in *A World of Difference*, in which she takes on Paul De Man by asking whether "self-resistance, indeed, may be one of the few viable postures remaining for the white male establishment" (45).

16. This comes from Gallop's discussion of postmodernist thinkers such as Derrida, who she argues "celebrates Nietzsche's 'femininity' while attacking feminists' 'masculinity'" (160).

17. Schor, *Reading in Detail*, 17, here quoting Jean Larnac, author of *Histoire de la littérature féminine en France* (1929).

18. These terms are Teresa De Lauretis's, from an essay in *The Essential Difference* in which she writes: "The question, for the female philosopher, is how to rethink sexual difference within a dual conceptualization of being, 'an absolute dual,' in which both being-man and being-woman would be primary, originary forms" (16). Her idea of "an absolute dual" both excites and troubles me—it excites insofar as it is part and parcel of some very important practical endeavors, such as the attempt to get the UN to recognize the rights of women and girls as human rights, but troubles insofar as it preserves the binarism at the core of so much thinking about gender, even as it attempts to alter its implications (thus leaving all those who feel themselves somewhere "in-between" "being-man" or "being-woman" out in the cold).

19. I'm not all that interested in going to bat over what constitutes an "authentic avant-garde," but I would point out that the idea of the New York School as the "last" one elides countless other avant-garde scenes in the United States from the sixties to the present, including Black Arts; the birth of rap, hip-hop, and free-styling; punk and post-punk writing by writers such as Kathy Acker, Patti Smith, and Dennis Cooper; L=A=N=G=U=A=G=E writing; the girls' art movement Myles talks about at the end of chapter 5; African American collectives such as Dark Room and Black Took; and so on.

20. Mayer, interview with Jarnot, 6; Myles, see contributors' index in the back of Waldman, *Out of This World*, 663; Notley, from email interview with the author, 9 February 2002.

21. See Myles in *Narrativity*. Virginia Woolf's *Mrs. Dalloway*—which famously charts the progress of a single day in the life of Clarissa Dalloway—is a notable female predecessor here. It interests me, however, that the book's resurgence in popularity at the turn of the twenty-first century was due to Michael Cunningham's 1998 book (then movie) *The Hours*—another meditation/mediation of women's daily lives by a gay man. I don't mean to impugn Cunningham's project—rather, I am wondering about how the marketing of and/or reception to such classics of the "female quotidian" would differ, or do differ, when the directors or authors are women or lesbians themselves.

22. See Mary Douglas's 1966 classic *Purity and Danger: An Analysis of the Concepts of Pollution and Taboo*, 181–190, as well as Anne Carson's essay "Dirt and Desire" in *Men in the Off Hours*, and my discussion of such in regard to Mayer in chapter 4.

23. Though the whole topic of whether American poetry is dead may seem a little passé, somehow the conversation still tumbles along, mostly in mainstream venues. For example, as I was finishing this book in 2003, the mainstream line seemed to be that American poetry "mattered" again, partly due to the well-publicized opposition of many poets to the Iraq war, crystallized in Sam Hamill's organized boycott of Laura Bush's "Poetry and the American Voice" event, and his consequent submission of an extensive collection of antiwar poems to deliver to the White House. (For more on this movement, which continues, see Hamill's "Poets against the War" website, http://www.poetsagainstthewar.org/.) But given the disdain for political engagement shown by many of the men who have written about the death of poetry and/or the avant-garde, the circumstances of this "revival" strike me as quite ironic. For more on this issue—particularly as it relates to the rise of MFA programs in the USA—see Eric McHenry's "An Anti Anti MFA Manifesto," in *Poets and Writers Magazine*, May–June 2003, in which McHenry discusses Gioia's "change of heart" in Gioia's new introduction to *Can Poetry Matter?* as well as work on the subject by David Alpaugh and Neal Bowers.

1. ABSTRACT PRACTICES

1. See Steiner, *The Colors of Rhetoric*, 183. Most assume Stein didn't mean this as praise; Warhol, on the other hand, was enraptured by exactly that connection, and eventually developed the ecstatic mantra: "Sex Is So Abstract" (see Koestenbaum, *Warhol*, 182).

2. This "broad, slippery, and vague employment" is a pitfall which I have tried to avoid but have undoubtedly fallen into at times throughout this study. Some of the trouble lies in Abstract Expressionist rhetoric itself, as critics from the period regularly made the leap of treating "abstract" and "transcendent" as synonymous terms—a leap which had more to do with a particular art-historical agenda than with a desire for linguistic exactitude. Another part of the problem stems from the fact that the word "abstract" means quite differently depending upon the context, or the language game, in which it is being used—imagine its varying uses, for example, in ancient philosophy, Continental philosophy, American pragmatism, art criticism, literary criticism, mysticism, and so on. For a discussion of how one might relate to the term decades after the Abstract Expressionist moment, see the introduction of Ann Eden Gibson's *Abstract Expressionism: Other Politics*, in which she explains how and why she aims to consider "abstract art" as "a sign whose meaning is determined by its use" (xxxvii). Armed with this Wittgensteinian approach, Gibson is able to reconsider the Abstract Expressionist canon and focus attention on neglected abstract work of the period done by women, people of color, and gays and lesbians, including Thelma Johnson, Rose Piper, Norman Lewis, Alice Trumbull Mason, Nell Blaine, Beauford Delaney, Ruth Abrams, and many others.

3. I'm not going to spend much time here arguing that Guest be returned to her rightful status as one of the core members of the New York School, mostly because other critics have recently done such a good job elucidating the matter—see the essays by DuPlessis, Keller, Kinnihan, and Lundquist in *The Scene of My Selves*, for example. I would reiterate, however, the "scandalousness" DuPlessis notes in her discussion of Guest's "shocking erasure" from the movement "in which she had been a key participant" (190)—an exclusion epitomized for many by her absence from *An Anthology of New York Poets*, edited by Ron Padgett and David Shapiro and published by Random House in 1970, which included only one female poet (a very young Bernadette Mayer) among twenty-six men. Not surprisingly, a parallel phenomenon transpired in the art world around the same time: Henry Geldzahler's 1969 blockbuster show at the Met, "New York Painting and Sculpture 1940–1970," included Helen Frankenthaler as the only female among forty-three male artists.

4. "The Club" was a volatile group formed in 1949 whose New York meetings served as "the primary forum for Abstract Expressionism through

the 1950's" (Kertess, 16). Originally The Club intended to exclude women and homosexuals from its meetings, but Mitchell ended up one of a handful of female members invited to join; O'Hara was also a regular visitor. See Gibson, xxv. See also Nina Leen's photograph of "The Irascibles," which appears at the beginning of this book's introduction, and in which the lone woman, Hedda Sterne, hovers at the back/top of The Club.

5. There also many other collaborations of import that I'm not taking up here: Mitchell collaborated with the poets J. J. Mitchell, Jacques Dupin, Pierre Schneider, Chris Larsen, Charles Hine, and Nathan Kernan (see "Biographical Chronology," Kertess, 179–183), and Guest collaborated with female painters such as Abbott and Hartigan. For the latter, see Lundquist's discussion in "Another Poet among Painters," in *Scene of My Selves*; see also Guest's *Dürer in the Window: Reflexions on Art*, ed. Africa Wayne.

6. Thinking back to Warhol's "sex is so abstract" for a moment, we can also see how the converse might function: as Koestenbaum explains in his biography, the more blatantly "material" the tools of Warhol's art became, as in his piss paintings and come paintings, the more abstract the work. Warhol also considered his series of Polaroids of cropped body parts—about 70 percent portray male asses, Koestenbaum testifies—abstract works, and called them "landscapes" (Koestenbaum, 183–185).

7. The galleries were Cheim and Read ("The Presence of Absence: Selected Paintings 1956–1992"); Lennon, Weinberg ("Petit: Small Paintings, Works on Paper"); Edward Tyler Nahem Fine Art; and Tibor de Nagy ("Working with Poets: Pastels and Paintings").

8. The silkscreens, along with Mitchell's collaborations with Schuyler and J. J. Mitchell, were all on view at the Tibor de Nagy in the summer of 2002, in "Working with Poets." The monograph with the foreword by Ashbery is *Joan Mitchell 1992* from the Robert Miller Gallery in New York.

9. See Marjorie Perloff's *Frank O'Hara: Poet among Painters*, the first edition of which usefully focuses on O'Hara's relationship to Action Painting, the second edition of which discusses how she missed or underplayed the connection to Johns and Rauschenberg on the first go-round. Lately this purview of O'Hara's collaborations has grown infinitely wider, in large part due to the publication of the twin-titled compendiums *In Memory of My Feelings: Frank O'Hara and American Art* (ed. Russell Ferguson) and *In Memory of My Feelings: A Selection of Poems*, ed. Bill Berkson, as well as several museum exhibitions.

10. This question also relates to Myles's focus on dogs, notable from early titles such as *The Irony of the Leash* (1978) all the way through to her many tributes to her dog Rosie throughout her forthcoming novel, *The Inferno*, which is about the hell (and the heaven and purgatory) of being a female poet. See also Notley's heavy use of animals as totems (owls, most notably), and hybrid animal-human forms in "White Phosphorous," *Alette*, and

Disobedience, and Mayer's play with Stein's "I am I because my little dog knows me" in poems such as "Hendecasyllables on Catullus #33" (*Selected*, 113), and so on. Schuyler's poetry also courts a similar dynamic, in that landscape, light, color, and weather often function in his work as his intimate, even social, companions. See, for example, his poem "I think," which begins: "Dear June Fifth, / you're all in green, so many kinds," and ends by imploring the color itself, "Green, / stick around / a while" (*Collected*, 161).

11. Not to be misleading, there were certainly other female Abstract Expressionist painters who *were* invested in innovation, as well as those (like Mitchell) who innovated whether or not they "cared" about doing so. The most frequently cited example of formal innovation among female painters from the period is usually that of Helen Frankenthaler—her experiments with staining the unprimed canvas, as in her "breakthrough" painting from 1952, *Mountains and Sea*, which inaugurated the practice of "stain-gesture." See Sandler's description of the influence of *Mountains and Sea* in *The New York School*, 59–68. His discussion of Frankenthaler's discovery of "false space" through stain-gesture—a space which he describes as both "atmospheric and flat"—is relevant not only to the concerns of this chapter but also to the discussion of "empty space" at the end of chapter 2. I would also here add that Frankenthaler's "drawing with color" seriously complicates the *disegno* vs. *colore* dichotomy as laid out by Batchelor later in this chapter. For more on this complication, especially as it relates to issues of "feminine painting" and the "stain-gesture" as feminized "leakage," whether menstrual or otherwise, see Lisa Saltzman's essay "Reconsidering the Stain: On Gender, Identity, and New York School Painting" in Landau, *Reading Abstract Expressionism*.

12. See Cavell, "Thinking of Emerson," *Senses of Walden*, 127–129. Here Cavell is drawing a distinction between Emerson and Kant; the argument goes something like this: Kant also says the universe "wears our color," but extrapolates that subjectivity is inherently solipsistic. Emerson, on the other hand, via his contention that "sense-experience is to objects what moods are to the world," is out to "destroy the ground on which [the problem of subjectivity vs. objectivity] takes itself seriously." While not feminist per se, this "destruction" bears some similarity to Irigaray's wager about the repressed feminine, which jams or disrupts the theoretical machinery.

13. See, for example, Mitchell's *Between* paintings from 1985—paintings which the poet Kathleen Fraser has described as "small pictures in which each initially empty canvas isolated and captured a detail up-close—as in a lens marking arbitrary boundaries within which a small part of a larger, perhaps more complex and amorphous landscape can be looked at in blown-up detail" (*Moving Borders*, 645).

14. See Guest's *Selected Poems*, 34, 21. One might also connect Guest's poetic investigation of color and mood with the obsession with "red feel-

ings" that saturates Anne Carson's 1998 novel-in-verse, *Autobiography of Red*; Guest's latest collection is called *The Red Gaze* (2005).

15. See Charles Rosen, "Mallarmé the Magnificent" rev. of Mallarmé's *Oeuvres complètes*, vol. 1, ed. Bertrand Marchal. *New York Review of Books* 46, no. 9 (May 20, 1999). Online at http://www.nybooks.com/articles/article-preview?article_id=487 (8 December 2006).

16. For more on Guest and the heroic, see Sara Lunquist's essay in *Scene of My Selves*, in which she considers the Hartigan-Guest collaborations as commentaries on the "heroic style" of Abstract Expressionism, as well as forays into new, unexplored forms of female heroism (253-264).

17. For more on this concept as it relates to Breton and Surrealism, see Rosalind Krauss's essay "No More Play" in *The Originality of the Avant-Garde and Other Modernist Myths*, in which she analyzes the "magisterial example" of the opening of Breton's *L'amour fou*, in which Breton and Giacometti are randomly claimed by "seemingly useless objects" while wandering around a flea market—objects which Krauss later calls "overdetermined" (see 43, 72). Guest's image of the poem as "going from place to place" and eventually "finding its own subject" might be productively tied to this flea market scene, with its romantic aura of overdetermined drifting.

18. William James moved this way, too; see his 1904 essay "Does Consciousness Exist?" See also Wittgenstein (*PI*, no. 501), where he asks, If the purpose of language is to express thoughts, then "what thought is expressed, for example, by the sentence: 'It's raining'?"

19. See also Lynn Keller's discussion of this poem in "Guest and the Feminine Mystique," *Scene of My Selves*, 217-218, in which she makes a similar point.

20. One could also extend Kinnihan's point even further, and into the realm of the debate over the role that universalism should (or shouldn't) play in feminism in general. As Joan Scott explains in a brief but illuminating essay entitled "Universalism and the History of Feminism," the apparent choice between the particular (sexual difference) and the universal (equality) has not really been a choice at all. Considering the history of feminism in France, Scott explains this dynamic: "To the extent that it acted for 'women,' feminism produced the 'sexual difference' it sought to eliminate. This paradox—the need both to accept *and* refuse 'sexual difference' as a condition of inclusion in the universal—was the constitutive condition of feminism as a political movement throughout its long history" (7). Scott goes on to explain how such dilemmas were "not wholly of [feminists'] own making," and are better understood as "symptoms of the contradictions of individualism." The greater point here is that although the "equality/difference conundrum returns whatever side feminists appear to take," it helps to place this recurrence, as Scott does, within the history of feminism itself—which is not, as Scott puts it, "the history of available

options or the unconstrained choice of a winning plan (either equality *or* difference)," but rather "the history of repeated attempts to solve the unsolvable" (11).

21. See *Art Journal*, Winter 1999, 8. The respondents included Amelia Jones, Susan Bee, Shirley Kaneda, Johanna Drucker, and several others; the occasion coincided with several other events, including the symposium "The F-Word: Contemporary Feminisms and the Legacy of the Los Angeles Feminist Art Movement" at the California Institute of the Arts (1996) and the panel discussion "What Ever Happened to the Women Artist's Movement?" at the New Museum of Contemporary Art in New York (1998), organized by Mira Schor.

22. See Kaneda's article "Painting and Its Others: In the Realm of the Feminine," in which she attempts to theorize a "'feminine' painting that disregards the gender of its maker," in an effort to think about abstract painting by women that does not fit into (male, modernist) paradigms.

23. As far as poetry goes, there are too many female poets currently working in abstract idioms of all kinds to list here, but a few strong, younger poets that first come to mind include Renee Gladman, Matthea Harvey, Claudia Rankine, Frances Richard, Deborah Richards, Bhanu Kapil Rider, Lisa Robertson, Juliana Spahr, Karen Weiser, and Elizabeth Willis. See also Sloan's *Moving Borders*, Rankine and Spahr's *American Women Poets in the Twenty-first Century*, and the anthology of women poets also edited by Rankine and Spahr, forthcoming from Wesleyan University Press.

2. GETTING PARTICULAR

1. See Lehman's arguments against this portrayal of O'Hara, 170–175. I don't mean to suggest here that the studies done by Shoptaw and Gooch are unimpeachable, only that their focus sends up a red flag for some. Certainly the reasons for discontent with both works are quite varied. For example, LeSueur himself calls Gooch's biography a "cold, deadly account of Frank's life" (291); anyone hostile to dense, theoretical criticism probably won't like Shoptaw's study, etc.

2. The exclusion of Koch's work from this discussion may seem willfully ahistorical, and the complications of his being the only straight poet of the "Big Four" are certainly worthy of extended discussion, as is his work itself, and his collaborative projects with women such as Nell Blaine. For my purposes here I am admittedly slighting this discussion. See also n. 11 about humor and gender in chapter 4, which touches on some of the ways that Koch's treatment of women in his work stands apart from the feminine identifications and valorizations that this chapter charts. I note these things not to diminish Koch's remarkable writing, teaching, and

legacy, but rather to explain why he is not one of the principal subjects of this chapter, and to offer potential ideas for further inquiry.

3. Giorno, like other artists who made a point of being "in-your-face-gay" during the period, remains "appalled" by Ashbery's closetedness: "He's always been a fag, in your face. It only goes to show how professional he was about his career. It only goes to show how things were at Artforum and all those publications" (*Nerve*). As if in testament to the fact that literary history is as subjective as any other narrative, LeSueur offers a very different take on the scene: "Frank did hang out with some pretty big names: de Kooning, Kline, and Guston come to mind. All of them fairly macho, I suppose, but they accepted Frank as one of them, even invited him to become a member of The Club. So far as I know, only Jackson Pollock, probably the least secure and most conflicted of all the downtown painters, expressed hostility toward gays: 'a couple of faggots' he was said to have groused when Frank and Larry Rivers, at the height of their affair in 1954, turned up at the Cedar together—which, come to think of it, was about the time John Myers carried on about their appearance together one night on the staircase of City Center, at a New York City Ballet performance. 'There they were,' he simpered, in his usual excessive fashion, 'like Rimbaud and Verlaine, covered with blood and semen!'" (166).

4. For more on this phenomenon, see Douglass Shand-Tucci's book *The Crimson Letter: Harvard, Homosexuality, and the Shaping of American Culture* (2003), which argues something similar in its exploration of how Harvard University nurtured many powerful gay male intellectuals and artists even as it occasionally subjected them to intense harassment.

5. O'Hara was famous for his confidence, which some thought bordered on arrogance; Schuyler, who was perhaps the least outgoing or ambitious of the bunch (and the only one who didn't attend Harvard), once wrote in a 1959 letter to Ashbery, "Secretly, I don't think K. [Koch] believes anybody except you, he, Frank & me has anything to offer" (Lehman, 12). Schuyler is here referring to submissions to the magazine *Locus Solus*, not to the dimensions of the New York School itself (he's also referring to Koch's POV, not his own)—but Lehman skips over both distinctions in his book, in an effort to explain why he concentrates solely on Ashbery, Koch, O'Hara, and Schuyler, and to account for the paucity of women in both "the movement" and his history of it. The slippage brings up many interesting questions about where authority lies in the construction of the "mythic forms" of literary history.

6. There may exist some biographical reasons for this dynamic, for in contrast to the New York School writers, many of the queer or bisexual Beat poets—including Bowles, Burroughs, Kerouac, and Neal Cassady—married and/or fathered children at some point. Given the tensions within these marriages or families—some of which had to do with mismatched sexual

preferences, others of which with the difficulties of balancing bohemian restlessness with the responsibilities of domestic life—many of these situations were quite tortured, especially for the women who were left behind to raise the kids. (For more on this issue, see the "Muses" section of *Women of the Beat Generation: The Writers, Artists, and Muses at the Heart of a Revolution*, ed. Brenda Knight.) In this context, Corso's heckling of O'Hara—that O'Hara had it easy because he was queer, and would make a better father than Corso would—gains in pathos. In contrast, the gay New York School writers generally avoided these dilemmas; as LeSueur explains, "Like so many gays, we were young for our age, thus slightly giddy and sometimes heedless; we had no responsibilities beyond making enough money to pay the rent, buy food and booze, and go to the movies and the ballet as much as possible" (68-69).

7. See *The Haunting of Sylvia Plath*, 150-164, where Rose discusses all three of these thinkers and their effect on the Plath-Hughes saga. Also, for more on the lived experience of women in the Beat Generation, see the two classic memoirs from the period: Diane di Prima's *Memoirs of a Beatnik* and Hettie Jones's *How I Became Hettie Jones*.

8. There are crabbier ways to describe this dynamic—you could say the women were beards, or that the friendships were simply prototypes of the fag hag/queen dyad. John Simon, for example, explains the entourage that surrounded Bunny Lang as follows: "Bunny Lang was a fag hag. She was an exaggerated, overdone parody of femininity who cultivated around her a retinue of homosexual men who liked her for her outrageousness and outspokenness" (Gooch, 148). There may be some truth in Simon's account, but I don't share his distaste for Lang's "parody of femininity." We might also recall that, at the time, it was not uncommon for straight women with many gay male friends to be psychoanalyzed for the problem, as was the case with Mitchell; Grace Hartigan was allegedly encouraged by her therapist to give up her friendships with O'Hara and others for this very reason (which, apparently, she did). It requires a certain resistance to mainstream literary and art-history narratives to remember that women (like Lang, Guest, Mitchell, etc.) were integral parts of the scene because they were working writers, thinkers, and artists, not simply parodies, accessories, or attractions. As for the latter characterization, LeSueur himself takes credit for coining the term "art tart" to describe the "abject, sycophantic females who hung out at the Cedar" (161), and while I don't want to take his dismissive tone too seriously—LeSueur enjoyably mocks people of all stripes in his memoir—my interest is nonetheless sparked: Who were these art tarts, anyway?

9. Feminism has done much work to recognize and theorize the nature of this classic patriarchal move (i.e., asserting dominance over the mother and/or the maternal function, as in worship of God the Father and the fantasy of Immaculate Conception, and then expressing a generalized sorrow,

confusion, mourning, or amorphous existential despair over the disconnect or vanquishing). As far as the particular sagas of identification and dis-avowal performed by Wordsworth, Breton, and Hulme, I'm thinking of Wordsworth's envious yet distancing admiration for the "simpleness" of his wife, Mary, who (by his estimation), "welcomed what was given, and craved no more; / Whate'er the scene presented to her view, / That was the best"; Breton's glorification of the figure of Nadja, whose blurring of art and life he first exalts as "the extreme limit of the surrealist aspiration," but later rejects as madness—a madness which disgusts him because it lacks "that minimal common sense which permits my friends and myself, for instance, to *stand up* when a flag goes past"; and Imagist doctrine as laid out by Hulme, who went to great lengths to promote a poetics dedicated to "fancy" and sub-lunar detail that was simultaneously "all dry and hard," i.e., purged of Romantic slither—slither that he, Pound, and Eliot all connected (implicitly, and, at times, explicitly) with the polluting influence of both Jews and women. See Hulme's 1911–1912 essay "Romanticism and Classicism" for an elaboration of this last rhetoric, especially in its opening paragraphs, in which he aligns his literary vision with the political actions of the anti-Semitic group L'Action Française. For the others, see Wordsworth, *The Prelude*, 12. 158–160, and Breton's *Nadja*, 74, 143.

10. Johnson's essay examines this legacy in Keats and Mallarmé, and ends with a discussion of the film *The Piano* by Jane Campion. She concludes with the following crucial insight: "It is in this male two-step—the axe wielder plus the manipulative sufferer—*both* of whom see themselves as powerless, that patriarchal power lies. . . . If feminism is so hotly resis-ted, it is perhaps less because it substitutes women's speech for women's silence than because, in doing so, it interferes with the official structures of self-pity that keep patriarchal power in place, and, in the process, tells the truth behind the beauty of muteness envy" (153).

11. See Butler's essay, "Gender Is Burning," in *Bodies that Matter*, 127. Here Butler is discussing bell hooks's review of the movie *Paris Is Burning*, in which hooks criticizes some gay male drag as misogynist.

12. For more on the issue, see Sedgwick's chapter "How To Bring Your Kids Up Gay" in *Tendencies*, in which Sedgwick persuasively argues for the interruption of "a long tradition of viewing gender and sexuality as contin-uous and collapsible categories—a tradition of assuming that anyone, male or female, who desires a man must by definition be feminine; and that any-one, male or female, who desires a woman must be by the same token mas-culine" (157).

13. See Francine Prose's 2002 book *The Lives of the Muses: Nine Women and the Artists They Inspired*, for a more recent consideration of the topic. It could be argued that O'Hara's queerness is precisely what makes the dif-ference here (after all, Riding and Graves, like Hughes and Plath, were a

married couple), but even if that's the case, there is much to learn from his example—certainly gay men and straight women are not the only ones capable of reconfiguring the relationship between male artist and female muse that DuPlessis deplores. And there are many other notable gay male poets, such as James Merrill, who often participate in the kind of ideology DuPlessis is talking about, as is evident in Merrill's oft-anthologized poem "An Urban Convalescence," whose opening lines figure a mechanized crane as filthy and female: "watching a huge crane / Fumble luxuriously in the filth of years. / Her jaws dribble rubble. An old man / Laughs and curses in her brain, / Bringing to mind the close of *The White Goddess*." Very seldom in New York School writing does one come across such rote gendering of the urban landscape—or the pastoral, for that matter (though I admit that the invocation of Graves's book here may be a little tongue-in-cheek).

14. For more on this issue, see Perloff's article "Normalizing John Ashbery," in which Perloff considers the "revisioning" of Ashbery in more conservative circles. For example, she notes that Shetley, in *After the Death of Poetry*, mistakenly, and "with some satisfaction," announces that Ashbery did not even appear in Donald Allen's "antiformalist" anthology *The New American Poetry*. But as Perloff points out, Ashbery did appear there, and in fact gets ten pages of the anthology.

The subject of Ashbery and his influences has proved a popular one: Perloff and Vendler, for example, have been involved in a longstanding, not-altogether-unfriendly debate about whether Ashbery should be tethered to a lineage that would include the Romantics, Eliot, and Stevens (as Vendler would have it), or a "poetics of indeterminacy" as represented by agitators such as Rimbaud, Pound, Cage, and the Language poets (as Perloff would have it). As if exasperated by all the conjecture, Ashbery himself finally weighed in on the subject in his book of lectures, *Other Traditions*: "How does it happen that I write poetry? What are the impetuses behind it? In particular, what is the poetry that I notice when I write, that is behind my own poetry? Perhaps someone wondered this. In the end, I decided this possibility was the one most likely to fulfill expectations. I'm therefore going to talk about some poets who have probably influenced me (but the whole question of influence appears very vexed to the poet looking through the wrong end of the telescope, though not to critics, who use this instrument the way it was intended—but I don't think I'll go into that now, though it may well creep in later)" (4). The lectures that follow discuss the "certifiably minor poets" John Clare, Thomas Lovell Beddoes, Raymond Roussel, John Wheelwright, Laura Riding, and David Schubert: in short, none of the usual suspects on either Vendler's or Perloff's list.

15. The role of their actual mothers in the poetry is a distinct and fascinating topic, although not one I'm prepared to tackle here. Schuyler's last epic, "A Few Days," meditates throughout on his mother's death, and ends:

"Margaret Daisy Connor Schuyler Ridenour, / rest well, / the weary journey done." And though Ashbery insists that *Flow Chart* is not really "about" his mother, the original idea behind it was to write a one-hundred-page book about his late mother over the course of a year, to be started and finished on his birthday (see Shoptaw, 302). O'Hara's relationship with his mother—as is evident in poems such as "To My Mother," which ends, "Have you escaped yet? if you / haven't I hope you've killed someone, / or suicide's grown curious of someone, / or someone's accidentally died"—was much more tortured; in a 1963 letter to Larry Rivers he describes her as "bitchy selfish stupid hysterical self-pitying ungrateful ignorant etc." (Gooch, 404).

16. Schuyler is the only poet of the three to whom it doesn't seem a stretch to apply the adjective "feminist"—partly because he outlived O'Hara, who died before the women's movement (though I imagine O'Hara might have been a natural feminist, as he loved and respected his female friends, and wrote poems with lines such as "I live above a dyke bar and I'm happy") and partly because Ashbery is so famously shy of anything smacking of politics. In comparison with the disgust with female genitalia as expressed by Spicer and Ginsberg—for example, "The female genital organ is hideous," Spicer writes in "For Joe"; "the hang of pearplum / fat tissue / I had abhorred" is how Ginsberg describes pussy in "This Form of Life Needs Sex"—Schuyler's attitude was quite different, as when he writes in his *Diary*: "When I woke up I thought I was going to hop out of bed and write an ode to bisexuality, which was quite clear to me, but all that remains is the ending: 'and remember that / cunt is where it's at'" (142).

17. Herring's essay "Frank O'Hara's Open Closet" takes on a similar topic. Herring argues that "personism creates an intimate artistic space through which impersonal identification can occur," a dynamic he relates to that of an "open closet" by which one manages to be "*open* but not violated," as Grace Hartigan once said of O'Hara's poetry (see Herring, 416–417).

18. Although Nelson is right that Lowell places himself as a "particular person in a particular place and time," there still exist potent differences—namely, Lowell often uses this particularity in an attempt to use his biography or body as a microcosm or metaphor for the body politic at large, a gesture also prevalent in Beat writers such as Allen Ginsberg, who famously tells America that he is "putting his queer shoulder to the wheel." The New York School poets' use of specificity, on the other hand, seems to be more for the sake of specificity itself. Drawing attention to the importance of speech and/or the speaking body in New York School poetry, Charles Molesworth puts it this way: "Unlike Whitman, O'Hara never sings *of* his self; rather, his self is the instrument *on* which the poet sings." See Molesworth's essay in *Frank O'Hara: To Be True to a City*, ed. Elledge, 210. Also, for an alternative reading of Lowell's "Skunk Hour," see Perloff's discussion in chap. 3 of her book on Lowell, *The Poetic Art of Robert Lowell*.

19. For more on O'Hara and race, see Benjamin Friedlander's essay "Strange Fruit: O'Hara, Race, and the Color of Time," in *Scene of My Selves*, 123-141. See also Michael Magee's *Emancipating Pragmatism: Emerson, Jazz, and Experimental Writing*.

20. For the quotation regarding Strauss, see Timothy Jackson. The panel I'm referring to was entitled "Poets and Painters," and featured John Ashbery, Larry Rivers, and Diane Kelder, moderated by Roberta Smith, and took place at the Graduate Center of the City University of New York on April 22, 2002.

21. "Nancy" is of course slang for "fag," as well as the name of the Ernie Bushmiller comic strip character that Joe Brainard appropriated to place in all kinds of hilarious situations ("If Nancy Was an Ashtray" and "If Nancy Was a Boy" are but two titles of Brainard drawings from the seventies).

22. As chapter 1 suggests, Ashbery is not alone in this desire to confuse the divide between idealism and realism. Treating ideas as things—another spin on the notion of a true abstraction—has been something of an American preoccupation, from John Edwards to John Dewey, with both religious and pragmatic roots. See Thoreau's *Walden*, for example: "The bullet of your thought must have overcome its lateral and ricochet motion and fallen into its last and steady course before it reaches the ear of the hearer, else it may plough out again through the side of his head" (1708), or William James's *Principles of Psychology*: "Annihilate a mind at any instant, cut its thought through whilst yet uncompleted, and examine the object present to the cross-section thus suddenly made; you will find, not the bald word in process of utterance, but that word suffused with the whole idea" (282). The idea that art can or should be a means of conjoining thought and sensation is not, of course, a particularly American one: Hegel theorized that "art's peculiar feature . . . consists in its ability to represent in sensuous form even the highest ideas, bringing them thus nearer to the character of natural phenomena, to the senses, and to feeling" (Richter, 362), and many poets—Keats immediately comes to mind—have treated their art as a means of rendering thought "sensuous"; Keats's lovely phrase for this was "ideas on the pulses."

23. There remains, of course, this big difference between Ashbery and Darger: Ashbery knew he was writing a book, and a book that would be published by Farrar, Straus, and Giroux, while Darger labored in a self-imposed, superstitious obscurity: "All the Gold in the Gold Mines / All the Silver in the world, / Nay, all the world / Cannot buy these pictures from me," he warned ominously—see the copyright page of *Henry Darger: In the Realms of the Unreal*, ed. John MacGregor. Given that Ashbery is "devoted to the impossible," as Schuyler once said, I imagine that part of Ashbery's attraction to Darger's work—especially at this late point in his career, after he has been consistently deemed one of the twentieth century's great

poets—lies precisely in Darger's total insulation from the eye of critics and audience, and in the consequent maniacal, unedited sprawl of his vision.

24. I would also point out here that as imaginative and outsiderish as Darger's vision may have been, it is also true that the dismemberment, torture, murder, and bodily decay of little girls falls fairly centrally on our psychic and cultural radar screens. Indeed, the nightly news, that most mainstream of forums, is constantly fixated on a dead or missing (white) girl. Much like the Surrealist excursions into the collective unconscious in the first part of the twentieth century, Darger's vivid fantasies about the bloody slaughter of naked girls (usually via disembowelment or strangulation) may perhaps make no new discovery, but rather amplify a particular strand of the infatuation with sexual violence which already permeates our everyday lives.

25. Though he is better-known for his interest in childhood than girlhood per se, Koch's extensive investment in teaching poetry to children is relevant here; see his two classics, *Rose, Where Did You Get That Red?: Teaching Great Poetry to Children*, and *Wishes, Lies, and Dreams: Teaching Children to Write Poetry*.

26. Interestingly, in his later life, when he became very religious, Darger was particularly bothered by cross-dressing in the church, and wrote a letter to the priests at St. Vincent de Paul about the issue. A priest wrote back to explain that as long as cross-dressing did not lead to the "unnatural sin of sodomy," it was OK by the Holy Scriptures. See MacGregor's account, 528. MacGregor usefully relates this vacillation about cross-dressing to Darger's childhood experience at the Lincoln Asylum for Feeble-Minded Children, where boys were made to dress up like little girls as a form of punishment.

27. Much has been written on the potential relationship between this far-reaching "absorbency" and the American obsession with manifest destiny and cultural and military imperialism. This debate raged in the 1950s in regard to Abstract Expressionist painting, as painters such as Motherwell were becoming famous for the huge scale of their paintings just as the U.S. was solidifying its rise to cold war ascendancy. For more on the topic, see Leja's *Reframing Abstract Expressionism*. Interesting as this connection may be—and it hasn't become dated, for the debate about the far-reaching voraciousness of U.S. interests has never been more fierce—I am also wary of mapping political policy too crudely onto aesthetic impulses. With regard to New York School poetry, for example, I don't think that its "aesthetics of monstrous absorbency" is necessarily complicit in any imperialist design; as my chapter on Mayer makes clear, there are many kinds of prolificacy—like that of female speech or bodily functions (or, more ominously, of terrorist "sleeper cells")—that can potentially be quite threatening to the so-called powers that be.

28. See Lehman: "The association of Ashbery as an aesthetic force with Andy Warhol is to my mind as tendentious an interpretation of Ashbery's

poetry as that which alleges he is secretly a political poet," (354) and Ward: "To read O'Hara, Ashbery and Schuyler as they deserve, is to open their work to, and see refracted in it, the full retrospect of the American Renaissance, and of the changing structures of European poetry from Romanticism to the present. To lower one's sights, and in particular to pander to the notion that poetry should be modest and casual, is to block out knowledge of the challenges to which these three poets have at least risen. O'Hara's work takes on more than either the ephemeral sixties 'happenings' or the boxed-in ironies of the Movement with which it is contemporary" (4).

29. Here I'm talking primarily about the downtown scene around the Poetry Project—clearly there were many other scenes in New York at the time, such as the one around the Black Arts Repertory Theater in Harlem, founded in 1967 by Amiri Baraka. And despite the Poetry Project's hopes for openness and all-inclusiveness, it has had many dissenters, who argue that it has epitomized and perpetuated precisely the cliquey-ness that has in some sense characterized New York School poetry itself. Charles Bernstein, for example, writes that its "preference for the local (the neighborhood) and the stylistically familiar (tried) has sometimes clouded a larger view of what is happening in the art" (see his endnote in Waldman, *Out of This World*, 621); others have noted that the Project has never really shed its original image as a haven for educated, white, middle-class bohemians. "There are still persistent problems [at the Poetry Project], such as the lack of non-white women editing and publishing through the Project. . . . This goes for non-white men as well," says Marcella Durand, who has worked at the Project in various capacities—see Kane, 205. For more on the role "coterie" has played in this milieu, see Lytle Shaw's *Frank O'Hara: The Poetics of Coterie*; see also Michael Davidson's chapter "Ennabling Fictions" in *The San Francisco Renaissance*, for a discussion of the role exclusivity and oppositionality can play in the construction of literary communities.

30. In his study *Destructive Poetics: Heidegger and Modern American Poetry*, Paul Bové makes a similar point: "I want to offer for consideration the idea that certain strong poets exist in the mediate without experiencing the trauma [Bloom] describes. Or, rather, their response to the 'trauma' is not a defensive lie against time, a mastering of anxiety by an act of deceitful will, but an open and projective poetry. . . . They do not unwillingly extend the decayed and decaying death of the revisionist to the death of poetry itself" (31). Though Bové is more concerned with Black Mountain poets such as Olson and Creeley (hence the reference to "projective poetry"), his remark has relevance here.

31. In addition to its relation to New York School writing, the dance analogy Jacobs offers here also prognosticates the very aesthetic of postmodern dance that will become dominant in the Judson Church and other experimental dance venues in downtown New York in the sixties, in the

non-dancerly, pedestrian work of Yvonne Rainer, Steve Paxton, Simone Forti, Deborah Hay, and many others.

32. This "public poetry which does not abolish the private" is precisely the point of tension upon which Myles situates her poetic performance (see chapter 5); it is also the primary subject of Herring's piece on O'Hara, in which he argues that Personism is a queer retailoring of "a postwar poetics of impersonality" rather than a rejection of it (426). For the Yau comment, see "The New York School Symposium," videotape of a panel at St. Mark's Church in 1988, with Charles North, John Yau, Dore Ashton, Tony Towle, and Jane Freilicher, moderated by Anne Waldman (New York: Thin Air Video, 1988. Videographer Mitch Corber, 68 min. Available at the New York Public Library).

33. Incidentally, LeSueur says that O'Hara's "Personism" was in fact originally called "Personalism," and that O'Hara changed it after LeSueur told him that a "dopey philosophy founded in southern California" went by that name. See LeSueur, xxiv.

34. Though first-generation New York School poetry is rarely associated with Marxist philosophy—more often it is seen as a symptom or celebration of bourgeois consumerism—one might also note that its poetic production coincided with a tremendous amount of (primarily Continental) theorization about "everyday life" from a Marxist standpoint, a discourse which links everything from Marx and Lenin to the Surrealists to the Frankfurt School to the Situationists to the events in France in May–June 1968. The French historian and sociologist Henri Lefebvre eloquently summarizes the scope of this discourse in his book *Critique of Everyday Life*, using terms that echo the New York School interest in skimming the surface of self or daily life: "Our search for the human takes us too far, too 'deep,' we seek it in the clouds or the mysteries, whereas it is waiting for us, besieging us on all sides. We will not find it in myths—although human facts carry with them a long and magnificent procession of legends, tales and songs, poems and dances. All we need to do is simply to open our eyes, to leave the dark world of metaphysics behind and the false depths of the 'inner life' behind, and we will discover the immense human wealth that the humblest facts of everyday life contain" (132).

35. The psychologist Carol Gilligan has even set forth an entire system of ethics based on granting primacy and value to a feminized notion of "caring"—see her *In A Different Voice: Psychological Theory and Women's Development*, and the anthology *Women, Girls, and Psychotherapy: Reframing Resistance*, ed. Gilligan, Annie G. Rogers, and Deborah L. Tolman (1991).

36. Schuyler stands a bit apart from his peers in that he didn't go to Harvard; while O'Hara worked as a curator at the Museum of Modern Art, and Ashbery and Koch ended up with jobs in the academy (Bard and Columbia, respectively), because of a host of physical and mental problems, Schuyler may very well have become someone you stepped over on the sidewalk had

it not been for the patronage that installed him in the Chelsea Hotel in his later years (as Myles, who worked as an assistant to Schuyler at the Chelsea, once put it). Nonetheless, Schuyler's poetry still concerns itself with the pinnacle of what he calls "East Fifties queen taste," and his early travels in Europe, where he met and worked for W. H. Auden, most certainly familiarized him with a brotherhood at the heart of the poetry world (though he later rejected Auden's poetry, explaining, "I would type something of Wynstan's and think, 'Well, if this is poetry, I'm certainly never going to write any myself'" [Lehman, 259]).

37. Anne Waldman's poem "Makeup on Empty Space" (and her performances of it) is of import here (as is her "Fast Talking Woman" poem and persona, especially in light of the conversation about "fast talk" poetics discussed in chapter 4). See the essays on Waldman in *Jacket* 27 (http://jacketmagazine.com/27/index.shtml [19 December 2006]), especially Akilah Oliver's "Hold the Space: Anne Waldman's Poetics," Jena Osman's "Tracking a Poem in Time: The Shifting States of Anne Waldman's 'Makeup on Empty Space,'" and Rachel Blau DuPlessis's "Anne Waldman: Standing Corporeally in One's Time." I would also note that Notley has continued to work explicitly on the theme of the freedom and isolation of empty space, and has recently tethered it to a more overtly explicitly political attitude. In a 2001 interview, she explains: "I am writing something now in which there's a concept called 'negative space,' and there are a lot of dead women in the book—this book is about dead women, actually, though they're not all dead, the dead women, because I'm one of them. But since we have no role in [political] events, particularly now, we withdraw into negative space and take no part in it" (Dick). This epic—*Alma, or the Dead Women*—was published by Granary Books in 2006, just as this book was going to print.

3. WHAT LIFE ISN'T DAILY?

1. I admit at the outset that my focus on these two particular works slights other aspects of Mayer's career, but thankfully there are many others who have written or are currently addressing its other aspects—Kane, Vickery, Spahr, Lee Ann Brown, Michael Gizzi, Peter Baker, Stephen Cope, Nada Gordon, among others. Also, a plethora of papers on Mayer were presented at the 1999 Barnard conference.

2. See *A Secret Location on the Lower East Side: Adventures in Writing, 1960–1980*, edited by Rodney Phillips and Steven Clay, for documentation of many of these publications.

3. For a fuller discussion of Mayer's workshops, collaborative projects, and performance stunts, see Kane, 187–201, and Vickery's chapter "Desire Not a Saint: The Pathography of Bernadette Mayer."

4. For examples of Mayer's work in these genres, see her books *Story* (*o to 9*, 1968), *The Basketball Article*, written with Anne Waldman (Angel Hair, 1975), *Incidents Reports Sonnets* (Archipelago Books, 1984), *Utopia* (United Artists Books, 1984), *The Art of Science Writing*, by Mayer and Dale Worsey (Teachers and Writers, 1989), *Sonnets* (Tender Buttons, 1989), *The Formal Field of Kissing* (Catchword Papers, 1990), and *The 3:15 Experiment*, written with Jen Hofer, Lee Ann Brown, and Danika Dinsmore (Owl Press, 2001).

5. I'm not really concerned, however, with "claiming" Mayer as a New York School poet as opposed to a Language poet. For reasons explored earlier, all of the women at issue here complicate such divisions. As Myles recently said: "There was a time when the poetry I felt most immediately affected by split, and labels were affixed that said 'you're New York School,' and 'you're Language,' as though these were really different things, when in fact Language came out of the New York School, and New York School came out of French Surrealism and Russian Futurism and John Cage and Lana Turner. It is one flow" (Richard, 26–27).

6. See the work not only of Mary Kelly, but also of Carolee Schneeman, Yoko Ono, Marina Abramović, Linda Montano, Cindy Sherman, Eleanor Antin, Adrian Piper, Karen Finley, Jenny Holzer, and Barbara Kruger.

7. See Louis Zukofsky's introduction to the 1931 "Objectivist" issue of *Poetry*, in which he privileges "information" alongside "sincerity" and "objectification" as one of poetry's goals: "When sincerity in writing is present the insincere may be cut out at will and information, not ignorance, remains" (283).

8. In fact I can't think of too many others, though Carole Maso's pregnancy journal, *A Room Lit with Roses* (2000), Claudia Rankine's poetry collection *Plot* (2001), and Rachel Zucker's *The Last Clear Narrative* (2004) are intriguing recent contributions to the field.

9. At times in *Midwinter* Mayer's preoccupation with this question leads her into dubious territory, as when she pleads near the end of the book, "So just because we're married / Don't dismiss us, don't forget to include us / In all the gay anthologies as a family / We are still crazy" (108). It's not hard to understand how this appeal might annoy some people—being "crazy" (or bohemian or poor or whatever) is clearly not the same as being gay, and Mayer's comfort with the slippage between them in a book so devoted to taking stock of a hetero family ("today our combined ages add up to 71 years / And all together we weigh 350 pounds" [*MD*, 54]) can be a little unsettling. Later works of Mayer's—specifically, 1989's *Sonnets*—delve more fully into the pleasures and difficulties of unclassifiable sexuality; Spahr has written well on this topic in her essay "'Love Scattered, Not Concentrated Love,'" in which Spahr considers Mayer's sonnets in relation to queer theory's "resistance to regimes of the normal" (110). One might also note that in the two decades or more since the composition of *Midwinter Day*, Mayer

has moved further away from the subjects of marriage and children—in the Jarnot interview, she asserts: "I think [monogamy] sucks. Yeah, I'm against monogamy . . . I'm against marriage. The only reason I'll get married now is if someone needs a green card and will pay me a lot of money" (8). The point here isn't Mayer's personal belief system or biography, but rather that her negotiation of domestic relations grows in scope when we recognize that these early books do not necessarily dead-end into a Molly Bloomesque "yes I said yes I will Yes" embrace of married life, with all its flaws and disappointments. Rather, they represent the beginnings of a long journey into ambivalent, often uncharted waters.

10. The Notley quote about dreams comes from an email interview with the author, 4 February 2002. For the Irigaray, see *This Sex Which Is Not One*, 123.

11. Stein's personal attitudes toward childbearing were actually quite fascinating, as a recently discovered Stein essay from the early 1900s, "Degeneration in American Women," suggests. In the essay, Stein argues (to the surprise, and perhaps horror, of many feminists) that "the only serious business of life in which [women] cannot be entirely outclassed by the male is that of child bearing." Her primary distaste lies with college-educated women who delay or ignore childbirth, though she admits that there are "a few women in every generation . . . who are exceptions to the rule"; one imagines that Stein must have placed herself in this latter category. For more on this issue, see Brenda Wineapple's book *Sister Brother: Gertrude and Leo Stein*; Wineapple discovered this unpublished, handwritten essay by Stein in a Princeton University archive while doing research for her book. See also Mina Loy's writings on the subject, which are similarly fascinating and vexing—see, for example, her poem "Parturition" and her "Feminist Manifesto," which echoes the eugenics movement in its proclamation that "every woman of superior intelligence should realize her race-responsibility, in producing children in adequate proportion to the unfit and degenerate members of her sex" (*The Lost Lunar Baedeker*, 4, 155).

12. Mayer's conflict with Stein began as far back as *Memory*. About the project's conception, she has said, "Part of the reason I did it was to be nasty to Gertrude Stein who always said you can't write remembering, so I wanted to say that maybe you could . . . But in a spirit of fun, I was doing it *with* Gertrude Stein" (*Disembodied Poetics*, 98–99). *Midwinter Day* inherits something of this same relationship, a relationship I find interesting for its commitment to "being nasty" and "having fun" at the same time.

13. Not to be misleading, I should add that though Maso thoroughly enjoys her pregnancy, her accounts of birth and afterbirth veer into terrifying territory, as she recounts the deep pain of childbirth and the even deeper disorientation of a postpartum depression.

14. Think, for example, of Schuyler's comment (in a 1971 letter to Gerard Malanga) about the Lower East Side, where Mayer and many other "second-generation" poets made their home in the seventies and eighties: "It's a remarkably dreary day out here and I think I'll be staying more at my New York pad, on East 35th—a nice blah sort of neighborhood, unostentatious middle class, my dish exactly. I admire my friends who [have] the courage to live on the lower East side; I certainly haven't." Quoted in Kane, 18.

15. For an exciting recent revisioning of this "trash aesthetic" in poetry, see Brenda Coultas's *A Handmade Museum*, whose female narrator-heroine is preoccupied by dumpster-diving and garbage.

16. The issue of rage as it relates to Mitchell's work and life, and to feminism in general, is an important and fascinating one; see Nochlin's essay on the subject, "A Rage to Paint," in Livingston's monograph.

17. See Rifkin's account in "My Little World" in *Jacket* 7. Rifkin here discusses *Unnatural Acts*, the magazine devoted to collaborative writing procedures which stemmed from a 1972 Mayer workshop, a workshop which included an eight-hour collaborative writing session. Mayer's direction about "working yr ass off" appears in the version of Mayer's "Experiments" that Bernstein and Andrews include in *The Language Book*, 83. Ironically, "don't ever get famous" is now the title of a book of critical work edited by Daniel Kane, *Don't Ever Get Famous: Essays on New York Writing after the New York School*, which appeared as this book was going to print.

18. For a more theoretical, cultural-historical, and wide-ranging examination of these "not-nice" feelings, see Sianne Ngai's book *Ugly Feelings*, which discusses the political and aesthetic roles of "non-cathartic" affects such as envy, irritation, paranoia, and disgust as they play out in the work of Stein, Melville, Nella Larsen, Alfred Hitchcock, Ralph Ellison, John Yau, Bruce Andrews, and others.

4. DEAR DARK CONTINENT

1. For my purposes here I have had to forgo a richer discussion of Notley's contributions to the field of women, the epic, and the visionary. For work focused on the topic, see Page DuBois's essay in *Differences*; also see the essays by Susan McCabe, Claudia Keelan, and Libbie Rifkin in *Interim* 23, nos. 1–2, as well as Notley's own words on the subject in conversation with her son, Anselm Berrigan, in *Interim*, 96–98.

2. This shift also echoes that made by Anne Waldman, though Notley has made interesting comments on why she doesn't consider works such as Waldman's *Iovis* or DuPlessis's *Drafts* epics: see her conversation with Berrigan in *Interim*, 96.

3. It's probably misleading to treat *Alette* as the pivot point in her career; Notley has always written long poetic sequences. Before *Alette* she had already worked with the form in early pieces such as *Sorrento* (1984) and the two "fictive" books published together in *The Scarlet Cabinet, Close to me & Closer . . . (The Language of Heaven)* and *Désamère*. See her description of this shift in conversation with Eleni Sikelianos in *Interim*, 113-114.

4. The archives can be found at the University of California at San Diego, Geisel Library, Mandeville Special Collections, Register of the Alice Notley Collection, 1969-1997, and online at http://orpheus.ucsd.edu/speccoll/testing/html/msso319a.html (3 December 2006).

5. In 2006, Wesleyan University Press published Notley's *Grave of Light: New and Selected Poems 1970–2005*. As this beautiful, expansive volume was not yet in print at the time of this book's composition, all references to Notley's *Selected* that appear here refer to the slimmer 1993 volume published by Talisman.

6. In Freud's text, the phrase "dark continent" appears in English, and is justly famous not only for its feminist ramifications, but also for its metaphorical coupling of female sexuality with a racialized Africa, and by extension, other countries with a "dark" populace.

7. Sexton's book is *To Bedlam and Part Way Back* (1960). Sexton takes her epigram from an 1815 letter from Schopenhaeur to Goethe, and arguably uses it to position herself, as poet, as Oedipus, en route to discovering "the awful truth," and the reader as a sort of Jocasta, "who begs Oedipus for God's sake not to enquire further." Sexton's unfashionable interest in "the awful truth," specifically in religious truth at the end of her career (as in *The Awful Rowing toward God* [1975]), may also bear some relation to Notley's.

8. Selinger notes this connection with Rich's poem in his essay on Notley, and argues that "writing in the Mainstream American Tradition set Notley apart from the two most obvious models for feminist poetry in the early 1970s: the fierce, resistant mythologizing handed down from Plath; and the feminist exploration of women's 'essential connection' to each other, and to their children, sponsored by Rich. The earliest poems included in her Selected, which proceeds in chronological order, glance at both models for guidance." See Selinger, 313.

9. It's tempting to contrast Notley's embrace of Williams, Whitman, O'Hara, and so on with her lack of interest in the poetry of Sexton, Plath, and Rich, and to see the latter as a perplexing, and perhaps disappointing, rejection of her female contemporaries or recent predecessors. But such a reading skips over the fact that to many "bohemian" artists of the day, the work and reputations of those women appeared compromised by their more mainstream, Boston Brahmin milieu, which stood aesthetically and socially far afield from the more experimental, anti-academic poetry scene

that Donald Allen aimed to showcase in *The New American Poetry*. (Rich is obviously a different case from Plath and Sexton, because of her politicized departure into feminist and lesbian inquiries, but even her most "experimental" poetry tends to remain ghosted by the formality with which she began her career.) In an autobiographical essay about her development as an artist during this period, the poet Kathleen Fraser offers a relevant summary of this distinction: "It was Olson's declared move away from the narcissistically probing, psychological defining of self—so seductively explored by Sylvia Plath, Anne Sexton, and Robert Lowell in the early and mid-1960s, and by their avid followers for at least a generation after—that provided a major alternative ethic of writing for women poets. While seriously committed to gender consciousness, a number of us carried an increasing skepticism towards any fixed rhetoric of the poem, implied or intoned" (*Moving Borders*, 642). Though Fraser is focused on Olson whereas Notley is not, Fraser's account echoes comments Notley has made about her attraction to O'Hara at around the same time: "Much of mainstream poetry seems more narcissistic than O'Hara's, say: he never says, Admire my emotion, or as Adrienne Rich often seems to, Admire my emotion which is Our emotion. He's saying Together we will make a little fun of my emotion, which may also be yours, while I try to demonstrate how emotion is the glue of our existence" (Foster, 81).

10. See Gooch's description of the circumstances surrounding the poem's writing, in *City Poet*, 322–325, and LeSueur's in *Digressions*, 219–222.

11. To preserve the look of the text of *The Descent of Alette*, which employs double quotation marks throughout as a form of measure, I use single quotation marks to enclose and mark excerpts from it.

12. This problem rears its head most starkly in critical discussions of Kenneth Koch, whose poetic treatment of women can be uncharacteristically tiresome. Many critics hastily rush to defend this aspect of Koch's work by invoking Koch's own commitment to humor—for example, after quoting the lines of Koch's poem "The Art of Love" which imagine jumping on a woman tied up to a bed until she's "all flattened / and splayed out," the critic David Spurr writes: "'It's supposed to be funny,' Koch once remarked in conversation to an outraged female acquaintance" (*Scene of My Selves*, 352). Not to be misleading, I should note that Spurr's essay in *Scene*—"Koch's 'Serious Moment'"—is unique in its willingness to take seriously the role of violence and sadomasochistic fantasy in Koch's work. Elsewhere, one repeatedly gets the sense that even to broach the subject is to invite being tarred as a spoilsport, or as "righteously indignant," as Lehman has put it (205).

13. To try to write what "poetry needs next" can be taken as another version of Myles's comment that the poet has to address "the room of the culture"—and it is precisely here that Notley's "hermetic" poetry takes on

its public dimensions. For more on the public aspects of her work, specifically as it relates to the function of the epic and the role of the poet/seer/sayer, see her conversation with Sikelianos in *Interim*, 112–114.

14. Though my study is not focused on the rich history of live poetry performances from the Beat era to the present, I would point out here that this "fast talk" on the page is but one element of a city and scene that were teeming with live talk, be it poetry-performance talk, telephone talk, bar talk, pillow talk, or stoop talk, and that this explosion of speech links up the New York School and Warhol's writings, poetry slams, performance art, and much more. See Kane's chapters "Oral Poetics on the Lower East Side" and "Bob Holman, the Poetry Project, and the Nuyorican Poets Café," Reva Wolf's study *Andy Warhol, Poetry and Gossip in the 1960s*, and Hazel Smith's *Hyperscapes in the Poetry of Frank O'Hara: Difference, Homosexuality, and Topography* for more on "poetry off the page" during the period.

15. It should be noted here that Notley's preoccupation with ghosts partakes in a lineage of women's literary interest in ghosts and ventriloquism, especially since "woman" herself, or as Castle has it, the lesbian, is very often the "ghost in the machine" of literary history. For more on "spiritualism," especially in relation to the modernist period, see Helen Sword's *Ghostwriting Modernism*.

16. Notley goes on in the interview to address the important and vexing issue of audience or lack thereof for poetry in general: "I think that so-called popular poetry underestimates the verbal intelligence of so-called ordinary people, who in turn haven't been properly taught poetry in school," she explains. "Meanwhile so many people's careers in the academy and in poetry seem to depend on their obfuscating poetry, making it as theoretical and intellectual as possible. The consequence is that ordinary people think they can't understand poetry, and popular poetry talks down to them. . . . My books are for anyone, anyone who feels like taking the chance, and the time. Of course, that still won't be a lot of people" (Goldman, 6).

17. Notley's means of challenging an obsolete but still functioning patriarchy by dreaming up new worlds and giving them voice participates in a long tradition of mythic and utopian storytelling that has appealed to many feminist writers, from Christine de Pizan's medieval feminist epic *The Book of the City of Ladies* (1405) to Margaret Cavendish's comedic play *Convent of Pleasure* (1668) to Charlotte Perkin Gilman's *Herland* (1915) to Monique Wittig's lesbian-warrior epic *Les Guérillères* (1969) to a whole host of recent science fiction. Other feminist utopia writers include Joanna Russ, Marge Piercy, Suzy McKee Charnas, Margaret Atwood, Christiane Rochefort, E. M. Broner, Ursula LeGuin, Pamela Sargent, Luce Irigaray, Hélène Cixous, Joan Slonczewski, and many, many others. Their visions vary wildly, of course; for more on the subject, see Frances Bartkowski's book *Feminist Utopias*. See also Mayer's *Utopia* (1984).

18. In this context—as discussed in chapter 3 in regard to Mayer's *Midwinter*—this Tomkins principle is essentially a declaration of freedom, insofar as it refocuses attention on the human subject's capacity to "invest any and every aspect of existence" with any one of a whole range of positive to negative feelings, from "the magic of excitement and joy" to "the dread of fear or shame or distress" (Tomkins, 54), instead of the fixed effects that one would expect certain stimuli to occasion (the latter being a moralist's universe, without a doubt). Chappell discerns the workings of this principle in *Alette*, although it distresses him: "The images [in *Alette*] point toward meanings beyond themselves only during the time it takes an incident concerning them to occur. Then the meanings shift. This is the obverse of Dante. . . . [In *Alette*] the motivic images—snake, meadow, cavern, tree, mask, lapis, and so forth—recur constantly but there are no steady root meanings" (153).

19. Though the two books differ dramatically in tone and substance, Notley's project in *Mysteries* bears an intriguing relationship to Roland Barthes's *Roland Barthes by Roland Barthes*. Barthes remains far more enraptured by the principle "that *the subject is merely an effect of language*," but much of the pleasure of his book lies in his perverse unwillingness to grasp this fact. "Do I not know that, *in the field of the subject, there is no referent?*" he asks himself at one point (56), the more interesting part of the sentence being not the semiotic truism but rather the complexity of its self-reproach. Notley's navigation between the constancy and inconstancy of "self" produces a similar effect, as the "I" she inhabits cannot be properly understood as a consolidated lyric speaker or as fragmented linguistic predicament. For Barthes, the enigma that muddles up the neatness of poststructuralist platitude is the body—his body—and its "anarchic foam of tastes and distastes"; for Notley, it is the concrete existence of "soul." Both "autobiographies" are shaped by a horror of the doxa—"Public Opinion, the mind of the majority, petit bourgeois Consensus, the Voice of Nature, the Violence of Prejudice," as Barthes defines it (47)—and an urgent desire to evade its sway at every turn. Barthes focuses on the sensual and cerebral pleasures of this evasion; Notley prefers impassioned dissent.

20. For more on this conflict as it relates to feminist writers and Notley's legacy in particular, see Catherine Wagner's "fake interview" with Notley in *Interim*, in which Wagner says to Notley, "As a younger poet who's been influenced by your work I'm in a bind when I read your 'Poetics of Disobedience' talk, because, to be very simplistic, if I disobey the world I'm obeying you, and if I obey the world I'm disobeying you. I want to go along with you by disobeying the world because gosh how exciting, but that means finding a way to rebel against you as well. My little rebellion against you ends up sounding sort of milquetoast." (To which Wagner has Notley reply, "I accuse you of money" [89].) In my own negotiation of Notley's influence,

I've felt a similar bind—a bind which, while occasionally quite unnerving, can also be quite productive, as the energy of Wagner's imagined dialogue with Notley indicates. In the end it pushes one to define the terms and stakes of one's own disobedience, which can become its own form of self-liberation.

5. WHEN WE'RE ALONE IN PUBLIC

1. I am keenly aware that the word "lesbian" has barely appeared in my study thus far. In fact, while writing about the many male ghosts that populate Notley's work, I could not help but feel haunted by another specter, that of the "apparitional lesbian," as Terry Castle has put it—i.e., the lesbian that patriarchal culture "ghosts," then exorcises—that it drains of corporeality, sensuality, danger, and authority, then conveniently disappears. In her book *The Apparitional Lesbian* (1993) Castle begins by articulating the by now standard (yet still potent) objections to the umbrella term "queer." In a section entitled "*[The lesbian] is not a gay man*," Castle explains: "As soon as the lesbian is lumped in—for better or for worse—with her male homosexual counterpart, the singularity of her experience (sexual and otherwise) tends to become obscured. We 'forget' about the lesbian by focusing instead on gay men" (12). Thus far, this study has entertained this all-too-familiar peril.

2. See Myles's comments in "Chewing the Fat about AIDS—Arts Today with Eileen Myles," from *Artery: The AIDS-Arts Forum*. Myles has never flinched from addressing the complexities of the links that can exist between gay men and lesbians, links which the AIDS crisis rendered acute throughout the eighties and early nineties. See her remarks on the topic at the end of this study's afterword.

3. See Patrick F. Durgin's entry on Myles in *Dictionary of Literary Biography*, here cited from the online version at Literature Resource Center 3.1, Author Resource Pages. Durgin notes that Myles uses the term "proprioceptive" in a letter.

4. The writer-dancer Deborah Hay is the only artist I know of to elaborate explicitly on this "cellular" idea—see her book *My Body, The Buddhist* (Wesleyan University Press, 2000), in which she describes her body as her "53-trillion-celled teacher," and her dance practice as the observation of "cellular consciousness." Muriel Rukeyser also insisted that her poetry came from her female body in a more expansive way; see Kate Daniels's preface to Rukeyser's *Out of Silence: Selected Poems*, in which Daniels reports that Rukeyser once told Cynthia Ozick at a 1976 panel, "You, Cynthia, write from the mind, but I write from the body, a female body" (xv).

To be fair, Pinsky admits that there do exist other kinds of poetry: "Other conceptions of poetry might include flamboyantly expressive vocal delivery, accompanied by impressive physical presence, by the poet or performer; or the typographical, graphic appearance of the words in itself, apart from the indication of sound." But he quickly adds: "Those areas are not part of this book's conception." Fair enough, but such an exclusion complicates his earlier claims about what poetry essentially "is," and uses a kind of sleight of hand to make entire dimensions of the art disappear. (I won't even get into the word choice of "flamboyant," with its connection to the "flaming" queer spectacle, and so on.)

5. Critics who disapproved of the personal theater of Plath and Sexton customarily used the word "exhibitionistic" to denigrate their work ("narcissistic" coming in a close second); Myles's relaxed reclamation of the term points further toward her difference. As Patrick Durgin puts it in his essay on Myles in the *Dictionary of Literary Biography*, "A confession, strictly speaking, insinuates that readers are made privy to something which, in Myles's aesthetic, was always in the fore, assuming the nature of traditional wisdom. Her type of disclosure precludes the tension inherent in coming clean." See also Myles's poem "Edward the Confessor" in *Not Me*; see also Chris Kraus's review of *Cool for You* in the *Nation*, in which Kraus makes the important point that "like Acker, Myles values the most intimate and 'shameful' details of her life not for what they tell her about herself but for what they tell us about the culture."

6. The 1949 Plath quotation is cited by Rose (145); the second is from *The Unabridged Journals of Sylvia Plath* (77). Of course, potent class distinctions come into play here, as "walking the streets" has historically posed a different kind of problem for "good" middle- or upper-middle-class girls (like Plath) with a reputation to protect. For a story that depicts the dangers faced by a lower-class "slut" hitchhiking in America in the late sixties, see Cookie Mueller's humorous and disturbing autobiographical story, "Abduction and Rape–Highway 31 Elkton, Maryland–1969," in which Mueller tries to avoid getting raped by using the following logic: "I have always been an astute observer of sexy women and unsexy women, and in all my years I've never seen a crazy woman get chased by a man. Look at bag ladies on the street. They rarely get raped. And look at burnt-out LSD girls. No men bothered with them much. So I decided that I would simply act crazy. I would turn the tables. I would scare him" (49).

7. To take a more global view, it bears noting that in a number of countries the prohibition against women in the public sphere is enforced by violent retribution—sometimes legally sanctioned, sometimes just culturally so—as in the so-called honor killings of women who appear in public with a man who is not a family member. The website http://womensissues.about.com/cs/honorkillings reports that honor killings have been reported in Bangladesh, Brazil, Ecuador, Egypt, India, Israel, Italy, Jordan, Morocco, Pakistan, Sweden, Turkey, Uganda, and the United Kingdom, and remarks

that although they are prevalent in Muslim countries, "many Islamic leaders and scholars condemn the practice and deny that it is based on religious doctrine." The UN estimates as many as five thousand women are murdered via honor killings each year.

8. The most immediate precursor of the "skinny column" poem is Schuyler, and Myles—who worked for Schuyler—testifies that his skinny lines stemmed from a similar process: "When he was an art writer he used small books . . . that's actually why Jimmy's poems look like that too" (Foster, 52). Myles explains that once she's at home, "the legal pad becomes [her] material of choice, and the poems get fatter" (Foster, 52); one suspects that Schuyler might have shared aspects of this compositional process, as his fattest poems, such as "A Few Days" and "The Morning of the Poem," seem most clearly set at his desk, in repose.

9. Schuyler struggled with obesity and diabetes, and his *Diary* is filled with beautiful and poignant lines about food and weight. "Yesterday an early supper at Grand Central, six Wellfleet, sweet and cold, and oyster stew, OK, but I really wanted a pan roast," he writes on 16 April 1988; "I lost four pounds. A pound a week, which [the doctor] says is fine," he reports a few days later (213–214, 216).

10. Notley, by contrast, nominally shuns the communal: "We is a difficult word," she told me in an email interview. "And I don't use it in *Mysteries*" (4 February 2002). Compare this attitude with the title of Myles's pamphlet *We, the Poets*, and at least one point of divergence between them becomes clear.

11. The links to Antonin Artaud and Barthes are no accident, in that Myles's autobiographical writing may bear more kinship with European traditions of experimental "life writing" than with the American "tell-all" memoir. See Kraus's review of *Cool for You* for more on this issue, in which she smartly distinguishes between the sort of life writing practiced by Acker and Myles and the more traditional forms of the American "memoir," especially what Kraus calls the "Female Madness Tale."

12. These distinctions between "self" and "character" are more complicated still, as Myles explains in an interview: "There are certain ways I didn't know who I was until I developed that character, so it gets a little dicey. Really the character is more firm than I am. . . . So of course it's easy to get up and do her in a reading, because I know what she sounds like" (Richard, 29).

13. Given her commitment to the complexity and risks of her "dirty secret," Myles has little patience for critics who dismiss her work as "too personal." "I've actually been criticized in my writing for being 'personal.' Like that's not so important . . . I mean in some reviews I got for *Chelsea Girls*, the reviewer was saying that what was trivial and unimportant about my work was how personal it was. It's a funny way of making their objec-

tions to my writing sound abstract. They basically just didn't like hearing about a woman, a lesbian" (Foster, 60–61). *Chelsea Girls* pleasurably anticipates this criticism within the text: the epigraph to the story "Toys R Us" is an excerpt from a *Village Voice* review that reads: "Myles's social observations are scattershot, and when she turns her eye exclusively on herself, as too often she does, she sinks to sharing sappy diary entries." The story then humorously begins: "That's when I knew my play was over" (145). The disobedient trope of merging a review into a story gets inverted and expanded in Myles's own review of her friend Tim Dlugos, in which she writes: "I've written tons of reviews of books of poems. I consider it an act of politics, to review poetry, especially if I'm able to sneak a review by on an editor who either doesn't know or whom I've managed to convince that the poet isn't a friend of mine. There's this bizarre myth in the teeny subfiefdom of the books pages of papers and magazines and journals that there's something wrong with reviewing friends, and so we see such good examples of 'objective journalism' as when a *Times* reviewer is assigned to Kathy Acker who could only shit on her head, but the reviewer doesn't 'know' her at least" (*Mississippi*, 226).

14. Myles's treatment of breath in the story of her father's death may actually have more in common with the fragile *Atemwende*, or "breath-turn," as theorized by Paul Celan, than the blustery "breath-line" elaborated upon by Walt Whitman, Charles Olson, or Allen Ginsberg. In Celan's "The Meridian Speech," he writes: "Poetry is perhaps this: an *Atemwende*, a turning of our breath. Who knows, perhaps poetry goes its way—the way of art—for the sake of just such a turn? . . . Nobody can tell how long the pause for breath—hope and thought—will last." Celan's breath-turn emphasizes the deep uncertainty that breathing—along with hoping and thinking—will continue: the abyss of death and silence is always right around the corner, ready to shape, deform, or exterminate poetic expression. Myles is similarly haunted—she knows that "breaths can suddenly go false and shallow and the bowl of you can be perched, still, and then shatter from everything that doesn't return—air, life." The last lines of O'Hara's "The Day Lady Died"—"while she whispered a song along the keyboard / to Mal Waldron and everyone and I stopped breathing"—are also relevant here.

15. This dual capacity—our capacity to witness, sustain, and help each other, and our equally real capacity to abandon each other, or at least be unable to protect each other from our inevitable deaths—might also be taken as yet another manifestation of the caring/not-caring conundrum at issue throughout this study. Taken as a whole, *Cool for You* makes a crucial contribution to this discussion by exploring this drama on an institutional level: the novel couples an unflinching record of time spent working in institutions that supposedly "care" for people—a school for severely retarded adult males, a nursing home—with a painful inquiry into the life

and death of Myles's grandmother, Nellie Myles, who lived for seventeen years as a mental patient in a state hospital before dying there.

16. Myles's ideas about class and the speaking subject have much in common with the aesthetic theories of Mikhail Bakhtin, who emphasized "the shifting planes of intention that can occur whenever one language meets another" (see Richter, 528). Both Bakhtin and Myles care deeply about the political ramifications of *heteroglossia* ("the word of another") and dialogical discourse; both actively despise the stultifications of mono-logical discourse, of authoritative speech which "tries to have its say in a vacuum" (Richter, 528). A rich comparison could be made, for example, between Bakhtin's description of the "discourse-address" of Dostoevsky's Underground Man and Myles's self-conscious consideration of "where [she is] performing and who [she is] performing for . . . and thinking what would be political for this particular group of people." See Richter, 547.

17. This task is particularly important in that it's so much easier to lament the nonexistence or inefficacy of a movement (be it an avant-garde art movement, an antiwar movement, etc.) than it is to create or articulate one. Thus, in addition to facing the real deficiencies of current forms of resistance—be they aesthetic or political—we might also ask hard questions about our practiced cultural deafness to dissent (a deafness which the cur-rent Bush Administration, for example, has brought to new heights in the face of widespread global and domestic opposition to the ongoing war on and occupation of Iraq). For the relationship between this deafness and lit-erary history, see Erica Hunt's essay "Notes for an Oppositional Poetics," in which she writes: "The principle of cooptation is this: that dominant cul-ture will transfer its own partiality onto the opposition it tries to suppress. It will always maintain that it holds the complete world view, despite the fissures. Opposition is alternately demonized or accommodated through partial concessions without a meaningful alteration of dominant culture's own terms." She then goes on to discuss how such a dynamic can replicate itself in the land of literature (*Moving Borders*, 685).

18. Though it may have hit a peak in the nineties, the reclamation of the term "girl" remains an ongoing cultural phenomenon—one that is per-haps best understood as part and parcel of the feminist demand that grown women be called women (instead of "coeds," "office girls," and so on). To insist that others call you a woman is to demand that the world stop infan-talizing you; to call oneself a girl is to refuse and resist "becoming a woman" in all the pernicious senses of the phrase—entering the heterosex-ual marketplace, renouncing clitoral sexuality, becoming defined (or "defiled") by menstruation or heterosexual intercourse, allowing male desire to take precedence over one's own, giving up one's name in mar-riage, bearing children in a compulsory fashion, and so on. To reclaim the term "girl" is to insist on remaining in a more inchoate place, before

enthusiasm, self-assurance, and desire become thwarted or codified. It is also to refute the power of reproaches such as *You fight like a girl, you throw like a girl, you cry like a girl*—condemnations which seamlessly merge misogynistic taunt with homophobic ridicule.

This girl movement has been contemporaneous with a powerful outpouring of clinical interest in the particular problems that girls face as they head into adolescence, spearheaded by the psychologist Carol Gilligan, a founding member of the Harvard Project on Women's Psychology and Girls' Development. See Gilligan's essay "Reframing Resistance" from the collection *Women, Girls, and Psychotherapy* (1991), in which she explains how despite a "remarkable convergence of clinical observation, developmental findings, and epidemiological data, pointing repeatedly to a striking asymmetry between girls' and boys' development—and one which has clear implications for preventing suffering and fostering development—this persistent observation of difference has, until recently, remained unexplored and unexplained theoretically" (14). As the title of her essay indicates, Gilligan—along with feminists in a number of different fields—is invested in understanding how and why girls resist socialization around the time of adolescence, and how their resistance might be read as a "protest against the available fictions of female becoming," as Nancy Miller has put it in a literary context (see Heilbrun, 18).

19. Idiosyncratic genius abounded in these workshops—and here I'm thinking of people such as Annie Iobst and Lucy Sexton, who performed as the duo Dancenoise; screenwriter/playwright/fiction writer Laurie Weeks; video artist Cecilia Dougherty; artist/boxer Nancy Brooks Brody; rock musicians Anne Kugler and Cynthia Nelson; art writer Nathan Kernan; painters Jennie Portnof and John Juray; photographer Shannon Ebner; artist/restauranteur Tanya Rynd; and countless others.

20. For more on *affidamento*, see the work of Italian feminist Luisa Muraro, who describes the relationship as follows: "You tie yourself to a person who can help you achieve something which you think you are capable of but which you have not yet achieved" (124). Such a relation is based on the still radical presumption that women have something to offer each other beyond knitting-circle secrets of how to get by in a man's world. *Affidamento* presumes that women can claim, wield, and exchange power.

AFTERWORD

1. It might seem as though I'm leaning here in the direction of a certain essentialism that suggests that women are "naturally" antiwar; I know this is a troublesome proposal, complicated by many factors, including the increasing presence of women in combat forces around the world, the role

of women in the torture of prisoners at Abu Ghraib, hawkish female politicians such as Condeleezza Rice, the rising number of female suicide bombers, and so on. I would also here point out the startling statistic that prior to WWII, women and children traditionally constituted about 5 percent of wartime casualties; now they constitute 95 percent. Some progress, indeed. (For more on the issue, see the anthology *Women on War: An Anthology of Writings from Antiquity to the Present*, ed. by Daniela Gioseffi [New York: Feminist Press, a not-for-profit NGO of the United Nations, 2003], which contains 150 perspectives from around the globe, from Sappho to RAWA in Afghanistan, and includes everything from theoretical work to firsthand survival stories.) Also, to defuse this essentialism, I would offer up this very helpful distinction made by the organizers of a 2002 conference at the Barnard Center for Research on Women entitled "Responding to Violence, Rethinking Security," who wrote in their published report on the conference: "Feminists have developed new understandings of the causes of violence and they have also developed creative alternatives for response and prevention. Feminists can offer these alternative viewpoints not because women are somehow more peaceful, but because feminists don't share the set of assumptions that make violence appear inevitable and even ennobling" (2).

2. See Notley's talk "Homer and Postmodern War," given at Poets' House on December 5, 2002, a section of which was reprinted in the guide to the 2003 People's Poetry Gathering, quoted here from p. 5. See also Notley's *Alma*, and Weil's *The Iliad: A Poem of Force*.

3. See Dan Cameron's essay "Passion in the Wilderness" in *Fever*, ed. Scholder, a monograph produced as part of a retrospective exhibition of Wojnarowicz's work at the New Museum of Contemporary Art in New York City in 1999. See also *David Wojnarowicz: A Definitive History of Five or Six Years on the Lower East Side*, interviews by Sylvère Lotringer, ed. Giancarlo Ambrosino.

4. This melding is on display in nearly all of Carson's work, but see especially "The Glass Essay" in *Glass, Irony, and God*, the collections *Plainwater* and *Men in the Off Hours*, and her most recent collection, *Decreation* (2005).

5. I've also noticed—especially when teaching adults—that the figure of the impoverished, bohemian poet chronicling her drug use, nomadic wanderings, sexual adventuring, and lack of bourgeois "extras" (such as adequate healthcare) reads quite differently when the poet is a mother as opposed to a man, even if that man is a father. The "get a job" judgment comes down much faster and harder, and the financial sacrifices the writer makes for the sake of her art strike some readers as less immediately "justifiable." (Notley responds to this line of criticism quite hilariously in *Mysteries*, in a poem which recounts her early life with Berrigan and their two

kids: "we're always looking for money to borrow / five ten or twenty dollars / we only want to have / just enough money, today / . . . they think it all 'goes for pills' / how much do they think pills cost" [65].)

6. Myles's forthcoming "poet's novel" *The Inferno* makes this audacity even more literal, in that its last section takes the form of a "career narrative," such as the kind one has to produce in support of a Guggenheim application—an application Myles has made (unsuccessfully) many times over the years. Also, on the topic of how these economies have shaped the book you are now reading, I would note the funding crises afflicting university presses across the land, and the financial pressure that many are feeling to publish books which might find a more "general" audience rather than a "scholarly" one. This squeeze is a result of many factors, including declining funding from host universities, a steep falloff in library subscriptions and sales, the diminished importance of research in the humanities as compared to the sciences, the cultural backlash against "esoteric" academic scholarship, the advent of chain bookstores and the consequent dwindling of independent bookstores, and so on. For more on the subject of cultural capital, especially as it relates to the university system and canon formation, see John Guillory's classic by that name.

SELECTED BIBLIOGRAPHY

Abelove, Henry, Michele Aina Barale, and David M. Halperin, eds. *The Lesbian and Gay Studies Reader*. New York: Routledge, 1993.

Adorno, Theodor. *Aesthetic Theory*. Trans. Robert Hullot-Kentor. Minneapolis: U of Minnesota P, 1997.

Albers, Josef. *Interaction of Color*. New Haven: Yale UP, 1963.

Allen, Donald. *The New American Poetry*. New York: Grove Press, 1960.

Ambrosino, Giancarlo, ed. *David Wojnarowicz: A Definitive History of Five or Six Years on the Lower East Side*. Interviews by Sylvère Lotringer. Coeds. Chris Kraus, Hedi El Kholti, and Justin Cavin. Los Angeles: Semiotext(e), 2006.

The American Heritage Dictionary. 2nd College Ed. Boston: Houghton Mifflin, 1982, 1985.

Andrews, Bruce, and Charles Bernstein, eds. *The L=A=N=G=U=A=G=E Book*. Carbondale: Southern Illinois UP, 1984.

Ashbery, John. *Flow Chart*. New York: Alfred A. Knopf, 1991.

——. Foreword. *Joan Mitchell 1992*. Ed. John Cheim. New York: Robert Miller Gallery, 1992.

——. *Girls on the Run*. New York: Farrar, Straus and Giroux, 1999.

——.*The Mooring of Starting Out: The First Five Books of Poetry*. Hopewell, NJ: Ecco Press, 1997.

——. *Other Traditions*. Cambridge: Harvard UP, 2000.

——. *Reported Sightings: Art Chronicles 1957–1987*. Ed. David Bergman. New York: Knopf, 1989.

——, and James Schuyler. *A Nest of Ninnies*. Hopewell, NJ: Ecco Press, 1997.

Ashton, Dore. *The New York School: A Cultural Reckoning*. Berkeley: U of California P, 1992.

Austin, J. L. *How to Do Things with Words*. Cambridge: Harvard UP, 1975.

Bahktin, Mikhail. "The Topic of the Speaking Person" and "Problems of Dostoyevsky's Poetics." Trans. Caryl Emerson. *The Critical Tradition: Classic Texts and Contemporary Trend*, 530–547. Ed. David Richter. Boston: Bedford Books, 1998.

Baker, Peter. Entry on Bernadette Mayer. *Dictionary of Literary Biography*. Vol. 165: *American Poets Since World War II*. 4th series. Detroit: Gale Group, 1996. Online at Literature Resource Center 3.1–Author Resource Pages, Gale Group.

Barthes, Roland. *Camera Lucida*. Trans. Richard Howard. New York: Noonday Press, 1981.

——. *Mythologies*. Trans. Annette Lavers. New York: Noonday Press, 1957, 1972.

——. *The Pleasure of the Text*. Trans. Richard Miller. New York: Hill and Wang, 1975.

——. *Roland Barthes by Roland Barthes*. Trans. Richard Howard. New York: Farrar, Straus and Giroux, 1977.

Bartkowski, Frances. *Feminist Utopias*. Lincoln: U of Nebraska P, 1989.

Batchelor, David. *Chromophobia*. London: Reaktion Books, 2000.

Benjamin, Walter. *Illuminations*. Trans. Harry Zohn. New York: Harcourt, Brace, and World, 1968.

Benstock, Judith. *Joan Mitchell*. New York: Hudson Hills Press, 1988.

Berkson, Bill. "Frank O'Hara and His Poems." *Art and Literature* 12 (Spring 1967): 53–63.

——, ed. *In Memory of My Feelings: A Selection of Poems*. New York: Museum of Modern Art, 2006.

——. Untitled essay on Joan Mitchell, printed for *Working with Poets*, a show at the Tibor de Nagy Gallery, Summer 2002.

——, and Joe LeSueur, eds. *Homage to Frank O'Hara*. Bolinas, CA: Big Sky, 1988.

Bernstein, Charles. "Stray Straws and Straw Men." *The L=A=N=G=U=A=G=E Book*, 39–45. Ed. Bernstein and Bruce Andrews.

——, and Bruce Andrews. *The L=A=N=G=U=A=G=E Book*. Carbondale: Southern Illinois UP, 1984.

Berrigan, Ted. *On the Level Everyday: Selected Talks on Living and the Art of Poetry*. Jersey City: Talisman House, 1997.

——. *Selected Poems*. Ed. Aram Saroyan. New York: Penguin, 1994.

Bowles, Jane. *My Sister's Hand in Mine: The Collected Works of Jane Bowles*. New York: Ecco Press, 1978.

Bové, Paul. *Destructive Poetics: Heidegger and Modern American Poetry*. New York: Columbia UP, 1980.

Breton, André. *Nadja*. Trans. Richard Howard. New York: Grove, 1960.

Butler, Judith. *Bodies That Matter*. New York: Routledge, 1993.

——. *Excitable Speech: A Politics of the Performative*. New York: Routledge, 1997.

——. *Gender Trouble*. New York: Routledge, 1990.

——. "Imitation and Gender Insubordination." *The Lesbian and Gay Studies Reader*, ed. Abelove, Barale, and Halperin, 307–320.

——, Ernesto Laclau, and Slavoj Zizek, eds. *Contingency, Hegemony, Universality*. London: Verso, 2000.

Cage, John. *Conversing with Cage*. Ed. Richard Kostelanetz. New York: Limelight Editions, 1988.

——. *Silence*. Middletown, CT: Wesleyan UP, 1961.

——. *A Year from Monday*. Middletown, CT: Wesleyan UP, 1969.

Capote, Truman. Introduction. *My Sister's Hand in Mine: The Collected Works of Jane Bowles*, v–xi. New York: Ecco Press, 1978.

Carr, C. "Portrait in Twenty-Three Rounds." *Fever: The Art of David Wojnarowicz*, 69–89. Ed. Amy Scholder. New York: New Museum of Contemporary Art and Rizzoli Books, 1998.

Carson, Anne. *Autobiography of Red*. New York: Vintage, 1998.

——. *Decreation: Poetry, Essays, Opera.* New York: Knopf, 2005.

——. *Economy of the Unlost.* Princeton, NJ: Princeton UP, 1999.

——. *Glass, Irony, and God.* New York: New Directions, 1992, 1995.

——. Interview with Stephen Burt. *Publisher's Weekly* 247, no. 14 (April 3, 2000): 56.

——. *Men in the Off Hours.* New York: Knopf, 2000.

Castle, Terry. *The Apparitional Lesbian: Female Homosexuality and Modern Culture.* New York: Columbia UP, 1993.

Cavell, Stanley. *The Senses of Walden.* Expanded ed. Chicago: U of Chicago P, 1981.

Celan, Paul. "The Meridian Speech." Trans. Rosmarie Waldrop. *Poems for the Millennium* 2: 408–409. Berkeley: U of California P, 1998.

Chappell, Fred. "The Contemporary Long Poem: Minding the Kinds." *Georgia Review* 51, no. 1 (Spring 1997): 141–154.

Clark, T. J. *Farewell to an Idea: Episodes from a History of Modernism.* New Haven: Yale UP, 1999.

Cooper, Dennis. Rev. of *Maxfield Parrish* by Eileen Myles. *ArtForum*, Summer 1996: 26.

Cotter, Holland. "Everything about Warhol But the Sex." *New York Times*, July 14, 2002.

——. "Poetry Soaked in the Personal and the Political." Profile of Eileen Myles. *New York Times*, May 30, 2001.

Coultas, Brenda. *A Handmade Museum.* Saint Paul: Coffeehouse Press, 2003.

Creeley, Robert. *Tales Out of School: Selected Interviews.* Ann Arbor: U of Michigan P, 1993.

Cunningham, Michael. *The Hours.* New York: Farrar, Straus and Giroux, 1998.

D'Agata, John. Rev. of *Girls on the Run* by John Ashbery. *Boston Review*, February–March 2000. Online at http.bostonreview.net/BR24.6/dagata.html (3 December 2006).

Davidson, Michael. "Compulsory Homosociality." *Cruising the Performative: Interventions into the Representation of Ethnicity, Nationality, and Sexuality*, 197–216. Ed. Sue-Ellen Case, Philip Brett, and Susan Leigh Foster. Bloomington: Indiana UP, 1995.

——. *The San Francisco Renaissance: Poetics and Community at Mid-Century.* Cambridge: Harvard UP, 1991.

De Certeau, Michel. *The Practice of Everyday Life.* Trans. Steven Rendall. Berkeley: U of California P, 1984.

De Kooning, Elaine. Response to Linda Nochlin. *Art and Sexual Politics: Women's Liberation, Women Artists, and Art History*, 57–71. Ed. Thomas Hess and Elizabeth Baker. New York: Collier Books, 1971.

De Lauretis, Teresa. *The Practice of Love.* Bloomington: Indiana UP, 1994.

De Man, Paul. "Autobiography as De-facement." *MLN* 94, no. 5 (Dec. 1979): 919–930.

Di Prima, Diane. *Memoirs of a Beatnik.* New York: Penguin, 1988.

Diggory, Terrence, and Stephen Paul Miller, eds. *The Scene of My Selves: New Work on New York School Poets.* Orono, ME: National Poetry Foundation, 2001.

Dillard, Annie. "Sight into Insight." *The Norton Reader: An Anthology of Expository Prose*, 6th ed., 1182–1192. Ed. Arthur M. Eastman. New York: Norton, 1984.

Dlugos, Tim. *Powerless: Selected Poems 1973–1990*. Ed. David Trinidad. New York: Serpent's Tail/High Risk Books, 1996.

Douglas, Mary. *Purity and Danger: An Analysis of the Concepts of Pollution and Taboo*. London: Routledge, 1966, 2002.

Drucker, Johanna. "In the Early 70s." *Art Journal* 58, no. 4 (Winter 1999): 13.

DuBois, Page. "'An Especially Peculiar Undertaking': Alice Notley's Epic." *Differences* 12, no. 2 (2001): 86–97.

DuPlessis, Rachel Blau. "Manifests." *Diacritics* 26, nos. 3–4 (Fall–Winter 1996): 31–53.

Durgin, Patrick. Entry on Eileen Myles. *Dictionary of Literary Biography*. Vol. 193: *American Poets Since World War II*. 6th series. Detroit: Gale Group, 1998. Online at Literature Resource Center 3.1–Author Resource Pages, Gale Group.

Dworkin, Andrea. "Writing." *Hotel Amerika* 1, no. 1 (Fall 2002): 35–38.

Eliot, T. S. *Selected Prose of T. S. Eliot*. Ed. Frank Kermode. New York: Farrar, Straus and Giroux, 1975.

Elledge, Jim, ed. *Frank O'Hara: To Be True to a City*. Ann Arbor: U of Michigan P, 1990.

Emerson, Ralph Waldo. *The Portable Emerson*. Ed. Carl Bode with Malcolm Cowley. New York: Penguin, 1981.

Evans, Steve, ed. "After Patriarchal Poetry: Feminism and the Contemporary Avant-Garde." Special issue. *Differences* 12, no. 2 (Summer 2001).

Felman, Shoshana. "Turning the Screw of Interpretation." *Literature and Psychoanalysis*, 94–207. Ed. Felman. Baltimore: John Hopkins UP, 1982.

Felski, Rita. *Beyond Feminist Aesthetics: Feminist Literature and Social Change*. Cambridge: Harvard UP, 1989.

——. *The Gender of Modernity*. Cambridge: Harvard UP, 1995.

Ferguson, Russell, ed. *In Memory of My Feelings: Frank O'Hara and American Art*. Berkeley: U of California P, 1999.

Foster, Edward, ed. *Poetry and Poetics: A New Millennium*. Jersey City: Talisman, 2000.

Foucault, Michel. *History of Sexuality*. Vol. 1, *An Introduction*. 1978. Trans. Robert Hurley. New York: Vintage, 1990.

Fraser, Kathleen. "Translating the Unspeakable: Visual Poetics, as Projected through Olson's 'Field' into Current Female Writing Practice." *Moving Borders*, 642–654. Ed. Mary Margaret Sloan. Jersey City, NJ: Talisman House, 1998.

Freud, Sigmund. *The Freud Reader*. Ed. Peter Gay. New York: Norton, 1989.

Frost, Elizabeth. *The Feminist Avant-Garde in American Poetry*. Iowa City: U of Iowa P, 2003.

Gage, John. *Color and Meaning: Art, Science, and Symbolism*. Berkeley: U of California P, 1999.

Gallop, Jane. *Thinking Through the Body*. New York: Columbia UP, 1988.

Gander, Forrest. "Often a Strange Desire." Rev. of *Girls on the Run* by John Ashbery. *Jacket* 8, at http://jacketmagazine.com/08/gand-r-ashb.html (3 December 2006).

Gass, William. *On Being Blue: A Philosophical Inquiry*. Jaffrey, NH: David R. Godine, 1976.

Gevirtz, Susan. "Belief's Afterimage." Rev. of Barbara Guest. *Jacket* 10, at http://jacketmagazine.com/10/gues-by-gevi.html (3 December 2006).

Gibson, Ann Eden. *Abstract Expressionism: Other Politics*. New Haven: Yale UP, 1997.

Gilligan, Carol. *In A Different Voice: Psychological Theory and Women's Development*. Cambridge: Harvard UP, 1982.

——, Annie Rogers, and Deborah Tolman, eds. *Women, Girls, and Psychotherapy: Reframing Resistance*. New York: Haworth Press, 1991.

Gioia, Dana. *Can Poetry Matter?: Essays on Poetry and American Culture*. Saint Paul: Graywolf Press, 1992, 2002.

Giorno, John. Interview. Conducted by Daniel Nester. Nerve.com, June 2002, at http://www.nerve.com/poetry/nester/pornyesterday (3 December 2006).

Goldin, Nan. *The Ballad of Sexual Dependency*. New York: Aperture Foundation, 1986.

Gooch, Brad. *City Poet: The Life and Times of Frank O'Hara*. New York: Random House, 1993.

Greenberg, Clement. *The Collected Essays and Criticism*. Ed. John O'Brian. Chicago: U of Chicago P, 1986.

Greer, Germaine. *The Female Eunuch*. New York: McGraw-Hill, 1971.

Guest, Barbara. *Dürer in the Window: Reflexions on Art*. Ed. Africa Wayne. New York: Roof Books, 2003.

——. *Miniatures and Other Poems*. Middletown: Wesleyan UP, 2002.

——. *Poems: The Location of Things, Archaics, The Open Skies*. Garden City, NY: Doubleday, 1962.

——. *Quill, Solitary Apparition*. Sausalito: Post Apollo Press, 1996.

——. *The Red Gaze*. Middletown: Wesleyan UP, 2005.

——. "Remarks," from "Barnard Conference: Statements from 'Where Lyric Tradition Meets Language Poetry: Innovation in Contemporary American Poetry by Women.'" *Fence* 3, no. 1 (Spring–Summer 2000): 122–124.

——. *Rocks on a Platter: Notes on Literature*. Middletown: Wesleyan UP, 1999.

——. *Seeking Air*. Santa Barbara, CA: Black Sparrow, 1978.

——. *Selected Poems*. Los Angeles: Sun & Moon Press, 1995.

Guilbaut, Serge. *How New York Stole the Idea of Modern Art: Abstract Expressionism, Freedom and the Cold War*. Trans. Arthur Goldhammer. Chicago: U of Chicago P, 1983.

Guillory, John. *Cultural Capital: The Problem of Literary Canon Formation*. Reprint. Chicago: U of Chicago P, 1995.

Hainley, Bruce. Rev. of *Autobiography of Red* by Anne Carson. *Nation* 266, no. 20 (June 1, 1998): 34.

Haronian, Mary Jo. "Language Experiment: Science, Gender, and Discourse in the Works of Margaret Fuller." PhD diss., Graduate Center of the City University of New York, 1998.

Hay, Deborah. *My Body, the Buddhist*. Middletown: Wesleyan UP, 2000.

Heidegger, Martin. *Basic Writings*. Ed. David Farrell Krell. Various translators. San Francisco: HarperSanFrancisco, 1993.

———. *Poetry, Language, and Thought*. Trans. Albert Hofstader. New York: Harper and Row, 1971.

Heilbrun, Carolyn. *Writing a Woman's Life*. New York: Norton, 1988.

Hejinian, Lyn. "Some Notes Toward a Poetics." From "Barnard Conference: Statements from 'Where Lyric Tradition Meets Language Poetry: Innovation in Contemporary American Poetry by Women.'" *Fence* 3, no. 1 (Spring–Summer 2000): 114–119.

Herring, Terrell Scott. "Frank O'Hara's Open Closet." *PMLA* 117, no. 3 (May 2002): 414–427.

Hess, Thomas B., and Elizabeth C. Baker, eds. *Art and Sexual Politics: Women's Liberation, Women Artists, and Art History*. New York: Macmillan Publishing Co., 1973.

Hong, Cathy. "Weather Vein." Rev. of *Skies* by Eileen Myles. *Village Voice*, April 2, 2002.

Howe, Susan. *The Birth-Mark: Unsettling the Wilderness in American Literary History*. Middletown: Wesleyan UP, 1993.

Howes, Victor. "Happy-making Poet and Others." Rev. of Anne Sexton. *Christian Science Monitor*, March 20, 1969.

Hulme, T. E. "Romanticism and Classicism." *The Collected Writings of T. E. Hulme*, 59–73. Ed. Karen Csengeri. Oxford: Oxford UP, 1994.

Irigaray, Luce. *This Sex Which Is Not One*. Trans. Catherine Porter. Ithaca: Cornell UP, 1985.

Jackson, Timothy. Online entry on Richard Strauss's *Symphonia Domestica* for the American Symphony website, at http://www.americansymphony .org/dialogues_extensions/97_98season/5-hconcert/strauss.cfm (20 June 2002).

Jacobs, Jane. *The Death and Life of Great American Cities*. New York: Vintage, 1961.

James, Williams. *The Principles of Psychology*. 1890. Reprint. New York: Dover, 1950.

Jardine, Alice. *Gynesis: Configurations of Women and Modernity*. Ithaca: Cornell UP, 1985.

Jarman, Derek. *Chroma*. Woodstock, NY: Overlook Press, 1994.

Johnson, Barbara. *The Feminist Difference: Race, Gender, Literature, and Psychoanalysis*. Cambridge: Harvard UP, 1998.

———. *A World of Difference*. Baltimore: Johns Hopkins UP, 1987.

Jones, Hettie. *How I Became Hettie Jones*. New York: Penguin, 1990.

Juno, Andrea, and V. Vale, eds. *Angry Women*. Re/Search 13. San Francisco: Re/Search Publications, 1991.

Kane, Daniel. *All Poets Welcome: The Lower East Side Poetry Scene in the 1960s*. Berkeley: U of California P, 2003.

——, ed. *Don't Ever Get Famous: Essays on New York Writing after the New York School*. Normal, IL: Dalkey Archive Press, 2006.

Kaneda, Shirley. "Greenbergian Formalism." *Art Journal* 58, no. 4 (Winter 1999): 19.

——. "Painting and Its Others: In the Realm of the Feminine." *Arts Magazine* (Summer 1991): 58–64.

Kaufman, Robert. "A Future for Modernism: Barbara Guest's Recent Poetry." *American Poetry Review* 29, no. 4 (July–August 2000): 11–16.

Keller, Lynn. "Becoming 'a Compleat Travel Agency': Barbara Guest's Negotiations with the Fifties Feminine Mystique." *Scene of My Selves*, 215–227. Ed. Diggory and Miller.

Kertess, Klaus. *Joan Mitchell*. New York: Harry N. Abrams, 1997.

Kimmelman, Michael. "In Joyous Colors, a Hint of Joys Lost." Rev. of Joan Mitchell's exhibition at the Whitney Museum. *New York Times*, July 5, 2002.

Kinnihan, Linda A. "Reading Barbara Guest: The View from the Nineties." *Scene of My Selves*, 229–243. Ed. Diggory and Miller.

Koch, Kenneth. *Rose, Where Did You Get That Red?: Teaching Great Poetry to Children*. New York: Vintage, 1990.

——. *Wishes, Lies, and Dreams: Teaching Children to Write Poetry*. New York: Harper, 2000.

Koestenbaum, Wayne. *Andy Warhol: A Penguin Life*. New York: Viking, 2001.

——. *Cleavage: Essays on Sex, Stars, and Aesthetics*. New York: Ballantine, 2000.

——. *Double Talk: The Erotics of Male Literary Collaboration*. New York: Routledge, 1989.

——. "Epitaph on Twenty-third Street: The Poetics of James Schuyler." *Parnassus* 21, nos. 1–2 (Winter 1995): 33–57.

——. *The Queen's Throat: Opera, Homosexuality, and the Mystery of Desire*. New York: Vintage, 1993.

Knight, Brenda, ed. *Women of the Beat Generation: The Writers, Artists, and Muses at the Heart of a Revolution*. Berkeley: Conari Press, 1996.

Komunyakaa, Yusef. Introduction. *The Best American Poetry 2003*. Ed. David Lehman. New York: Scribner, 2003.

Kraus, Chris. "Ecceity, Smash, and Grub," in *French Theory in America*, ed. Sylvère Lotringer and Sande Cohen. New York: Routledge, 2001.

——. "Girls, Interrupted." Rev. of Myles's *Cool for You*. *Nation*, January 1, 2001. Online at www.thenation.com/doc/20010101/kraus and at Myles's website, at http://eileenmyles.com/coolrev.html (3 December 2006).

Krauss, Rosalind. *Bachelors*. Cambridge: MIT Press, 1999.

——. *The Originality of the Avant-Garde and Other Modernist Myths*. Cambridge: MIT Press, 1986.

Kunin, Aaron. "A Poetics of Color for 1945." Unpublished essay.

Landau, Ellen G., ed. *Reading Abstract Expressionism: Context and Critique*. New Haven: Yale UP, 2005.

Lang, V. R. ("Bunny"). *Poems and a Play with a Memoir by Alison Lurie*. New York: Random House, 1975.

Lefebvre, Henri. *Critique of Everyday Life*. 1947. Trans. John Moore. London: Verso, 2000.

Lehman, David. *The Last Avant-Garde: The Making of the New York School of Poets*. New York: Doubleday, 1998.

Leja, Michael. *Reframing Abstract Expressionism: Subjectivity and Painting in the 1940s*. New Haven: Yale UP, 1993.

Leslie, Alfred, dir. *The Last Clean Shirt*. Subtitles by Frank O'Hara. Museum of Modern Art, 1964.

LeSueur, Joe. *Digressions on Some Poems by Frank O'Hara*. New York: Farrar, Straus and Giroux, 2003.

Lippard, Lucy. *Six Years: The Dematerialization of the Art Object from 1966 to 1972*. Berkeley: U of California P, 1973.

Livingston, Jane. *The Paintings of Joan Mitchell*. New York: Whitney Museum, 2002.

Lowell, Robert. *Life Studies, For the Union Dead*. 1964. New York: Farrar, Straus and Giroux, 1984.

Loy, Mina. *The Lost Lunar Baedeker*. Ed. Roger L. Conover. New York: Noonday Press, 1996.

Lundquist, Sara. "Another Poet Among Painters: Barbara Guest with Grace Hartigan and Mary Abbott." *Scene of My Selves*, 245–264. Ed. Diggory and Miller.

Luyckx, Marjorie. *The Spirit of Abstract Expressionism: Selected Writings*. New York: Braziller, 1994.

Lyons, Kim. Rev. of Notley's *Mysteries of Small Houses*. *Poetry Project Newsletter* 171 (October–November 1998): 23–25.

MacGregor, John. *Henry Darger: In the Realms of the Unreal*. New York: Delano Greenidge Editions, 2002.

Magee, Michael. *Emancipating Pragmatism: Emerson, Jazz, and Experimental Writing*. Tuscaloosa: U of Alabama P, 2004.

Marcus, Jane. *Art and Anger: Reading Like a Woman*. Columbus: Ohio State UP, 1988.

Martin, Ronald E. *American Literature and the Destruction of Knowledge: Innovative Writing in the Age of Epistemology*. Durham: Duke UP, 1991.

Maso, Carole. *A Room Lit by Roses: A Journal of Pregnancy and Birth*. Washington, DC: Counterpoint Press, 2002.

Mayer, Bernadette. *Another Smashed Pinecone*. New York: United Artists Books, 1998.

——. *A Bernadette Mayer Reader*. New York: New Directions, 1992.

——. *The Desires of Mothers to Please Others in Letters*. West Stockbridge, MA: Hard Press, 1994.

——. "Dream Tape Transcribed–Hypnagogic Images." *The World*, annual publication of the Poetry Project (2000): 9.

——. "From: A Lecture at Naropa." *Disembodied Poetics*, ed. Anne Waldman and Andrew Schelling, 95–102.

——. Interview with Lisa Jarnot. *Poetry Project Newsletter* 168 (Feb.–March 1998): 6–9.

——. *Memory.* Photographs and text. Exhibited in New York City, 1972. Plainville, VT: North Atlantic, 1975.

——. *Midwinter Day.* Berkeley: Turtle Island Foundation, 1982.

——. "The Poetry of Everyday Life." Lecture given at the Poetry Project on April 7, 1988. Quoted from unpublished manuscript in the Poetry Project archives, by permission of Bernadette Mayer.

——. *Scarlet Tanager.* New York: New Directions, 2005.

——. *Sonnets.* New York: Tender Buttons Press, 1989.

——. *Studying Hunger.* Berkeley, CA: Serendipity, 1975.

McCabe, Susan. "Alice Notley's Epic Entry." *Antioch Review* 56, no. 3 (Summer 1998): 273–281.

Menand, Louis. "All That Glitters: Literature's Global Economy." *New Yorker* (Dec. 26, 2005–Jan. 2, 2006): 136–140.

——. *The Metaphysical Club: A Story of Ideas in America.* New York: Farrar, Straus and Giroux, 2001.

Merrill, James. *Collected Poems.* Ed. J. D. McClatchy and Stephen Yenser. New York: Knopf, 2001.

Miller, Nancy K. "Representing Others: Genders and the Subject of Autobiography." *Differences* 6, no. 1 (1994): 1–27.

Motherwell, Robert. *The Collected Writings of Robert Motherwell.* New York, Oxford: Oxford UP, 1992.

Mueller, Cookie. *Walking through Clear Water in a Pool Painted Black.* New York: Semiotext(e), 1990.

Muraro, Luisa. "Bonding and Freedom" (1985). *Italian Feminist Thought: A Reader,* 123–126. Ed. Paola Bono and Sandra Kemp. New York: Blackwell, 1991.

Myers, John Bernard. *Tracking the Marvelous: A Life in the New York Art World.* New York: Random House, 1981.

——, ed. *The Poets of the New York School.* Philadelphia: University of Pennsylvania P, 1969.

Myles, Eileen. *Chelsea Girls.* Santa Rosa: Black Sparrow Press, 1994.

——. "Chewing the Fat about AIDS–Arts Today with Eileen Myles." Symposium talk published online at http://www.artistswithaids.org/artery/symposium/symposium_myles.html (3 December 2006).

——. Contribution to *Narrativity* 2 (December 2001), online at http://www.sfsu.edu/~newlit/narrativity/issue_two/myles.html (3 December 2006).

——. Contributor's note. *The Best American Poetry 2002.* Ed. Robert Creeley. New York: Scribner, 2002.

——. *Cool for You.* New York: Soft Skull Press, 2000.

——. *A Fresh Young Voice from the Plains.* New York: Power Mad Press, 1981.

——. Interview. Conducted by Michelle Alb for Naropa Summer Writing Program, Summer 1998, online at http://www.naropa.edu/swp/myles.html.

——. Interview. Conducted by Liz Galst. *Boston Phoenix*, July 1994.

——. Interview. "Never Real, Always True: An Interview with Eileen Myles." Conducted by Frances Richard. *Provincetown Arts*, 2000: 24–29.

——. *Maxfield Parrish: Early and New Poems*. Santa Rosa: Black Sparrow Press, 1995.

——. "My Intergeneration." *Village Voice*, The Queer Issue (June 21–27, 2000): 75.

——. "Myles Ahead." Profile in *Time Out New York*, November 2, 2000. Available at http://66.111.110.102/newyork/DetailsAr.do?file=features/267/267.ft.myles.html (16 December 2006).

——. *Not Me*. New York: Semiotext(e), 1991.

——. *On My Way*. Cambridge: Faux Press, 2001.

——. *School of Fish*. Santa Rosa: Black Sparrow Press, 1997.

——. *Skies*. Santa Rosa: Black Sparrow Press, 2001.

——. "Tim: A Review." *Mississippi Review* 31, no. 3 (2003): 226–231.

——. *We, the Poets*. Unpag. pamphlet. New York: belladonna* 38, Winter 2003.

——, and Liz Kotz, eds. *The New Fuck You: Adventures in Lesbian Reading*. New York: Semiotext(e), 1995.

Nelson, Deborah. *Pursuing Privacy in Cold War America*. New York: Columbia UP, 2002.

Ngai, Sianne. *Ugly Feelings*. Cambridge: Harvard UP, 2005.

Nietzsche, Friedrich. *Beyond Good and Evil*. Trans. R. J. Hollingdale. New York: Penguin, 1973.

Nochlin, Linda. Interview with Joan Mitchell at the Westbury Hotel in New York, April 16, 1986. Transcript at www.aaa.si.edu/collections/oralhistories/transcripts/mitche86.htm (3 December 2006).

——. "A Rage to Paint." *The Paintings of Joan Mitchell*, ed. Livingston, 49–59.

Notley, Alice. *Alma, or The Dead Women*. New York: Granary Books, 2006.

——. *At Night the States*. Chicago: Yellow Press, 1988.

——. *Close to me & Closer . . . (The Language of Heaven)*. Oakland, CA: O Books, 1995.

——. *Coming After: Essays on Poetry*. Ann Arbor: U of Michigan P, 2005.

——. *The Descent of Alette*. New York: Penguin, 1992.

——. *Disobedience*. New York: Penguin, 2001.

——. "Epic and Women Poets." *Disembodied Poetics*, ed. Waldman and Schelling, 103–109.

——. *Grave of Light: New and Selected Poems 1970–2005*. Middletown: Wesleyan UP, 2006.

——. Interview. Conducted by Jennifer Dick. *Doublechange* magazine, January 16, 2003.

——. Interview. Conducted by Judith Goldman. *Poetry Project Newsletter* 164 (Feb.–Mar. 1997).

——. Interview. Conducted by Brian Kim-Stefans in *Jacket* 15 (December 2001). Online at http://jacketmagazine.com/15/stef-iv-not.html (3 December 2006).

——. *Margaret & Dusty*. Saint Paul: Coffee House Press, 1985.

——. *Mysteries of Small Houses*. New York: Penguin, 1998.

——. "The Poetics of Disobedience." Published online at the Electronic Poetry Center at SUNY Buffalo, at http://wings.buffalo.edu/epc/authors/notley/disob.html (3 December 2006).

——. *The Scarlet Cabinet* (with Douglas Oliver). New York: Scarlet Edition, 1992.

——. *The Selected Poems of Alice Notley*. Jersey City: Talisman House, 1993.

——. "Voice." *Interim* 23, nos. 1–2 (2005): 146–156.

O'Hara, Frank. *Art Chronicles 1954–1966*. New York: Brazillier, 1975.

——. *The Collected Poems of Frank O'Hara*. Ed. Donald Allen. Berkeley: U of California P, 995.

Oliver, Douglas. "Poetry's Subject," in *PN Review*, Sept.–Oct. 1995: 52–58.

Olson, Charles. "Projective Verse." *The New American Poetry*, 386–397. Ed. Donald Allen. New York: Grove, 1960.

Oppen, George. *Collected Poems*. New York: New Directions, 1975.

The Oxford English Dictionary. Compact Edition. Oxford: Oxford UP, 1971.

Padgett, Ron, and David Shapiro. *An Anthology of New York Poets*. New York: Random House, 1970.

Peirce, Charles Sanders. *The Essential Writings*. Ed. Edward Moore. Amherst, NY: Prometheus Books, 1998.

Perloff, Marjorie. *Frank O'Hara: Poet among Painters* (1977). Chicago: U of Chicago P, 1997.

——. "Normalizing John Ashbery." *Jacket* 2, January 1998, at http://jacketmagazine.com/02/perloff02.html (3 December 2006).

——. *The Poetic Art of Robert Lowell*. Ithaca: Cornell UP, 1973.

——. "Whose New American Poetry? Anthologizing in the Nineties." *Diacritics* 26, nos. 3–4 (Fall–Winter 1996): 104–123.

——. *Wittgenstein's Ladder: Poetic Language and the Strangeness of the Ordinary*. Chicago: U of Chicago P, 1996.

Phillips, Adam. *Terrors and Experts*. Cambridge: Harvard UP, 1995.

——. *Winnicott*. Cambridge: Harvard UP, 1988.

Phillips, Rodney, and Steven Clay. *A Secret Location on the Lower East Side: Adventures in Writing, 1960–1980*. New York: Granary Books, 1998.

Pinsky, Robert. *The Sounds of Poetry*. New York: Farrar, Straus and Giroux, 1998.

Plath, Sylvia. *The Collected Poems*. Ed. Ted Hughes. New York: Harper and Row, 1981.

——. *The Unabridged Journals of Sylvia Plath*. Ed. Karen V. Kukil. New York: Anchor Books, 2000.

Poirier, Richard. *Poetry and Pragmatism*. Cambridge: Harvard UP, 1992.

Pollock, Griselda. *Vision and Difference: Femininity, Feminism, and the Histories of Art*. New York: Routledge, 1988.

Prose, Francine. *The Lives of the Muses: Nine Women and the Artists They Inspired*. New York: HarperCollins, 2002.

Puniello, Francoise, and Halina R. Rusak, eds. *Abstract Expressionist Women Painters: An Annotated Bibliography*. Lanham, MD: Scarecrow Press, 1996.

Rankine, Claudia. *Don't Let Me Be Lonely: An American Lyric.* Saint Paul: Graywolf Press, 2004.

——. *Plot.* New York: Grove Press, 2001.

——, and Alison Cummings. "Afterword and Conception." From "Barnard Conference: Statements from 'Where Lyric Meets Language Poetry: Innovation in Contemporary Amerian Poetry by Women.'" *Fence* 3, no. 1 (Spring–Summer 2000): 124–127.

——, and Juliana Spahr, eds. *American Women Poets in the Twentieth Century: Where Lyric Meets Language.* Middletown, CT: Wesleyan UP, 2002.

Rasula, Jed. "Ten Different Fruits on One Tree: Experiment as a Claim of the Book." *Chicago Review* 43, no. 4 (Fall 1997): 28-39.

Rattray, David. *How I Became One of the Invisible.* New York: Semiotext(e), 1992.

Rich, Adrienne. *On Lies, Secrets and Silence: Selected Prose, 1966–1978.* New York: Norton, 1979.

Richard, Frances. "Never Real, Always True: An Interview with Eileen Myles." *Provincetown Arts,* 2000: 24–29.

Richter, David, ed. *The Critical Tradition: Classic Texts and Contemporary Trend.* Boston: Bedford Books, 1998.

Rifkin, Libbie. "'My Little World Goes On at St. Mark's Place': Anne Waldman, Bernadette Mayer, and the Gender of an Avant-Garde Institution." *Jacket* 7, online at www.jacketmagazine.com/07/rifkin07.html (3 December 2006).

Riley, Denise. *"Am I That Name?" Feminism and the Category of Women in History.* Minneapolis: U of Minnesota P, 1988.

Rorty, Richard. *Philosophy and the Mirror of Nature.* Princeton: Princeton UP, 1979.

Rose, Jacqueline. *The Haunting of Sylvia Plath.* Cambridge: Harvard UP, 1992.

Rosen, Charles. "Mallarmé the Magnificent," review of Mallarmé's *Oeuvres complètes. New York Review of Books* 46 (May 20, 1999). Online at http://www.nybooks.com/articles/article-preview?article_id=487 (8 December 2006).

Rothenberg, Jerome, and Pierre Joris, eds. *Poems for the Millennium.* 2 vols. Berkeley: U of California P, 1995.

Rukeyser, Muriel. *Out of Silence: Selected Poems.* Ed. Kate Daniels. Evanston, IL: TriQuarterly Books, Northwestern University, 1992.

Saltz, Jerry. "Hardcore." Rev. of Charline von Heyl. *Village Voice,* March 10, 2006, online at www.villagevoice.com/art/0611,saltz,72474,13.html (3 December 2006).

Saltzman, Lisa. "Reconsidering the Stain: On Gender, Identity, and New York School Painting." *Reading Abstract Expressionism,* 560–579. New Haven: Yale UP, 2005.

Sandler, Irving. *The New York School: Painters and Sculptors of the Fifties.* New York: Harper and Row, 1973.

Scalapino, Leslie. "Pattern—and the 'Simulacral.'" *Artifice and Indeterminacy: An Anthology of New Poetics*, 130–139. Ed. Christopher Beach. Tuscaloosa: U of Alabama P, 1998.

Scholder, Amy, ed. *Fever: The Art of David Wojnarowicz*. New York: New Museum of Contemporary Art and Rizzoli Books, 1998.

Schor, Mira. "From Liberation to Lack." *Art Journal* 58, no. 4 (Winter 1999): 23.

———. *Wet: On Painting, Feminism, and Art Culture*. Durham: Duke UP, 1997.

Schor, Naomi. *Bad Objects*: *Essays Popular and Unpopular*. Durham: Duke UP, 1995.

———. *George Sand and Idealism*. New York: Columbia UP, 1993.

———. *Reading in Detail*: *Aesthetics and the Feminine*. New York: Methuen, 1987.

———. "Re-reading in Detail: or, Aesthetics, the Feminine, and Idealism." *Criticism* 32, no. 3 (Summer 1990).

Schuyler, James. *Collected Poems*. New York: Farrar, Straus and Giroux, 1993.

———. *The Diary of James Schuyler*. Ed. Nathan Kernan. Santa Rosa: Black Sparrow Press, 1997.

———. *Selected Art Writings*. Ed. Simon Pettet. Santa Rosa: Black Sparrow Press, 1998.

Scott, Joan. "Universalism and the History of Feminism." *Differences* 7, no. 1 (1995): 2–14.

Sedgwick, Eve Kosofsky. *Epistemology of the Closet*. Berkeley: U of California P, 1990.

———. *Tendencies*. Durham: Duke UP, 1993.

Selinger, Eric. "That Awkward Grace (Recent Publications by Ted Berrigan, Alice Notley, and Ron Padgett)." *Parnassus: Poetry in Review* 21 (1996): 298–322.

Sexton, Anne. *The Complete Poems*. Boston: Houghton Mifflin, 1981.

Shand-Tucci, Douglass. *The Crimson Letter: Harvard, Homosexuality, and the Shaping of American Culture*. New York: St. Martin's Press, 2003.

Shaw, Lytle. *Frank O'Hara: The Poetics of Coterie*. U of Iowa P, 2006.

Shelley, Mary. *Frankenstein*. Ware, Hertfordshire: Wordsworth Editions Limited, 1993.

Shetley, Vernon. *After the Death of Poetry: Poet and Audience in Contemporary America*. Durham: Duke UP, 1993.

Shoptaw, John. *On the Outside Looking Out: On John Ashbery's Poetry*. Cambridge: Harvard UP, 1995.

Shulevitz, Judith. "The Close Reader: Sing Muse . . . Or Maybe Not." *New York Times Book Review*, November 24, 2002.

Silverman, Kaja. *The Subject of Semiotics*. New York: Oxford UP, 1983.

Sloan, Mary Margaret, ed. *Moving Borders: Three Decades of Innovative Writing by Women*. Jersey City: Talisman, 1998.

Smith, Hazel. *Hyperscapes in the Poetry of Frank O'Hara: Difference, Homosexuality, Topography*. Liverpool: Liverpool UP, 2000.

Smith, Patti. *Complete: Lyrics, Reflections, and Notes for the Future*. New York: Doubleday, 1998.

Sontag, Susan. *Against Interpretation*. New York: Anchor Books, 1966.

Spahr, Juliana. *Everybody's Autonomy: Connective Reading and Collective Identity*. Tuscaloosa: U of Alabama P, 2001.

——. "'Love Scattered, Not Concentrated Love': Bernadette Mayer's *Sonnets*." *Differences* 12, no. 2 (2001): 98–119.

Spicer, Jack. *The Collected Books of Jack Spicer*. Ed. Robin Blaser. Santa Barbara: Black Sparrow Press, 1996.

Stein, Gertrude. *The Autobiography of Alice B. Toklas*. New York: Vintage, 1933.

——. *Everybody's Autobiography*. New York: Random House, 1937.

——. *Selected Writings of Gertrude Stein*. New York: Random House, 1962.

Steiner, Wendy. *The Colors of Rhetoric: Problems in the Relation between Modern Literature and Painting*. Chicago: U of Chicago P, 1985.

——. *Exact Resemblance to Exact Resemblance: The Literary Portraiture of Gertrude Stein*. New Haven: Yale UP, 1978.

Stiles, Kristin, and Peter Selz, eds. *Theories and Documents of Contemporary Art: A Sourcebook of Artists' Writings*. Berkeley: U of California P, 1996.

Sword, Helen. *Ghostwriting Modernism*. Ithaca: Cornell UP, 2002.

Thoreau, Henry David. *Walden, or Life in the Woods* (1854). *The Norton Anthology of Literature*, 3rd ed., vol. 1. New York: Norton, 1989: 1635–1808.

——. *A Year in Thoreau's Journal, 1851*. New York: Penguin, 1993.

Tomkins, Silvan. *Shame and Its Sisters*. Ed. Eve Kosofsky Sedgwick and Adam Frank. Durham: Duke UP, 1995.

Vendler, Helen. "Frank O'Hara." *Part of Nature, Part of Us: Modern American Poets*, 179–194. Cambridge: Harvard UP, 1980.

Vickery, Anne. *Leaving Lines of Gender: A Feminist Genealogy of Language Writing*. Middletown: Wesleyan UP, 2000.

Waldman, Anne, ed. *Out of This World: An Anthology of the St. Mark's Poetry Project, 1966–1991*. New York: Crown, 1991.

——, and Andrew Schelling, eds. *Disembodied Poetics: Annals of the Jack Kerouac School*. Albuquerque: U of New Mexico P, 1994.

——, Lewis Warsh, and Clark Coolidge, eds. *Angel Hair Sleeps with a Boy in My Head*. New York: Granary Books, 2001.

Ward, Geoff. Rev. of Guest's *If So, Tell Me* in *Jacket* magazine 10, at http://jacketmagazine.com/10/ward-on-guest.html (3 December 2006).

——. *Statutes of Liberty: The New York School of Poets*. New York: Palgrave, 1993.

Warhol, Andy, and Pat Hackett. *POPism: The Warhol Sixties*. New York: Harcourt Brace, 1980.

Watkin, William. *In the Process of Poetry: The New York School and the Avant-Garde*. Lewisburg, PA: Bucknell UP, 2001.

Weed, Elizabeth, and Naomi Schor, eds. *The Essential Difference*. Bloomington: Indiana UP, 1994.

——. *Feminism Meets Queer Theory*. Bloomington: Indiana UP, 1997.

Weeks, Laurie. Rev. of *Cool for You* by Eileen Myles. *Index* 5, no. 4 (April–May 2001), available online at Myles's website, http://www .eileenmyles.com/coolrev.html (3 December 2006).

Weil, Simone. "The Iliad, or the Poem of Force," in *War and the Iliad*. Trans. Mary McCarthy. New York Review of Books Classics, 2005.

Willis, Elizabeth. Rev. of *Proper Name and Other Stories* by Bernadette Mayer. *Poetry Project Newsletter* 162 (October–November 1996): 18–19.

Wineapple, Brenda. *Sister Brother: Gertrude and Leo Stein*. Baltimore: Johns Hopkins UP, 1997.

Wittgenstein, Ludwig. *Culture and Value*. Ed. G. H. von Wright. Trans. Peter Winch. Chicago: U of Chicago P, 1980.

——. *On Certainty*. Ed. G. E. M. Anscombe and G. H. von Wright. Trans. Denis Paul and G. E. M. Anscombe. New York: Harper and Row, 1969.

——. *Philosophical Investigations*. Trans. G. E. M. Anscombe. Oxford: Blackwell Publishers, 1953.

——. *Remarks on Colour*. Trans. Linda L. McAlister and Margarete Schettle. Berkeley: U of California P, 1978.

——. *Tractatus Logico Philosophicus*. 2nd ed. New York: Routledge Classics, 2001.

——. *Zettel*. Ed. and trans. G. E. M. Anscombe. Berkeley: U of California P, 1967.

Wittig, Monique. *The Straight Mind and Other Essays*. Boston: Beacon Press, 1992.

Wolf, Reva. *Andy Warhol, Poetry, and Gossip in the 1960s*. Chicago: U of Chicago P, 1997.

Wojnarowicz, David. *Close to the Knives: A Memoir of Disintegration*. New York: Vintage, 1991.

——. *Memories That Smell Like Gasoline*. San Francisco: Artspace Books, 1992.

Wordsworth, William. *The Major Works*. Ed. Stephen Gill. Oxford: Oxford UP, 2000.

Yaeger, Patricia. "Toward a Female Sublime." *Gender and Theory: Dialogues on Feminist Criticism*, 191–212. Ed. Linda Kauffman. New York: B. Blackwell, 1989.

Yau, John. *In Company: Robert Creeley's Collaborations*. Niagara University, NY: Castellani Art Museum of Niagara University, 1999.

Yingling, Thomas E. *Hart Crane and the Homosexual Text: New Thresholds, New Anatomies*. Chicago: U of Chicago P, 1990.

Zucker, Rachel. *The Last Clear Narrative*. Middletown: Wesleyan UP, 2004.

Zukofsky, Louis. "Comment." *Poetry: A Magazine of Verse* 37, no. 5 (February 1931): 268–272.

INDEX

Abbot, Mary, 8

Abstract Expressionism, 7, 18–20, 52, 197; America and, 239n27; and gesture, 7, 15, 47, 221; rhetoric of, 17, 19, 228n2; women and, 206, 230n11, 231n16. *See also* New York School of painters

abstraction, 4–6; "abstract practice," 5, 32, 46, 104; Americans and, 12, 238n22; color and, 14, 22–28; dangers of, 4, 47–48; diversity in, 5–6; definitions of, 6, 34, 228n2; and landscape, 27, 229n6; in language, 5–6; "true abstraction," 13, 22, 50, 58, 74, 175, 238n22; and voice, 13; and women, 8, 46–48

Acker, Kathy, 171, 179, 227n19, 253n13

Action Painting, 14, 21, 229n9. *See also* Abstract Expressionism; New York School of painters

affidamento, 206, 255n20

AIDS, 71, 147, 212–214, 216, 220, 250n2

Albers, Josef: *Interaction of Color*, 28

Allen, Donald: *The New American Poetry*, 6, 31, 32, 48, 208, 236n14, 247n9

Altieri, Charles, 90

Amer, Ghada, 47

American Folk Art Museum, New York, NY, 49, 75

Andre, Carl, 108

Andrews, Bruce, 38, 152–153, 245n18

Apollinaire, Guillaume: "Zone," 190

Apollo and Daphne (myth), 56

Armantrout, Rae, 136, 225n8

Art and Language (group), 108

Artaud, Antonin, 195, 252n11

Ashbery, John, 6, 7, 8, 27, 30, 49, 50, 233n3, 238n22; and gender, 51, 59, 76, 77; influences, 60–61, 73, 74, 76, 236n14; and Mitchell, 14, 19, 27, 30; on New York City, 190; trash aesthetic and, 72–75; and "true abstractions," 74, 238n22

Ashbery's works: "Europe," 59; *Flow Chart*, 30, 33, 61, 73; "For John Clare," 74–75; *Girls on the Run*, 59, 75; "Idaho," 144; *The Mooring of Starting Out*, 30; *A Nest of Ninnies* (with Schuyler), 60–61, 93–94; "The New Spirit," 30, 43; *Other Traditions*, 34, 60, 74; "Self-Portrait in a Convex Mirror," 32; *Some Trees*, 40, 51; "The System," 80; *The Tennis Court Oath*, 79; "Thoughts of a Young Girl," 59; *The Vermont Notebook*, 72

Auden, W. H., 64, 242n36

Mayer's works: (*continued*)
119; *Proper Name and Other
Stories*, 116; "Public Lice," 121;
"Say Goodbye to Legacy," 220;
Scarlet Tanager, 217; "Sonnet
Welcome," 217; *Studying
Hunger*, 105; "Thanksgiving,"
217; "To a Politician," 212
McCarthy, Joseph, 68, 72–73
McClelland, Suzanne, 47
Mead, Taylor, 80
Menand, Louis, 219–220
Merrill, James, 8; "An Urban
Convalescence," 84, 236n13
metonymy, 196–197
Miller, Nancy K., 161–162, 255n18
"mimeograph revolution," 79,
102–103
mimesis, 4, 11, 18, 46
misogyny, 54, 164; and feminism,
10–11; in homosocial circles, 53,
235n11; in lyric poetry, 58; Myles
and, 193
Mitchell, Joan, 3, 5–6, 13–31, 45,
94, 102, 121; "abstract practice"
of, 5, 230n13; color and, 18,
20–24; friends, mentors,
influences, 14, 18–19; influence
of poetry on, 14, 20–22;
landscape and, 6, 16, 19, 27;
move to France, 18–19
Mitchell's works: *Blue Territory*,
22; *Bluet* and *Les Bluets*, 29;
Clearing, 20; *Evenings on 73rd
Street*, 18; *A Few Days after II
[After James Schuyler)*, 14; *Field
for Skyes*, 20, 21, 26; *George
Went Swimming at Barnes Holes,
but It Got Too Cold*, 17; *Girolata
Tryptych*, 22, 27; *Hemlock*, 18;
Hudson River Day Line, 30; *Iva*,
17; *La Vie en Rose*, 22; *Mooring*,
22, 30; *Salut Sally*, 22; *Skyes*, 17;

To the Harbormaster, 30; *Two
Sunflowers*, 30; *Wet Orange*,
20–21
modernism, 4, 7, 12, 18–19, 46,
232n22
Monet, Claude, 18, 19
Montagu, Lady Mary Wortley,
126–127
Moore, Marianne, 60, 64, 148
Moses, Robert, 87
mothers: actual, 236–237n15; as
literary influences, 62, 117
Motherwell, Robert, 18
Mueller, Cookie, 251n6
muses: dogs as, 17; female, 58, 62,
235–236n13
Museum of Modern Art (New
York), 110, 241n36
Myers, John Bernard, 8, 52, 78
Myles, Eileen, 13, 40, 81, 169–208,
254n16; body and, 170–173, 175;
class and, 93, 181, 202;
influences, 174, 195–96;
performative utterance and, 179,
184–185, 205; presidential
campaign, 187–189; and public
sphere, 180–88; on reclamation,
204–205, 208; writing
workshops, 206–207, 255n19
Myles's works: "An American
Poem," 182–185, 186, 216;
"Bath, Maine," 174; "A Blue
Jay," 176–177; *Chelsea Girls*,
174, 191, 193, 252–253n13; *Cool
for You*, 181, 191, 193–194,
200–203, 215, 253–254n15; "The
End of New England," 203–204;
"Exploding the Spring
Mystique," 200; *A Fresh Young
Voice from the Plains*, 187, 191;
Hell (libretto), 211–212; "Hot
Night," 189–190; "Inauguration
Day," 186; *The Inferno*, 257n6;